Looking North

Northern England and the national imagination

DAVE RUSSELL

Manchester University Press

Manchester and New York

distributed exclusively in the USA by Palgrave

Published by Manchester University Press
Oxford Road, Manchester M13 9NR, UK
and Room 400, 175 Fifth Avenue, New York, NY 10010, USA
www.manchesteruniversitypress.co.uk

Distributed exclusively in the USA by
Palgrave, 175 Fifth Avenue, New York,
NY 10010, USA

Distributed exclusively in Canada by
UBC Press, University of British Columbia, 2029 West Mall,
Vancouver, BC, Canada V6T 1Z2

British Library Cataloguing-in-Publication Data
A catalogue record for this book is available from the British Library

Library of Congress Cataloging-in-Publication Data applied for

ISBN   0 7190 5177 0   *hardback*
        0 7190 5178 9   *paperback*

First published 2004

13 12 11 10 09 08 07 06 05 04   10 9 8 7 6 5 4 3 2 1

Typeset in Adobe Garamond and Gill Sans by
D R Bungay Associates, Burghfield, Berks

Printed in Great Britain by CPI, Bath

Looking North

Published in our
centenary year

~ **2004** ~

MANCHESTER
UNIVERSITY
PRESS

STUDIES IN
POPULAR
CULTURE

General editor: Professor Jeffrey Richards

STUDIES IN POPULAR CULTURE

There has in recent years been an explosion of interest in culture and cultural studies. The impetus has come from two directions and out of two different traditions. On the one hand, cultural history has grown out of social history to become a distinct and identifiable school of historical investigation. On the other hand, cultural studies has grown out of English literature and has concerned itself to a large extent with contemporary issues. Nevertheless, there is a shared project, its aim, to elucidate the meanings and values implicit and explicit in the art, literature, learning, institutions and everyday behaviour within a given society. Both the cultural historian and the cultural studies scholar seek to explore the ways in which a culture is imagined, represented and received, how it interacts with social processes, how it contributes to individual and collective identities and world views, to stability and change, to social, political and economic activities and programmes. This series aims to provide an arena for the cross-fertilisation of the discipline, so that the work of the cultural historian can take advantage of the most useful and illuminating of the theoretical developments and the cultural studies scholars can extend the purely historical underpinnings of their investigations. The ultimate objective of the series is to provide a range of books which will explain in a readable and accessible way where we are now socially and culturally and how we got to where we are. This should enable people to be better informed, promote an interdisciplinary approach to cultural issues and encourage deeper thought about the issues, attitudes and institutions of popular culture.

Jeffrey Richards

To my friends in the North,
wherever they were born

Contents

List of tables

General editor's foreword

There is a popular composite image of the North of England. It comprises cloth caps and whippets, clogs and shawls, brass bands, cobbled streets, tripe and black pudding, trouble at mill, Rugby League, Wigan Pier, George Formby and Gracie Fields, L. S. Lowry, *Coronation Street* and Andy Capp. It has grown up over two centuries and is deeply rooted in the popular consciousness. It is essentially urban, industrial, working-class and in many respects nineteenth-century. In his fascinating, wide-ranging, thought-provoking and immensely readable new book, Dave Russell sets out to deconstruct and analyse this image of the North. He brings to the project all the knowledge, insight and understanding that he demonstrated in his previous outstanding works of cultural history, *Popular Music in England* and *Football and the English*. Having carefully defined his terms historically and geographically, he ranges widely across every area of popular culture, travel writing, dialect literature, novels, plays, films, music and sports, to explore and explain the creation of the image of the North. Along the way he discovers many contradictions, variations and distinctions but he returns again and again to the ideas of the bracing air of the moors, the plain-speaking, commonsensical, down-to-earth folk and the concept of hard, honest graft as defining characteristics of the North. What seems to have ensured the deep rooting and long-lasting nature of the image is that is has been promoted by northerners as a robust and unashamed celebration of the North constructed in specific opposition to the idea of an effete, decadent and corrupt South. But at the same time it has been propounded by metropolitan Southern sophisticates as a way of dismissing the North as blighted, benighted and backward. With its wide range of reference, its freshness of approach and its sympathetic understanding this book represents a significant contribution to cultural history.

Jeffrey Richards

Acknowledgements

I first considered writing this book in the early 1990s, finally started work on it in 1997 and staggered over the line six years later. Over the course of this period I have benefited from the assistance and kindness of many people. The staffs of the British Library, British Newspaper Library and the central libraries of Bradford, Halifax and Manchester have been as helpful as always, as have those in a new place of resort, the TV Heaven facility at the Bradford Museum of National Museum of Photography, Film and Television. I was awarded an AHRB research leave grant in 2001–2 and the project would simply have been abandoned without it. The support of Neville Kirk and Jeffrey Richards at this stage was absolutely crucial. As series editor, Jeffrey Richards has been steadfast in his support and encouragement throughout the entire process and Alison Whittle and Jonathan Bevan at Manchester University Press showed great patience and helpfulness in the face of endless delays over the last two years. The interest shown at key moments by a number of people including Robert Colls, Richard Cox, Jeff Hill, Dick Holt, Bill Lancaster, Gavin Mellor, Stuart Rawnsley (his pioneering work in the early 1990s was an important initial spur), Mike Paris, Chris Riley, Keith Vernon and Wendy Webster was far greater than they ever realised. My colleagues at the University of Central Lancashire put up with the extra burdens that flowed from my unexpected absence on research leave in 2001–2 without making me feel too guilty; the support of the Head of Department, Joe Pope, during this period was especially gratefully received, as indeed was his unfailing helpfulness in all matters during his stewardship of the Department from 1987 until his retirement in 2003. Within the Department I also owe a huge debt to Steve Caunce whose endless ideas and stimulating argument on many trans-Pennine train journeys have played a big part in shaping the end product. The debt to John Walton is equally large; his boundless enthusiasm, bibliographical assistance, suggestions on draft material and ridiculous levels of knowledge were invaluable. Three cohorts of MA students helped keep my interest in this topic alive and the footnotes testify to how highly I valued them. Finally, Veronica Russell once again proved a willing listener, a source of ideas and a calming influence. I hope the final product is worthy of this collective generosity.

Defining the North of England

Key:

- ·—··—··—· Country boundaries
- ············ Pre 1974 County boundaries

1 — Approximate line of division between 'far' and 'near' Norths

2 - - - Southern boundary of 'seven-county North'

3 -··-··- Severn-Wash line

4 ····· Approximate traditional dialect line

NORTHUMBERLAND
Newcastle
Sunderland
CUMBERLAND
DURHAM
WESTMORLAND
LANCS
North Riding
YORKSHIRE
1
4
West Riding
York
East Riding
Bradford
Leeds
LANCASHIRE
Manchester
Sheffield
2
Liverpool
Lindsey
LINCOLNSHIRE
CHESHIRE
DERBYSHIRE
NOTTINGHAMSHIRE
Nottingham
Kesteven
3
STAFFORDSHIRE
Holland
R. Trent
Birmingham
Northampton
LONDON
GLC
3

0 miles 50
0 kilometres 100

Introduction

When the first uncertain ideas for this book began to form in the early 1990s, I started collecting examples of what I termed 'northern grit', the simple, factual errors about northern England that blow around within the national media. The *Guardian* provides a useful start. In August 1994, it illustrated a story about the potential for cultural tourism within England with two photographs captioned 'Huddersfield town hall, left, squares up to the Louvre'. Unfortunately, the Huddersfield picture selected was of its neo-classical railway station, a building that admittedly would put many a town hall to shame. Four years later, an *Observer* sports reporter decided in his turn to embellish a report of a Halifax Town football match with some local knowledge. 'There's a saying in these parts', he confidently asserted, '"From hellhole and Halifax preserve us"'. In fact, the phrase (part of an apocryphal beggars' litany alluding to Halifax's maintenance of a gibbet until 1680), is more normally rendered as 'From Hull, Hell and Halifax may the good Lord deliver us.' In June 2001, the *New Statesman*'s Ziauddin Sardar made his modest contribution to the art after being parachuted into the North to investigate racial tensions. In Bradford's Manningham district he found himself somewhere that he consistently called 'Lamb Lane'; Bradfordians know it rather better as Lumb Lane. Several days later, after riots in Manningham, Radio Four's John Humphrys informed listeners that the area was a council estate, when it is mostly an area of privately owned Victorian housing.[1]

Mistakes get made – and most certainly not just about the North – and the examples noted here are clearly extremely minor in themselves and of interest to only relatively small numbers. Nevertheless, tiny fragments can point to a bigger narrative and the trail of northern grit signals a much larger pattern of unequal relationships between the northern periphery and the metropolitan core within which the national media is largely focused and the representation of the 'regions' largely (although not exclusively) constructed. Some argue that the North, its culture and its relationship with London and the south-east are tired topics that will reveal little. The North–South divide apparently 'gets written about *ad nauseum*' and there is no doubt that an easy and predictable characterisation of the North – what an exasperated Dennis Potter once termed the 'slate-grey rain and polished euphoniums ... eh-bah-goom heritage' – has become so taken for granted within the national comic grammar that is easy to smile (or wince) on meeting it and move on.[2] This book, however, is rooted in the belief that the issue of the North's place and representation within the national culture remains significantly under-examined and that, at a time when regional devolution and regeneration are key elements of contemporary political and economic debate, provides an important field of study.

What follows has been conceived as a serious academic investigation synthesising existing writing on northern England and northern identity and building on it through research into previously neglected or little considered areas. Nevertheless, it has also been fuelled by a personal desire to make sense of northern England's place within the national culture. While the following couple of paragraphs might then appear as so much self-indulgent autobiography, they are a genuine attempt to identify the motives and personal prejudices that underpin this work. Like another recent historian of the North, much of my academic interest in it stems from my own and my family's history.[3] Raised in the south of England in the 1950s and 1960s, I had never ventured further north than Villa Park, Birmingham until a school trip took me to the Lake District aged 18. I was dimly aware of the North's existence but in a suitably stereotypical way, my mental images culled from an amalgam of Al Read and Jimmy Clitheroe radio programmes and a few meetings with a branch of my family that hailed from Stockport. I remember them being welcomed them at West Croydon Station with phrases such as 'come on mother' and 'are you courting?' delivered in cod northern accents. A ritual greeting in the form of a handkerchief, suitably knotted in each corner and placed on my father's head, also comes to mind, but perhaps my memory is playing tricks. I hope so. Overall, though, the North seemed far way (it was before the establishment of a motorway network and high-speed trains) and exotic in a rather comical way. Most of my friends thought the same way, with our idiosyncratic sense of geography demonstrated when one of them described her decision to pursue higher education in Coventry as a move 'up to the North'.

An entirely haphazard process of choice found me arriving in York as an undergraduate in 1971. Within weeks I had decided that, beyond a few trips to see friends, family and my mother's washing machine, I did not want to return to the South. The rootless, often southern, middle-class male seeking a new identity through association with proletarian or non-white culture has become a literary and sociological cliché since the 1980s, but at the time I was a little less 'knowing'. Yorkshire was my Mississippi Delta. Quite simply, for someone raised in Croydon, Slough and the rapidly expanding commuter suburbs of Reading, the north of England represented 'authenticity', 'real life', 'difference', 'working-class culture'. (York was then a decidedly working-class, manufacturing town, for all its other associations.) The many changes in the northern cityscape and the greater exposure given to versions of northern life in the popular media perhaps make it harder to appreciate just how 'different' the North could feel to new arrivals even just thirty years ago. For months after moving to the far more classically northern industrial landscape of Bradford in 1975, I walked to the end of the street to look out in fascination across the valley at mill chimneys, cobbled streets, and distant moorland. The Thames Valley it was not. The feeling of novelty has faded with familiarity, but it can still be conjured up. When combined with the sense of the North's isolation from the metropolitan centre that can only be experienced by living there, it becomes easy to feel part of, if not another nation, then at least a decidedly separate place.

But southern accents and cultural ties are hard to shed. For all my dalliances with small-town northern football clubs since 1971, my allegiance has always ultimately been to a London team. Similarly, I still adhere to my father's dictum that 'in cricket, I am unbiased. I don't care who beats Yorkshire', and am particularly pleased when it is Surrey that does so. Again, I have often been struck and occasionally genuinely irritated by the odd views of the South held by some northerners. It was apparently, I learnt on arrival, a place largely inhabited by golf-playing merchant bankers with trophy wives and privileged and privately educated children, trained to speak by the authors of 1930s elocution manuals. Moreover, as I stood and listened to fans at northern football grounds terming the players and fans of Cambridge United, Ipswich Town, Oxford United and other decidedly non-metropolitan clubs 'Cockneys', I began to realise that it was not just the inhabitants of Reading that needed geography lessons.

My attempt to make sense of some of these attitudes and perceptions is an exploratory cultural history attempting to meet John Walton's call for regional histories that 'pay sustained heed to the myths that are imposed upon the region's people and the myths by which they live'.[4] It does this by examining the nature, cause and consequence of the numerous representations of the North and 'northernness' and the discourses surrounding them that have operated in a number of cultural fields since the mid-nineteenth century. This concentration upon cultural representation in no sense implies a rejection of modes of investigation rooted in the history of actual events and observable, measurable patterns; certain material realities are indeed considered here. However, most people outside the North and many within it have come to know the region not through personal experience but via the versions they encounter in the field of culture. To explore the constructed 'North' then, is to engage not with some peripheral academic plaything but with a major factor in the definition of popular mentalities.

Four closely interrelated concerns are pursued here. One fundamental task has been the analysis of the many and sometimes apparently contradictory images of the North that circulate within the national (specifically here the *English*) imagination, of those 'True Norths' that can be grim and beautiful, comic and threatening, untutored and artistically sensitive. Attention has been paid not only to the role that this imagery has played in building external views of the region but also to the issue of self-image and self-expression. The existing literature often underestimates the extent to which the region has been active in its own making and it is important to remember the 'national imagination', while undoubtedly receiving its most influential molding in that loosely defined territory we call the 'South', is shaped and experienced in many different locales including the North. Secondly, the book tries to identify the major functions served by the North within the national culture since the mid-nineteenth century and its key moments of prominence within either that culture as a whole, or some aspect of it. A third concern, and one that enthusiastically acknowledges the importance of 'objective realities' to the cultural historian, is with the measurement of the contribution made by northerners and northern institutions to particular aspects of English cultural life. Most of the thematic chapters therefore have introductory sections that try to establish orders of magnitude and to pin down northern contributions to the national whole with rather more precision than is normally the case. Finally, the book interrogates the concept of 'northern identity' and 'northern consciousness' and examines the complex interrelationships between regional and other forms of collective identity. Key questions here include the extent to which we can speak of a single 'northern' identity and whether regional patriotisms can hold their own against the often-conflicting demands of locality at one extreme and class and nation at the other. The relationships between regional and class identities are especially interesting in the North where the conscious deployment of populist 'northern' discourses and cultural practices by elite groups have long served as a central hegemonic strategy.[5]

Scholars from many disciplines have opened up these and other related questions and their insights and arguments will emerge at relevant points in the text rather than through sustained analysis at this point. However, it is worth identifying some of the key works and intellectual contexts that have shaped both this work and the study of northern image and identity more widely. Historians have long had the North, especially its manufacturing districts, under intense scrutiny. Indeed, given that academic discourses are as much part of the process of cultural production as any other, their treatment has played a not insignificant role in building certain limited and limiting images of the region as harsh, industrial, grimy and the particular province of the working-class. Its culture, identity and broader relationships with other parts of the country, however, have been far less frequently considered. There were signs that this was to change in the 1960s with Donald Read's *The English Provinces, c.1760–1960* (1964) especially important. Similarly, Asa Briggs consistently stressed the need for work on the North–South divide, suggesting in an oft-quoted aphorism that a 'nineteenth-century conflict between North and South was as much a leading theme of English as American history'.[6] One of the finest contributions at this time came from outside academia in the shape of Graham Turner's *The North Country* (1967).[7] The kind of book likely to earn journalism a good name, it provided an excellently researched interrogation of the North in all its complexity and has proved a rich source for this study.

Interestingly, however, the North and, indeed, the whole area of regional identity, remained at best a marginal element of the historian's research agenda, displaced almost as soon as it had appeared by the contending claims of class, a topic that so absorbed historians in the 1960s and 1970s. Only in the 1980s did an ever-widening intellectual space open up within which regional issues could be debated in various forms. As ever, academia took much of its flavour from the wider political arena. The weakness of industrial and political labour in the face of the rise of Thatcherism helped draw attention away from of class as a determinant of social action, while the economic travails of the decade placed the North–South divide on the agenda more firmly than at any time since the 1930s. Discussion of Scottish and Welsh devolution and, by the 1990s, even that of the English regions gave a further boost. Accompanying these domestic concerns was the much wider influence of the various epistemological currents gathered under such convenient umbrellas as 'post-modernism' and the 'linguistic turn', and which turned attention much more fully to the construction, and multi-layered nature of personal and collective identities.

Although Charles Dellheim's pioneering 1986 study of Victorian images of Lancashire and Yorkshire was the first significant attempt to re-engage with the topic, arguably the crucial moment for the historical study of the North came in the early 1990s with the publication of three – albeit very different – works.[8] Patrick Joyce's *Visions of the People* (1991) was not exclusively concerned with the North but the substantial attention paid to northern identities by an innovative and prominent social historian gave added credibility and visibility to the subject area.[9] Frank Musgrove's wide-ranging 1992 survey of the North from Roman times to the present was largely (and perhaps strangely) unconcerned with issues of northern identity, but his attempt to identify and explain key moments of 'particular northern distinction, importance and power', generated much material and many ideas.[10] Helen Jewell's *The North–South Divide. The Origins of Northern Consciousness in England* (1994), a study of the emergence of that divide from the fifth to the mid-eighteenth century, was perhaps more successful in demonstrating the region's territorial distinctiveness and outsiders' attitudes to it than the actual formation of the 'northern consciousness' that her book's sub-title promised.[11] Nevertheless, after Jewell, there could be no lingering possibility that the North–South divide might be seen as a product of the industrial age. Overall, the collective weight of these books announced the clear arrival of 'The North' as organising concept and valid topic within English history and opened the way for the more specialist studies that are now becoming part of the fabric of contemporary scholarship.[12]

Historians have by no means had sole charge of northern territory. One brief but important contribution made during their relative absence in the 1970s was that of geographers Pocock and Hudson in their *Images of the Urban Environment* (1978).[13] Working from the perspective of 'perception theory' with its emphasis on 'the subjective manner of construing reality' and 'the relevance to personal and social life and behaviour of … mental representations, rather than those of objective realities', one section of their study focused on literary representations of the North in order to demonstrate how the cumulative impact of cultural experiences allows people 'to know, and hold opinions about, many places never actually visited'.[14] Although the authors tended to a rather hypodermic model of the relationship between text and reader, the debt that this work owes to their basic position will already be obvious and demands acknowledgement here. As within history and as the result of similar political and intellectual imperatives, it was the period from the 1980s that saw a real gathering of interest in the North across disciplines. Particularly in the 1980s, much of this was concerned with economic issues but the range of both subject matter and approach has been consistently extended.[15] One piece that has been especially important for this study has been the rich chapter on the 'North–South divide' in Rob Shields' theoretically sophisticated cultural geography of marginal and liminal spaces, *Places on the Margin* (1991). Using literature, 'New Wave' cinema and the press coverage of the 1980s, Shields examined the northern 'place-image' – 'the discrete meanings associated with real places or regions regardless of their character in reality' – in ways that paid attention both to the varied and contradictory elements found within that image and to the role it played in locating the region in a national spatial hierarchy radiating from London.[16]

Intellectual currents and projects that have not always directly engaged with the region can, of course, also enhance discussion of the North. One of the most fertile such debates in recent years has focused on 'Englishness' (and more recently, 'Britishness'). The term, of late twentieth-century coinage, would not have been familiar to the historical actors to whose culture it has been applied, and has rarely been closely defined; this study uses the term simply to denote people's sense of what it was to be English. The key terms of the debate were laid down in the 1980s by Martin Wiener in his study of the values and mentalities of the nineteenth- and twentieth-century English elites and by the contributors to an important set of essays on English culture from 1880–1920 edited by Robert Colls and Philip Dodd.[17] In essence, these argued that dominant classes threatened by currents of modernism, urbanism and political radicalism sought to construct a distinctive and defensive type of Englishness, utilising a rich repertoire of cultural practices that celebrated the pre-industrial past and an idealised rural 'Deep England' in which the south of England was often stood proxy for the nation as a whole.[18]

While these arguments still predominate within interpretations of English history from 1880 to about 1950 (and sometimes beyond), they have not been without challenge. Peter Mandler has suggested in a trenchant critique that the 'rural-nostalgic vision of "Englishness" remained the province of impassioned and highly articulate but fairly marginal groups' and that an 'aggressively urban and materialistic' tone marked the national culture far more clearly at this time.[19] In a sparkling study, David Matless has shown that celebration of countryside need not imply an embrace of conservative ideologies and has also noted the importance of East–West oppositions within national identity, setting Anglo-Saxon rationality against Celtic mysticism and demanding consideration alongside the standard North–South polarity.[20] Despite this necessary corrective, a further criticism might be that the Englishness debate has actually still not engaged closely enough with the role of the North and its inhabitants. It would be sad irony indeed if the 'exclusive Englishness of the twentieth century ... developed precisely to eliminate the dirty, unpalatable working parts of England from influence and power' was so effectively internalised by the scholarly community that the region was denied a place in discussion.[21] The North's rich mixtures of urban and rural and its host of powerful local and regional identities in fact make it an excellent site for observing contending versions of national identity and this study will examine the extent to which notions of the North and northernness have complemented, augmented or challenged that identity.

On a yet wider scale, two other important influences must be noted. Although by no means immune from criticism, Edward Said's *Orientalism* (1978) has been one of the truly formative academic texts of modern times.[22] While there is no attempt here to see the North of England as essentially an internal colony in the period under study, as will be argued shortly, Said's exploration of colonial discourses offers immensely valuable ways of looking more generally at relationships between dominant and subordinate cultures and not least the English 'South' and 'North'. Benedict Anderson's *The Imagined Community* (1983) has similarly gained enormous currency. His now classic formulation of the 'imagined community' with its central tenet that 'all communities larger than primordial villages of face-to-face contact (and perhaps even these) are imagined' is used here in full awareness of some of its potential problems but with equal appreciation of its extraordinary value as a shorthand encapsulation of a complex process.[23]

The study of the North or any other region must be open to many and varied influences in these days of usefully blurring disciplinary boundaries. While eclectic borrowing rather than any one single theoretical or methodological tendency thus guides this study, it is useful to identify two of its fundamental assumptions. The book is predicated on a belief that that the 'national culture', in terms of both the mentalities and the institutions that form them, has always been largely constructed from within London and its immediate environs and that the 'North' has therefore been defined in that culture as 'other' and ultimately, as inferior. This is not to deny that the region can serve extremely important functions within national life, that particular aspects of its culture earn consistently high approbation and that it can exert some control over its representation.[24] Its sheer size, the centrality of its contribution to national life and the efforts of its many spokespeople (often holding key positions within the metropolitan elite) to argue its case have ensured that. Indeed, those in other significant regions such as the 'South-west', 'East Anglia' and perhaps above all, the ill-defined and oft-ignored 'Midlands', have been marginalised within the regional hierarchy by the sheer power of the North's sense of place and by the dominant discourse of the 'North–South divide'. In the opening paragraph of Lettice Cooper's 1938 novel *National and Provincial*, for example, her heroine, *en route* from London to Leeds waits until Sheffield to 'rouse herself to look out of the window. The placid and uneventful Midlands, heavy with the green of July, slid by her unnoticed'. That lack of interest captures well the plight of a region sandwiched between the two most culturally laden spaces within the nation's imaginary geography.[25]

For all its importance, however, the North has never been able to enjoy a sustained or broad-based cultural leadership. In *Orientalism* Said speaks of a 'flexible positional superiority', a strategy 'which puts the Westerner in a whole series of possible relationships with the Orient without ever losing him the relative upper hand' and this, if used carefully, is extremely helpful in the context of North/South relationships within England.[26] Relationships between the English centre and its internal regions were vastly more equal than those that Said explores and the South obviously never had or required the level and apparatus of control over the 'production' of the North that typified European relationships with the Orient. The North has therefore enjoyed some degree of agency and been celebrated, even cherished, but always on terms dictated by the centre and its positional superiority and in ways that do not fundamentally challenge perceived truths about the nature of English identity.

A second point relates to the duality of 'image' (or 'representation') and 'reality' that has run rather loosely around this introduction to date. This work is not concerned with identifying a set of images and then testing them out against supposedly objective realities. Rather, it attempts to explore the complex interrelationship between the two. It accepts that many of the myths and stereotypes that surround the region may well be rooted in measurable, material conditions. In the words of Castells and Walton 'Regional identities are the discursive products of the collective invention and recreation of traditions, but they are also grounded in the ways in which people made their own livings and lived their lives'. Sidney Pollard has similarly suggested that the association of marginal places within Europe with such characteristics as on the one hand backwardness and ignorance and, on the other, resourcefulness, bravery and a certain unspoilt nobility – all qualities often attributed to the North – may well be rooted in actual relationships between society and environment.[27] The ultimate concern here, however, is with the way in which regional imagery, no matter how 'truthfully' conceived or 'accurately' portrayed, has been disseminated and deployed in the interest of the agendas of competing and contending social groups.

The first chapter discusses definition of the North, describes some of the region's ascribed characteristics and tries to place it within the wider national culture. Seven thematic chapters examining the ways in which the North has been constructed by a particular cultural form or practice then provide the core of the work. The chosen areas are tourist literature; fiction; dialect, dialect literature and sound broadcasting; the stage; film and television; music and sport. They are obviously by no means neatly sealed categories. Gracie Fields and George Formby were stars of both stage and screen; dialect is an issue in the novel, film and television as much as it is the specific field of dialect literature; Keith Waterhouse's 1959 novel *Billy Liar* was subsequently dramatised, filmed, televised and turned into a stage musical. The eventual placing of specific individuals and specific texts is thus often somewhat arbitrary and there is doubtless some repetition across chapters. However, this should be compensated for by an increased awareness of the distinct contribution of specific cultural forms and by the presentation of a series of discrete narratives for readers with particular interests. The final chapter discusses the various overlapping forms of social and personal identity that emerged from both the objective and subjective experiences of being 'northern'.

The seven themes have been chosen for a number of reasons beyond intrinsic importance. The range is certainly large enough to draw attention to the relative autonomy of individual cultural forms. While there was so often an ultimate unity at least in regard to external views of the region deriving from a high degree of intertextuality, different cultural arenas could treat it in quite distinctive ways. For example, while the North might be seen as bleak, industrial, proletarian and thus eminently avoidable in some tourist discourses, those same characteristics could be celebrated as progressive and stimulating both in, and in writing about, Edwardian drama or 1950 and 1960s 'New Wave' cinema. Again, the selection allows for consideration to be given to culture as *text* as in the novel or film and as *practice* as in music making and the playing and consumption of sport. Finally, it also provides a reasonably balanced mixture in terms of the illumination of cultural representations largely generated externally (tourism and film, for example) and of those (such as dialect writing and sport) that allow for greater levels of self-representation.

Most writers acknowledge the limits of their writings and the provisional nature of their findings and I am no exception. The decision to cover a fairly lengthy time span means that the establishment of general trends and tendencies is more common than close scrutiny of specific instances. Again, representation of the North and its culture can be met literally everywhere and considerations of space and limits to personal competence ensure that not all potentially relevant forms of cultural representation and activity are dealt with here. The press could sustain a full-length study of its own but is used here to provide a body of evidence rather than as a central focus. Fine art and photography are obvious omissions and inclusion of poetry and sculpture would have modified some of the comments on the marginal nature of the North's cultural contribution and status.[28] Attention to patterns and styles of consumption would have proved a further useful addition. Nevertheless, the resultant content and structure should generate at least some sense of broad changes and continuities in a number of significant cultural arenas over the period since the mid-nineteenth century. If other writers are sufficiently interested (or irritated) by what they read here to engage in debate and fill the many gaps, my efforts will have been worthwhile.

Notes

1 *Guardian*, 5 August 1994; *Observer*, 8 March 1998; *New Statesman*, 4 June 2001; Radio Four, 'Today Programme', 16 August 2001.

2 P. Barker, 'Cloth caps and chips it isn't', *New Statesman*, 9 January 1998; quoted in *British Bandsman*, 7 December 1963.

3 H. Jewell, *The North–South Divide. The Origins of Northern Consciousness in England* (Manchester: Manchester University Press, 1994), p. vii.

4 J. K. Walton, 'Professor Musgrove's North of England: a critique', *Journal of Regional and Local Studies*, 12, 2, 1992, p. 29.

5 Unless otherwise stated, whenever attempts are made to examine intra-northern relationships the 'North' has been referred to the as the 'region'; elements within it such as administrative counties or a collection of communities as 'sub-regions' and specific towns, cities and villages as 'localities'.

6 A. Briggs, *The Age of Improvement* (London: Longman, 2000 edn), p. 42.

7 G. Turner, *The North Country* (London: Eyre and Spottiswoode, 1967).

8 C. Dellheim, 'Imagining England: Victorian views of the North', *Northern History*, xxii, 1980, pp. 216–30.

9 P. Joyce, *Visions of the People. Industrial England and the Question of Class, 1848–1914* (Cambridge: Cambridge University Press, 1991); H. Jewell, *The North–South Divide. The Origins of Northern Consciousness in England* (Manchester: Manchester University Press, 1994).

10 F. Musgrove, *The North of England. A History from Roman Times to the Present* (Oxford: Oxford University Press, 1992), p. 1.

11 For a rich review, K. Wrightson, 'Northern identities: the long durée', *Northern Review*, 2, 1995, pp. 25–34.

12 For example, R. Colls and B. Lancaster (eds), *Geordies: Roots of Regionalism* (Edinburgh: Edinburgh University Press, 1992); J. Richards, *Stars in their Eyes. Lancashire Stars of Stage, Screen and Radio* (Preston: Lancashire County Books, 1994); J. Hill and J. Williams (eds), *Sport and Identity in the North of England* (Keele: Keele University Press, 1996); R. Samuel, 'North and South', in *Island Stories. Unravelling Britain* (London: Verso, 1998); N. Kirk (ed.), *Northern Identities. Historical Interpretations of the 'The North' and 'Northernness'* (Aldershot: Ashgate, 2000). Although far from exclusively about the North, E. Royle (ed.), *Issues of Regional Identity* (Manchester: Manchester University Press, 1998), has several northern essays and, as befits a festschrift for John Marshall, is an invaluable stimulus for the student of regionalism.

13 D. Pocock and R. Hudson, *Images of the Urban Environment* (London: MacMillan, 1978), chapter 8.

14 Ibid., pp. 1, 110.

15 D. Smith, *North and South* (London: Penguin, 1989); P. Balchin, *Regional Policy in Britain. The North–South Divide* (London: Paul Chapman, 1989); P. J. Taylor, 'The meaning of the North: England's "foreign country" within?', *Political Geography*, 12, 1993, pp. 136–55 and 'Which Britain? Which England? Which North?', in D. Morley and K. Robbins (eds), *British Cultural Studies* (Oxford: Oxford University Press, 2001), pp. 127–44. The journal *Regional Studies* provided a constant and rich source of debate on economic and political ideas.

16 R. Shields, *Places on the Margin* (London: Routledge, 1991), pp. 207–51, 60.

17 *English Culture and the Decline of the Industrial Spirit, 1850–1980* (Cambridge: Cambridge University Press, 1981); R. Colls and P. Dodd, *Englishness. Politics and Culture, 1880–1920* (Beckenham: Croom Helm, 1986). See also Robert Colls, *Identity of England* (Oxford: Oxford University Press, 2002), a stimulating attempt to consider English identity by mixing 'the history of events with the history of ideas about those events' (p. 6). It is not possible to list all of the numerous books on English/British identities. Colls' *Identity* provides a very good guide. See also J. K. Walton (ed.), *Relocating Britishness* (Manchester: Manchester University Press, 2004).

18 This phrase is from Patrick Wright's, *On Living in an Old Country* (London: Verso, 1985), especially pp. 81–7. Wright stresses the importance of the penetration of dominant 'pastoral and green' imagery into every day life 'whatever the situation in which it is lived' (p. 87).

19 P. Mandler, 'Against "Englishness": English culture and the limits to rural nostalgia', *Transactions of the Royal Historical Society*, sixth series, vii, 1997, p. 170. See too his 'The consciousness of modernity? Liberalism and the English "National Character", 1870–1940', in M. Daunton and B. Rieger (eds), *Meanings of Modernity. Britain from the late-Victorian era to world war 11* (Oxford: Berg, 2001), pp. 119–44, a perceptive analysis that seeks to distinguish between 'Englishness' and 'English national character'.

20 D. Matless, *Landscape and English Identity* (London: Reaktion Books, 1998), pp. 17–20.

21 Taylor, 'Which Britain? Which England?, p. 135. Taylor has been one of the few to place the North within the debate. See too, M. Saler, 'Making it new: visual modernism and the "Myth of the North" in interwar England', *Journal of British Studies*, 37, 4, 1998, pp. 419–60 and D. Gervais, *Literary Englands. Versions of Englishness in Modern Writing* (Cambridge: Cambridge University Press, 1993), pp. 271–2.

22 E. Said, *Orientalism* (New York: Pantheon Books, 1978). A helpful introduction is provided by J. McLeod, *Beginning Postcolonialism* (Manchester: Manchester University Press, 2000).

23 B. Anderson, *Imagined Communities. Reflections on the Origin and Spread of Nationalism* (London: Verso, 1985 edn), p. 15. For a sensitive critique, see A. D. Smith, *Nationalism and Modernism* (London: Routledge, 1998), pp. 130–42.

24 For a study showing unusual sensitivity to the possibility that the North might sometimes burrow to the centre of Englishness, albeit in a very narrowly defined way, Saler, 'Making it new'.

25 L. Cooper, *National and Provincial* (London: Victor Gollancz, 1938), p. 9.

26 Said, *Orientalism*, p. 7.

27 L. Castells and J. K. Walton, 'Contrasting identities: north-west England and the Basque Country', in Royle (ed.), *Issues of Regional Identity*, pp. 76–7. S. Pollard, 'Regional character: the economic margins of Europe', in Royle, *Regional Identity*, pp. 14–24. For an idiosyncratic attempt to explore 'regional personality' through assessment of objective criteria (in this case, consumption patterns), D. E. Allen, *British Tastes. An Enquiry in to the Likes and Dislikes of the British Consumer* (London: Hutchison, 1968).

28 Leading northern-born poets include W. H. Auden, Basil Bunting, Tony Harrison, Ted Hughes, Roger McGough and Norman Nicholson. Two of the world's leading twentieth-century sculptors, Henry Moore (b. 1898) and Barbara Hepworth (b. 1903), were born just a few miles apart in the West Riding. See especially, Saler, 'Making it new'.

1

Defining the North

It is widely accepted that regions are dynamic, shifting entities and that 'static conceptions and boundaries always come to grief'.[1] The 'North' is no exception and, lacking any fixed formal existence, it is undeniably 'as much a state of mind as a place'.[2] Nevertheless, awareness of the impossibility of neat definition runs alongside an equally insistent appreciation that workable boundaries must be established in the interests of clarity and consistence of purpose. It is, after all, really quite useful to know exactly what is being talking about when discussing the 'North's' contribution to the national sporting culture or comparing its production of novelists to that of other areas. The approach taken here is to acknowledge the fluidity of a region that can be viewed in many ways, most of which send it spilling untidily across administrative units, while also adopting a specific definition based precisely upon such structures. The most obvious and the most convenient choice here falls upon the historic counties that existed throughout the period until the implementation of the 1972 Local Government Act in 1974.

Attempts at defining the North are more frequently made than is the case for other English regions. This is clearly suggestive of its status as England's most important region, but it also underlines its essentially subordinate relationship to the 'South', an area so unconsidered that it can stand for anything from a greater London, to that late nineteenth century invention the 'Home Counties', and through to a territory stretching from Dorset to Essex and from the south coast to wherever it is that the 'midlands' begins. The North has been imagined in various ways according to time, context, subject matter and, crucially, angle of vision. While from Scotland, the whole English North looks rather like the British Midlands, from the north-east of England the immediate terrain can seem 'truly' northern and cities such as Sheffield and Manchester distantly and satisfyingly southern. Again, in its borderlands, and especially southern ones, geographical demarcation can become a matter of individual perspective with boundaries defined according to family tradition, place of occupation and location of leisure activities. Writing in 1967, Graham Turner noted the 'unexpected' propensity of some south Yorkshire dwellers to 'think of themselves as Midlanders', with two Rotherham waitresses informing him, 'We're Midlands. Don't forget when they talked on t'radio about bombing raids in t'war, they put us wi' them.'[3]

Obviously, not all aspects of the definitional task are problematic. The east coast takes care of one problem and the Scottish and Welsh borders to some degree of two more, although the many ties that continue to link communities along either side of these political boundaries suggest somewhat softer frontiers than might at first be expected. There are certainly arguments for seeing Liverpool as the capital of north Wales and a number of commentators have noted the shared affinities between Northumberland and the Scottish border country.[4] The most difficult element, however, is undoubtedly the southern boundary, which has been subject to widely differing interpretation. In contemporary popular discourse, its southernmost lines are often drawn in such phrases as 'foreigners start north of Watford' or 'the North begins at Watford Gap', actually a small Northamptonshire village some fifty miles north of its better-known namesake and famed for its motorway service station. In 1964 the Oxford Union introduced another revealing variant when debating the motion 'When going North, wogs begin at Barnet'.[5] Clearly, these 'definitions' would draw millions of people into the North who have absolutely no sense of belonging there, and while they indicate intriguing intimations of northern 'otherness' and of a chauvinism held with varying degrees of seriousness within and around the metropolis, they have little practical value. Some scholarly contributions have also given the North fairly generous dimensions, positing the so-called Severn-Wash line as its southern boundary. (Interestingly, Watford Gap sits very close to this.) This has been especially favoured by writers examining twentieth-century economic divisions, which, put very crudely, have seen the country's most prosperous regions increasingly being found to the south and east of this line.[6] Such an approach has great value within its own terms of reference, but it once again colonises large numbers of people who have no meaningful connection with the region and is thus unhelpful in terms of defining a culture of shared interests and experiences recognisable both from within and by informed observers from without.[7] Given that these are central concerns here, narrower definition must be sought.

In working toward this, this study is much informed by the work of Helen Jewell, who has produced probably the most detailed exploration of the southern boundary. Although focusing on periods far earlier than that covered

in this study, Jewell clearly sees her findings as having contemporary significance arguing that,

> I am satisfied that we have, from Humber to Mersey, with attention to the Trent in
> between, a border which would be recognised by people on both sides of it as gen-
> erally accepted as the beginning of the north of England, when travelling north, or
> the end of it, when travelling south, for more than a millennium.[8]

Her analysis lays most stress on political boundaries, with the Humber, the southernmost point of the Saxon kingdom of Northumbria, and the Trent, increasingly recognised by governments as an administrative dividing line from the
thirteenth century, gaining their significance in this way. However, she is also
alert to a range of other physical, climatic, economic and cultural issues, not the
least important of which has been the tendency for early modern topographers
and travel writers to see the Trent as marking an effective northern boundary. The
testimony of the many later commentators who, like David Smith in 1989, have
found that when journeying northward 'it does feel like another country' when
arriving 'just south of Sheffield', reinforces the sense that this Humber–Mersey
'line' has genuine and long-standing meaning and purchase.[9]

   Jewell's border allows eleven counties to be considered northern but as she
argues, 'quite different degrees of northernness in feeling as well as geography
can be detected'.[10] While the pre-1974 counties of Northumberland, Durham,
Westmorland, Cumberland, Yorkshire and Lancashire all fall squarely in the
North as she defines it, her telling reference to the need for 'attention to the
Trent in between' and other acknowledgements of the flexible and provisional
nature of the boundary renders the exact status of much of Cheshire,
Derbyshire, Staffordshire, Nottinghamshire and Lincolnshire uncertain. At
various times and to a varying extent, these counties have formed quite close
attachments to their northern neighbours, while at others they have kept their
distance.[11] This is all a gloriously messy and enjoyable business, but, as noted
earlier, analysis sometimes demands the imposition of rather boring hard lines
rather than soft and interesting ones. While it is fully acknowledged that all or
parts of the eleven counties noted above (and perhaps even others too) can happily be considered northern, there is value in concentrating on a more minimalist core that many would agree upon. This study therefore adopts a
seven-county North as a unit for measurement and as a focus for the thematic
studies that follow, comprising of Cheshire, Cumberland, Durham, Lancashire,
Northumberland, Westmorland and Yorkshire. Cheshire is undoubtedly the
most troublesome, with its industrial region abutting Merseyside clearly of the

North, but other areas including the city of Chester and the 'swell belt' dormitory communities such as Alderley Edge and Knutsford that are scattered in and around the older industrial locations, linked to it but far less obviously anchored in it. However, it has been included as the least problematic of the border counties. In the future, there will hopefully be studies tracing the existence (or otherwise) of communities of shared interest within these border counties and the core North. The drawing of a necessarily thick line should encourage the search for thinner and less certain ones.

The issue of divisions *within* the North will be dealt with in the next section but broad underlying principles can once again be established here. The same problems that befall attempts to define a wider North reoccur in this context. Neat administrative lines certainly do not necessarily provide clear communities of interest recognisable to those inside and without. Cumberland and Westmorland formed part of the 'North' Standard Planning Region from the 1940s along with Durham, Northumberland and the North Riding of Yorkshire, but then found themselves (now, broadly, as Cumbria) placed with Lancashire and Cheshire as part of the 'North West' when the Government Offices for the Regions were established in 1994. Even counties are not necessarily sacrosanct. While Phythian-Adams, for example, is happy to see Yorkshire as a clear 'cultural province', Neave has argued strongly for the climatically, economically and architecturally distinctive East Riding to be capable of study 'as a separate entity' to the rest of the county.' Similarly, Caunce has pointed out that Lancashire 'often felt as if it was divided at the Ribble and Morecambe Bay, something never given institutional form but which was very real in both economic and cultural terms'.[12]

Certain broad lines of demarcation can nevertheless be observed. Following standard practice, the most basic division posited here is that between a 'far' and 'near' North.[13] Purely in terms of county-based definition, Durham, Northumberland, Cumberland and Westmorland are the clearest components of the 'far North', tending to share a harsher climate than some of their southern counterparts and obviously experiencing a much more acute sense of distance from the capital. The problems with county boundaries have been discussed already, however, and other demarcations can be suggested. The most promising builds on Caunce's division of Lancashire at Morecambe Bay noted above and then takes the boundary line from the north Lancashire coast, across north Yorkshire and then roughly along the line of the River Wharfe and then finally to the Yorkshire coast at Flamborough Head. This places north Lancashire and most of north Yorkshire in the 'far North', something that many residents of the two areas would recognise (see map, p. xii). Indeed, the 'North' Standard Planning Region from the 1940s to 1974 (when the North Riding was lost to Yorkshire and Humberside) came quite close to achieving this division. There are also objective factors operating here. The line, adhering reasonably closely to the southern boundary of the Saxon kingdom of Northumbria, defines the fundamental point of transition between traditional dialects sharing various features with Scotland and those that do not.[14] It also runs a little above the limit of intense industrialisation in Yorkshire and Lancashire and draws attention to the substantial rural belt that separates the North's two major industrial clusters south of the Ribble and north of the Tees.

Obviously, while 'far' and 'near' North can never be defined precisely the terminology provides a useful shorthand that will inform the rest of the book. The two areas can obviously be endlessly sub-divided in their turn. The 'north-east', bounded by the Tees to the south, the Tweed to the north and the Pennines to the west, makes up one distinctive area with in the far North, while the Pennine textile towns of west Yorkshire and east Lancashire offer a less immediately obvious but nevertheless recognisable sub-region in the near North.[15] All that can be asked of historians drawn to this rich variety of interlocking communities of interest is that they define working boundaries as closely as possible and don't stray too far from them

Describing the North

However the North is ultimately defined, it comprised a substantial part of the English nation. Even in its relatively minimalist seven-county form, it takes up just under 30 per cent of England's landmass and contained 25 per cent of the population of England and Wales in 1801, rising to 30 per cent by 1861 and 33 per cent by 1921. By 2001, despite significant outflows of population, it still stood at close to 30 per cent. Lancashire and Yorkshire, or at least its West Riding, were especially heavily populated, with Lancashire's population reaching 4.9 million by 1921 and Yorkshire's 4.1 million. Lancashire's population at this stage almost matched Scotland's and outstripped Ireland's and both counties were larger than a number of European states including Denmark, Finland and Norway. It is hardly surprising that these two counties, and their industrial areas in particular, came to play such a large role in the nation's mental map of the North.

'The concept of a homogeneous North, so dear to many of the participants in the recent popular debate about North and South, is a dangerous simplification.

The variety of the North requires at least as much explanation – historical and otherwise – as the difference between North and South.'[16] Asa Briggs' wise counsel has lost none of the authority it commanded when first offered almost forty years ago, for the North of England is a place of remarkable contrast and complexity that defies easy characterisation. A leisurely and not entirely direct journey of some 180 miles from Liverpool in the west to Scarborough in the east, would traverse innumerable geological, climatic, linguistic, historical and archi- tectural zones, probably far more than could be found in any part of England. Some of the physical and human geography, the smaller red-brick towns of textile Lancashire or the sandstone towns of West Yorkshire, the Pennine moorlands between Manchester and Huddersfield, and the more plebeian parts of Scarborough would 'feel' northern to an outsider raised on the region's stock imagery. Other parts, however, such as the rich, flat arable lands of the Vale of York, the chalk cliffs of Flamborough Head and Manchester's affluent southern suburbs and exurbs might surprise and confuse. Similarly, a circuitous journey from north to south ending on the west coast would embrace both the largest tract of English land containing a population density of less than 6 people per square kilometre, running from the Scottish borders to the southern end of the Yorkshire Dales National Park, and the largest continuous tract of English land to record average densities of over two hundred people per kilometre in the form of an extended strip of land stretching from the Mersey across to Leeds and then swinging down towards Nottingham and Derby. It is this great variety that has fed so much of the debate about the 'essence' of the region, allowing critics and celebrants alike to pick and chose their own 'true North'.

Alongside these physical differences, the region has always been the site of internal economic, political and cultural tensions. The many nuances arising from this will be traced across the book, but some key divisions can be identified here. Concentrating for the moment on purely territorial antagonisms, a variety of sub-regional and local conflicts have tended to fracture the wider North. The best-known rivalry is that between Yorkshire and Lancashire, visible throughout the period under review and surviving even into new forms, expres- sions and contexts of popular culture. A Manchester United fanzine, for example, used chants of 'Y.R.A. … Yorkshire Republican Army' by visiting Leeds United fans ('Neanderthals'), as the basis of a comic piece on an inde- pendent 'Yaarkshire' inhabited largely by a race of male chauvinistic, homo- phobic and racist 'large eared daft people'.[17] This opposition, however, has arguably been far less significant than is sometimes assumed. Even the gen- uinely intense sporting battles between the two (with the exception of football since the 1990s) have disguised a considerable degree of mutual recognition and respect and a body of shared values. The real significance of this often good-natured competition has been that the publicity afforded to it has provided two counties anyway dominating external views of the region with an even greater sense of distinctiveness and special status within it. Notably edgier relations can be found between the north-east and Yorkshire, with some in the former area angered by what they see as the assumed leadership of the wider North by their southerly neighbour. One recent writer has suggested, for example, that it is perhaps time to place J. B. Priestley, 'in the reserve stock on the crowded "Visiting Yorkshiremen" shelf', reward for the largely unflattering section on the north-east in his 1934 travelogue *English Journey*. A long history can be sensed in that short phrase.[18] (Although relationships with Manchester have been problematic, Lancashire and Cheshire are generally too distant and inadequately linked with the north-east for this to become a full-blown conflict of 'far' versus 'near' Norths.)

The most potent conflicts have tended to develop between the 'city-states' that came to political and economic prominence in the late eighteenth and nineteenth centuries. Manchester and Liverpool have an especially long history of mutual mistrust, rooted in political and economic rivalries extending back into the eighteenth century. Manchester's status as 'capital of the North', partly self-proclaimed but partly awarded by southern-based commentators in the nineteenth century was a source of particular annoyance, with Liverpool countering with claims to be the 'second metropolis' and the 'second city of Empire'.[19] Tension between the two was often expressed in the most forcible language, particularly in Liverpool where the ambitions of its *parvenu* rival rankled bitterly. In 1964, an editorial in a Liverpool newspaper saw Manchester's malign influence as a major factor in Liverpool's growing economic difficulties and its representation in the national media as 'a city of thugs, down-and-outs and juvenile delinquents'. It talked of Manchester's 'absurd and harmful pretensions' and likened it to 'an upas tree, [that] drains all that its branches overhang or its roots undermine. The thin and peeling veneer with which Manchester in so many ways attempts to disguise its purely commercial fabric as a cultural one deceives a few, but repels many more'.[20]

Manchester's 'capital' status (until 'leadership' passed to Birmingham in the 1860s, it was also often seen as capital of the provinces more generally) caused problems with most other major regional centres across the North.[21] This issue is of some importance to many of the topics discussed in this book and it is worth probing it a little further here. Manchester's role in the new industrial and commercial order was obviously vitally important, enabling it to join medieval York as the only northern city ever to 'have presented anything like a challenge to London's authority'.[22] The regional capital of one of the nation's most dynamic industrial areas, the birthplace of both the Anti-Corn Law League in 1839 and the National Charter Association in 1840 and a source of fascination to visitors from all over the world, Manchester was at the very core of the forces that appeared to be shaping society between the 1830s and 1850s. Influential cultural responses such as Disraeli's *Sybil* (1845) and Mrs Gaskell's *North and South* (1855) as well as a raft of journalism and social commentary added yet more to its status.

Obviously, the claims of capital city status have no literal substance simply because the North is not a formal territory for any individual city to be the 'capital' of. However, used in the looser sense of Manchester being the region's leading or most influential city, it is convincing in many ways. It was so clearly the most nationally significant northern city of the nineteenth century in the fields of politics and economics, while in the later nineteenth and early twentieth centuries the efforts of Sir Charles Hallé and Annie Horniman made it a major centre of art music and theatre respectively. From the 1920s, it built on strong nineteenth-century foundations (as well as being home to the *Manchester Guardian*, the city had become a major national centre for the sporting press) to become the 'most important centre of the newspaper industry outside London', while its choice as the BBC's northern headquarters in 1928 confirmed its importance as a major media centre more generally.[23] Conversely, it is undeniable that many northerners were affected little or not at all by its influence on a daily basis and that its own claims for leadership, often based on a too easily repeated but rarely considered litany of past glories (the 'thin and peeling veneer' as viewed from Liverpool), were ever less convincing as the twentieth century wore on. Whatever the case, the crucial outcome was twofold. As noted earlier, tensions between Manchester and other major northern cities became a major feature of northern life and, particularly at the level of popular sentiment, remain so.[24] Perhaps more importantly, the attention Manchester received, especially in the early and mid-nineteenth century, gave the city a centrality in the mental imagery of those from outside the North and thereby helped fix a rather simplistic notion of both it and the North within the popular imagination.

While there have been many 'Norths' and many tensions between them, it is undeniable that the region shows features that, although rarely unique, help both to distinguish it from other parts of the country in objective terms and to feed powerfully into the space-myths that have accrued around it. In terms of physical geography, with the exception of a small part of Dartmoor, all English land over 2,000 feet (*c.* 610 metres) is to be found from the Derbyshire Peak District northward. The North also has larger and more continuous tracts of land over 500 feet than other parts of the country. This distinctive topography is partly responsible for its clear meteorological characteristics. Although the ever-widening strip of lowland running southwards from Middlesbrough through the Vale of York and toward Lincoln is one of the driest parts of England, regularly receiving under 25 inches (625 mm) a year, the North is generally both slightly wetter and colder than the rest of the country.

Most important are a cluster of characteristics stemming from the economic changes of the late eighteenth and nineteenth centuries. Industrialisation was obviously in no sense a phenomenon suddenly encountered at Sheffield and agriculture did not disappear at the same spot, forming, as it did, the dominant economic activity of substantial parts of the North for much of the last two hundred years. Nevertheless, it is undeniable that the seven northern counties and their immediate hinterlands contained much of the core activity associated with the so-called industrial revolution, activity which shaped physical and mental landscapes as much as economic ones. In 1921, when the industrial North of the nineteenth century was poised for its accelerated decline into the twentieth, 50 per cent of all English coalface workers were found in the seven county North, along with some 75 per cent of those employed in steel works and steel rolling mills and well over 90 per cent of those engaged in textile production.[25] While such macro-measurement disguises considerable regional variations in the distribution of these industries, the key role of the North in the growth and development of heavy industry is clearly apparent. Certainly, the de-industrialisation that took place gradually over the twentieth century and particularly rapidly since the 1980s, has, along with the concomitant growth of the tertiary sector, partially reduced the North's economic separateness. Even here, however, the intense media scrutiny that charted and debated the decline of manufacturing and extractive industries was so often focused on the region, that that separateness continued to be underlined. Unsurprisingly, the region's economic history gave it a larger working class and a far smaller middle class than most others, especially the South. In 1912 London and the Home Counties region held just over a fifth of the population but 'about half of the English middle class'.[26]

Closely related to the commercial and industrial expansion of the North has been the growth of urbanisation. In 1801 London was the only English (or British) town with a population of over 100,000. By 1911 there were 35 Urban

Districts and Boroughs with population at this level of which 21 were in the seven-county North.[27] Of the six English 'conurbations' recognised by contemporaries from the late nineteenth century but only classified thus for census purposes from 1951, four (South-east Lancashire/North-east Cheshire, Merseyside, West Yorkshire and Tyneside) are to be found in the North. Perhaps even more important than simple numbers, especially between about 1775 and 1850, was the sheer pace of expansion associating the region not just with urban growth, but a transformation of the environment and of styles of living. Once again, there must be no pretension to uniqueness. Alongside the obvious case of London, 'exceptional growth' could be found in the later nineteenth and early twentieth centuries in such places as the railway town of Swindon, the agricultural servicing centre of Ipswich and the resorts of Hastings and Southend.[28] Nevertheless, the North was at the heart of change.

The role of the industrial and the urban has in turn helped shape the North's political history. Although there have been moments when the national political geography (especially in electoral terms) can be usefully depicted in terms of a North/left–South/right divide – elections between 1979 and 1992 met this picture to varying degrees – the general picture has usually been far more complex. Nevertheless, the North's experience of industrial and demographic change has made the region, or significant parts of it, a forcing ground of radical working-class political culture. While Chartism was undoubtedly a national phenomenon with London, Birmingham and other cities and regions playing a major part in its development, the North, and especially the textile districts of Lancashire, Cheshire and the West Riding, was critical to its history. Royle has referred to this latter region as being 'overwhelmingly important' to English Chartism and as 'having stamped its peculiar nature on Chartism as a whole'. He also identifies the north-east as another important centre.[29] The late nineteenth-century socialist revival saw parts of Lancashire emerge as a key area for the Social Democratic Federation, while the Independent Labour Party was founded in Bradford in 1893 and drew the overwhelming body of its founding delegates from the North. Trade unionism can also be characterised as having a decidedly northern flavour. In 1892, while trade union membership per head of population attained its regional peak at 11 per cent in Northumberland and Durham and reached 8.6 per cent in Lancashire, it fell to below 1 per cent in 16 southern counties.[30] Obviously, this is only one selected snapshot but it captures a situation that remained broadly true thereafter. In 2000, the North East, North West and Yorkshire and Humber were the only English regions with levels of union membership above the UK average.[31]

It was inevitably those parts of the North most affected by these striking changes in the economic and social order that fixed a particular image of a complex region so firmly in the national imagination. Fascinated, repelled or merely curious, representatives from the entire cultural field were drawn to the industrialising North in the late eighteenth and earlier nineteenth centuries and their observations have provided a convenient set of references and images ever since. While, as the next chapter shows, the timeless, pre-lapsarian North had its celebrants and its distinctive role to play, the North of England as 'the land of the working class' and urban/industrial monolith clearly came to predominate in the productive interchange between objective reality and discursive practice.

North and South

The previously often marginal North moved far more towards the forefront of national economic and political life over the course of the eighteenth and nineteenth centuries, only to experience, sometimes extremely painfully, a relative decline in fortunes over the twentieth. This section outlines this difficult trajectory. Although the 'South' and London are by no means co-terminous, consideration of the capital's role in national life in comparison to that of the North and 'provincial' England more generally provides an obvious route here. Its is, after all, London and its hinterlands – particularly the south-east – that has always been the particular target for northern hostility. London's striking dominance of English life in the later medieval and early modern periods, rooted in its marriage of the nation's key political, economic and cultural functions, is well documented.[32] By the middle of the seventeenth century it was home to perhaps 375,000 people at a time when its nearest rivals, Bristol, Newcastle and Norwich, had populations of barely 25,000. About 10 per cent of the nation's population lived in the capital at any one time and about 15 per cent spent some part of their life there. No other European state exhibited this level of capital city 'primacy' and the extraordinary levels and longevity of political, economic and cultural power that London enjoyed helped secure the capital's advantages and structure its relationship with the rest of the country in ways that appertain to the present day. However, although London continued to hold a little over 10 per cent of the population throughout the eighteenth century, from the late seventeenth century, observers were increasing aware of the growing significance of the expanding commercial and industrial centres in the north and midlands; by about 1760, it was obvious that important alterations were occurring in the balance of power between the capital and what was generally termed the 'country' but was about to become known as the 'provinces'.

The term came into common parlance from about the last decade of the eighteenth century. It was very much a metropolitan-centred concept, acknowledging the importance of the new industrial and commercial centres but placing them in a dependent relationship with capital: 'provincial', after all, already had clear pejorative connotations of intellectual narrowness and a lack of refinement and the new term carried these inflections with it.[33] Nevertheless, both labels were increasingly appropriated by regionally based politicians and used to symbolise the dynamic role that their areas played in the new order. This was given shape in the raft of vigorous political, social and economic movements that began in earnest with Christopher Wyvill's Yorkshire Association in 1779 and that was to make the nineteenth century 'the heyday of provincial initiative and independence in economic and political affairs'.[34]

Although Birmingham proved one of the most fertile sources of political and social activity and the flowering of provincial culture was genuinely nationwide, the larger northern cities generally and Manchester particularly were at the heart of much of this new enterprise.[35] Provincial energy and vitality was constantly contrasted with London's role as holder of unfair monopolies (Liverpool bitterly resented restrictions on the shipping trade before the 1830s) and the undeserving and wasteful recipient of both the material wealth and the human talent created elsewhere. It was also seen as temperamentally and structurally geared to political apathy. In a famed rebuke, the Chartist *Northern Star* argued that 'London is always the last to stir, or when it takes the initiative, such is its overwhelming bulk, and the consequent segregation of its parts, that no powerful and well compacted concentration of popular energy is produced … How different all this is in a provincial town'.[36] Obviously, not all views of London were negative. Its rich career opportunities drew many ambitious northerners and its innumerable attractions enthralled tourists and visitors. Nevertheless, a sense outside the metropolis that the provinces inhabited a world morally superior to that of the capital was a core nineteenth-century mentality and one that was endlessly reinforced and reshaped in the twentieth. It will be a recurring theme in this book.

In the light of the economic and political realities of the twentieth century, it is not surprising that such symbolic capital has been so enthusiastically preserved and cherished within the North. Just how far the balance between South and North had changed in the period to about 1890 is not clear. In the economic sphere especially, there is much debate as to the respective wealth and power of the northern manufacturing and commercial centres on the one hand and the

City of London on the other. Whatever the situation, many in the North clearly believed that the nineteenth century essentially belonged to their region. The period from the 1890s, however, saw a fundamental shift back in favour of London and the south-east. The change began gradually, with initial developments usefully described as 'subterranean' by one historian.[37] The increased penetration of the national press into the markets of their local and regional counterparts and the national advertising and sale of branded goods were important here, as was the increasing migration of political, economic and cultural institutions to the capital. Significantly, there was nothing new in this. In 1785, at the very moment when the provincial renaissance was in early maturity, a decision to place the headquarters of the General Chamber of Manufacturers in London was defended with the argument that 'as the seat of government, and the grand magazine of the kingdom, [London] must obviously be the place of general union'.[38] The Anti-Corn Law League's move from Manchester to the capital in 1842 was perhaps the ultimate testimony to its hegemony. Nevertheless, many institutions were able to remain in the North or other provincial locations, feeding out of and into, local interests and expertise. By the 1920s, and probably earlier, such a decision looked increasingly eccentric in many spheres.[39]

Significantly, it was in this period (from about 1880 to 1920) that what Donald Horne has called the 'Northern Metaphor' lost out to its southern equivalent. Horne was not attempting to define North and South or to capture images of them but rather to identify national self-images that could be broadly attributed to distinct territories.

> In the *Northern Metaphor* Britain is pragmatic, empirical, calculating, Puritan, bourgeois, enterprising, adventurous, scientific, serious and believes in struggle. Its sinful excess is a ruthless avarice, rationalized in the belief that the prime impulse in all human beings is a rational, calculating, economic self-interest. In the *Southern Metaphor* Britain is romantic, illogical, muddled, divinely lucky, Anglican, aristocratic, traditional, frivolous, and believes in order and tradition. Its sinful excess is a ruthless pride, rationalized in the belief that men are born to serve.[40]

The victory of the southern metaphor with its resultant celebration and sanctification of certain types of cultivated rural landscape most often associated with the 'south country', renewed respect for the ancient and the pre-industrial and tendency to view the 'Home Counties' as something akin to an English 'homeland', was at the core of the reconstructed 'Englishness' of the late nineteenth and earlier twentieth centuries. While 'southern' victory was neither as complete as is sometimes suggested or fixed for all time, it had certainly gone far enough in this period significantly to devalue 'both the locales of and the qualities that had made, the industrial revolution'.[41] The North arrived in the twentieth century with its greatest days tainted and its future increasingly under threat.

The shifting balance between North and South became brutally clear over the course of the inter-war period above all in the economic sphere; the idea of a North–South economic divide indeed appears to have passed into popular parlance in the late 1920s. Crudely put, the North as principal location of staple industries such as coal, textiles and shipbuilding suffered more severely than other sectors of the economy from loss of world markets and weak domestic demand. Conversely, the South and much of the midlands, economic potential unlocked by the spread of the electricity grid and by the growth of local consumer demand, enjoyed the benefits of expanding light industry, typified by the manufacture of motor cars and electrical goods. The consequent economic indices are eloquent testimony to the changes wrought. The population of London and the south-east grew by 9 per cent in the decade 1921–31, for example, a clear indication of its new prosperity. Although patterns of unemployment were complex, with high rates recorded in some southern locations and extremely low ones in certain northern ones, regional variations were only too apparent, with rates in the North above the national average, those in the south-west, south-east, London and the midlands below. Even during the relative recovery in 1937 unemployment in the north-west and north-east still ran at 14 per cent and 11 per cent respectively, compared with 7.2 per cent in the midlands and 6.3 per cent in London. Again, sections of the north-east along with west Cumberland were the only English regions to be given special designation under the 1934 Special Areas Act.[42] At the same time, the establishment of the BBC, clearly driven by a metropolitan-national agenda, the emergence of other southern-based cultural industries and the further penetration of the national press into the North gave a further push to centripetal forces. For those outside of the region, its economic difficulties placed a new layer of otherness over old ones that had at least associated industrial landscapes with wealth creation. For many of its residents old fears about the power of the centre transmuted into the elegies for lost talent that so marked the 1930s. An editorial in the *Heaton Review*, a remarkably rich church magazine published in Bradford from 1927, speaks well for wider sensibilities. 'We are rich as a province in the wealth of ability which is native to our northland, though we deplore the magnetic and insistent call of the Metropolis and the South, which makes its gaping inroads into our possessions and weakens our hopes for a more concrete provincial character.'[43]

The exigencies of war followed by post-war recovery and a political settle-
ment that saw both major parties 'assign a key role to regional policy' in the
1950s and 1960s, held regional economic imbalances in check and perhaps –
opinion is divided – even began to redress them in some cases.[44] At the same
time, the North became fashionable within the cultural field, albeit in Graham
Turner's useful phrase, 'in a rather strange and oblique sort of way'.[45] Its very
'otherness' in terms of landscape and its image as the land of the working class
and thus supposedly a site for honesty and authenticity, briefly made it the ideal
space for the working out of issues relating to the contemporary condition of an
England and a culture dominated by the South and its middle class.

Between about 1957, with the publication of John Braine's *Room at the Top*,
and the mid-1960s, northern literature, film, television and popular music penetrated the national culture to an extent hitherto unknown. Indeed, there was a
kind of 'northernisation' of the national culture at this time with Richard
Hoggart's sociology of mass culture-cum-autobiography of Hunslet life, *The
Uses of Literacy*, published in the same year as *Room at the Top*, crucial here.
David Gervais has argued suggestively that the 'axis of Englishness' has moved
northward over the course of the twentieth century, with nostalgia for the lost
communities of the industrial north increasingly generating sensibilities once
reserved for the rural 'South Country' and Hoggart's book is central to this
process.[46] The success of the Beatles was in its turn immensely important and to
Liverpool in particular. The 'Merseysound' of 1963 indeed provided a distinct
second phase of this northern cultural moment, building on the successes of
1957 and beyond but moving the focus from the 'textile North' that been the
dominant setting until that point. Finally, but crucially, the emergence of a
regional commercial television network from 1955 meant that the North had
the potential to portray itself to the rest of the nation on its own terms far more
easily than in the past. For all the turn to 'Swinging London' in the mid-1960s a
tradition of northern cultural production and dissemination has continued to
feed into and influence the national culture from this point. The urban/indus-
trial North felt good about itself, moreover, with local magazines and newspa-
pers celebrating the image of modernity offered by new high-rise flats and
shopping centres.[47]

Yet even at the height of the North's cultural triumphs, countervailing tendencies were all too easily apparent with none more symbolic than the
Manchester Guardian's decision to remove its home city from the masthead in
1959 and to decamp to London five years later.[48] The region became at the same
time ever more the focus of an often affectionate but disabling humour playing

with notions of it being 'grim up North'. More fundamentally, the oil crisis of 1973 and its consequences, followed by the election of Margaret Thatcher's free market Conservative government in 1979, ushered in economic changes which were to accelerate and intensify the divide between North and South. By the mid-1980s the language of that divide had become a staple of political and economic discourse and a few simple indicators show why.[49] Between 1979 and 1986 the number of people in employment in the North fell by 1.1 million while in the South numbers rose by 356,000. Critically, the South far outstripped the North in the generation of jobs in the new hi-tech industries such as computing. By 1984, the south-east (*excluding* London) alone enjoyed 27.5 per cent of such employment in comparison to Yorkshire and Humberside's mere 3.4 per cent. Similarly, the South's long established role as the administrative centre of the national economy became even more entrenched. By the late 1980s, while 485 of Britain's 1,000 biggest companies had their headquarters in London, only 15 were sited in the whole of the North Standard Government Region.[50] While it is difficult to sustain any reading of 'North–South' relationships over the longer term in truly colonial terms, it is not surprising that some politically engaged northerners began to view themselves as living under precisely such an arrangement from the 1980s.[51]

In a painful cultural accompaniment to all this, so many of the North's previous positive associations were challenged and tarnished. Raphael Samuel's account of this process cannot be bettered.

> The very qualities which had recommended it to the 'new wave' writers and filmmakers now served as talismans of narrowness. The rich associational life, such as that of the workingmen's club, was seen not as supportive but as excluding, a way in which the natives could keep newcomers and strangers at bay ... The solidarities of the workplace were reconceptualised as a species of male bonding, a licence for the subjugation of women; while the smokestack industries which had been the pride of the North now appeared, retrospectively, as ecological nightmares. In another set of dialectical inversions, the modernizations of the 1960s were stigmatised as planning disasters, imprisoning the local population in no-go estates and tower blocks.[52]

There were undoubtedly varying degrees of painful reality in these critiques and they affected communities, especially working-class ones, throughout the country. Nevertheless, reaction to deindustrialisation impacted most damagingly upon northern England, rendering it in Samuel's phrase 'a byword for backwardness'. Liverpool suffered more than most. Although always associated in the popular imagination with a 'rough' working-class culture, the 1960s had overlain far more positive images. Now, a highly publicised mixture of economic decay

and political and industrial militancy saw the city defined as 'Britain's Beirut' a
'"showcase" of everything that has gone wrong in Britain's major cities'. Football
crowds, especially but not exclusively in the South, began to sing (and still do) 'I'd
rather be a Paki than a Scouse'.[53]

In recent years there has undoubtedly been convergence in such key indicators as regional unemployment rates and, as ever, both intra- and inter-regional
complexities cut across neat lines of division. Within the North, for example,
Cheshire enjoyed a per capita GDP 3 per cent above the European Union
average in the mid-1990s while neighbouring Merseyside's fell some 26 per cent
below that average. Similarly, while one postcode sector in Bradford recorded
the lowest average household income in Yorkshire and Humberside in 1998
(£9,562), some 25 miles away in Wetherby, the region's wealthiest sector
enjoyed an average of £42,433.[54] At the same time, evidence of serious economic and social deprivation can be found in the South, especially in parts of
Essex and Kent and in certain areas of inner London, always at the bottom of
any national index of wealth and prosperity.[55] Yet another complicating factor
has been added by claims that an 'East–West' divide is actually more revealing
of the English (and indeed, British) condition, with the area to the west of the
Pennines, the M1 and the Solent disadvantaged by an inferior transport system,
a larger legacy of problems and a greater distance from the new markets in
Europe.[56] Overall, however, most close observers still see a sharp North–South
division that is as strong as ever in economic terms.[57]

Crucially, it is also a divide that still exists in many people's heads. This is
often expressed at a humourous, somewhat ironic level, but real passion can
come through. When journalist Robert Chesshyre visited the North in June
2000, he found anger expressed about the patronising attitude to northern
accents and culture ('if you wear a suit and can say "entrepreneurship", they're
gobsmacked'); the London media's failure to cover northern events, the government's tendency to spend on prestige projects in the South to the detriment of
the North and much more.[58] Moreover, the nascent movement for regional
devolution, initially rooted in the harsh 1980s, has actually gained a slightly
increased momentum in the more optimistic climate accompanying the recent
regeneration of some northern townscapes. Old antipathies can be sustained by
confidence as much as by anger. While the North–South divide is undoubtedly
both a powerful rhetorical device often misused by those in the North seeking
to simplify difficult issues and, alternatively, an easy source of humour for
anyone who cares to use it, it captures and has long captured some fundamental
economic and cultural realities. This is perhaps one reason why northerners are

so inexact in their definition of the 'South', seeing it in the abstract as a source of misdirected power rather than an objective geographical entity.

Knowing the North, imagining the North

England is a small country with its southern capital not excessively distant from anywhere. London lies 160 miles from Sheffield, 185 from Manchester, 274 from Newcastle and 301 from Carlisle and, by the late nineteenth century, was comfortably within a half-day's travel from all but the most remote northern destinations. The spread of the motorway system and high-speed rail links from the late twentieth century have (given good luck) put the capital and its hinterlands in even easier reach. Yet, one of the most striking features of the North's place in the national culture is that relatively few people from outside the region have ever gained much personal experience of it. Certainly, very few have ever lived there. In 1901, for example, approximately 75 per cent of the populations of Durham, Lancashire and Westmorland had been born in their county of residence, with most of the remainder hailing from neighbouring northern counties. Those born in the south of England, defined here as London and six nearby counties, made up only 1.3 per cent of the total residents of these three counties: in some industrial towns the percentage fell below 1 per cent.[59] Obviously, a census snapshot cannot capture the full story. Itinerant workers, such as building workers, commercial travellers and military personnel with northern postings will have enjoyed periods of varying length in the region, while from the later twentieth century the expansion of higher education has also been a mechanism attracting 'migrants' into the north. Most of these are short-term residents but some cities have been able to hold growing numbers after graduation: one fifth of students from outside West Yorkshire were staying in Leeds after graduation by 2000.[60] Not only students but also their families have often enjoyed an initial introduction to the North through the now obligatory ferrying of bags, baggage and music centres along the English motorway network. However, these additional forms of quasi-residence and recent increases in geographical mobility have not fundamentally altered the basic pattern.

Many outsiders, even in the later twentieth century, have indeed been almost frightened of the region, and desperately reluctant to go there. In the late 1960s, Graham Turner noted that many managerial recruits to the north-east, especially southerners, admitted to expressing 'horror' on hearing of their postings. Most saw their spells in the region as effectively a spell of emigration (the word 'posting' does seem especially apt), beneficial only for its offer of cheaper housing, increased pay and better prospects on 'return'. Twenty years later, the Chief Executive of a major Bradford company admitted that 'When I told my wife I was going to take a job in Bradford, she said "Oh God!"'[61]

Potentially the most practicable and fertile source for outsiders seeking personal experience of the North has been tourism but, even here, the outcome has been limited. Even with the advent of mass tourism since the 1950s and the emphasis placed on tourism within the northern economy since the 1970s, the seven-county North has an improving but still only modest share of the national market. In 1999, the four regional tourist board areas within the North attracted between them 26 per cent of all English tourists at a time when the far smaller west country region, England's premier holiday destination, attracted 22 per cent.[62] Moreover, the North draws most of its tourists from within. A 1988 survey showed that of the four areas, only the north-west attracted less than half of its tourists (46 per cent) from the North of England (Blackpool is critical here). Significantly, only about 20 per cent of visitors to the North as a whole came from the south-east.[63]

It should also be acknowledged that much of the North has also been *terra incognita* for its own residents. When Phyllis Bentley sought tuition for a B.A. examination in 1913, it never occurred to her to look just twenty miles east to Leeds; even her middle-class Halifax family 'knew nothing' of the nearby city.[64] On a larger geographical scale and in a later period, writer Keith Waterhouse did not made the forty-mile journey from his native Leeds to Manchester until he was 21, while author Graham Turner, born into a Cheshire family of keen fell walkers in the 1930s, did not visit either the Yorkshire Dales or the Lake District until journalistic research took him there in the 1960s.[65] Clearly, certain locations such as Blackpool long served as a common reference point and increased mobility in the later twentieth century altered personal geographies in often unexpected ways. While visiting a particularly popular working men's club in the small south Yorkshire town of Greasborough in the 1960s, Turner encountered coach parties from as far away as County Durham.[66] Nevertheless, life for many northerners (and most English people for that matter) has often been intensely local, with even neighbouring towns remaining unvisited if they are not part of long-established patterns of community or family linkage. All this underlines the huge importance of cultural forms in constructing and reinforcing notions of 'the North'; most people from outside the region (and many in it) have only 'known' it through the various cultural representations that form the core of this book.

As already implied, there have been moments when the North has enjoyed, if that is always the correct word, an especially prominent share of those representations within the national culture. It is possible to identify four moments of intensified interest, namely the 1840s and earlier 1850s; the 1930s; the years 1957–*c*.1964 and the 1980s. Significantly, all bar the third period were times when the North was suffering from either intense economic difficulty and/or generating major political challenges that included significant elements of working-class mobilisation. The North generally intruded, it would appear, when it was troubled and troublesome. This periodisation provides a chronological template for the thematic studies that follow, although not a rigid formula: while some forms adhere to this outline extremely closely, the relative autonomy of culture ensures that others do not. The exceptional circumstances of wartime should also be noted here, especially those relating to the 'People's War' of 1939–45 when the North was warmly embraced for its distinctive contribution to a wider Englishness or Britishness. The British Board of Film Censors' decision in 1940 to allow a screen adaptation of the previously undesirable *Love on the Dole*, a version that consigned northern mass unemployment to what was portrayed as distant history in its closing sequence, is an obvious example.[67] This was not just a matter of propaganda or manipulation, however, for attitudes were changed at least for brief periods in both North and South. One Yorkshire writer saw 'a new, half-envious respect for southern England' emerge within the North from 1940.[68] The issue of war and regional identity would certainly repay the attention not afforded to it in this study.

The final task here is to outline the key images of the North and ideas about it that will be encountered in the ensuing chapters. The genealogy of northern stereotyping needs far more research but it would seem that both standard external and internal representations are long established. The North was being constructed from the centre in a definite and opinionated way from at least the twelfth century and while northern self-representation may have lagged behind somewhat – the evidence is patchy – it was certainly visible by the sixteenth century and possibly before. Internal and external characterisation of the region often focused on similar elements of landscape, behaviour and mentality but, as will be seen, interpretation of their meanings could vary dramatically. In terms of the external view, twelfth-century chronicler William of Malmesbury was happy to use 'disparaging adjectives' about the earlier Northumbrian kingdom, referring to their haughtiness of its inhabitants, noting 'the prevalence of degenerate manners' and deeming them 'a ferocious race of people … ever ripe for rebellion'. Some Tudor chroniclers viewed what indeed in their era could be a distant and sometimes rebellious region as a place where the populous were 'savage and more eager than others for upheavals'.[69] Such a picture was reinforced and embellished by the depictions of a primitive, unsophisticated place blessed with a harsh climate and bleak environment that were a staple of the travel literature emerging from the sixteenth century.[70] Celia Fiennes and Daniel Defoe certainly had plentiful problems with northern manners, accent, climate and scenery.[71] How influential such works were at the time – readership would have been confined to the 'middling sorts' and upward – is unclear, but there is some evidence that pejorative views of the North, or at least specific parts of it, were entering into popular discourse. As early as the mid-seventeenth century, for example, 'to put Yorkshire of a man' served as a phrase for cheating, while Henry Carey could entitle his 1736 ballad opera *A Wonder, or, An Honest Yorkshireman.*[72]

The North thus entered the period of the 'industrial revolution' with a powerful set of negative images already attached. As Jewell, Musgrove and others have argued, the economic and social upheavals associated with rapid industrialisation did not therefore create a new image of the North, but, rather, allowed existing ones to be sharpened, expanded and made available to a wider audience. To older notions of the North as harsh and bleak were added innumerable descriptions of the horrors of northern townscapes. Reportage of working-class political and industrial movements in the 1830s and 1840s (although not confined to the North) revived old notions of the region as rebellious and truculent and, as Rawnsley shrewdly notes, 'when such fears subsided, images of the northern working class as stubborn, independent and unruly, remained'.[73] The sense of the North as unsophisticated was given a distinctive twist from the late eighteenth century as the new industrial and commercial middle classes fell victim to the charge of 'philistinism'. In 1821, *Blackwood's Edinburgh Magazine* famously described the Manchester elite as 'gentlemen, whose erudition, we believe, consists in the playing whist, drinking port and damning "form"'.[74] What was often, as in this case, specifically Tory propaganda aimed at political enemies, became a more generalised discourse in this period. When travel writer Walter White walked the streets of Hull in the 1850s he saw 'evidences enough of – to use a mild adjective – an unpolished population. The northern characteristics were marked'.[75]

This is not to deny the many extremely positive external views of the region. From at least the late seventeenth century many travellers saw the North as a place of hard work, progress and achievement and its industrial sites increasingly became places of pilgrimage.[76] Again, with the Romantic Movement transforming attitudes to landscape from the late eighteenth century, northern hills and mountains increasingly became a focus for artistic celebration and sites of physical, moral and emotional regeneration rather than the sources of terror they had been only had a century before. Parts of the North, especially the Lake

District, therefore became favoured elements of the national landscape even if they were sometimes represented as somehow not quite of the North, accidentally part of its physical geography but deserving of a better fate.[77] Metropolitan 'flexible positional superiority' clearly allowed the North space to serve crucial and valued functions within the national culture. Celebratory depictions were, nevertheless, decidedly secondary to far less flattering ones.

Far less is known about northern *self*-image in the pre- and early industrial periods than its external equivalent. Some within the North were certainly aware of outside prejudice: when the citizens of York petitioned for a university in 1652, they noted how 'we have been looked upon as a rude and barbarous people'.[78] It is also clear that the North increasingly had the power to imagine itself and thus to structure the creative tensions that gave territorial conflicts shape and meaning. Although, as Shields argues, northerners undoubtedly 're-worked, accepted or rejected' images of their region 'produced in the cultural hub of London', this claim for agency is actually not forceful enough: they were increasingly producers as much as they were active consumers in this process.[79] There are clear hints of this self awareness within specific sub-regions if not across the North as a whole. The tentative beginnings of a written dialect tradition from the late seventeenth century and more continuously from the second half of the eighteenth provided an early but important source of local and subregional self-representation. Although there have been intense academic arguments over the class provenance and ownership of the late eighteenth-and early nineteenth-century Tyneside songs that established 'Bob Cranky' as the archetypal hard-working but harder drinking collier and set 'Canny Newcastle' and its heroes against presumptuous London, the very existence of these pieces shows regions at work in shaping the representation of their own worlds.[80]

The stock language and imagery used of the North actually changed very little between the medieval period and the nineteenth century. By the third quarter of the nineteenth century 'northern character' was a remarkably settled thing in both external and internal representations. While Peter Mandler has seen 'national character' as a fluid and multi-faceted construction from its emergence as a liberal ideology in the 1840s through to its far more heterogeneous depiction in the inter-war period, regional character appears remarkably static and free of contextual influences.[81] National character was malleable in the face of changed circumstance, always defined with attention both to international considerations and to class politics. The stress on hierarchy and the gentlemanly ideal that became important in the twentieth century, for example, was to some degree an elite response to the rise of a mass electorate. Its regional and local equivalents, conversely, were domestic and trans-class. As such they could remain fixed and, indeed, had to if both insiders and outsiders were to use them effectively. While Mandler suggests that the notion of national character became ever less useful because it became so contradictory and confusing, regional character ran the very different risk of becoming so rigid that it became a cliché that offered easy comic potential for outsiders while denuding internal versions of any real power.[82]

This is to run ahead far too swiftly, however, for it is first necessary to examine the ascribed key elements of the North and 'northern character' and the various interpretations that they have been open to. Focusing rather more on the characteristics of people than environment, table 1 captures some of the most frequently encountered attributes claimed for the region and is intended as a general signpost for what is to come.[83] Rather than just listing, it emphasises contestation, drawing attention both to the way in which a particular trait or feature can be interpreted according to the spatial perspective of the relevant social actors and across the broad lines of 'North–South' conflict. The middle column acts as the point of reference from which these processes can be observed.

While stereotypes must contain sufficient observable reality to allow them to function, interest is here rooted solely in the way that they function as myths, in the accepted anthropological sense of stories we tell each other and about each other in order to make sense of society. 'Image' and 'reality' are not being measured against each other. To some eyes this depiction probably looks too obvious, a litany of well-paraded clichés.[84] However, the fact that such notions have become so much part of our common sense is indicative of their power and thus of the need to study them. The table may also look too confrontational and possibly is. Much of the 'North–South' discourse in England has always operated at a relatively humorous level (although humour can be cruel and disabling) and regional differences have often been sunk in wider English, British and imperial mentalities. At the same time, the external view has been represented at its most extreme. The positive attributions in the first column should not be ignored and it must not be forgotten that many outsiders have found the North stimulating and refreshing sometimes precisely because of its 'otherness'. Nevertheless, a stress on tension does direct attention the rich repertoire of mutual suspicion and misunderstanding that has surrounded so many northern engagements with the 'South'. At the same time, it draws attention once again to northern 'agency' and leads to an appreciation that northern popular culture was capable of constructing an inner view worked out often in contradistinction (but not necessarily in reaction) to London and the South.

Table I Imagining the North

External (especially southern) images of the North	Northern self-image	Northern images of the South
Character		
Truculent/carrying chip on shoulder	Independent	Subservient
Rude/lacking social graces	Blunt/straight-talking	Evasive/duplicitous
Hardworking	Hard-working/physically tough	Effete/wasteful/absorbing efforts and energy of the rest of the country
Over-competitive/ungentlemanly	Competitive	Dilettante/lacking spirit
Philistine/unpolished, albeit highly musical	Practical/productive	Snobbish/wasteful/superficial
Mean	Careful with money	Wasteful
Homely	Friendly/hospitable	Unfriendly/unsociable
Parochial	Proud of roots and identity	Cosmopolitan/rootless
Working-class	Meritocratic/egalitarian	Nepotistic/elitist
Prejudiced/biased	Knowledgeable/holding strong views	Evasive/equivocal
Humorous if crude	Humorous/witty	Quick-witted but overly fond of *double entendre*
A breed apart	A breed apart	A breed apart
Landscape and geography		
Relentlessly urban/bleak/site of much open, often wild countryside	Varied in nature	Soft countryside/London an exciting place offering much opportunity, but too dominant and too marked by extremes of wealth
Wet/cold/bracing	Harsh but better than often claimed	Warm/pleasant
Industrial	Industrial but economically more varied than usually appreciated	Financial/place of consumption rather than production

Clearly, broad sweeps of this type do miss out the many subtle differences in characterisation *within* the North. Notions of 'Yorkshireness' particularly influence the first and second columns. This is to some degree justifiable. Yorkshire has enjoyed a deserved reputation for an especially intense county pride, and one probably established earlier than elsewhere in the region, with one late nineteenth-century writer claiming with the knowing hyperbole so typical of Yorkshire writing that the county was 'the most birthproud member of the human race'.[85] It has certainly imposed itself and been imposed upon the characterisation of the North. However, distinctions between and within different sub-regions have often been posited by both internal and external sources. Lancashire, for example, has been viewed as softer, friendlier and less financially oriented than its eastern neighbour.[86] Similarly, the easy bonhomie and drink-fuelled cheeriness of the Tyneside 'Bob Cranky' archetype, sits a little uneasily with the slightly dour Yorkshire 'tyke'.[87] Liverpool provides yet another variation, its strong Celtic heritage and large pool of both casual labour and transient seafarers supposedly giving the city an ebullient, extrovert, non-conformist edge and a quick, often surreal sense of humour (a similar humour is sometimes claimed for the north-east) that marks it out from the rest of the North in one respect and provides an apotheosis in another.[88] Even within Yorkshire, where a single county identity was more likely to be broadly accepted, interesting variations could emerge. The steel city of Sheffield, for example, long saw itself as morally superior to Leeds, a place almost southern in its association with easy profits and a tailoring trade 'hardly worth the time, effort and skill of real men'.[89] In the nineteenth century, claims for intra-county differences were often tied to racial arguments. Walter White proclaimed three types of Yorkshireman, the 'broad-shouldered rustic' Saxon and the Scandinavian in the east and north, 'the Celt, short, swarthy, and Irish-looking' in the west. Commenting on the ugliness of some working-class women of the West Riding, he noted their being remarkable 'for that protruding lower jaw which so characterises many of the Irish peasantry'.[90] More positively, many prized the Yorkshire Dalesfolk and other upland rural dwellers as repositories of old values and as individuals in a mass society, almost as holy innocents; Teesdale farmer Hannah Hauxwell, focus of an immensely successful Yorkshire Television documentary and subsequent series of books, received such treatment as late as the 1970s and 1980s.[91]

Although most of the characteristics outlined above were usually ascribed to the population as a whole, the North has generally been coded as masculine (albeit in a more complex way than might be assumed) and set against a more effeminate South. The region is often perceived as, and in reality has been, a site of much hard, demanding physical labour with one of its emblematic occupations, coal-mining, exclusively male from the 1840s. Women, of course, have had more than their share of such work but in a society where the male breadwinner norm has been assumed from the mid-nineteenth to the late twentieth century, male work has often been uppermost in public perception. Physical toughness in sport, a male republic for most of the period, has been much celebrated and seen as an extension of this experience of daily 'graft'. Again, many of the North's representative characters whether real life ones, such as the brass bandsman or the professional sportsman, or fictional ones such as Joe Lampton and the other 'Angry Young Men' of the 1950s and 1960s, have been male.

Women have tended to be closely associated with particular northern attributes such as the generic 'homeliness' and the phlegmatic quality and lack of 'fuss' that were seen as distinctive Yorkshire traits, but these are obviously characteristics that easily attach to them.[92] On some occasions, however, they have been allowed a far more radical representation. The North has certainly been the key site for England's 'strong' women, again both real and fictional. Individuals as varied as the Brontë sisters, politicians Bessie Braddock and Barbara Castle and the racing cyclist Beryl Burton have been both and represented and imagined as, path-breaking women empowered to at least some degree by their nothernnness.[93] From Harold Brighouse's Maggie Hobson in *Hobson's Choice*, to Walter Greenwood's Sally Hardcastle in *Love on the Dole*, Willy Russell's Rita White in *Educating Rita* and beyond, the cultural field has been populated with determined, resolute, admirable (young in these examples) northern women. It is significant that all three of the above examples are drawn from texts set in Lancashire, seen by many as more of a matriarchal society than any other in the North as a result of its relatively high level of female employment, at least in the cotton districts.[94] The north-east, with its very different occupational structure, has certainly produced fewer fictional characters of this type, at least until recently. These issues will be pursued throughout the book to some degree, although the topic deserves a study of its own. For the moment, however, future projects must wait. It is now time to pursue the central themes of this one.

Notes

1 N. Evans, 'Regional dynamics: north Wales, 1750–1914', in E. Royle (ed.), *Regional Identities* (Manchester: Manchester University Press, 1998), p. 201.

2 J. Hill and J. Williams, 'Introduction', *Sport and Identity in the North of England* (Keele: Keele University Press, 1996), p. 6. The Standard Government Region has

never comprised more than the historic counties of Northumberland, Durham, Cumberland, Westmorland and the North Riding of Yorkshire.

3 G. Turner, *The North Country* (London: Eyre and Spottiswoode, 1967), p. 14.

4 E. Vale, *North Country* (London: Batsford, 1937), p. 2.

5 N. Rees, *Phrases and Sayings* (London: Bloomsbury, 1995), pp. 350, 514. These phrases appear to have been coined the 1960s and 1970s although they reflect older mentalities.

6 P. Balchin, *Regional Policy in Britain. The North–South Divide* (London: Paul Chapman, 1989), pp. 1–2, for example. The notion of such a boundary appears to have taken on increased popularity in the late 1920s. N. Rees, *Bloomsbury Dictionary of Phrase and Allusion* (London: Bloomsbury, 1991), p. 242.

7 Cornwall, for example, often becomes a part of the North in such analyses.

8 H. Jewell, *The North–South Divide. The Origins of Northern Consciousness in England* (Manchester: Manchester University Press, 1994), p. 25. For the whole discussion, see pp. 8–25.

9 D. Smith. *North and South* (London: Penguin, 1989), p. 266.

10 Jewell, *North–South Divide*, p. 24

11 M. Tebbutt, '"In the midlands but not of them": Derbyshire's Dark Peak – an imagined northern landscape', in N. Kirk (ed.), *Northern Identities. Historical Interpretations of 'The North' and 'Northernness'* (Aldershot: Ashgate, 2000), pp. 163–94.

12 D. Neave, 'The identity of the East Riding of Yorkshire', in E. Royle (ed.), *Issues of Northern Identity* (Manchester: Manchester University Press), p. 199. S. Caunce, 'Urban systems, identity and development in Lancashire and Yorkshire: a complex question', in Kirk (ed.), *Northern Identities*, p. 61.

13 These terms show that academics are no less prone to London-centredness than any other group, with the capital obviously the point of reference here. 'Upper' and 'lower' might be more usefully neutral terms but I have stayed with normal conventions.

14 P. Trudgill, *The Dialects of England* (Oxford: Basil Blackwell, 1990), p. 34. See below, chapter 4.

15 On defining the north-east, see N. McCord, 'The regional identity of north-eastern England in the nineteenth and twentieth centuries', in Royle (ed.), *Issues of Northern Identity*, pp. 102–17; W. Stokes, 'Definition of a financial region', in ibid., pp. 118–53.

16 A. Briggs, 'Issues in Northern History', *Northern History*, 1, 1966, p. 3.

17 *United We Stand*, 120, April 2003, p. 25.

18 A. Myers, 'Being beastly to Priestley', *Northern Review*, 1, Spring 1995, p. 62. See too, David Byrne's description of Labour Party's regional office as the 'Yorkshire mafia'. Ibid., p. 33.

19 J. Belchem, *Merseypride. Essays in Liverpool Exceptionalism* (Liverpool: Liverpool University Press, 2000), pp. xii, 3. Glaswegians begged to differ.

20 *Liverpool Daily Post*, 20 April 1964.

21 Many academic works still use this designation.

22 F. Musgrove, *The North of England. A History from Roman Times to the Present* (Oxford: Oxford University Press, 1992), p. 17. See especially, A. Briggs, *Victorian Cities* (London: Penguin edn, 1968), pp. 88–138; G. S. Messinger, *Manchester in the Victorian Age. The Half-Known City* (Manchester: Manchester University Press, 1985); A. Kidd, *Manchester* (Keele: Keele University Press, 1996 edn).

23 For the BBC and the North see below chapter 3, for Horniman chapter 4 and Hallé chapter 6. Kidd, *Manchester*, p. 193.

24 Local elites have possibly become more ecumenical. In 2001, Liverpool established formal structures in order to learn from Manchester's success in the field of urban regeneration.

25 Rounded figures based on county occupational tables in 1921 census.

26 R. Colls, *Identity of England* (Oxford: Oxford University Press, 2002), pp. 261–2.

27 N. Tranter, *British Population in the Twentieth Century* (Basingstoke: Macmillan, 1996), p. 9; Census of England and Wales, 1931, General tables, table 8B.

28 P. J. Waller, *Town, City and Nation. England, 1850–1914* (Oxford: Oxford University Press, 1983), pp. 73–4, 3–4. Waller defines 'exceptional growth' as at least one period of 'intercensal growth of over 25 per cent'.

29 E. Royle, *Chartism* (Harlow: Longman, 1980 edn), pp. 65, 62.

30 F. Musgrove, *The North of England*, pp. 267–8.

31 *Regional Trends* 36, 2001, p. 74. The North East, where 39 per cent of all workers were unionised, had the nation's highest level. The UK average was 30 per cent.

32 E.A. Wrigley, 'A simple model of London's importance in changing English society and economy, 1650–1750', *Past and Present*, 37, 1967, pp. 44–70. The following is based on P. Clark and P. Slack (eds), *English Towns in Transition, 1500–1700* (Oxford: Oxford University Press, 1976); P. J. Corfield, *The Impact of English Towns, 1700–1800* (Oxford: Oxford University Press, 1981).

33 D. Read, *The English Provinces c.1760–1960. A Study in Influence* (London: Edwin Arnold, 1964), pp. 1–3. 'Country' was never entirely displaced, however. For examples in fiction, see Arnold Bennett, *A Man from the North* (1898, London: Hamish Hamilton edn 1973), pp. 21, 47; J. L. Hodson, *Harvest in the North* (1934, London: Author publ. edn., 1955), p. 370.

34 Read, *English Provinces*, p. xi.

35 Read remains an excellent starting point, but see also P. Borsay, *The English Urban Renaissance. Culture and Society in the Provincial Town, 1660–1770* (Oxford: Clarendon, 1989); J. Brewer, *The Pleasures of the Imagination. English Culture in the Eighteenth Century* (London: HarperCollins, 1997), part vi; S. Gunn, *The Public Culture of the Victorian Middle Class. Ritual and Authority and the English Industrial City, 1840–1914* (Manchester: Manchester University Press, 2000).

36 *Northern Star* 21 Dec. 1850, quoted in D. Read, *English Provinces*, p. 117.

37 J. Harris, *Private Lives, Public Spirit. A Social History of Britain, 1870–1914* (Oxford: Oxford University Press, 1993), p. 19.

38 D. Read, *English Provinces*, p. 29.

39 Ibid., pp. 207–31.

40 D. Horne, *God is an Englishman* (Sydney: Angus and Robertson, 1969), pp. 22–3.

41 Wiener, *English Culture*, p. 42.

42 B. Robson, 'Coming full circle: London versus the rest, 1890–1980', in G. Gordon (ed.), *Regional Cities in the UK, 1890–1980* (London: Harper and Row, 1986), p. 222; S. Constantine, *Unemployment in Britain Between the Wars* (Harlow: Longman, 1980), pp. 18, 70.

43 *Heaton Review*, vol. vii, 1934, p. 68.

44 *North and South*, pp. 29, 78–96. Balchin, *Regional Policy*, pp. 68–70.

45 *North Country*, p. 399. Still the best study of this period, albeit for a class rather more than a regional perspective, is Stuart Laing's *Representations of Working-Class Life, 1957–1964* (London: Macmillan, 1986).

46 D. Gervais, *Literary Englands. Versions of Englishness in Modern Writing* (Cambridge: Cambridge University Press, 1993), pp. 271–2. E. P. Thompson's canonical *The Making of the English Working Class* (London: Victor Gollancz, 1963), 'written in Yorkshire, and … coloured at times by West Riding sources', is another work of significance in this context. *Making* (Pelican, 1968 edn), p. 14.

47 For example, Kathleen Binns, 'Everyone's talking about Bradford', *Bradford Pictorial*, September 1966.

48 Robson, 'Full Circle', p. 225.

49 R. Shields, *Places on the Margin* (London: Routledge, 1991), pp. 207–51.

50 P. Balchin, *Regional Policy*, pp. 10, 13–14, 17.

51 J. Osmond, *The Divided Kingdom* (London: Constable, 1988), p. 54; P. J. Taylor, 'The meaning of the North: England's "foreign country" within?', *Political Geography*, 12, 1993, p. 147.

52 R. Samuel, 'North and South', in *Island Stories. Unravelling Britain* (London: Verso, 1998), p. 166.

53 Belchem, '"An accent exceedingly rare": Scouse and the inflexion of class', in his *Merseypride*, p. 55; L. Back, T. Crabbe and J. Solomos, *The Changing Face of Football* (Oxford: Berg, 2001), pp. 55–9.

54 *Renewing the Regions* (Sheffield: Regional Policy Commision, PAVIC Publications, Sheffield Hallam University, 1996), Appendix, 'North-west profile'; *Bradford and District Economic Profile, 7* (Bradford: Bradford TEC, 2001).

55 *Renewing*, Appendix, 'South-east profile'.

56 *Guardian*, 7 Dec. 1999.

57 K. Morgan, 'The English question: regional perspectives on a fractured nation', *Regional Studies*, 36, 7, 2002, pp. 799–800.

58 'And is there honey by the Tees?', *New Statesman*, 3 July 2000, pp. 9–11. Most of his interviewees were admittedly, 'on the left'.

59 The counties are Berkshire, Essex, Kent, Middlesex, Surrey and Sussex. All data here derives from the 1901 census. The choice of 1901 admittedly disguises the level of migration into the North from Ireland, Scotland, Wales and some English counties such as Cornwall that met the labour needs of industrialisation and urbanisation earlier in the century.

60 For a negative view of the consequences, 'Two square miles of housing hell', *Guardian*, 24 October 2000.

61 G. Turner, *The North Country* (London: Eyre and Spottiswoode, 1967), pp. 357–69; *Bradford Telegraph and Argus*, 8 November 1986; See also *Liverpool Echo*, 11 November 1963, for recruitment to Ford's Halewood plant; and D. Pocock and R. Hudson, *Images of the Urban Environment* (London: Macmillan, 1978), pp. 110–27, for the general issues.

62 British Tourist Authority, *Tourism Intelligence Quarterly*, 22, 4, 2001, table 3. A tourist here is defined as an individual taking at least one overnight stay while on holiday. The North's share had risen from 21 per cent in 1996.

63 R. Burton, *Travel Geography* (London: Pitman), 1991, p. 207, table 17.17.

64 P. Bentley, *O Dreams, O Destinations* (London: Victor Gollancz, 1962), p. 84.

65 K. Waterhouse, *City Lights* (London: Hodder and Stoughton, 1994); Turner, *North Country*, p. 275.

66 Turner, *North Country*, p. 245.

67 N. Pronay and J. Croft, 'British film censorship and propaganda policy during the Second World War', in J. Curran and V. Porter (eds), *British Cinema History* (London: Weidenfeld and Nicholson, 1983), p. 150.

68 L. Cooper, *Yorkshire. West Riding* (London: Robert Hale, 1950), p. 79.

69 Jewell, *North–South Divide*, pp. 37–8, 58.

70 E. Moir, *The Discovery of Britain. The English Tourists, 1540–1840* (London: Routledge and Kegan Paul, 1964).

71 D. Defoe, *A Tour through the Whole Island of Great Britain, 1724–6*; Jewell, *North–South Divide*, pp. 118–51 on southern perceptions in the early modern period.

72 D. Hey, *Yorkshire From AD 1000* (London: Longman, 1986), p. 5: M. Bradford, *The Fight for Yorkshire* (Beverley: Hutton Press, 1988), p. 24; A. Kellett, *Basic Broad Yorkshire* (Ilkley: Smith Settle, 1991), p. 109.

73 S. Rawnsley, 'Constructing 'The North': space and a sense of place', in N. Kirk (ed.), *Northern Identities*, p. 7.

74 Quoted in J. Seed, '"Commerce and the liberal arts": the political economy of art in Manchester, 1775–1860', in J. Wolff and J. Seed (eds), *The Culture of Capital. Art, Power and the Nineteenth Century Middle Class* (Manchester: Manchester University Press, 1988), p. 45.

75 W. White *A Month in Yorkshire* (London: Chapman and Hull, 1858), pp. 15–16.

76 E. Moir, *Discovery*, pp. 35–7.

77 See below.

78 Quoted in Wrightson, 'Northern identities', p. 33.

79 Shields, *Margins*, p. 207.

80 D. Harker assisted by F. Rutherford, *Songs From the Manuscript Collection of John Bell* (Durham Publications of the Surtees Society, vol. 196, 1985); R. Colls, *The Collier's Rant. Song and Culture in the Industrial Revolution* (London: Croom Helm, 1977), especially pp. 14–54.

81 P. Mandler, 'The consciousness of modernity? Liberalism and the English "national character"', in M. Daunton and B. Rieger (eds), *Meanings of Modernity* (Oxford: Berg, 2001), pp. 119–44.

82 Ibid., pp. 121–2, 132, 137. Mandler may predate the death of the idea, which he puts at about 1950.

83 C. Dellheim, 'Imagining England: Victorian views of the north', *Northern History*, XXII, 1986, pp. 126–30 has been influential here; as argued, such views are as much twentieth and even twenty-first century as Victorian.

84 See, for example, A. Room, *A Dictionary of Contrasting Pairs* (London: Routledge, 1988), p. 167.

85 James Burnley, cited in C. Dellheim, 'Imaging England', p. 220. On Yorkshire Societies in early modern London, P. Clark, *British Clubs and Societies, 1580–1800* (Oxford: Clarendon Press, 2000), pp. 281–2.

86 For example, Vale, *North Country*, p. 7; W. Pickles, *Between You and Me* (London: Werner Laurie, 1949), p. 67–70; D. E. Allen, *British Tastes. An Enquiry in to the Likes and Dislikes of the British Consumer* (London: Hutchison, 1968), pp. 136–9.

87 For 'Bob Cranky' and much else on Tyneside popular culture, see Colls, *The Collier's Rant*.

88 Turner, *North Country*, pp. 140–58; J. Belchem, '"An accent"', pp. 31–64.

89 Turner, *North Country*, p. 231.

90 White, *Month in Yorkshire*, pp. 52–3, 279.

91 Barry Cockcroft's 'Too Long a Winter' (1973) for Yorkshire Television began the cult. Boundary changes in 1974 pushed Hannah's farm into County Durham.

92 Bentley, *O Dreams*, p. 114. See also V. Brittain, *Testament of Friendship. The Story of Winifred Holtby* (London: Macmillan, 1941), pp. 282–3.

93 Writer Nicole Ward Jouves has noted how the 1970s serial killer Peter Sutcliffe disrupted the image of Yorkshire specifically as a place of powerful women which she had generated from youthful reading of Brontë novels. N. W. Jouves, *The Street Cleaner. The Yorkshire Ripper Case on Trial* (London: Marion Boyars, 1986).

94 For the cultural sphere, see J. Richards, *Films and British National Identity. From Dickens to Dad's Army* (Manchester: Manchester University Press, 1997), pp. 258–9. Rita, as a hairdresser from Liverpool, a city with very distinctive employment patterns, is in this sense something of an honorary member of 'cultural Lancashire'.

2

Discovering the North[1]

As the late Ian Ousby so eloquently claimed, travel creates 'a habit of vision and a corresponding habit of blindness: seeing our environment, getting to know a region of England or an aspect of its life, increasingly become a matter of appreciating particular sights from a particular angle'. Travel writing (and equivalents in radio, television and elsewhere) has been fundamental in nurturing these habits by creating the expert discourses directing what John Urry has termed 'the tourist gaze' and this chapter explores the role played by such writing in negotiating and constructing images of the North.[2] Visitors to the region have been as much influenced as any tourist group by commentators making judgments on places and the people within them via the identification of routes, vantage points, places of interest and, by default, of non-interest. Through this process of exclusion and inclusion, of enthusiastic endorsement and studied silence, travel writing generated ways of thinking and seeing that probably had greater apparently quasi-scientific status than any other cultural form considered in this study. Herein lay much of its power and significance.[3]

'Travel literature' is not an easily definable entity, shading as it so obviously does into many other literary fields.[4] Many of those categorised as travel writers have indeed shown a resistance to the label, with one contemporary author in the field claiming that no other genre has 'suffered this weird allergy to itself'.[5] It is useful, then, to try and impose some order on this vast literature. Neat categorisation is clearly impossible but on those occasions when it seems helpful to draw attention to a book's particular flavour or style, this study uses a broad tripartite division designating works as 'factual/descriptive', 'promotional' and 'discursive'. The first category refers to works largely written as sources of information to guide visitors around specific areas or particular locations. Usually including a gazetteer of 'key sites' often embellished by some kind of ranking system, such titles are clearly far less neutral than the label adopted here suggests, structuring views by a hidden process of selection if not by direct comment. 'Promotional' material specifically intended to boost a particular town or agency has been especially prevalent from the later twentieth century and parades its biases rather more obviously. So too does the final and loosest of the three categories, the 'discursive', a shorthand term to cover the many subjective travelogues in search of England and its soul that have become so crucial to the shaping of the national imagination especially from the 1920s. A number of authors who might more normally think of themselves, or be thought of, as investigative journalists or social critics, can be placed here; George Orwell through his *The Road to Wigan Pier* (1937) is a good example. Although not considered in this chapter, it must be stressed that novels, films, television series and all manner of other cultural forms can also serve both as a type of tourist literature and provide a context for it. This has been especially important since the late 1970s when the increased importance of popular cultural pilgrimage has seen England increasingly divided into 'Last of the Summer Wine Country' and other such entirely new imaginative spaces.

Not all tourists to and within the North have necessarily used guidebooks and other forms of travel guidance. With even cheaper works beyond many working-class budgets until at least the 1950s, it is likely that for much of the period readership rarely penetrated far below the upper-working class and was most firmly rooted at a higher social level. Moreover, it must not be assumed that these works shaped mentalities in ways that might be supposed by early twenty-first century readers. Travel literature is as open to multiple and alternative readings as any other cultural form and it can be challenged by both other sources of imagery and the personal 'joy of discovery [available] to the enterprising or the unconventional traveller' that many guidebooks sought to encourage.[6] However, there can be no denying its potential capacity to shape and reinforce attitudes to and images of the North and especially those of visitors coming to the region for the first time. Crucially, the reach and potential impact of these works went far beyond actual visitors. 'Most people journeyed by book' and such readings from a distance, emptied of even the possibility of the challenge to expectation provided by personal experience, may have indeed exerted a more significant influence on the national imagination than those absorbed *in situ.*[7]

Gazing at the North

This chapter is mainly concerned with the representation of specific parts of northern England but it is helpful to consider the region's more general position within travel literature. With all due allowance for change over time, the most striking point here is the region's generally secondary, even marginal place. Both the single volume guide to England and Britain and the multi volume series have tended to focus on the south-east, Devon, Cornwall and 'Shakespeare's England' at the expense of the North and other regions. Only the Lake District and Yorkshire, the biggest and the most varied of English counties, have consistently earned themselves an early and guaranteed place in the many series devoted to the English regions. They were certainly the seven-county North's only representatives amongst the 20 English regions selected in Edward Stanford's 'Tourist Guides' series in 1880, the 10 in Dulau's 'Thorough Guides' in 1902 and the 14 in Black's 'Beautiful Books' series in 1908. (The Peak District, northern in some definitions, also featured in many series.) In comparison, 13 of Stanford's titles and 10 of Black's dealt with locations in London, the Home Counties and the south-west.

The inter-war period saw a continuance of the trend. One quarter of John Prioleau's single volume *Car and Country* (1929) was concerned with Kent, Sussex and Surrey alone, while Robert Hale's 'County Books' series began with studies of the same three counties.[8] Catherine Brace has defended Batsford's inter-war 'Face of England' series against charges of a southern-centric bias, but while it certainly ranged wider than many, even here, only two of the thirteen titles concerned with England dealt with the seven-county North.[9] There were undoubtedly exceptions to this picture, with the *Blue Guide. England* providing the English regions, including the North, with coverage in almost exact proportion to their actual size from its inception in 1920. The overall pattern, however, is hard to ignore. Only in the 1970s and 1980s, with a growing interest in industrial archaeology and the emergence of tourist initiatives in almost every part of the country, did a more balanced picture emerge. Significantly in the context of previous practices, the publication of the first 'Shell Guide' to County Durham in 1980 saw the series editor describe Durham as one of England's previously 'maligned counties'.[10] For all the new developments, however, the city of York and the Lake District were the only northern venues in the *Fodor Guide 2000*'s fourteen-day 'Highlights of Britain' tour.[11] All this is not to claim a conspiracy against the North. Hard commercial decisions were operating here and patterns of guidebook production largely followed those made by tourists. The North's secondary position within the literature remains, nevertheless, an important issue when assessing the overall balance of cultural power within England.

Accompanying this unequal representation, has been the crucial fact that the 'gaze' directed at the North has invariably come from the South and most usually from London. The metropolitan location of the major publishing houses is a factor here but more significant has been London's role as point of departure – people rarely set out from the North to 'search for England' – and often return. All factual guidebooks begin in the capital and move northward while those works offering discursive tours invariably begin their journeys in the capital and sometimes end there, giving the impression of a return to a fixed central point and safe haven. This is especially marked in the closing words of J. B. Priestley's *English Journey* (1934) where the author, a proud northerner now resident in the capital, recalls returning through the fog to London where 'a lamp was cutting the fog away from a charming white gate. Doors were opened. Even the very firelight was familiar. I was home.'[12] Yet again, so many writers from the South talked of the North as a 'foreign' or 'strange' country and judged it as such. As Rob Shields has argued of Orwell's *The Road to Wigan Pier*,

> the *authority* to pronounce upon the 'real' character of the British North is implic-
> itly based on being not just a foreigner seeing the landscape with new eyes but also
> a foreigner from 'the South'. Significantly, being from the North would not give
> one the same sort of authority to pronounce upon the South.[13]

For all these reasons, therefore, a genre that speaks in many tones but most of them in some degree authoritative and commanding, has invariably laid the North out for inspection, classification and judgment from a specifically metro-politan perspective.

The sheer variety of human and physical geography on offer in the North of England has been nowhere more apparent or richly the source of cultural negotia-tion and manipulation than in the field of travel writing. A five-category classifica-tion, developed in table 2, has been adopted here in order to establish a working taxonomy of northern tourist locations that captures some sense of this com-plexity. Not all of the labels would have been recognisable to past generations and it is acknowledged that these apparently neat categories are actually far from that. The modern Lake District, for example, offers a wide range of separate experiences, from the commercial sites of Windermere, to the literary tourism of Grasmere and the tops of the Lakeland fells. Nevertheless, here are five useable versions of the region with which to flavour the national imagination, five broadly recognisable tourist 'Norths' that compete, contend or coalesce within the literature.

Two central arguments inform this interpretation of the resultant fertile process. First, it must be acknowledged that tourist literature provided some of the most positive images of the North ever to emerge, allowing the region to exhibit characteristics that made it properly, fully English. These representations,

Table 2 Major categories within travel literature on the North

Classification	Main features	Examples
Historic	Historic towns and cities; castles, country houses, religious buildings and remains	City of York; Castle Howard; Fountains Abbey; Lindisfarne
Rural/scenic	Coastal scenery; meadowland; moorland and mountain	Flamborough Head; River Wharfe; Lakeland fells
Literary/artistic/televisual	Birthplaces and residences; areas associated with particular individuals; galleries	Dove Cottage, Grasmere; Haworth Parsonage; Catherine Cookson Country; 'Emmerdale'; 'Last of the Summer Wine Country'
Resort-based	Seaside; spas	Blackpool; Whitby; Harrogate
Urban/industrial	Large cities and industrial areas; industrial museums; regenerated industrial and commercial sites	Saltaire industrial village; Beamish; Albert Dock, Liverpool

even though they were so often concerned with those areas that corresponded closely to town and landscapes (often southern) most favoured within the national culture, need far greater attention than they have traditionally received, illuminating as they do the full complexity of national identity and the North's place in shaping it. However, this powerful imagery ultimately failed to challenge the region's subordinate ranking. Indeed, it often depended upon the denial or downplaying of the industrial-urban society that formed the daily experience of so many northerners and had been the major engine of British economic growth in the nineteenth century. Ironically, celebration of the North often carried the seeds of the region's potential denigration.[14]

True North, true England

As Catherine Brace has argued, from the late nineteenth century, England was to a considerable degree imagined as a sum of its unique parts, with national identity forged through a broad 'celebration of regional character, defining England through a tapestry of landscapes and people'.[15] While some regions were definitely prized above others, there were always opportunities for parts of the North to connect with key national themes. Yorkshire was especially favoured, its size and variety allowing for a helpful marriage of the regional and the national. Here was an 'epitome of England; whatever is excellent in the whole land being to be found there' and a region that 'contained' the nation within it, clearly had at least some purchase within that nation's culture.[16] Unsurprisingly, the North was seen most positively in treatments of the 'historic', the 'rural/scenic' and the 'literary/artistic', discussion of which always comprised by far the largest component of the factual guides and usually formed the bulk of much discursive literature. Although detailed content analysis has not been attempted, a survey of Yorkshire travel literature suggests that the historic-scenic-literary matrix was especially powerful between about 1880 and the 1960s, and particularly so in the inter-war period.[17] Even as late as 1996, some 70 per cent of the *England. The Rough Guide*'s coverage of the county fell into these categories.

For much of the nineteenth and well into the twentieth century, travel writers defined 'history' in a very specific way, coming perilously close to 1066ian full stop with the restoration of the monarchy in 1660. 'With the exception of some royal visits and several risings in the manufacturing districts, occasioned by commercial distress and the introduction of machinery, the subsequent history of this county presents no events deserving special notice', confidently asserted one 1858 guide to Yorkshire. The same work similarly asserts that after the plague of 1665 there were apparently 'no remarkable events in the subsequent history of Leeds'.[18] Beyond the polite architectural heritage of the eighteenth century little of more modern times slid through this particular interpretative net. This perspective was, in fairness, by no means confined to externally based commentators, with northern writers sharing very similar views, and neither was it peculiar to travel writers.[19] Nevertheless, the modern urban North became interesting for most writers only when, as in this discussion of Leeds's Kirkstall Abbey, it offered 'something very striking in the contrast between these relics of a former age, and the factories and roads that encircle them'.[20] In a crucial sense, it was denied a history.

The first half of the twentieth century saw little fundamental change. Indeed, the many writers troubled by the contemporary condition of urban-industrial England arguably celebrated this distinctively constructed pre-industrial North even more enthusiastically in this period for its capacity to generate a sense of rootedness and belonging. In 1941, when wartime exigencies added another layer of apprehension, the 'King's England' volume on Yorkshire drew powerfully on this sensibility.

> The history of this great county is part of the history of England itself, for its people, with their Lancashire neighbours, have been the backbone of the nation in its rise to power and its struggle for freedom. Among its historic battlefields are Stamford Bridge where our Saxon King Harold won his last victory before he fell at Hastings; Standard Hill, where the Scottish king was beaten by King Stephen; Towton where the Red and White Roses fought; and Marston Moor where Cromwell turned the tide.

York was similarly described as a place for those 'deeply moved by the sense of something running through our ancient story like a thread of time, binding age to age'. S. P. B. Mais echoed this sentiment when visiting Hadrian's Wall a few years later. 'Over 1800 years have passed since the Great Wall was built yet it is no dead thing. It is a living tribute to the Great Empire from whom the western world first learnt its sense of discipline and order.'[21]

Armed with this clear sense of what constituted the past, travellers in the North were firmly directed to its key sites. As implied above, the walled city of York was especially significant. J. B. Priestley, who, unusually, did not much like the city, aptly termed it the 'guide-book man's paradise ... if you want the past, here it is, weighing tons'.[22] It invariably absorbed at least 10 per cent of guide-books to Yorkshire from the nineteenth century and was (and still is) invariably the most extensively discussed northern location in national guides. Durham was not far behind, its Norman cathedral and castle and the 'surprise' view of their dramatic situation from the railway line – modernity had its saving graces – key elements of guidebook itineraries throughout the period. The region's rich Christian heritage clearly played a distinctive role in the construction of the historical North. Ecclesiology was central to factual guidebook literature until at least the 1950s and later some cases. The 1973 edition of the 'King's England' Lancashire volume, for example, gave almost as much attention to Blackpool's churches as it did to the resort's entertainment features.[23] The North was extraordinarily well placed to meet this aspect of tourist need. York was once again especially celebrated, the Minster alone taking up some seven per cent of Murray's 1867 *Handbook for Yorkshire Travellers*. Combined with the walls and substantial medieval housing it created 'a peaceful, astonishingly beautiful medieval town' a spectacle 'too good to be true', according to an adoring H. V. Morton in the 1920s, while for Mais, in 1948, it was 'to England what Rome is to Italy, the Sacred City'.[24] The monastery at Lindisfarne, established by St

Aidan in 635 AD in the north-eastern most corner of Northumberland and one of the cradles of English Christianity, was as 'treasured in the history of the North as is our first little church of St Martins in Canterbury'.[25] The cathedrals of Beverley, Durham and Ripon, monastic sites at, amongst others, Furness and Whalley in Lancashire, Fountains, Rievaulx, Byland and Whitby in Yorkshire, Fichale in Durham and Tynemouth in Northumberland and the rich variety of parish churches that led Mrs Rodolph Stowell (like many others) to devote a quarter of her *Motor Tours In Yorkshire* (1908) to a chapter entitled 'chiefly old churches', were enthusiastically classed among the region's – and the nation's – major attractions.

Historic sites have accrued further status if associated with scenic beauty or literary/artistic merit. A number, most notably the ruined Bolton and Fountains Abbeys in North Yorkshire, have managed both. The former bene-fited from its striking setting on a curve of the River Wharfe, with one early twentieth-century writer claiming that there was 'no lovelier four miles of river-scenery in the kingdom' than that between the Abbey and Barden Bridge. The Abbey and its surrounds inspired paintings by Turner in 1808–9 and 1832 and poetry by Wordsworth in 1807. Turner also painted Fountains Abbey, a site used more frequently as a frontispiece for Yorkshire tour guides than any other, in 1798 and 1815.[26]

This rich historic legacy enabled many parts of the North to be claimed for the idea of England as 'old country' that became such a key element of national self-imagination from the later nineteenth century.[27] While the apparently superfluous reminder in the 'King's England' volume that Yorkshire's history 'is part of the history of England itself' is perhaps unwitting testimony to the North's generally marginal position, a focus on its castles, churches and remains made it as securely English as the region could ever be. A similar claim can be made in terms of its scenic qualities. Attitudes towards different types of land-scape have changed over the period and different interest groups have sought to appropriate the countryside in distinctive ways, but the 'rural-scenic' North has undoubtedly earned the region some of its most potent cultural capital.

Celebration of the rural was probably at its height from approximately 1890 until 1939, reflecting varying degrees and forms of concern with an increasingly urbanised (and *sub*urbanised) environment that was reinforced by the emo-tional displacement generated by the First World War. The many writers and travellers who went in search/pursuit/discovery of England found much to excite them north of the Trent. Many went to great lengths to stress that the North of England had never been the urban/industrial monolith of stubborn popular opinion and labelled its non-industrial parts in a revealing act of judg-ment, the 'true' or 'real' North. H. V. Morton was quick to appreciate the prox-imity of open countryside to northern towns, noting that 'their inhabitants can be lost in green fields and woodland within a few minutes. London is much more distant from a real wood than Warrington'. Indeed, he depicted the North as quintessentially rural, and worked hard to challenge the dominant stereo-type.

> In the south of England we suffer from a false idea of the manufacturing north. It is almost within the times of our grandparents that the coal-fields of the north became more important than the cornfields of the south…The commercial prominence of those recent giants, Liverpool, Manchester, Leeds, Sheffield, Bradford and Halifax, blinds us to the real north, which, apart from those areas of dense population, remains, as it has always been, one of the most romantic and naturally beautiful divisions of England … Leeds, Sheffield and Bradford are the small circles in a land of abbeys, churches, castles, wild moorland and beautiful dales, unchanged in parts since that time when the first monks went through Northumbria with the first crucifix.[28]

In his 1936 contribution to the intriguing 'Right Book Club' series, W. S. Shears was anxious to point out that 'the industrial north is vastly more than a gloomy succession of slag heaps and smoking towns' and that 'we find nearly three-quarters of Lancashire, Durham and Yorkshire still agricultural'. The 'King's England' series expressed similar sentiments in its 1941 Yorkshire volume:

> It has some of the ugliest towns ever seen in the world, heartbreaking to a traveller who rides through them in his car and realises that these long depressing streets are England. But they are not the true Yorkshire. The vast populations living in them can escape with ease to mountain and moor, woodland and dale.[29]

It was the remarkable variety of northern scenery alluded to in that last sentence that struck so many writers. The 'middling landscape', the 'man-fashioned' environment that blended tranquil, cultivated landscapes with ancient build-ings was much celebrated as the classic English landscape and the North offered rich abundance.[30] The special attractions of the area around Bolton Abbey already been noted but other rural pockets situated almost anywhere in the region had their enthusiasts. Relatedly, while lacking the importance of the Cotswolds, Sussex or parts of the south-west, the North has played its part in constructing 'traditional village England'. Downham, near Clitheroe in Lancashire has often featured in surveys of emblematic English villages, while Gainsford in Durham has been described as 'the immemorial English village …

on the green, everything is out of sight except the white cottages, the pub at one corner, and patches of blue sky peeping through thick overarching foliage'.[31] The irresistible conjunction of scenery and weighty historical association found on the east coast, especially from Flamborough Head northwards, has added yet another dimension. Scarborough with its castle, Whitby, with its Abbey, fishing quays, cliffs, nearby village of Robin Hood's Bay and literary links ranging from Caedmon to Dracula, and the 'historic' Northumberland coast from Warkworth to the Scottish border, were long-standing guidebook staples, always gaining far greater attention than their more commercially-oriented sisters in the west.

It is, however, the Lake District that has generally been taken as the (literal) pinnacle of scenic beauty in the North. Here, according to one nineteenth-century guidebook publisher, was scenery attaining 'that high pitch of excellence which marks the most celebrated tourist-resorts of the Kingdom', and which thus placed it alongside the Scottish Highlands, North Wales and Killarney.[32] The region has endured a variety of different treatments from travel writers and served many purposes for sometimes competing clienteles. Until the eighteenth century it was a terror-inducing landscape, 'the wildest, most barren and frightful of any that I have passed over' in Defoe's well-known phrase.[33] However, shifts in taste toward the picturesque, the romantic and the sublime, stimulated by the rash of writing on the district that began in the 1760s and 1770s, soon made it 'a serious challenge to the aesthetic supremacy of the European Grand Tour'.[34] Many of its first visitors were drawn from elite groups and although the social base of its tourism widened across the nineteenth century and an increasing number of 'heavy char-a-bancs from Blackpool, Morecambe, Preston and elsewhere' arrived in the 1920s, the area was still essentially a middle-class resort well into the twentieth century.[35] Nevertheless, the increased spread of car ownership, the designation of the Lake District as a National Park in 1951 and the astonishing success of the walking guides of Alfred Wainwright from 1955, eventually earned the Lake District a special place in the affections of a substantial social and geographical cross-section of the English population. Visitor figures to the National Park reached 17 million by the 1990s.[36]

It was what Wendy Joy Darby has termed 'Wordsworthshire', the lakes and the cultivated valley bottoms around and adjacent to them, that first attracted attention and have always continued to inspire.[37] However, the mountain scenery soon had its celebrants and the region increasingly became one of the most prized destinations for walkers and climbers. Crucial to the power of 'upper Lakeland' has been its combining of aesthetic and physical stimulation in ways which encouraged relaxation, repose and the possibility of mental healing. 'The tourist who comes here for rest and change, to enjoy the beauties of nature, and to be braced for future work by mountain air and exercise, will, it is hoped, find this book a useful and practical guide', expounded the 1882 edition of Jenkinson's *Tourist Guide to the Lake District* in the no-nonsense tones of later Victorian self-improving rational recreation. An almost spiritual quality could be claimed, as when, in 1948 Mais described it as a place to experience 'a sense of harmony and serenity ... to regain a sense of continuity and true perspective in this disjointed age'.[38] Although the Lake District was at the forefront of such interpretation, other areas of northern upland, most notably the Yorkshire Dales, received similar treatment. Both areas, especially the Lake District, also saw their status enhanced yet further by their literary and artistic associations. The Lake poets made the area, and above all Wordsworth and Dorothy's Dove Cottage at Grasmere, arguably one of the nation's leading sites of literary pilgrimage and writers as diverse as John Ruskin and Beatrix Potter cemented the process. Yet more *kudos* was generated by its close association with the National Trust, one of whose founders in 1895 was the Vicar of Crosthwaite, Canon Rawnsley, and which has acquired far more properties in the Lake District than in any other part of the North.[39]

Representations of the North focusing on the historic and scenic undeniably resonated powerfully with some of the key organising principles of 'Englishness', giving the region, in these guises at least, an important place in the national culture. This discussion might be extended fruitfully into yet other territories. Harrogate, for example, the 'most important inland watering-place in the north of England' as it was described in 1867, remained one of the North's and Britain's most exclusive tourist attractions well into the twentieth century, enticing visitors from all over Britain and a number from continental Europe.[40] Here was sophistication and refinement enough to meet the most challenging of critics.

Care must be taken not to overstate the centrality of the North within the undeniably southern-centric notions of Englishness. Donald Horne has made the telling point that 'Things that are rural or ancient are at the very heart of English snobberies, even if they occur in the north'.[41] Cultural phenomena that do not fit into pre-existing ideas of what comprises the 'North' can thus become detached from their real geographical moorings and be claimed as 'southern' or 'national'. The North's greatest attractions are, then, always open to acts of appropriation that denude the region's cultural status or at least reduce it. This argument is pursued in John Urry's stimulating account of travellers' treatments of the Lake District.[42] After acknowledging the range of possible readings, Urry is ultimately convinced that the region's association with elite leisure from the late eighteenth century, its literary and cultural associations and its landscape, wild but partially tamed by its quiet valley bottoms and villages and increasingly *managed* since the 1949 National Park legislation, makes it 'not quite of the north. It is almost an honorary part of the south-east … The Lake District is rather like Nice, Madeira, the Alps, The Dordogne – places made as part of the English south-east and its elite metropolitanism'.[43] There is clearly much in this view. The albeit often artfully 'surprised' tone of the many visitors who discovered, like Morton, that they had a 'false view' of the North when they reached some its more scenic parts, implies a feeling that it might not be as bad after all because it fits another altogether more acceptable and superior model. (Many northern dwellers will have heard from visitors, or even used themselves, a phrase such as 'it doesn't feel like the North'). However, for all its interpretative power, the 'honorary south' perspective can obscure other ways in which northern features play a key role in national identity on their own terms. This is especially important in regard to its wilder moorland and mountain landscapes. Whether specifically associated with the 'south country' or not, the most celebrated English landscape from the later nineteenth century (and beyond) was 'rolling and dotted with woodlands. Its hills are smooth and bare, but never rocky and craggy'.[44] Much upland northern terrain is precisely the opposite of this, even in the more managed National Park era. The walker struggling up the final boulder strewn path to Scafell's summit, lost in mist around Yorkshire's Gaping Ghyll, or slithering along the wettest sections of the Pennine Way (added duckboards, stepping stones and all) in the manner so comically but not entirely inaccurately described in Barry Pilton's *One Man and his Bog*, will in no sense feel that they are in a tamed, classically English landscape.[45] It was this wildness, this refreshing and cleansing aspect of the northern uplands that was celebrated by locals and visitors alike. Here was 'the high, grey desolation with the winds shooting over [it]', the country 'Thibetan in its height and emptiness' that Priestley rediscovered in Upper Wharfedale in 1934; the 'solitary country, best seen in solitude [and] best appreciated when it is in its most savage mood … A cruel, austere, but a very awe-inspiring land' that so invigorated S. P. B. Mais in the Trough of Bowland a couple of years earlier.[46] With all allowance for the complexity of northern upland scenery, the possibility for other regions to fulfil the same function and the romantic imaginations of travel writers, here is the North fulfilling, literally, its distinctive and special role within English culture as breath of fresh air, as a necessary counter to the moderate, sometimes anodyne south. Its uplands were certainly only for temporary inhabitation and usage, marginal places refreshing the centre, but they mattered. 'Other' the North might always ultimately be, but in some facets that very otherness has served English culture in important and positive ways.

'Black England'

While respect and recognition for certain aspects of northern heritage and landscape abound in travel writing, the uncomfortable corollary was the shadow that this cast on the region's urban and industrial regions. These were at the absolute core of the 'black England' that writers invoked so often from the early twentieth century, a phrase sometimes applied specifically to mining areas but often used to stand more generally for industrial landscapes and larger towns and cities.[47] The defence of the North mounted by writers like Morton and Mee, anxious to downplay the extent of urban and industrial change in order to assert the continuities of English history and landscape, meant that those areas containing 'some of the ugliest towns ever seen in the world' were inevitably foils for the 'true North' of ruined abbeys and open country. They were thus 'other' even in their own domain, a ruined Eden 'naturally beautiful but spoilt from a picturesque point of view by the deleterious character of the commercial pursuits carried on in them'.[48]

As ever, blanket generalisation about the treatment of the industrial North is not helpful. In the eighteenth and early nineteenth centuries, industry was novel, evidence of British progress and development and therefore of great interest. 'To have been at Newcastle, and men of curiosity too, without seeing a coal-pit, would have been a sin of the most unpardonable nature', proclaimed one traveller in 1780. Especially when set in attractive rural surroundings, early industrial sites were soon important points on the tourist circuit and not least in the Lake District, with lead mines in Borrowdale deemed to exhibit 'a variety of romantic views which should not be neglected by the tourist' according to one guide of 1819.[49] Some of the new cities, particularly Manchester, were also visited with varying degrees of enthusiasm. Even after 1850 when industrial and urban landscapes became ever more mundane and far less appealing, major sites were never without visitors. Northerners were certainly always aware of the attractions within their region. In 1878, the *Halifax Courier* noted the Liverpool's popularity as a destination with local holidaymakers, 'its great diversity of attractions both on water and land having a special charm to the toiling thousands of this district'.[50] Outsiders were also kept aware of possibilities. The model industrial community at Saltaire, near Bradford, Marshall's flax mills in Leeds and the larger forges and cutlery shops of Sheffield, were just some of the Yorkshire attractions regularly listed in guidebooks up to 1900 and beyond, while a number of factories made themselves available for visits even in the 'ruralist' highpoint of the 1920s and 1930s.[51] The1920 *Blue Guide* argued that Liverpool at least 'surpasses the average manufacturing city in the number and splendour of its public buildings' and gave its docks a one-star rating, thus placing it on a par with Eton College, Beachy Head and the New Forest.[52]

Industrial tourism has always been a minority interest, however, and for much of the period most travel literature neglected, traduced or damned the industrial North with faint praise in about equal measure. Significantly, many volumes did not bother to define their purpose or the territory they sought to cover, simply assuming that readers would expect their 'journeys', 'glimpses' and 'gleanings' to embrace the rural, the historic and the resort. Those that did were uncompromising. H. A. Piehler informed readers of his *England for Everyman* (1933) that 'the great manufacturing cities – Birmingham, Liverpool, Manchester, Sheffield etc. – are omitted, and all also the predominantly industrial areas such as the Black Country, the Potteries, and the cotton and wool areas of Lancashire and Yorkshire. Throughout the volume nothing is mentioned unless it is worth seeing.'[53] Morton famously chose to 'skirt Black England', pausing to visit only the music-hall joke town of Wigan.[54]

References to manufacturing areas and suggested journeys through them usually took up only a very small proportion of most titles and often focused mainly on the few scenic or historic sites scattered across them. Gordon Home's *Yorkshire*, published in 1908 is fairly typical in giving only 5 per cent of its space to the 'Manufacturing District', concentrating on Kirkstall Abbey, Selby Cathedral and other monuments when getting there and devoting only one of the author's 71 colour paintings to an industrial theme. Even here, his 'Iron Foundries at Brightside, Sheffield' was included because of the artistic potential generated by the subject matter and not because of any intrinsic interest.[55] Certain regions such as parts of south-west Lancashire and east Durham were deemed so unworthy that they effectively ceased to exist on this particular mental map of England. As late as 1969, the *King's England* volume on Lancashire failed to include an entry on St Helens, a town with a population of 105,000.[56]

In terms of actual physical description, the most hostile comments tended to stem from journeys through broad territories rather than visits to specific places. While Mais discovered a 'nightmare uniformity of ugliness' during his drive from Stockport to Bolton, 'especially after the gracious meadows and lawns of the south country', he was not especially critical of Bolton itself.[57] (The mode of transport might have played an important role here, with the broad impressions of arterial roads gained through a windscreen hardly open to the subtlety made possible by excursions on foot.) A few locations, however, were singled out and probably nowhere so than the steel and cutlery town of Sheffield. Its proximity to fine countryside led to it regularly being described as 'a dark picture in a golden frame' but there were many worse depictions. It was 'the blackest, dirtiest and least agreeable' town in Yorkshire according to one guide in 1867, a city that 'could justly claim to be called the ugliest town in the old world' in Orwell's words ('And the stench! If at rare moments you stop smelling sulphur it is because you have begun smelling gas.'), and one that would not tempt 'any but the most diehard of tourists' in those of the 1996 *Rough Guide*.[58] Negative treatment of industrial areas often resulted in the neglect of attractive rural areas or other sites of interest in the immediate vicinity. Even in the late twentieth century, for example, many national guidebooks failed or were slow to draw attention to the emergence of the much-altered West Yorkshire mill town of Hebden Bridge as a potential destination. Lazy depiction of the North strayed from tourist literature into other genres. C. N. Parkinson, a professor of Economic History who might have been expected to know better, claimed that during the industrial revolution 'a walk out of Manchester merely brought you to Salford; a walk out of Bradford end[ed] merely in Leeds'.[59] Clearly his map of Bradford looked only eastward.

There were exceptions to these patterns. Edmund Vale's *North Country* produced for Batsford's 'Face of Britain' series in 1937, managed a skilful balance in both text and photographs between 'Open Country', 'Industry' and 'Towns', even including a section on slum clearance. This, however, was discursive travel literature at its closest to investigative journalism and it was in this type of writing that the North was most likely to receive full treatment. Ironically, given that such books, especially in the inter-war period, had to engage with the issues of poor housing, industrial relations and unemployment, the very act of giving coverage often rendered the industrial North as problematic. Priestley's *English Journey* (and especially the chapter on 'East Durham and The Tees') and Orwell's *The Road to Wigan Pier*, both works that have been hugely influential with later generations, serve as powerful examples in this regard.[60]

Representation in the discursive literature of some of the region's most popular seaside resorts, and above all Blackpool, might also have compromised the industrial North. This is admittedly a highly speculative point. As the English seaside's premier historian has argued, Blackpool's image has shifted over time and according to the context in which comment has been passed.[61] It is also the case that some of the most detrimental comments about the town, such as Paul Theroux's comments on the 'the swollen guts and unhealthy fat of its beer-guzzling visitors', came in the late twentieth century often as part of a not always well informed discourse on the decline of the English resort.[62] Nevertheless, there has long been a tradition of focusing on the brash and vulgar aspects of the town's working-class holiday trade, seeing it as a place where the industrial North came to play hard and spend up. Much writing of this type is intended to be affectionate, with Edmund Vale, for example, finding 'a great deal about Blackpool that is quite charming in that it reflects the simple-heartedness of the Lancashire people'. Moreover, there is probably much in Tony Bennett's argument that Blackpool provided its northern visitors with a robust and positive identity to set against the supposedly restrained and restrictive southern and metropolitan versions of Englishness.[63] It is hard to escape the feeling, however, that for some outside eyes (and perhaps some northern ones too), Blackpool and other resorts with large working-class publics added a popular cultural overlay to the wider distaste for the industrial North. A place where 'the sands themselves are quite invisible' under the weight of visitors and the human traffic had to be controlled by 'beach-watchers and notice-boards' might show a lovable side of northern character but it was decidedly not the 'true' North.[64]

The *people* of the industrial North emerged from all this extremely positively. Despite, or even because of their environment, they were invariably viewed as humorous, hard-working, warm-hearted and friendly, if, especially in Yorkshire, 'more forthright and outspoken than in the south of England. [If] this is taken in the right way it can be very beneficial'.[65] Here, perhaps, was yet another example of the North's necessarily bracing impact on the national culture. The places in which they lived, however, were clearly not so favoured. There are perfectly obvious reasons for this and there must be no anachronistic critique of previous viewpoints. As industrial areas have become cleaner and greener in recent decades it is easy to forget the environmental blight of earlier periods; it really could be grim up North. It is no surprise that residents of one of the most urbanised and industrialised countries in Europe have found York preferable to Leeds, the Lake District to St. Helens. As Baddeley's 'Thorough Guide to Yorkshire' argued in 1902, 'The tourist or other holiday-maker, would hardly thank us for cumbering his pocket with full descriptions of the places he wishes to avoid rather than visit'.[66]

The cultural ramifications that flowed, however, were considerable. It is obviously not possible to provide objective measurement of how these twin strands of strict avoidance and negative coverage impacted on readers' interpretations of other more celebratory coverage of the North. It is certainly possible, however, to see how they might at least nullify and at worst undermine such coverage, thus ultimately leaving the region's standard bleak image largely intact. The very fact that most northerners lived in industrial areas and that these were the places most often encountered in the media and other cultural forms, can have only added to the sense of the 'true' North being exceptional and not really of it. As will be argued in later chapters, the industrial North might be celebrated as the forcing ground of such key areas as sport, popular entertainment and popular music. In its own terms, however, it has been for the most part decidedly a place on the margins.

The northerner's North

Most of this chapter has focused on works produced (in as far as authorial biography can be ascertained) by those hailing from outside the North and written for a national market. Before assessing whether the late twentieth century brought a new view of the industrial North, it is useful to explore the work of those writers operating from within the region. Internal travel writing came in many guises from the essays of major figures such as Priestley to, more typically, a crucial although generally unconsidered body of literature. This includes the town histories and local topographies so popular feature in the nineteenth and early twentieth centuries; local newspaper articles offering travel hints for days out and often eventually published in book form; the monthly 'county' magazines and the many mini-guides and pamphlets dealing with specific sites or aspects of tourism. Some ventures have become important parts of the regional literary landscape. *The Dalesman*, a magazine of rural Yorkshire life (the Dales receive special but not exclusive attention) founded by *Yorkshire Post* journalist Harry Scott in 1939, enjoyed a circulation of 60,000 and an estimated readership of 300,000 in the late twentieth century.[67] Although *The Dalesman* and similar publications such as *Cheshire Life* (1934), *Lancashire Life* (1946) and *Cumbria and Lake District Magazine* (c. 1950) were not conceived or intended as tourist or travel literature, their concern with the landscape, village life and local history made them an important adjunct to it.[68] Such publications and indeed, the field of regional travel writing in general, have provided an important entrée into writing for women. Often focused on the individual's immediate locality and

accessible hinterland, as with the regional novel, it provided women perhaps
denied access to full-time careers and wider geographical mobility with crucial
opportunities. The Yorkshire writers Marie Hartley (b. 1906), Joan Ingilby
(1912–2000), Ella Pontefract (1897–1945), Phyllis Bentley (1894–1977) and
Lettice Cooper (1897–1994) all exemplify this at some stage of their careers.

Northern writers often talked about their region in a manner and tone very
similar to that of outsiders. They were not shy in illustrating the problems of some
urban environments and were enthusiastic celebrants of the historic and the
scenic. However, those writing from within sometimes offered subtleties that
softened and refined the depiction found in many external representations.
Much more systematic work is needed in this area, but it is probable that regionally rooted travel writing was at its most effective in this regard between about
1930 and 1970, a time when many strands of local and regional literary and historical practice were at their height. This was especially marked in coverage of the
relationship between rural and urban. Many visitors tended to posit a binary
opposition, with Morton's notion of towns and cities as 'mere black specks [in]
the great green expanse of fine country' being fairly typical.[69] While, as noted
above, Morton and others were making an important partial corrective to stereotypes of northern geography, it tended to be locals who caught the more complex
situation that existed especially in Pennine Durham, the West Riding of
Yorkshire and industrial Lancashire. Writing of the nineteenth century, Charles
Dellheim has argued that indigenous writing stressing the region's rural beauty
and rich historical legacy undercut 'the southern stereotypes of the Northerner as
an upstart living in a rootless society'.[70] This is an important point, but the most
potent writing not only praised those aspects of northern life that were definitive
indicators of English identity, but which also tried to change the terms of the
debate and mount a defence of the North in all its complexity.

Here, the external's emphasis on rural versus urban was replaced by the
internal's stress on the rich and varied mixture of both. In her discursive text,
Yorkshire. West Riding (1950), Lettice Cooper noted the existence of 500 farms
within the County Borough of Bradford and talked of the 'typical West Riding
valleys, half industrial and half pastoral'. Similarly, while her mental image of
the area included rows of houses sprawling up hillsides and innumerable mill
chimneys 'pouring out smoke' it also included towns growing *into* the heather
moors, rolling hills and stone walls.[71] Her description of Bradford captures the
nearness of open space which some felt even in the city centre. 'I shall not have
made Bradford alive at all unless I make clear this hinterland of moors just
beyond the farthest chimneys. You cannot see them from the heart of the city,

but you can feel their presence, just as you are always aware that you are in a sea-side town even if you are out of the sight of the sea…' Again, she notes enthusi-astically how Priestley's novel *Bright Day*, set in pre-1914 Bradford, demonstrates the ease with which individuals could fish in solitude in the River Wharfe in the afternoon and attend a city centre music hall just hours later.[72] Such writing also often included a spirited defence of the urban-industrial North within its own terms. In an essay on Yorkshire and Humberside for the *New Shell Guide to England* (1970), the novelist and sometimes topographer and historian, Phyllis Bentley offered a plea for the mill chimney ('skilful and beautiful structures … most unjustly disliked'); a celebration of the county's achievements in music and sport; praise of its variety of amateur societies, 'all democratically run by properly elected committees' and a mild rebuke to south-erners. 'Yorkshire people are often vexed by the attitude of more southern coun-ties, who seem to regard us as uncultured barbarians, as if we had not yet recovered from William's fire and sword.'[73]

Clearly, not all Yorkshire folk had the financial and cultural capital necessary to enjoy the landscape or imagine the cityscape in the ways envisaged by the county's champions. Nevertheless, these are shrewd observations recognisable to many past and present dwellers in the county specifically and the North more widely. Northerners were certainly not alone in sharing these possibilities of bal-ancing the rural and urban but they probably enjoyed more opportunities than most. Here perhaps is a subtle northern/provincial variant of 'Deep Englishness' typified by affection for the rural, for the spaces that Priestley found 'more wide and open to me than all Montana or the Rhodesian plains', but accepting of the urban feast even when offered in less than attractive set-tings.[74] George Orwell was only one who believed northerners to be inured to their unprepossessing surroundings arguing that 'they have got used to that kind of thing and do not notice it'. This was far from the case. Rather, as exem-plified when Lettice Cooper termed the West Riding 'one of the ugliest and most beautiful' of places, they had simply learnt the art of managing both modernity and tradition.[75] Such writing obviously contained a tongue-in-cheek element, but it could carry serious intent particularly in the hands of writers like Bentley and Cooper who, as will be seen in the next chapter, consciously sought to interpret their native heath to the rest of the nation. A clear sense of local, sub-regional or even a wider northern pride is clearly evident here as the North was unapologetically laid out in all its guises.

In the last decades of the twentieth century, the tone has become more hesi-tant and the sense of pride less confidently asserted. While Cooper, Bentley and others were operating in a climate when industrial landscapes were, if not always appreciated by outsiders, at least accepted as the basis of economic strength, de-industrialisation, changing attitudes to the environment and the expectations raised by the heritage industry have placed their successors in a much altered context. Northern writers have always had to operate to some extent within the discourses generated by external commentators but the new situation appears to have intensified this process and with significant consequences. Thus when Jessica Lofthouse described post-1974 Lancashire as having 14 districts 'of which only six are urban and industrial', she certainly did not intend to marginalise the industrial sector but readers could easily be left with such an impression. Similarly, a 1983 photo-essay on Lancashire claimed that the county was 'perhaps more often and more thoroughly traduced than any other in Britain … The entire Palatinate is envisaged as a gigantic Lowry landscape dominated by dark satanic mills'. Its response was to focus on the rural areas and to treat those industrial sites that were included as almost exotic. An evocative picture of mills behind a foreground of farmland, for example, is captioned, 'Leigh has mill chimneys as the town of San Gimignano in Tuscany, has towers'.[76] These tendencies become more pronounced and more problematic within the promotional and quasi-promotional literature that has accompanied the rise of industrial tourism since the early 1980s. The following extract, although drawn from a relatively low circulation publication and perhaps offering a rather extreme version of the argument, is nevertheless instructive.

> In many people's imagination, Lancashire is still a county of cloth caps, smoke-belching mills and factories, cobbled streets and terraced housing. However, in reality, the economic changes of recent years have removed many of these eyesores from the scene, although terraced housing still remains a feature of some towns. Factories and their drab surroundings have often disappeared to be replaced by attractive landscaping.[77]

This attempt to remove an accretion of negative imagery from the county simply results in the structures that fed and clothed local communities and fuelled national wealth for decades becoming 'eyesores' ripe for replacement with non-productive but pleasant landscapes. In such versions, good intentions encourage the denial of historical realities and dilute regional pride with a sense of insecurity.

Regenerating the North

Northern cities and industrial regions have always enjoyed some tourism and indulged in what America would later term 'civic boosterism'. The Manchester

Art Treasures Exhibition of 1857, which attracted around one and half million visitors and at which 'the new made city hurls back upon her detractors the charge that she is too deeply absorbed in the pursuit of material wealth to devote her energies to the finer arts', is perhaps the best-known example.[78] However, the new tourist strategies of the late twentieth century were very different phenomena, attempts not to civilise manufacturing industry but to help survive its decline and, eventually, perhaps even to replace it.

Ironically, the new approach was rooted in reaction to the urban renewal of the 1950s and 1960s that had given the image of the industrial North a short-term boost, an architectural accompaniment to the popular cultural triumphs of the period. Even Sheffield was praised, with one 1969 guidebook claiming that it led the North of England in its 'exciting post-war rebuilding' with the result that the 'picture [was] now worthy of the frame'.[79] The actual or threatened demolition of historic (usually Georgian or Victorian) sites that such programmes entailed, however, encouraged a flurry of conservationist activity from voluntary civic trusts whose work help shape the growth of the 'heritage industry' from the early 1970s.[80] This was accompanied by a growing interest in working-class history and awareness of the problems faced by traditional industries that together stimulated a renewed interest in industrial archaeology and vernacular housing: the opening of the North of England Open Air Museum at Beamish in County Durham in 1970 was a landmark date here. The gradual recognition within northern communities that economic problems of the later 1970s presaged something rather more fundamental than another phase in the pattern of boom and slump gave further crucial impetus for reconsideration of the recent past. Bradford was the first inland, industrial district to evolve a tourist strategy but others followed rapidly.[81]

Some of the earlier exponents of industrial archaeology and the new urban tourism seemed to share the picturesque tastes of their forebears. Writing in 1970, the academic L. T. C. Rolt equated 'modern industrialism' with a 'large scale and dreary uniformity [which] spells death to landscape' but saw many eighteenth and early nineteenth sites as 'at best comely and at their worst dramatic or idiosyncratic'. Only a decade later, however, a *Shell Guide* to County Durham was recommending a visit to the steelworks at Consett and suggesting that the pit village of Esh Winning was 'not to be missed ... for Durham atmosphere'.[82] The 1989 edition of the *Blue Guide* proudly announced that it had been substantially rewritten in acknowledgement of a new taste 'which now makes travellers take note of industrial sites and Victorian town centres ... as well as cathedrals, castles and picturesque villages'.[83] By the early 1980s most large cities and many smaller towns had embraced tourism as a force for economic growth and urban regeneration, resulting in a variety of projects designed to celebrate industrial heritage and/or to convert decaying industrial and commercial buildings into a plethora of retail outlets, museums, galleries and arts centres.[84] Amongst the most high profile outcomes were the establishment of the Castlefields Industrial Heritage Park in Manchester and Salford (1982), which was eventually to embrace industrial and scientific museums, Roman remains, the Granada Television Studios (opened for public visits in 1988) and a number of fashionable bars; Liverpool's Albert Dock complex, emerging from 1984 and attracting 3.5 million visitors by 1990, and the Wigan Pier Heritage Centre (1986). The conscious devolution of museums and gallery provision and the availability of Heritage Lottery and Millennium Commission funding boosted urban tourism still further. These factors led to the relocation of the National Armoury from London to Leeds (1996) and the establishment of such projects as the Earth Centre in Doncaster and the National Glass Centre in Sunderland (1998); the National Centre for Popular Music in Sheffield (1999); Magna in Rotherham (2000); the Lowry and the Imperial War Museum North in Salford (2001 and 2002); the National Football Museum in Preston (2001) and the Baltic Exchange in Gateshead (2002).[85]

These ventures have generally been hugely successful in environmental terms, doing much to improve depressed and depressing cityscapes. It is much harder to judge the complex issue of *economic* success, which is anyway beyond the scope of this study. Suffice it to say that it is often difficult to decide whether the undoubted growth in tertiary employment in bars, restaurants, hotels and so forth often claimed by tourist professionals as evidence of their success can be credited to their efforts or to a combination of wider economic and social changes. Moreover, the gap between official rhetoric and economic reality can be significant. While Bradford Council continually stressed the value of tourism in rebuilding the city's economy, a survey in 2001 noted that the city was still the sixth most depressed authority in England and Wales in terms of employment and the fifth in terms of income.[86] While tourism might have helped at the margin it was clearly not driving the economy forward. Even in the most successfully 'regenerated' northern cities often chronic problems of social exclusion and poverty, perhaps even exacerbated by the process, remain.

The issue of what might be termed image management, the central concern here, is equally complex. There have undoubtedly been successes but for many northern locations urban and industrial tourism has been at best a mixed blessing and, in the worst cases, a mechanism for polishing up traditional stereotypical images and the provision of some problematic new ones. There have certainly been a number of difficult contextual factors at work and not least the fact that the very strategy soon came under considerable attack. Beginning in earnest with Robert Hewison's influential polemic *The Heritage Industry* (1987), the 1980s and early 1990s saw the emergence of a powerful critique of attempts to compensate for the loss of traditional industries through heritage oriented tourism and consumption. A loosely defined heritage industry was variously accused of producing a sanitised and saleable past bearing little resemblance to historical 'reality'; restricting opportunities for creative thinking about the present by hiding in that past and of replacing a high wage, high skill economy with its direct opposite.[87] Whatever the strength of such arguments or of those offered in response, an air of doubt and uncertainty was cast over efforts at the re-thinking of industrial communities. Although the North was not the exclusive victim of such treatment, its ownership of such high profile sites as Wigan Pier Heritage Centre, one of Hewison's main targets, placed it very much at the forefront.

As the earlier listing of new attractions indicates, tourism's place in urban regeneration had been well established and was less frequently criticised by the mid-1990s. Nevertheless, issues surrounding the status and success of northern (and wider provincial) provision have continued to surface. Certainly, the devolution of national museums has benefited the North, or parts of it, far more than most other parts of England. Of the 24 'Non-London' national museums that existed in England in 2000, 14 were in the North with Liverpool, a particular focus for art galleries, housing 9 of these. The result of this is a partial inversion of the normal North-South divide in terms of museum and gallery funding.[88] These museums, however, are usually under-resourced and often showing collections that would otherwise have been in store.[89] In this sense, the North enjoys a branch plant status in the culture industry much as it enjoys one in the wider economy. Equally important has been the often quite vocal opposition raised against the siting of major museums and galleries in the North, the marginalisation of their achievements and much negative coverage of any difficulties. Those involved with the establishment of Bradford's National Museum of Photography, Film and Television (1983) were intensely aware of the prejudices the location faced. Its first Keeper of Film and Photography, Colin Ford, noted how 'when the decision [to establish it] was announced, a certain well-known London museum director said no-one would travel up to Bradford to see 250 old cameras in a disused ice rink'.[90] Similarly, many northern and provincial-based curators and administrators have expressed concern that projects have only tended to receive attention when they have failed to attract visitors – the financial difficulties faced by the Royal Armouries Museum in Leeds and the collapse of Sheffield's National Centre for Popular Music in 1999 and Bradford's Transperience and Life Force in 1997 and 2001 respectively, certainly gained extensive media coverage – and that they are constantly starved of publicity. Amanda Nevill, Head of the Bradford Photographic Museum, claimed that despite attracting over one million visitors annually by 2000, 'we still don't get talked about or written about nationally. I sometimes think I don't care if they tear us apart as long as they write something about us. If we had been in London we would have been celebrated by now!'[91] Clearly, institutional politics and personal prejudices are sometimes operating here and it would be foolish to claim that coverage is always hostile or limited. Nevertheless, there is a sense that even at its moment of partial transformation and success the North can still be constructed as secondary and peripheral.

Urban tourism specifically, and the urban North more generally, have also been the focus of some troublesome modes of travel writing. This was perhaps especially the case in the 1980s, when, as Raphael Samuel argued, the 'decline of the north was a leitmotiv of [contemporary] writing', and the region became the favoured subject of the various sepulchral narratives that surveyed Britain's industrial wastelands.[92] These varied in terms of intent and the nature of the prescription offered but they tended to sound a similar note. The American writer Paul Theroux's *The Kingdom by the Sea* (1983), the record of a tour around Britain's coastline, captures the style well. In the north-east, for example, Jarrow proved to be 'an area of complex ugliness … one of the dreariest landscapes I have ever seen', while at Hartlepool, 'even the sea was grim here – not rough but motionless and oily, a sort of offshore soup made of sewage and poison'.[93] There are strong echoes of much 1930s writing in this genre, but not always the same levels of sympathetic engagement.

While the doom-laden tones of the 1980s lightened a little in the next decade, that very lightness and the penchant for irony and cutting humour apparent in some of the decade's key works proved equally problematic. An interesting example is afforded by Charles Jennings' *Up North. Travels Beyond the Watford Gap* (1995), an often clever parody of both southern (especially his own suburban London) attitudes to the North and certain aspects of northern culture.[94] He is especially good on the former, alternately delighted and dismayed by the success or otherwise of various places in living up to his expectations. While, Manchester was 'spot-on, so far as this snotty Londoner was concerned', raising 'ugliness to new heights', Bradford, his expected 'jewel in the crown' of northern grit and grime was actually disappointing. It was *'cleanish . . .* and the air was only moderately polluted . . . it's all such a betrayal'.[95] Jennings is at best a shrewd and amusing observer and some of his strictures are impossible to deny but the humour is far from innocent. For all its post-modern knowingness and irony, Jennings' writing parades and thus to an extent reinforces all of the most tradi- tional stereotypes of the North even at those moments when acknowledging their datedness and reduced applicability. Moreover, his adoption of a humorous stance and his self-parodying allows him a considerable degree of rudeness and irreverence in regard to the North. This interpretation might be seen as overly serious, a failure to grasp the joke. The problem, however, is precisely that not all external readers (and most certainly not all internal ones) will get the joke in quite the way that Jennings might expect. The appetite for the mildly irreverent is also sometimes present in the factual literature, a genre that has generally eschewed humour as a vehicle. The 1996 *Rough Guide*, for example, referred to Bradford chasing visitors 'with a sort of grim determination, waylaying them on their way to Haworth'. The adoption of such a tone might be seen as welcome counter to the note of almost biblical authority that has sometimes predominated and to the exaggerated claims of tourist officers. However, as with Jennings, such observa- tions run the risk of reinforcing stereotypes. Indeed, this humorous literature as much as its earlier 'decline of England' equivalent ultimately somehow managed to diminish the urban North by reducing respect for it. Even the most negative comments of earlier generations were often softened by some sympathy for a people central to the nation's wealth production. 'It seems unfair that a district contributing so much to England's wealth should be repaid by gloomy skies and depressing landscapes' noted one 1908 guide to Yorkshire. Again, while Arthur Mee's 1936 'King's England' volume described Lancashire as 'littered with slag heaps and crowded cotton towns where beauty is hard to find', he both noted the rural and historic attractions that lay elsewhere in the county and chose the appre- ciative *Cradle of our Prosperity* as his sub-title.[96] In much recent travel writing, northerners are often either comic or tragic figures, adrift from their history, denied a valid contemporary role and offered little glimpse of a viable future.

The contemporary urban North is no monolith and some locations have benefited more than others from the new tourism. One of the most interesting consequences of this has been an increasing differentiation in the ways that the 'North' has been represented. Although there had always been some acknowl- edgement of the physical and economic differences with in the urban North, the popularity of such blanket phrases as 'black England' suggests that such discrimination was relatively limited. From about the mid-1990s, a status hierarchy has clearly emerged at least in regard to the major cities. While it has been flexible and open to the foibles of fashion, Manchester and Leeds have generally emerged at its head. Highly developed club, restaurant and bar cultures have been vital here, as has the 'Madchester' musical moment of the late 1980s and early 1990s (and dealt with in chapter 8).[97] Newcastle has also been favourably reviewed albeit quite often in ways which tie it, via its famed Bigg Market drinking culture, rather more to the work hard and play hard 'Bob Cranky' stereotype than some locals might like. However, its partnership with neighbouring Gateshead in its (ultimately unsuccessful) campaign to secure the prize of European Capital of Culture for 2008, which added the highly acclaimed Gateshead Baltic Gallery and Music Centre to Tyneside's cultural stock, has earned the city much enthusiastic media coverage and generated much local excitement.[98]

At the other extreme, Liverpool, Sheffield and Bradford have enjoyed far more problematic experiences. Liverpool's case admittedly demonstrates just how rapidly fashions can turn in this area. As late as 1996, *The Rough Guide* could describe it as 'the one city in England [that] could be said to stand as a symbol of a nation in decline'. By the early twenty-first century, both its objective situation and representations of it appeared to be improving and its success in becoming the European Capital of Culture for 2008 can only accelerate this rapid reversal.[99] The same cannot be said for the other two cities, with Bradford providing an extreme case study of the risks involved in exposing a city to the external gaze through tourism.[100] Faced in the late 1970s with acute economic difficulties and a serious image problem resulting from its association with serial killer Peter Sutcliffe (the 'Yorkshire Ripper') and racist 'humour' focused on its large south Asian community, it certainly needed a degree of re-invention. Set in extensive open countryside and with the leading literary pilgrimage site of the Brönte's Haworth falling within its Metropolitan boundaries, the turn to tourism seemed a sensible one. Its extension of provision to the urban and industrial has enjoyed many successes including the National Museum of Film, Photography and Television (1983); the blossoming of the industrial village of Saltaire – awarded Unesco world heritage status in 2001 – with its '1853 Gallery' (1987) filled with the work of David Hockney; serious attempts through the 'Flavours of India' holiday package and other moves both to place Bradford's multi-cultural nature at the centre of the tourist initiative and to encourage Asian businesses and the simple fact of its offering inspiration to other 'non-traditional' tourist locations. However, the city has not been able either to disguise the genuine socio-economic problems that it has faced (in fairness, it has rarely sought to do so) or to find ways of challenging deep-rooted ideas about the city.

A product of industrialisation and an early victim of de-industrialisation, Bradford has so often seemed to be cast as paradigm case for the social and economic decline of northern industrial England. An added ingredient of major significance has been the city's large south Asian population, predominantly although by no means exclusively Muslim. The city has thus, in Susanne Schmid's words, become 'the "other" in a double sense: both as a Northern city and because of its multi-ethnic population'.[101] Serious rioting in predominantly Asian areas in 1995 and 2001, and media responses to that rioting, have been critical in this regard. Placed at the core of a discourse that drew on long established notions of the North as bleak and harsh and added to it a distinctive admixture of current economic crisis and Asian 'otherness', Bradford became shorthand for the region's (and perhaps the nation's) contemporary problems. As a result, the city was a particularly prominent victim of the 'decline of Britain' journalism noted above. In 1984, for example, a piece by Will Hutton for the *Listener*, tied in with a BBC 'Newsnight' feature on the city, showed much sympathy but saw little hope of redemption through tourism or much else. 'Poverty, disease and want are back; far from renaissance, the prospect is one of permanent and relentless decline'.[102] Popular cultural representations of the city in the plays and films of Andrea Dunbar, discussed in a later chapter, and in Kay Mellor's popular TV series *Band of Gold,* were also inadvertently unhelpful. Mellor's drama, for example, focused on a group of Bradford prostitutes and drew attention back to the city's association with sexual violence that the tourism initiative had been partly intended to combat. As noted above, some travel writing was problematic even when its sting was dressed in humour. Bill Bryson's comment in his best-selling *Notes From a Small Island* (1995) that 'Bradford's role in life is to make every place in the world look better in comparison, and it does this very well', is perhaps the ultimate example.[103]

Ironically, a final but crucial element of the imagery circumscribing Bradford's attempt at re-branding has come from within the discourses of more sympathetic travel writing and even of the local tourist industry itself. Especially in the early period, Bradford's tourist strategy appeared to lack a coherent narrative and fed instead from various versions of its past and present in ways which, while often gently humorous and self-deprecating, resonated with older, rather dated representations of the city specifically and the North in general. When Bradford's first 'official tourist', Sussex pensioner Edward Adams, arrived in October 1980, he was greeted by a brass band and the mayor brandishing a two-foot stick of

Bradford rock.[104] Similarly, the opening of the National Film and Photography Museum in 1983 was accompanied by a banquet of fish, chips and champagne. Even very recently, when the city's celebration of multi-culturalism, Victorian heritage and nearby rugged landscape has been coupled up into a rather more effective tale to tell visitors, unhelpful stereotypes can reassert themselves. When the city's bid to be European City of Culture was launched in August 1999, for example, a prominent councillor allowed himself to be photographed in the local paper sitting in a pavement café, wearing a red bow tie and holding a cup of tea aloft with little finger crooked. Admittedly, this was for local consumption, but the northern self-parody here rides too closely for safety to age-old southern claims of philistinism.[105]

Alongside this, even the best-intentioned and friendliest travel journalism has tended to play with and even accentuate old images of the city for the sake of comparison with the new project. The *Guardian* reported on the reception for the city's first official tourist thus. 'The sparrows woke up coughing, the pigeons flew backwards to keep the dirt out of their eyes and the day shift down the legendary "treacle mine" was hard at it. But everyday life in industrial Bradford was halted for a few hilarious minutes yesterday when a 71–year-old pensioner stepped from a train.' A more general piece in the *Sunday Times* in 1981 was headed 'The black pudding boom in tourism' and ended by a cartoon showing a 'Welcome to Bradford banner' suspended between two mill chimneys. *Classical Music* magazine told its readers in 1988 that, 'Yes, Bradford Council does employ a tourism officer. And, no, her time is not spent in guiding coach parties around tripe mines, black pudding co-operatives or potential sites for the Whippet Winter Olympics.'[106] As late as 2000 the *Observer* led a story concerning the city's European Capital of Culture bid with the headline 'Culture? There's Paris, Venice and Bradford'.[107] As with the internal civic modes discussed above, this is gentle, inoffensive, if lazy humour, but it is a habit that constantly perpetuates old jokes and images and embeds them in precisely the progressive discourse that is supposed to challenge those images. When in October 2002 the city failed to make the national shortlist for Capital of Culture the risks involved in placing the city in the public spotlight and attracting – and even encouraging – such troublesome representations were starkly apparent for all to see.

Historians are always at risk when peering into the future but the trajectory of the North's urban regeneration certainly invites if not prediction, then at least some speculation about how the region might be viewed by new generations of 'discoverers'. In a challenging article, Peter Taylor has suggested that the huge success of shopping malls and other consumer spaces in the North demonstrates a genuine transformation of the region and its external relationships. 'As consumer modernity has replaced industrial modernity throughout the western world, the old North-South divide looks more and more like a British obsession with an old myth.'[108] Without necessarily accepting this argument in total, potentially highly significant forces are undeniably at work with popular culture at the heart of much of this new activity. Historically, the region's close association with such areas as sport, the music hall and stand up comedy may have counted against it in some assessments, further proof of its lower status when set against a more sophisticated South. In the post-modern era when leisure and popular culture have a far more powerful purchase than ever before, the North may perhaps have found that an old hindrance has become a new opportunity. It is similarly noteworthy that some of the most successful aspects of northern industrial/urban tourism have been to some degree 'placeless', rooted in experiences and celebrating cultural forms that are in no real sense 'northern'. Bradford's National Museum of Photography, Film and Television is exemplary here: it could have been sited anywhere in Britain and it explores media that are international. Manchester and Leeds's success as centres of the café-bar and the club are rather similar. When young clubbers come to Leeds from other parts of the country, taking advantage of special train and hotel rates offered to them, they come in a sense not to the North but to a neutral space to dance to music that could be and is danced to in innumerable locations. Even those sites that are rooted in the region by virtue of their association with traditional industries are often ultimately centres of consumption, providing experiences that could take place anywhere in the western world. At Saltaire, where visitors wander amongst terrace housing and look at paintings by Bradford-born artist David Hockney in a gallery housed in a vast decommissioned weaving shed, the experience need not necessarily have 'northern' connotations. Hockney is, after all, a world brand, like the coffees served in the village's cafes.

These linkages between the local, regional, national and international are complex. Non-northerners visiting Manchester's clubs, Bradford's Film Museum or Gateshead's Baltic Exchange, will, of course, find many other reminders of their northern location during their stays. Again, northerners remain fiercely loyal to the region and their localities within it despite these new layers of provision, and sometimes because of them. It will be interesting to see, however, how far new economic ambitions will drive the post-industrial North to divest itself of its associations with the industrial and commercial past that defined its once distinctive place in English culture, and what the consequences for northern self-identity might be.

Notes

1 While alert to Keith Waterhouse's epigram 'I am a traveller, you are a tourist, he is a tripper', this chapter uses the first two phrases interchangeably and without assumption. Quoted in J. Urry, *The Tourist Gaze. Leisure and Travel in Contemporary Societies* (London: Sage, 1990), frontispiece.

2 I. Ousby, *The Englishman's England. Taste, Travel and the Rise of Tourism* (Cambridge: Cambridge University Press, 1990), p. 5; Urry, *Gaze*, pp. 1–15.

3 For histories of northern *tourism*, see E. Moir, *The Discovery of Britain. The English Tourists, 1540–1840* (London: Routledge and Kegan Paul, 1964); Ousby, *Englishman's England*; J. Vaughan, *The English Guidebook c.1780–1870. An Illustrated History* (Newton Abbot: David & Charles, 1974); J. K. Walton, 'The demand for working-class seaside holidays in Victorian England', *Economic History Review*, 34, 1981; J. Benson, *The Rise of Consumer Society in Britain, 1880–1980* (London: Longman, 1994; J. K. Walton, *The British Seaside. Holidays and Resorts in the Twentieth Century* (Manchester: Manchester University Press, 2000).

4 For a valuable study of origins, Vaughan, *Guide Book*.

5 Robyn Davidson, 'The trip trap', *Guardian*, 4 August 2001.

6 *The Blue Guide. England* (London: Macmillan, 1920 edn), p. v.

7 Robert Colls, *Identity of England* (Oxford: Oxford University Press, 2002), p. 266.

8 Details drawn from dust jacket adverts in the relevant Lake District volumes; A. Howkins, 'The discovery of rural England', in R. Colls and P. Dodd (eds), *Englishness. Politics and Culture, 1880–1920* (London: Croom Helm, 1986), p. 83; listing on sleeve of L. Cooper, *Yorkshire. West Riding* (1950).

9 C. Brace, 'Finding England everywhere: regional identity and the construction of national identity, 1890–1940', *Ecumene*, 6, 1, 1999, pp. 102–3.

10 H. Thorold, ed., *County Durham. Shell Guide* (London: Faber and Faber, 1980), acknowledgments page.

11 All of the listed sites (in a book, it must be said, aimed mainly at North America) were, in fact, in *England*.

12 J. B. Priestley, *English Journey* (Harmondsworth: Penguin, 1987 edn), p. 390. He had started in Southampton 'where a man might well first land'.

13 C. Dellheim, 'Imagining England: Victorian views of the North', *Northern History*, 22, 1986, p. 229. R. Shields, *Places on the Margin* (London: Routledge), p. 213.

14 For a brief but rich assessment of the industrial North in travel writing see P. Taylor, 'Which Britain? Which England? Which North?', in D. Morley and K. Robbins (eds), *British Cultural Studies* (Oxford: Oxford University Press, 2001), pp. 135–8.

15 Brace, 'Finding England', p. 102.

16 J. Murray, *Handbook for Travellers in Yorkshire* (London: John Murray, 1867), p. viii.

17 Texts consulted include *Black's Picturesque Guide to Yorkshire* (Edinburgh: A&C Black, 1858); W. White, *A Month in Yorkshire* (London: Chapman and Hull, 1858); Murray, *Handbook for Travellers*); G. Phillips Bean, *Tourist Guide to the West Riding of Yorkshire* (London: Edward Stanford, 1880); Gordon Home, *Yorkshire*

(Edinburgh: Adam and Charles Black, 1908); A. Mee, *Yorkshire. West Riding* (London: Hodder and Stoughton, 'The King's England' series, 1941).

18 *Black's Picturesque*, pp. 2–3, 148.

19 C. Dellheim, *The Face of the Past* (Cambridge: Cambridge University Press, 1982).

20 Murray, *Yorkshire*, p. 357.

21 Mee, *Yorkshire. West Riding*, pp. 10, 17; S. P. B. Mais, *The English Scene Today* (London: Rockcliff, 1948), p. 280.

22 Priestley, *English Journey*, p. 327.

23 F. Beckwith (ed.), *The King's England. Lancashire* (London: Hodder and Stoughton, 1973), pp. 23–4.

24 H. V. Morton, *In Search of England* (London: Methuen, 1927, 39th edn, 1949), p. 202; Mais, *English Scene*, p. 228.

25 W. S. Shears, *This England: A Book of the Shires and Counties* (London: The Right Bookclub, 1936), p. 594.

26 M. J. B. Baddeley, *Yorkshire Part 1* (London: Dulau and Company 'Thorough Guide' series, 1902, 4th edn), p. xiii; D. Hill, *Turner in the North* (New Haven: Yale University Press, 1997); A. Hindle, *Literary Visitors to Yorkshire* (Ormskirk: G.W. and A. Hesketh, 1981), pp. 134–6.

27 See M. Wiener, *English Culture and the Decline of the Industrial Spirit, 1850–1980* (Cambridge: Cambridge University Press, 1981), pp. 42–51; P. Wright, *On Living in an Old Country* (London: Verso, 1985).

28 Morton, *In Search*, pp. 202–3.

29 Shears, *This England*, p. 575; Mee, *Yorkshire. West Riding*, p. 2.

30 C. R. Perry, 'In search of H. V. Morton: travel writing and cultural values in the first age of British democracy', *Twentieth Century British History*, 10, 4, 1999, p. 437; Brace, 'Finding England', p. 102.

31 G. Bernard Wood, *The North Country* (London: Robert Hale, 1973), pp. 178–9. Downham, owned by Lord Clitheroe and the subject of his very strict regulations on TV aerials, power lines and other features of modern life, is therefore a particularly potent symbol of 'old England'.

32 Baddeley, *Yorkshire*, p. xiii.

33 Quoted in Urry, *Gaze*, p. 193.

34 M. Andrew, *The Search for the Picturesque. Landscape, Aestheticism and Tourism in Britain, 1760–1800* (Stanford: Stanford University Press, 1989), p. 153. For the shifting place and role of the Lakes in English culture, see W. Darby, *Landscape and Identity. Geographies of Nation and Class in England* (Oxford: Berg, 2000).

35 *Burrow's Guide to the Lake District* (London and Cheltenham: J. Burrow and Co, 1922), p. 7, quoted in B. McNaboe, '"Images of Arcadia". A Critical Examination of the Lake District Guidebook, 1750–1950', unpublished MA dissertation, University of Lancaster, 1994, p. 97.

36 J. Urry, *Consuming Places* (London: Routledge, 1995), p. 193.

37 Darby, *Landscape*, p. 212.

38 Quoted in McNaboe, '"Images"', pp. 65–6; Mais, *The English Scene*, p. 269.

39 In 2000, the 14 Lake District properties represented over 20 per cent of the Trust's holdings in the entire seven-county North.

40 Murray, *Yorkshire*, pp. 242–5. It relinquished spa status in 1968.

41 D. Horne, *God is an Englishman* (Sydney: Angus and Robertson, 1969), p. 38.

42 Urry, *Consuming Places*, pp. 193–210.

43 Ibid, p. 208. Also, Darby *Landscape*, p. 89.

44 A. Howkins, 'Discovery of rural England', p. 64 and his 'Rurality and English identity', in Morley and Robbins (eds), *British Cultural Studies*, pp. 145–56.

45 Published, London: Corgi Books, 1986.

46 Priestley, *English Journey*, p. 170; Mais, *This Unknown Island* (London: Putnam, 1932), p. 150.

47 It is not clear when the phrase was coined, but it was certainly prominent in the 1920s and a key element of the ruralist discourse.

48 Baddeley, *Yorkshire*, p. xiii.

49 Moir, *Discovery*, p. 91; MacNaboe, 'Arcadia', p. 37.

50 *Halifax Courier*, 22 June 1878.

51 For example, White, *A Month in Yorkshire*, pp. 279–85; Murray, *Yorkshire*, pp. 350–1; *Black's Guide to the County of York* (A & C Black: Edinburgh, 1888), p. 332; M. V. Hughes, *About England* (London: Dent, 1927), p. 276; A. Machin, 'Tourism and the industrial community: aspects of change', paper given at the 'Tourisms: Identities, Environments, Conflicts and Histories' Conference, University of Central Lancashire, 23 June 2001.

52 *Blue Guide*, p. 208.

53 H. A. Piehler, *England for Everyman* (London: Dent, 1933), p. vii. I am grateful to Alan Hughes for this reference.

54 Morton, *In Search*, pp. xiv, 181–5.

55 Home, *Yorkshire*, pp. 425–48. Even in the much-altered climate of 1996, only about 10 per cent of the Yorkshire chapter in *England. The Rough Guide* was dedicated to industrial areas.

56 The Pilkington Glass Museum was noted in an appendix.

57 Mais, *English Scene*, pp. 206–7.

58 Murray, *Handbook for Travellers in Yorkshire*, p. 471; G. Orwell, *The Road to Wigan Pier* (1937, Harmondsworth: Penguin edn, 1963), p. 95; *England. The Rough Guide* (London: Rough Guides Ltd, 1996), p. 609.

59 C. N. Parkinson, *Left Luggage. From Marx to Wilson* (London: John Murray, 1967), p. 10.

60 A. Myers, 'Priestley being beastly', *Northern Review* 1, Spring 1995, pp. 53–62.

61 J. K. Walton, 'Blackpool and the varieties of Britishness', in J. K. Walton (ed.), *Relocating Britishness* (Manchester: Manchester University Press, 2004).

62 P. Theroux, *The Kingdom by the Sea* (London: Hamish Hamilton, 1983), p. 173. See also, B. Bryson, *Notes from a Small Island* (London: Doubleday, 1995), pp. 213–15.

63 Vale, *North Country*, p. 50; T. Bennett, 'Hegemony, ideology, pleasure: Blackpool', in T. Bennett, C. Mercer and J. Wollacott eds., *Popular Culture and Social Relations* (Milton Keynes: Open University Press, 1986), pp. 135–54.

64 Vale, *North Country*, p. 50.

65 G. Gibbons, *Yorkshire. Britain's Biggest County* (London: Geographia Ltd, 1969), p. 6.

66 *Yorkshire*, p. xiii.

67 D. Joy (ed.), *The Dalesman. A Celebration of Fifty Years* (London: Pelham Books, 1989), p. vii. The initial title was the *Yorkshire Dalesman* but in April 1948 it decided to 'look over the Yorkshire border'.

68 Although *Cheshire Life* was originally founded by the Cheshire Publicity and Industrial Development Council as a mechanism for encouraging investors. For this and much else about county magazines, I am indebted to Andrew Hobbs.

69 Morton, *In Search*, p. 202.

70 C. Dellheim, 'Imagining England', pp. 227–8.

71 L. Cooper, *Yorkshire. West Riding* (London: Robert Hale, 1950), pp. 11, 113, 7, 111.

72 Ibid., pp. 108–9.

73 J. Hadfield (ed.), *The New Shell Guide to England* (London; Michael Joseph, 1981 ed.), pp. 678–79. See too, Cooper's observations in her *Yorkshire*, p. 7.

74 Priestley, *English Journey*, p. 171.

75 *The Road to Wigan Pier* (Penguin edn 1963), pp. 96–7; Cooper, *Yorkshire*, p. 7.

76 J. Lofthouse, *Portrait of Lancashire* (London: Robert Hale, 1977 edn), p. 10: N. Roberts and F. A. H. Bloemendal, *England in Colour. Lancashire* (London: Town and Country Books, 1983), pp. 5, 102. I am grateful to Steve Caunce for drawing my attention to this volume.

77 C. Price, *Tea Shop Walks in Lancashire* (Wilmslow: Sigma Leisure, 1997), p. 1.

78 *Illustrated London News*, 9 May 1857.

79 Gibbons, *Yorkshire*, pp. 80–1.

80 A. Machin, 'Tourism and the industrial community'.

81 'Developing Bradford's Tourist Industry', City of Bradford Metropolitan Council, 1994, p. 1.

82 Hadfield, *The New Shell Guide*, p. 57; Thorold, 'County Durham', pp. 75–6, 108. Interestingly, the language used of Consett is decidedly sublime.

83 I. Ousby (ed.), *Blue Guide. England* (London: A & C Black, 1989), preface.

84 Obviously, these features are as much local and regional resources as centres of tourism.

85 R. Burton, *Travel Geography* (Longman: 1991), pp. 213–14; C. Law, *Urban Tourism. Attracting Visitors to Large Cities* (London: Mansell, 1993).

86 *Bradford and District Economic Profile, vol. 7* (Bradford: Bradford TEC, 2001), p. 46.

87 R. Hewison, *The Heritage Industry. Britain in a Climate of Decline* (London: Methuen, 1987).

88 A. Babbidge, 'UK museums: safe and sound?', *Cultural Trends*, 37, 2000, pp. 12–16, p. 26.

89 S. Caunce, 'British, English or what? A northern English perspective on late twentieth century Britishness', paper delivered at 'Relocating Britishness' Conference, University of Central Lancashire, June 2000.

90 *British Journal of Photography*, 22 June 1989.

91 'Lottery projects paint ugly picture', *Observer*, 9 July 2000. In 2001 the Museum was the most visited provincial museum.

92 R. Samuel, 'North and south', in *Island Stories. Imagining Britain* (London: Verso, 1998), p. 166.

93 P. Theroux, *The Kingdom by the Sea. A Journey Around the Coast of Great Britain* (London: Hamish Hamilton, 1983), pp. 263–4.

94 There are shrewd comments on this in S. Schmid, 'Exploring multiculturalism: Bradford Jews and Pakistanis', *Journal of British Culture*, 4, 1–2, 1997, pp. 163–79. It is instructive to compare Jennings with the affectionate but unsentimental insider's view offered in Simon Armitage, *All Points North* (London: Viking, 1998).

95 C. Jennings, *Up North. Travels Beyond the Watford Gap* (London: Abacus edn, 1995), pp. 58, 190, 208.

96 Home, *Yorkshire*, p. 439; A. Mee, *Lancashire* (London: Hodder and Stoughton, 1936), p. 3. I am grateful to Mark Green for this reference.

97 'Six in the city', *Guardian*, 31 March 2001; *Fodor Guide, 2000*.

98 For the Bigg Market, *England. The Rough Guide*, 1996, p. 699; for the Tyneside cultural renaissance, 'When the hope comes in' and 'Expect the unexpected', *Guardian*, G2, 24 June 2002.

99 *England. The Rough Guide*, pp. 558–9.

100 For detailed treatment, see P. J. Buckley and S. F. Witt, 'Case studies of Bradford, Bristol, Glasgow and Hamm', *Tourism Management*, 6, 3, 1985, pp. 205–14; D. Davidson and R. Maitland, 'Case study A: Bradford', in their *Tourism Destinations* (London: Hodder and Stoughton, 1997), pp. 190–207; C. A. Hope and M. S. Klemm, 'Tourism in difficult areas revisited: the case of Bradford', *Tourism Management*, 22, 2001, pp. 629–36; D. Russell, 'Selling Bradford: tourism and northern image in the late twentieth century', *Contemporary British History*, 17, 2, 2003, pp. 49–68.

101 Schmid, 'Exploring multiculturalism', p. 165.

102 *Listener*, 1 November 1984.

103 B. Bryson, *Notes From a Small Island* (London: Doubleday, 1995), p. 153.

104 *Bradford Telegraph and Argus*, 21 October 1980; *Yorkshire Evening Post*, 20 October 1980.

105 *Bradford Telegraph and Argus*, 17 June 1983, 25 August 1999.

106 *Sunday Times*, 30 August 1981; *Classical Music*, 19 March 1988.

107 *Observer*, 29 October 2000.

108 Taylor, 'Which Britain?', pp. 138–9.

3

Writing the North

Virtually almost every form of writing has helped shape our image of the North. Travel literature demands a separate chapter, dialect writing a substantial section of another and the novel is at the core of this one, but so many other genres mentioned here merely in passing – poetry, autobiography and biography, journalism, school text books, academic literature and much else – deserve detailed exploration. This chapter engages with the widest possible range of literature from *Hard Times, North and South* and other 'classics' of the mid-nineteenth century to the popular sagas of the late twentieth century and much in between. Given that no similar broad survey exists and that academic discussion of literature and northern identity has tended to focus on small number of titles or specific genres, such eclecticism seems justifiable. The focus is essentially on works set in the North, although novels where northerners go 'down south' or feature as central characters in other locations are considered where appropriate. All genres, whether written by northerners or by outsiders, are brought together under the shorthand of 'northern fiction'.

The crucial issue of readership can only be dealt with here very briefly, but the key point is that northern fiction has increasingly enjoyed the power to reach the widest possible audience. In terms of geographical reach, many northern-based writers have undeniably written with a local or regional audience uppermost in mind, with the sheer level of local allusion suggestive of a desire to connect with a knowing audience. However, at first sight unlikely books could break out of their expected confines, as exemplified by William Riley's *Windyridge* (1912). Originally written by the Bradford-based manufacturer as a solace for two bereaved neighbours and with no thought of publication, over 300,000 copies had been sold by the time of Riley's death in the 1960s, and to an audience that stretched way beyond the West Riding.[1] While many works spoke most clearly to northern audiences, there was often enough extra-regional interest to make even determinedly regional novels a major force for the external construction and negotiation of ideas about the North.

A broadening of audience has also been apparent in class terms. While it is probable that the core audience for northern fiction in the nineteenth and earlier twentieth centuries came from the middle and lower-middle class, rising living standards and the growth of mass paperback publishing have exerted an impact from that point. Libraries afforded further improved literary access for poorer readers, while some titles such as *Hard Times* have long been entrenched in the school curriculum. As a result of these processes, some titles have reached remarkably large audiences. Probably the biggest sellers have been works by the critically unregarded saga writers. Catherine Cookson is an extreme case, but pioneering work by Val Williamson has shown that a select group of other writers have also garnered huge readerships. In 1999, for example, 6 of the 139 books published in Britain with sales of over 100,000 sales were sagas set in the north-west, with two titles from Josephine Cox enjoying a combined total of three quarters of a million and a sales value of £3.8 million.[2] While most of the titles considered in this chapter could not begin to approach that level of popularity, some care has been taken to survey books that appear to have had some commercial success. Although cultural history should not be obsessed with the marketplace, the type of analysis attempted here requires engagement with works that interested the public rather than merely intrigued critics or later scholars. Given that many novels set in the North can be categorised as sagas, family histories or popular romances, it is likely that a disproportionate number of readers have been women, always closely associated with these genres as both producers and consumers. This has perhaps been the case especially in the second half of the twentieth century when the saga market has expanded greatly, and most notably since the 1980s.

Literary histories and literary geographies

The 'literary north' is often generously defined so as to embrace, amongst other areas, D. H. Lawrence's north Nottinghamshire, Alan Sillitoe's Nottingham and Arnold Bennett's Potteries. Geographers Pocock and Hudson were happy to label all three writers as 'northern' in their groundbreaking study of the region's literary representation, and others have followed: the fact that Bennett entitled his 1898 study of an aspiring Staffordshire author in London *A Man from the North* certainly makes his inclusion all the easier.[3] The 'North' under scrutiny here remains the seven-county version, partly to maintain organisational neatness across the book but also because contemporary reviewers tended to place these 'borderland' writers elsewhere. The *Times Literary Supplement*, for example, located Bennett's *Anna of the Five Towns* (1902) in 'mid-England' and Lawrence's *Sons and Lovers* (1913) in 'the colliery districts of the midlands'.[4] It is nevertheless significant that a number of writers from adjacent regions can be so easily claimed for the North, and especially those authors closely associated with the industrial working class and/or despoiled industrial landscapes. Notions of the North as essentially industrial and proletarian clearly run deep.

The status of northern fiction in general and northern-born writers more specifically has varied considerably since the mid-nineteenth century. While northern-based literature has been produced throughout the period under consideration, it has enjoyed moments of especial national prominence and significance. Writing specifically of the regional novel (a term returned to shortly), Snell has seen the genre emerging, 'most strongly during periods when older interior ways of life were being threatened economically, and when changes in familiar and psychological "landscapes" affected even those who were economically secure'.[5] This seems to hold true for novels about the North. National penetration occurred at three moments of economic dislocation and consequent political response in the 1840s and 1850s, the heyday of the industrial novel; the 1930s and the 1980s, when the impact of, and responses to Thatcherism stimulated 'an unprecedented outpouring of English regional fiction'.[6] A fourth high watermark came in the late 1950s and early 1960s, although here the challenge to 'older interior ways of life', brought about by northern 'Angry Young Men', came from economic buoyancy and expanding consumer power. All four periods coincided with (and were partly responsible for) the key moments of wider interest in and/or concern about the North identified in chapter 1. Indeed, the fit between cultural production and this wider context was probably more exact in literature than any other field.

These periods of prominence, however, must be set against other much longer ones of relative neglect. This was especially the experience of regional writers working in the adjacent category of the 'working-class' novel. Jack Common's work might better known had he published his north-eastern novel *Kiddar's Luck* in 1961 rather than 1951, the year in which John Braine's initial synopsis for *Room at the Top* was rejected.[7] Even the mid-twentieth-century moment of social realism was very modest in terms of the number of works involved and short-lived in terms of critical acclaim and fashionable status. Although there are books such as Sid Chaplin's *The Day of the Sardine* (1961), 'probably the best novel about our new lost generation that we have yet had' according to one contemporary reviewer, that have tended to be overlooked by later critics, the major northern literary 'New Wave' arguably comprised only Braine's *Room at the Top* (1957) and (perhaps) *Life at the Top* (1962), Keith Waterhouse's *Billy Liar* (1959), Stan Barstow's *A Kind of Loving* and David Storey's *This Sporting Life* and *A Flight into Camden* (all 1960).[8] Many of these writers certainly produced more on a northern theme, with Storey's *Saville* winning the 1976 Booker Prize. However, the vogue for such work waned swiftly and its classic texts have been relegated to the margins of the critical canon. Regarded by some even at the time as overly anthropological – Storey's *This Sporting Life* was described as a predictable 'piece of field work in darkest Yorkshire' in which the author 'turns his back on literature with an all too thoroughgoing zeal' – they have increasingly become valued more for sociological insight than literary quality.[9] The space within which northern fiction could operate was always both restricted and allocated elsewhere.

In another and probably related dimension, northern-born writers have generally been under-represented within what might be termed the national literary elite. This is made apparent by even the briefest survey of the birthplace of authors featured in selected literary and bibliographical guides. Exercises of the type are unquestionably problematic: birthplaces are sometimes accidental and often only briefly inhabited and thus not necessarily a guide to a region's creative potential. Moreover, the literary guides that they are extracted from are cultural constructs reflecting varying degrees of editorial prejudice, current taste and straightforward happenstance. Indeed, such works can be explored for their revealing biases against the North and other regions just as much as they can be used as sources of 'objective' evidence. Robert Colls has noted the thin coverage of the north-east in the *Oxford Companion to English Literature* while the *Oxford Illustrated Literary Guide to Great Britain and Ireland* in its turn omits Walter Greenwood from its Manchester/Salford entry and ignores Bradford altogether, thus excluding John Braine and, indefensibly, J. B. Priestley.[10] Nevertheless, analysis of such material provides an indication of broad trends indicating rather more than just the combined idiosyncrasies of personal geography and editorial bias.

A comparison between London and the seven-county North is instructive here. Although both produced about 25 per cent of the 105 major English-born novelists active between 1835 and 1900 and listed in a leading bibliographical guide, they did so from markedly different population shares. London, with approximately 12 per cent of the population could, in other words, claim the same number of authors as a region holding some 30 per cent.[11] Amongst the much smaller canonical elite included within this body of writers, only the Brontë sisters and George Gissing were born in the North, although Mrs Gaskell's childhood in Knutsford, Cheshire and adult life in Manchester, in many ways made her a northern writer. Scrutiny of a similar group of 122 writers active between 1900 and 1980 and featured in a similar guide suggests that this basic regional imbalance was maintained across the next century, with the North producing 22 (18 per cent) and London 35 (28 per cent) of their number.[12] These overall figures do, however, disguise the fact that the region improved its contribution to the national literary stock over the course of the twentieth century in that more of its writers – Winifred Holtby and J. B. Priestley in the 1930s and then later Beryl Bainbridge, Pat Barker, Malcolm Bradbury, Melvyn Bragg, John Braine, A. S. Byatt, Margaret Drabble, Susan Hill, and David Storey, for example – attained major critical acclaim with varying degrees of permanence.

These patterns are in many ways easier to describe than explain. The relative under-representation of northern writers perhaps supports Frank Musgrove's argument that the North has largely exhibited a 'practical and pragmatic character' and that its militarised nature, pre-industrial lack of wealth and the rise of manufacturing and mining have proved 'disastrous for intellectual life'.[13] These ideas and his claim that 'the northern intellect in modern times has had a distinctly scientific bent' cannot be dismissed completely. Nevertheless, they tend to reinforce stereotypes rather than open them up to scrutiny. There can be no denying the general creative impulse within the North throughout the nineteenth and twentieth centuries, something this book attests to in all manner of ways. It is, then, surely likely that the fortunes of northern writers (especially those from working- or lower-middle-class backgrounds) have been shaped more by such limiting factors as financial hardship and distance from crucial networks in the capital, than the more general operation of some northern 'character'. Moreover, changes in taste, new patterns of readership and, above all, increased educational opportunities, have ironed out some of the regional imbalance from the 1950s. Ten of the 22 twentieth-century northern novelists noted above were born between 1929 and 1942 and were in many cases beneficiaries of the 1944 Education Act.[14]

The final issue in this consideration of northern literary exclusion and inclusion concerns the 'regional novel'. Given its significance in this chapter, some comment on definition is useful here. Keith Snell has seen its key elements as including a setting in a clearly recognisable region; a description of the life and culture of people therein; a strong sense of local geography and topography and the capacity to generate a sense of place through realistic dialogue, often involving dialect or demotic speech.[15] While some writers, notably W. J. Keith, have seen it as a rural genre, Snell acknowledges overlap with, and absorption into, other categories, including the industrial novel, women's romantic fiction, detective stories, children's literature and much else.[16] Given the remarkable success of some works in these latter categories in capturing a sense of place, Snell's broad reach seems entirely appropriate, even though the last section of this chapter will take a slightly narrower view.

For current purposes, however, definition is less of an issue than status. Although the label 'regional novelist' has been applied in certain situations to the works of Mrs Gaskell, the Brontës, Thomas Hardy, D. H. Lawrence and other major literary figures, the regional novel has generally lacked *kudos*. The term is too loaded with the pejorative connotations that cling to the term 'regional', itself too close a cousin of 'provincial'. As Raymond Williams so effectively put it, 'The life and people of certain favoured regions are seen as essentially general, even perhaps normal, while the life and people of certain regions, however interestingly and affectionately presented are, well, regional'.[17] London – explicitly excluded from most academic studies of the regional novel before Snell's intervention – and the Home Counties have unsurprisingly served as the 'non-regional' norm. The genre's close association for much of the twentieth century with the realist aesthetic and the traditions of ordered narrative that ran counter to the dictates of modernist critics from around 1920 has provided a further problem, as have, perhaps, its association with the mass market and with women, both as authors and audience.[18] For all these reasons, one of the most vibrant areas of cultural production in the North specifically, and the provinces more generally, has often found itself marginalised within critical discourses.

Alongside these relationships between the North and South, province and capital, some interesting *intra*-regional patterns of literary geography can also be discerned. The clearest point here is the dominance of Yorkshire and Lancashire both in terms of the production of authors and as sites of plot location. Of the northern writers working between 1875 and 1950 identified in Lucien LeClaire's pioneering 1954 bibliography of regional novelists, about 85 per cent were born in either Yorkshire or Lancashire.[19] Although LeClaire's guide is most certainly not definitive (the north-east is very patchily treated), this might suggest that writers from the 'far North' have sometimes found it difficult to attract publishers. In terms of settings, Keith Snell's more recent and richly thorough bibliography shows that about 70 per cent of regional novels set in the seven-county North between 1800 and 2000 were located in Lancashire and Yorkshire, more or less a reflection of their objective position within the wider region although probably also testimony to their highly developed sense of county identity.[20] (Cheshire, by comparison, was the focus of less than 1 per cent of the works listed by Snell.) Significantly for later discussions, it was the urban/industrial regions within these two counties that attracted by far the most attention. As in other cultural fields, the industrial north-east has featured far more consistently since 1950, and not least because of the phenomenal output and sales achieved by South Shields-born Catherine Cookson, whose first novel, *Kate Hannigan,* appeared in that year. By the late 1990s, her total career sales topped 100 million.[21] In general, however, as was so often the case, the industrial near North tended to stand for the region as a whole.

Northern images

In the light of this, it is not surprising that the industrial and urban novel is the main focus of this chapter. Other fictional Norths and their functions must certainly be acknowledged. The region's vast rural acreage and network of villages and country town have featured strongly, especially between about 1875 and 1939 when rural settings were at their most fashionable. Yorkshire was a significant site for such literature, with the Brontës a crucial inspiration. William Riley (1866–1961), James Keighley Snowden (1860–1947) and Halliwell Sutcliffe (1870–1932), novelists of the industrial West Riding's rural hinterlands, and Mary Beaumont (1849–1910) and Mary Linskill (1840–1891), interpreters of the northern dales and the North Yorkshire Moors respectively, were amongst the most celebrated writers of this type. Although in many ways a novelist of the politics and culture of the small-town East Riding, much of the work of Winifred Holtby (1898–1935) also captured the area's rural life. Other notable figures included M. E. Francis (Mrs Francis Blundell, 1859–1930), whose Lancashire short stories enjoyed a vogue in the Edwardian period, and Constance Holme, who achieved a significant following from about 1914 to the late 1930s with her Westmorland fictions and especially *Crump Folk Going Home* (1913) and *The Lonely Plough* (1914). After 1939, rural fiction in general was very much in decline, with novelists turning far more obviously to urban themes and locations.[22] Nevertheless, numerous northern writers have continued to find inspiration in rural settings. Melvyn Bragg's use of the Lake District and other Cumberland and Westmorland settings is a notable example and the autobiographical writings of North Yorkshire vet 'James Herriot', swiftly adapted for television and film, have demonstrated the enduring appeal of the wilder North.[23] Coastal locations boasting attractive scenery and historic attractions have also been much favoured, with Whitby, offering both, notice-ably popular. It was the 'Monkshaven' of Mrs Gaskell's *Sylvia's Lovers* (1863) and 'Port St. Hilda' and 'Danesacre' in the work of locally born writers Mary Linskill and Storm Jameson (1897–1986) respectively, while neighbouring Robin Hood's Bay became Bramblewick in the fishing stories of Leo Walmsley (1892–1966).[24]

Although they could add substantially to stereotypical views of the North, many of these non-industrial fictions often produced a rather softer, gentler ver-sion of the region than their industrial/urban counterparts. Many were specifi-cally intended to appeal to local, urban-based readers seeking imaginative escape from familiar townscapes and recognisable social problems and into worlds peopled with slightly exotic characters and associated with pleasure, relaxation and freedom. In both its choice of location and tone this was the fic-tional equivalent of the travel writer's 'true North'. It was never entirely devoid of engagement with contemporary concerns, although these were usually very specific. Especially in the inter-war period, for example, rural novels often fretted over the suburbanisation of the countryside. In William Riley's *Windyridge Revisited* (1928), heroine Grace Holden wonders whether she will return the eponymous cottage on the fringes of the industrial West Riding.

> Farewell Windyridge! I shall see you, I hope again – perhaps many times: and yet I do not know. The city is creeping out to the moors and the golfers are there. Townsfolk are building bungalows on the outskirts of the grey, old-world hamlet – horrible suburban dwellings with red-tiled roofs and gardens like miniature Earl's Courts. It is desecration! I rather think my Trianon days are numbered.[25]

In a related vein, senior Labour politician and proud Yorkshireman Lord Snowden used his introduction to a 1932 reprint of 'kinsman' James Keighley Snowden's *The Web of the Old Weaver*, to register 'my anxiety to see preserved the characteristics of a people which, I am afraid, are rapidly changing under the influence of modern transport and the uniformity of an educational system imposed by a central authority'. At least, he conceded, the village 'has been spared the affliction of a cinema'.[26] In these modes, the rural North is connected firmly with wider currents of 'Englishness', celebrating tradition, continuity and rural beauty, albeit beauty often of a distinctive variety.

Despite this substantial strand, the literary North has most often and most potently been urban and, even more specifically, industrial; the commercial city of Liverpool certainly failed to attract the interests of the Victorian social novelists.[27] Rather than 'skirt Black England' in the manner of many travel writers, novelists headed straight for its centre. For all their subtleties and nuances, their writings have done more to define the North as 'other' – as harsh, bleak, industrial and 'the land of the working class' – than any other single cultural form. The small but influential body of mid-nineteenth-century industrial novels that runs from Harriet Martineau's *Manchester Strike* (1832) to Mrs Gaskell's *North and South* (1854–55) was absolutely critical here, defining the North in highly specific ways and setting a context for so much of the writing and thinking about the region that followed.[28] Telling depictions of the despoiled physical landscape, the drabness of daily life and the mindset of 'alien' peoples, whether working- or middle-class, are legion in these texts. The Coketown of Dickens's *Hard Times* is

> a town of redbrick, or of brick that would have been red if the smoke and ashes had allowed it; but as matters stood it was a town of unnatural red and black like the painted face of a savage. It was a town of machinery and tall chimneys, out of which interminable serpents of smoke trailed themselves forever and ever, and never got uncoiled. It had a black canal in it, and a river that ran purple with ill-smelling dye, and vast piles of buildings full of windows where there was a rattling and a trembling all day long … it contained several large streets all very like one another, and many small streets still more like one another, inhabited by people equally like one another …[29]

Similarly, as Margaret Hale and her father approach Milton-Northern in the county of Darkshire en route from idyllic rural Hampshire in the early stages of *North and South* (the juxtaposition of the 'real' southern county with its mythical counterpart is interesting here), she sees a 'deep lead-coloured cloud hanging over the horizon in the direction in which it lay … Nearer the town, the air had a faint taste and smell of smoke … Quick they were whirled over long, straight, hopeless streets of regularly-built houses, all small and of brick.' As the book develops, these physical divisions elide with intellectual and emotional ones. When the manufacturer John Thornton discusses the iron laws of *laissez-faire* economics, 'Margaret's whole soul rose up against him while he reasoned in this way – as if commerce were everything and humanity nothing'.[30]

These novels also fed on older notions of the North as uncivilised and only half-tamed. The brutalised environment, physical violence between employers and employees and the machinations of the self-seeking political demagogues that featured in so many plots were central in this context. So too was the sense of the North's almost alien remoteness. Interestingly, it was Mrs Gaskell, that normally most sympathetic of chroniclers, who made one of the most crucial interventions here, albeit in her hugely influential *The Life of Charlotte Brontë* (1857) rather than in a work of fiction. The novels of the Brontës, and most notably Emily's *Wuthering Heights* (1847), had themselves played a major role in this process. In her attempt to explain the genius and the achievement of the family, Gaskell chose to accentuate this, portraying the sisters almost as castaways amongst a savage people, their talent all the more startling for (although also shaped by) their living amongst 'this wild, rough population'. For Gaskell, Yorkshire people were anyway more 'independent' and 'self-sufficient' than most other northerners, with even Lancastrians struck by their 'peculiar force of character'. In the moorland communities above Haworth, however,

> Their accost is curt, their accent and tone of speech blunt and harsh. Something of this may, probably, be attributed to the freedom of mountain air and of isolated hill-life; something be derived from their rough Norse ancestry. They have a quick perception of character, and a keen sense of humour; the dweller among them must be prepared for certain uncomplimentary, though most likely true, observations, pithily expressed ... there would be much found even at present that would shock those accustomed only to the local manners of the south; and, in return, I suspect the shrewd sagacious, energetic Yorkshire man would hold such 'foreigners' in no small contempt.[31]

As Brontë scholars have shown, such a picture misleads by failing to capture Haworth's role as a busy industrial community with many and varied links to the outside-world. However, 'her wonderfully evocative picture ... has become the essence of Brontë mythology' and, while it was a picture of only one part of the North, it could clearly stand for Yorkshire, and indeed, the North as a whole.[32] In this instance at least, a writer known for her understanding of northern popular character opted for stereotype and with significant consequences.

Both the purpose and narrative structure of these early Victorian writings helped fix a specific image for the North. The overtly didactic intent of the novels was crucial here. As Peter Keating has argued, 'nobody in an industrial novel laughs, makes jokes or dances ... to make the reader laugh would have been considered an act of bad faith, or even taste'. He cites the somewhat, melodramatic, one-dimensional working-class characters in *Hard Times* – certainly lacking the richness of many of Dickens's cockney low life creations – as prime examples.[33] The sense of 'otherness' was made all the more tangible by the fact of so many novels being written by outsiders and/or having narratives driven by outsiders, leading to an anthropological approach that laid the region out to be explored, to be pathologised. Disraeli's *Sybil* and Gaskell's *North and South* exemplify this, especially in their earlier descriptive passages; significantly, Disraeli's hero Egremont at one stage disguises himself as a journalist investigating the condition of the northern people. The industrial novel was often intended as a tool of reconciliation, a mechanism for encouraging or imagining better understanding between classes and regions. This undoubtedly demanded that some of these outsiders had to attain a better understanding of the region. *North and South*, the subtlest of these texts because of its depth of inside knowledge, increasingly interrogates the simple oppositions that shape the early chapters and are encapsulated in a title that folds all complexities into manageable binary form. Towards the close of the book we are clearly supposed to be amused by Margaret's aunt's metropolitan view of Milton-Northern, one rendered simplistic by her niece's experiences there. 'It was noisy, and smoky, and the poor people whom she saw in the streets were dirty, and the rich ladies overdressed, and not a man that she saw, high or low, had his clothes made to fit.'[34] Nevertheless, for all the opening of minds and social exchange through marriage and friendship that feature in these novels, northern voices never take control of the narrative. As a result, the North–South relationship can be readjusted but never equalised.

There is no originality in most of the above claims. Indeed, the quotation from *Hard Times* has been chosen precisely because of its familiarity. The crucial point is that a small number of highly influential texts established a distinct version of the North and then kept that view alive as a result of their continued popularity. Contemporary readers may indeed have been able to glimpse a slightly more complex North than later generations. Readers of *Hard Times* in its original serialised form, for example, will have been able to find elsewhere in their copy of *Household Words* positive pieces on Manchester's commercial architecture and Liverpool's economic achievements.[35] It is likely that many later readers will have approached these texts in a far less open manner. As recently as 1994, the jacket description on the 'Penguin Popular Classics' edition of *Hard Times* told would-be readers that 'It depicts Coketown, a *typical* red-brick industrial city of the north. In its schools and factories children and adults are caged and enslaved, with no personal freedom until their spirit is broken'. Dickens would have been pleased if perhaps surprised that his flying visit to Preston, the most likely original for the novel's setting, could have generated so much interpretative power for so long.[36]

While the fashion for the industrial novel had abated by the late 1850s, every major northern literary 'moment' from that point has continued to be heavily coloured by what Philip Dodd, admittedly in specific reference to the later twentieth century, has termed the 'Lowryscape'. Each of these has had its distinctive shading and emphasis.[37] Economic and social disruption, specifically the ramifications of mass unemployment, dominated the literature of the 1930s. The northern realist writing of the late 1950s and early 1960s had a very different set of concerns while remaining clearly urban/industrial and although Ian Haywood correctly argues that it is hard to date 'the action precisely, or to locate the influence of regionalism' in such novels as Pat Barker's *Union Street* (1982) or Livi Micheal's *Under a Thin Moon* (1992), the urban texture of these studies of a now de-industrialising northern England are certainly apparent.[38] Northern literature has long raised expectations of, and been rooted in, a highly distinctive geography.

From the later nineteenth century this geography has been far more securely in the hands of local practitioners than it was in the early Victorian period. Although, as will be argued below, this did not result in fundamental changes in the region's representation, in combination with the growing number of working-class and women authors it added to the range of perspectives shaping those representations. Moreover, by the later nineteenth century, those from outside the region who chose to write about it or populate their work with northern characters varied but little from local writers in their interpretation and description of the North and its people. Kipling's John Learoyd, a Yorkshireman significantly chosen alongside the cockney Ortheris and the Irishman Mulvaney to stand for the British soldier in his *Soldiers Three* stories, would not have looked out of place in a story produced in the character's native Bradford. The North has then, with some exceptions, been perhaps a little less vigorously 'other' than in earlier fictional accounts.

In terms of depiction from the inside, most northern writers have acted only as spokespeople for a relatively limited part of the wider region. As a result, important intra-regional differences in self-image are often apparent. Priestley's description of West Riding folk as individuals who 'use emphatic consonants and very broad vowels and always sound aggressive, who are afraid of nothing but mysterious codes of etiquette and any display of feeling', captures that dourness beloved by the county's literary representatives; to the west of the Pennines, friendliness and openness were more obviously prized.[39] These differences were ultimately largely only a matter of emphasis, however, and a broadly agreed northern self-image can be identified. It was often an extremely positive one. As might be expected from the 'identikit' offered in chapter 1, some of the most consistent and proudest claims made in regard to northern character were for a cluster of related values embracing independence of spirit, dislike of imposed authority and a natural egalitarianism. This was a hand that could be over-played. 'Isn't the rest of our country pretty well sold now on our bluff-and-gruff-but-hearts-of-gold tradition?' gently chided one reviewer in 1940. 'Our West Riding forthrightness, uprightness and downrightness already form the basis of a thriving literary industry – cloth bound so to speak'.[40] The very existence of this knowing, insider's joke, of course, reveals the strength of such representations as much as challenges them and they certainly continued to appear well after this date.

A particularly powerful stress was placed on the warmth and sustenance provided by the industrial working-class community. Certainly, there were numerous plots and sub-plots that showed the emotional and intellectual limitations that such communities could impose and a few works that dealt honestly with households failing to live up to patterns of sometimes clichéd fictional expectation. Barry Hines' *A Kestrel for a Knave* (1968), in which the dysfunctional Casper household offers something of a prelude to the 'underclass' novels of the 1980s, is a clear case in point. Nevertheless, the northern terraced street has become a powerful symbol of decency, compassion and survival. This has been especially the case in the immensely popular sagas and family histories that have been such a feature of the publishing landscape in the late twentieth century. They are most closely associated with Catherine Cookson although a skilful new set of authors have emerged since the 1970s, including Barbara Taylor Bradford, Josephine Cox, Olive Etchells, Audrey Howard, Marie Joseph, Sheelagh Kelly and Elvi Rhodes. Josephine Cox's memoir of her Blackburn childhood can stand almost exactly for the fictional world she and her fellow authors have created in which 'life was hectic and noisy, and often violent' but where 'people were warm and friendly, and every mother was mother to every child in the street'.[41] These writers, who have rooted a great deal of their work in the nineteenth century and the 1930s, have done much to maintain the 'mill town' version of the North. The attraction of such physical and chronological settings lays partly in their familiarity and their scope for generating dramatic action and sharp, oppositional characterisation, but they arguably capture a deeper need. David Gervais' perceptive suggestion that the 'axis of Englishness' has moved northward over the course of the twentieth century, noted in chapter 1, is useful here in helping to explain the popularity of these fictions. For all the material, mental and physical struggles found within them, the sense of community they convey may go some way in reacquainting readers with a world they have lost, or feel they have lost. (The later twentieth-century vogue for L. S. Lowry prints may also owe much to these sensibilities.)

Northern readers are possibly the more likely to read these books in this way but the possibilities are there for others to share. In this voice the North can speak most effectively for the nation.

Issues of gender intrude here, for it is women characters that have always been the strongest signifiers in depiction of the properly functioning community. This stems to a considerable degree from the close association of women writers with northern fiction and especially in the later twentieth century, a period that saw a substantial process of feminisation within the field, although male writers have always contributed their share to the stock of heroic wives and mothers. The representation of northern women in fiction almost demands a book of its own but the key point within this discussion relates to the centrality of the 'strong' or 'dominant' woman, those who hold together families and wider social networks in the face of poverty and personal tragedy. The most potent figures have tended to be either the young, single woman usually supporting an aged relative or younger sibling, or the older married woman bringing wisdom and a hard-edged kindness. Such characters probably constitute a minority within the literature as a whole. Indeed, the binary oppositions that drive the storylines actually demand that they be accompanied by a substantial number of the weak, the vacillating and the immoral. To give one random example, Joan Lowrie, the pit-brow lass in Frances Hodgson Burnett's *That Lass O' Lowrie's* (1877), gains her initial strength in the narrative through her protection of Liz, a young fellow-worker made pregnant and then abandoned by the mine owner's son, with his 'fine London ways'.[42] While many northern women are shown to be good at 'coping', it is these privileged few that give northern women and the North in general some of its most valuable cultural capital. Although consideration of this issue has been arrived at via discussion of the working-class community, powerful middle-class equivalents can be found just as easily. Alderman Mrs Beddow and her protégé, headmistress Sarah Burton, central characters in Winifred Holtby's *South Riding* (1936), and who work so hard for the good of East Riding coastal town of Kiplington, are fruitful examples here.

For all its importance in celebrating the North and generating complementary or even alternative forms of Englishness, it is still seems probable that industrial and urban fiction has bequeathed the region an awkward legacy. Even in the hands of 'insiders', it has tended to emphasis the bleaker aspects of life, with the popularity of late Victorian poverty or inter-war unemployment as an organising theme in the contemporary saga literature, telling cases in point. This has been compounded by the habit of some northern writers, often detached from their native communities as a result of education and other avenues of social mobility, to adopt something close to the anthropological tone of the early outside observers. Philip Dodd has argued persuasively for the presence of this internally generated otherness in treatments of the northern working class within a variety of later twentieth-century fiction and autobiography.[43] Similarly, the focus on working-class lifestyles, while far from exclusive, has run the risk of reinforcing the notion of the North as effectively a one-class society. The North is then often a rather one-dimensional place where only certain narratives, usually emphasising struggle, hardship and varying degrees of emotional repression seem to be allowable. This is obviously a generalisation that can be overturned with reference to specific texts and which must not be read as a denial of the working-class struggle and hardship that have been a major part of the reality of northern history. The powerful presence of one style of northern representation and the relative absence of others capturing a modernising, more cosmopolitan or simply a more mundane North, is nevertheless revealing, suggestive of the defensive nature of much northern regional ideology and the levels of cultural capital invested in particular versions of the region's history. As Dodd laments, 'I am forced to say – as the son of a Yorkshire miner – that the Lowryscape North has to be preserved in order that "We" can speak on its behalf, lament "Our" separation, and speak of its settled virtues'.[44]

The novels of the 1950s and 1960s arguably came closest to breaking away from traditional narratives and concerns. Their authors had far less obvious interest in defining and probing regional characteristics than previous generations and in some senses set out to dissolve such constructions. They were certainly little concerned with much of the daily texture of northern life and did not engage at any significant level with regionally distinctive topography, labour relationships, workplace practices or any of the other standard concerns of earlier northern fiction. Similarly, dialect was generally abandoned in favour of a looser regional demotic. (In the light of the earlier discussion of gender, it should be noted that they were most certainly not interested in strong and independently minded women.) All of these were of little interest to writers seeking to explore personal and inter-generational relationships at the moment when the 'traditional' working-class community was beginning to dissolve. It is interesting in this regard that these works are often grouped together as 'working-class novels'. In fact, in terms of characterisation at least, many leading characters are sometimes either not of the working class – Billy Fisher, central character of Keith Waterhouse's *Billy Liar*, works in an undertaker's office and is the son of a haulage contractor – or, like town hall clerk Joe Lampton in John

Braine's *Room at the Top* and draughtsman Vic Brown in Stan Barstow's *A Kind of Loving*, are so obviously on their way out of it.[45] While the label undoubtedly fits many titles and most of the writers had working-class backgrounds, its rather too general application says much about the power of the North's space-myth.

For all their change of perspective, however, even these works that had brought the North 'back into fashion in a rather strange and oblique way', have proved problematic for the region's image.[46] The very fact that they were less obviously rooted in a northern landscape than many predecessors is, ironically, an issue here. Readers, and especially those approaching the books without experiencing the far more overtly northern gloss added by their film adaptations, were arguably finding the North fashionable precisely because it did not fully resemble the North they had learnt to imagine. While these books were northern and 'other' enough to provide access to a supposedly more vibrant, edgy, relevant and democratic culture than that on view in most other post-war cultural arenas, they offered a version of the North that was universal in application. Concerns about sex, marriage, social and geographical mobility and much else, were obviously not peculiar to the North and, briefly, the region could speak for a much larger constituency. When that fashionable moment was over, however, older Norths quickly re-established themselves. Not everyone found the novels' subject matter attractive, of course, and reviews which talked of a book's interesting material being 'all but swamped by its dreary preoccupation with sex' will merely have associated the North in some minds with sordidness and the unwelcome intrusion of modern life.[47] Above all else, these works were critical in various degrees of many aspects of northern society and most especially its social snobberies, supposed sexual Puritanism and limited horizons. In that sense, some of the North's most celebrated cultural products undermined the region at the very time when they appeared to be making it fashionable. This crucial point is explored further at various stages in the next two sections.

The North has not been alone in being represented in some of the ways identified here. Other industrial areas have received similar treatment, especially at the hands of outsiders. Disraeli's 'Wodgate', set in a thinly-disguised Black Country, is described as 'the most hideous borough in the ugliest country in the world' inhabited by a people not immoral 'for immorality implies some forethought; or ignorant, for ignorance is relative; but they are animals; unconscious; their minds a blank; and their worst actions only the impulse of a gross or savage instinct'.[48] Similarly, 'Outcast London' and its horrors fascinated the Victorians and many since. However, London had numerous compensations while other industrial areas were either too small to receive consistent attention or were often anyway absorbed into a wider North within the popular imagination. The North, therefore, was always to carry the heaviest burden.

The road south

The issue of the relationship between the North and London and the south-east was perhaps worked out more fully in the field of literature than any other area, to some extent a reflection of the migration to London that was a reality for so many writers. David Storey's title *Flight Into Camden* provides a suitable leitmotif for the 1950s and 1960s and those who stayed, such as Stan Barstow, or who returned, such as Sid Chaplin, 'resented constantly being asked *why* they chose to live in the North, as if they were displaying some deplorable eccentricity'.[49] The complex mix of emotions engendered by southward migration coloured much writing. Whereas in the sports press and around the sports field, on the variety stage and in the pages of the dialect press, London was often reduced to a relatively simple formula variously defining it as pretentious, decadent, wasteful and generally morally inferior to the North, these often autobiographically inflected fictions often provided a more thoughtful, multi-faceted treatment.

There were three main ways in which a North/South, provincial/metropolitan perspective was treated. The first two involved inward journeys, either by 'outsiders' coming to live among a strange people or a 'local' returning home with, or in search of, a new perspective, while the third focused on the outward path taken by the aspiring northerner. All three variants could be found throughout the period from the mid-nineteenth century, although the latter was perhaps above all a late nineteenth- and twentieth-century phenomenon and was especially frequent from the 1950s and 1960s. Billy Fisher's ultimately unfulfilled love affair with an idealised version of the capital is central to Waterhouse's *Billy Liar*, while an actual move south frames Storey's *Flight into Camden* and *Saville*, Stan Barstow's *The Watchers on the Shore* (1965) and *The Right True End* (1976), Melvyn Bragg's *Kingdom Come* (1980), Margaret Drabble's *The Radiant Way* (1987) and much else.

Numerous versions of the North–South relationship emerged from these journeys in and out, with apparently contradictory attitudes sometimes present even within the same book. Without further research, there can be no attempt to draw up any kind of balance sheet weighing the frequency of particular responses but the 'South' was undeniably a frequent and often troubling presence. Many pictures of the capital and its surrounds, both in fiction and the discourses around it, were undeniably hostile and fed into the powerful critiques of metropolitan dominance embedded in all cultural arenas. There was much anger among northern writers and commentators that the capital drained the regions of its talent – a point developed in the final section of this chapter – and had a hugely inflated sense of its own importance. These sentiments can be found at any point but were most likely to surface at moments when the economic balance of power was shifting south. Gordon Stowell's trenchant defence of his novel of life in middle-class Leeds, *The History of Button Hill* (1929), captures well the spirit of some northern authors at this time. As well as stressing the need for novels of middle-class life, he saw his study as a counter to the idea that

> London is the only town in the world, or at least, the only place fit for the heroes of novels to live in … There are too many people who can only conceive of life outside the metropolis in terms of agriculture or slums. They find it difficult to grasp the demonstrable truth that the majority of English people do not live in London, and do not wish to live in London, not even the majority of educated or interesting people … I was once invited as an undistinguished make-weight to a gathering of the semi-intelligentsia in a London drawing-room. A certain lady was informed there that of all the more promising art students at the Royal College of Art at that time, the most promising ones had come from Leeds. She registered an amused incredulity and asked: 'Can anything good come out of Leeds?' I have never quite forgiven her.[50]

Its supposed privileges and wealth were another easy source of potential irritation. In *Standing Room Only* (1935) Walter Greenwood offers two responses to this. The first, significantly perhaps, displayed by an older and less acquisitive character, was to remain singularly unimpressed by all that London offered. In a set piece straight from the 'provincial innocent abroad' tradition of dialect literature and the stage, the mother of a northern playwright visits London for the premiere of his play and finds little to her satisfaction. She is disappointed that steps are not 'whitestoned'; deems Buckingham Palace 'more like a town hall' and only cheers up upon discovering that the King will not be present during her visit to the cenotaph. 'Y' get that mucky walking about, and I wouldn't like to bump into him lookin' like I do now.' The second response was rather sharper. When a well-dressed London theatrical agent walks into a Manchester public house the barmaid muses acidly, 'These London tarts know how to make up … Yes and anybody could dress like that if they'd the money. Besides, look at the choice one had in London.'[51] In a slightly more aggressive version of this, one late twentieth century best-selling popular fiction set in the 1930s, has a character accuse Londoners of ignoring the North's plight in the depression. She asks a southern visitor, '"Do they have the Means Test in London? ... It would do a lot of them snobs good to come up here and see what goes on. Folks up here are starving while they line their pockets.'[52] Such reconstructed versions of past mentalities resurrect old battles and hostilities for later generations.

Accompanying these less than flattering views was a propensity to celebrate the North as an essential counterbalance to London's claustrophobic embrace and its shallowness and superficiality. Especially in novels featuring the temporary returnee, the North is prone to be deemed physically and mentally bracing and refreshingly honest. William Riley's *Windyridge* gets much of its flavour from these ideas. Heroine Grace Holden, from a Yorkshire family but a lifetime resident in London, escapes north to avoid staying where her 'soul would be smothered' by the unpleasantness she finds during her philanthropic work. She finds peace in a village on the 'heather-covered moors, gloriously purple' beyond Airlee (Leeds), as does Philip, a local émigré eventually to be her husband, who at intervals leaves his legal work in London to 'refresh his soul with the Yorkshire burr ... my good spirit drives me north, where the air is not soft, but biting, and men speak their minds without circumlocution and talk to you without deference, and give you a rough and kindly thrust if they think you need it. And there I find vision and comfort.'[53] In another variant of the North as invigorating force, the returnee sometimes finds a strange beauty in even the most desolate and derided surroundings. In Lettice Cooper's *National and Provincial* (1938), Mary Welburn, a Yorkshire-born journalist returning to her native county, has such a moment when viewing the notoriously unscenic Sheffield. 'She was too familiar with such scenes to be struck by their ugliness, but she saw with a fresh eye their beauties, the subdued harmonies of grey and brown, the taut perfection of springing line in crane and chimney, all softened to-day in a sunlight thickened by smoke to a haze of gold.'[54]

There were certainly always narratives that counter-balanced this hostility to London and concomitant celebration of the North. The supposedly stultifying provincial mental climate was often set against London's supposed intellectual riches and social openness. The feeling that local life could quickly become exhausted and burdensome is certainly a central theme in literary autobiographies. Prolific Yorkshire-born author Joseph Smith Fletcher (b. 1863) argued that while the citizens of Bradford might believe their city 'is the full flower of all that is best in politics and mental culture', his experience there as a journalist made him believe that it and other provincial centres were 'only half-baked loaves of mental bread … I have always held, and hold now, there is only one town in England which is fit to live in, and that if you cannot live in London there is nothing to do but live in Arcadia'.[55] Neville Cardus recalled a youthful sense of having outgrown Edwardian Manchester and the dawning realisation that he 'was a provincial … One night I walked down the Palatine Road which goes southwards from Manchester, and with my imagination's vision I saw the glow of London, saw it as young Jude saw Christminster in the distance'.[56] Feeling 'unripe for London', he stayed, but the fact that a man with such an acute awareness of Manchester's cultural riches should feel this way is revealing.

This sense of frustration with the North, and the 'provinces' more generally, fuelled many fictional journeys southward. The naïveté and oversimplification that this process often involved, was wryly observed by Arnold Bennett's partly autobiographical *The Man From the North* (1898). 'There grows in the North Country a certain kind of youth of whom it may be said that he is born to be a Londoner. The metropolis, and everything that appertains to it, that comes down from it, that goes up into it, has for him an imperious satisfaction.'[57] Priestley also captured this well in *The Good Companions* (1929). Although Jess Oakroyd's much trumpeted sojourn 'down south' had actually involved a unexceptional six months in Leicester, whenever the unsettled Yorkshireman uttered the phrase 'he seemed to conjure up a vast journey towards the tropics and at the end of it a life entirely alien, fantastic'. Characters certainly often enjoyed London, a place of 'ambiguous satisfactions' in Ian Haywood's phrase, rather more in expectation than actuality.[58] Nevertheless, real pleasures were there to be experienced. Its sheer size and the opportunities this provided for personal reinvention or simple release from an all-seeing neighbourhood were much prized. 'I thrived on the anonymity', says Margaret Thorpe in *Flight into Camden* while, on a trip to London, Braine's Joe Lampton found that 'I didn't feel married, I didn't feel an employee … I threw off my Warley identities'.[59] Keith Waterhouse's Billy Fisher is sufficiently aware of this conceit to adopt it in one of his fanciful set-piece orations to girlfriend Liz. 'Do you know why I am so fascinated by London?' I said … 'A man can lose himself in London', I said. 'London is a big place. It has big streets and big people – I tailed off, because she would not be drawn, and in any case I had forgotten the end of the sentence.'[60] Billy never made it there, but for those who did it was a source of inspiration, a place that raised expectations. Thus in Storm Jameson's *The Lovely Ship* (1929), the fourteen-year-old Mary Hansyke is unsettled by a trip to London from her native Whitby. 'Her world, her simple and easily-compassed world, had been invaded ... by the monstrous heaving, swarming life of London. Living would never be a simple and easy process again.'[61]

It is this unsettling and disruptive presence of the capital that is so important. It can be positively so (Mary Hansyke is inspired to become a shipbuilder in Whitby), but more frequently it raises the possibility that a richer life might be being lived somewhere else. This is obviously so when characters such as Grace Holden in *Windyridge* or Mary Welburn in *National and Provincial* return to London after what turn out to be temporary northern sojourns. Whether this is occasioned in fictional terms by family responsibility, unrequited love or whatever, the sense that the North cannot hold on to its own or to its converts is always powerful. Again, while some characters do not reach London and others find it ultimately unsatisfactory and return home, a sense is often conveyed that such individuals are either weak or unadventurous, or settling for second best. Billy Fisher is the classic figure here, deliberately missing the train while girlfriend Liz, mirroring author Keith Waterhouse's own enthusiasm to move to London, seizes the opportunity.[62] Billy's 'reward' is that his eventual escape from Stradhoughton in *Billy Liar on the Moon* (1975) takes him only to the awful dormitory town of 'Shepford' where he must eventually accept the realities of adulthood. London's disruptive beckoning was a constant feature of northern fiction but it was especially prominent in novels of the 1950s and 1960s. It is one of the many ironies surrounding the North's most fashionable fictional moment that it was created by books working the themes of provincial entrapment and escape so intensely that they underlined the very cultural imbalance that they briefly appeared to be readdressing.

Regional novels and regional identity

The regional novel emerged as a European-wide phenomenon in the late nineteenth century at the very moment when the term 'regionalism' was both gaining currency as a political term and emerging as a political force in some European states.[63] Although regional government has occasionally featured on the British political agenda, it has never captured the popular imagination. Various cultural forms have filled this ideological vacuum and perhaps even contributed towards it by supplying more immediately satisfying modes of regional expression. This final section examines the role and function of the regional novel in this context, defining the form specifically so as to embrace those works produced by writers in the period between 1920s to the 1950s who sought with varying degrees of conscious intent to explain their chosen parts of the North both to local inhabitants and the wider world. The most passionate amongst them were to become the nearest equivalent to architects of a popular regional consciousness that England had yet seen.

The attempt to use the regional novel as a social tool was at its most developed in the 1920s and 1930s, suitably termed by Lucien LeClaire as the period of 'interpretative regionalism'.[64] Locally and regionally rooted fictions had admittedly always been to some degree 'interpretative'. The Brontës made explicit links between environment and character in the 1840s, as did Bennett, Lawrence and others half a century later. Much work was also often affectionate and anxious to promote regional patriotism, with Jessie Fothergill terming her industrial novel *Healey* (1875) a picture of 'certain phases of Lancashire life' by one of those who 'belong to this race and love it'.[65] However, the inter-war years saw a particularly determined attempt to provide an environmentalist interpretation of regional cultures and to provide an imaginative space for the consideration of their contemporary problems. This tendency was most marked in the North and its most influential 'theorist', if that is not too inflated a term, and certainly one of the most important practitioners, was Halifax-born Phyllis Bentley (1894–1973). Born into an upper middle class family with deep roots in the wool textile industry, her embrace of the regional novel was initially somewhat reluctant and largely unconscious. Educated at Cheltenham Ladies College, she found on her return that Halifax 'thought me odd and stuck-up' and herself 'apt to regard Halifax as ignorant and Philistine'.[66] After spells in London during the First World War, she returned to Halifax and gradually began a rapprochement with the West Riding that was to lead to an intense appreciation of, and identification with, its landscape, past history and present crisis. Invited to lecture on the 'regional novel' in 1924, 'I perceived for the first time that I myself was a practitioner'.[67] Her greatest success was undoubtedly *Inheritance* (1932), which went through nine editions in its first year of publication alone and was hailed in a review by Winifred Holtby (a close friend but an honest critic) as one of 'the three outstanding novels of 1932'.[68]

In her short but influential 1941 study, *The English Regional Novel*, Bentley defined the form uncontroversially enough as one 'depicting the life of that region in such a way that the reader is conscious of the characteristics which are unique to that region and differentiate it from others in the common motherland'.[69] However, in her hands and that of many contemporaries, such depiction and differentiation were pursued with far greater intent and thoroughness than had previously been the case. Attempts were made to attribute regional character, something which she and a number of other novelists also explored in travel writing, to specific geographical, and historical factors.[70] The West Riding's strong spirit of independence was, therefore, claimed to stem from a harsh climate that 'tends to produce a strong and independent race of men', the influence of the 'free spirit bred by hills' and the welding of society by the common experience of the textile industry.[71] She placed particular emphasis on history and her novels are heavily freighted with detail, often based on her own researches, designed not merely to provide colour to but to explain social processes. Of especial importance was her extremely developed sense of being 'at once a responsible unit of the West Riding community and its mouthpiece'. This latter role was most marked in her desire to explain North to South during the depression of the 1930s. While staying in London with Vera Brittain and Winifred Holtby in 1932 she was 'shocked to find how little was known in London of the plight of the industrial north', a plight that had deeply affected her family and many neighbours.[72] Lettice Cooper, a close friend of Bentley's, has a character establish the similarly 'educative' function of her novel *National and Provincial* at an early stage.

> We know more about Abysssinia here [in London] than we do about the provinces. To us they're either Beauty Spots or Distressed Areas. If something happens, we turn the limelight on them for a moment, but we never see their average life … I don't believe you can do anything much in England unless you've got the feeling of the provinces.[73]

A final but central task for regional fiction identified by Bentley was that it should acted as a bulwark against the 'whole trend of modern life today … towards uniformity'.[74] This is best examined not by reference to the novels but to the symbolism and the language used at the Yorkshire Authors Dinner in October 1938, an event organised by a committee including both Bentley and Cooper. Under the chairmanship of J. B. Priestley, 113 Yorkshire authors met at the suitably chosen Great Northern Hotel in Leeds. White roses, heather and bracken adorned the top table, a map of the county was placed behind the chairman and the centrepiece of the meal, a vast Yorkshire pudding, was brought in to the accompaniment of a mass singing of 'Ilkla Moor Baht 'At'. (Later courses included Cricket Ball Potatoes and Cauliflower Wensleydale.) There was obviously a light-hearted flavour to events – although probably not quite so light as would have been the case by the late century – and the regional sentiment expressed in no sense challenged wider English or British identities; the speeches and subsequent press comment stressed Yorkshire's contribution to the wider national community rather than any separateness. Nevertheless, long-established grievances and notions of distinctiveness were clearly expressed. Art historian and critic Herbert Read, a fierce advocate of provincial culture, hoped that 'not too many of us will make the trek south' and posited the idea of Yorkshire as being both a force within the national literature and a kind of moderate force within the national *British* character, neither 'as hard as the as the Scots and not so soft as the south'.[75] The Leeds-based *Yorkshire Post* followed up the event with an extended editorial developing these ideas. Beyond a belief that 'sturdy' northern character was behind Yorkshire's ability 'to win an author's county championship', its main related themes concerned London's dominance and the need for the provinces to make a distinctive, even idiosyncratic contribution to the national whole. Aspiring writers were certainly warned of the dangers of a metropolitan base.

> A young author, born in the provinces, is always strongly tempted to move to London as soon as he can afford it. Here, he feels he is in the capital of the Empire, is the heart and soul of literary life; here he will have the best chance of meeting influential persons, of getting known in the 'right' circles and of sharing at first hand in the most important intellectual movements of the day ... [But] if, after drinking deeply of northern air, he uproots himself and tries to acquire a veneer of Metropolitan polish, he may be crippling the most valuable sources of his inspiration. And even if the transformation succeeds, what he has been able to contribute to the literature of his time may well be less distinctive.

Moreover, London was prone to ephemeral fashions. The provinces must serve as a counterweight: 'less influenced by this cult of novelties [they] have a certain duty to stand for the more solid and enduring values in national life ... the aim of Northern culture, rooted in its native soil, must contribute its own best gifts to national life as a whole'.[76]

Much of the 'regionalist' agenda involved engagement with political and industrial conflict. It can no be no surprise that in this period and, indeed, in most others, a genre placing so much emphasis on shared roots and common purposes took on an essentially moderate, consensual political stance. Because academic writing has tended to focus on the so-called 'working-class' novel, the existence of this buoyant strain of work has been little commented on. This is not to minimise the achievements or importance of working-class writers such as Harold Heslop (b. 1898) with his tales of Durham pit village life or James Hanley (1901–85), who chronicled the Liverpool slums, or to deny the remarkable success of Greenwood's *Love on the Dole*. However, this latter work in particular has somewhat coloured our view of inter-war popular literature (and Greenwood's overall output) and rather hidden the far wider social landscapes and less obvious sense of unresolved class tension and division that typify many of the most popular books of the day. The depiction of a wide-ranging social cast was especially vital. This was not a creation of the inter-war period but it became a more common ploy, part stimulated, part assisted by the adoption of the family saga as a popular mode of delivery.

Bentley's work again stands as a useful if rather self-conscious example of these processes. Her autobiography records how she 'began reluctantly to extend' her sympathies not merely to 'the unemployed men lounging at the street corner with despair in their hearts, their anxious wives, their ill-fed children' but to 'their employers, fighting a tough battle daily with the forces of world economics, anxious, harassed, never certain whether they would be bankrupt or not by next week … But if only the two sides of industry would come together! … Their self-interest maddened me. Yet I began to love them.'[77] *Inheritance* (and much of her work in the 1930s) translates these feelings directly into literary form, climaxing in the final scene when the young David Oldroyd realises that 'by blood' he belongs to both employer class and working class, to the Luddite cropper who had attacked his family's frames in 1812 as much as to that family. As the train carrying his family from its failed business to a new life in the New Forest reaches the Yorkshire border, David jumps out.

> 'I can't leave the Ire Valley, father – I'm so sorry for the people, I don't see that I can help it – I can't break off in the middle of the fight; I must go on.'
>
> He jumped from the train, fell, rolled over, and picked himself up, bruised but laughing heartily … David strode up the lane, whistling cheerfully; he reached the road and set his face resolutely towards Marthwaite.[78]

Bentley was perhaps more explicit in her purpose than most others, but her work had many parallels. J. B. Priestley's enormously popular *The Good Companions* (1929), although working on national canvass, brings regions and classes together through the assorted characters that make up the eponymous concert party. J. L. Hodson's *Harvest of the North* (1934) depicts a society (Oldham during the 1920s) where economic vicissitudes affect lives across the social spectrum and where representatives of all classes have some sense of interdependence and respect for each other. A middle-class character, librarian and playwright, Henry Brierley, opens a small weaving shed with the last of his savings because 'I thought it was my job to try and provide some work'. In a minor but suitably symbolic moment of the plot, mill owner Edward Houghton waits for a tram with his workforce happy that he 'knew and liked and understood the work-people well enough to enjoy being close to them'. One of his young female workers addresses him directly and chirpily, and, smiling and 'almost blush[ing] now at her own boldness', she uses the much-vaunted northern independence of spirit as a force for the establishment of healthy social relations.[79] In her *National Provincial,* Lettice Cooper has her main character draw a wider point from her acknowledgement of the wide social base of her family and friends. 'Yes! If we ever do have to be sorted out into classes in England, especially in the West Riding of Yorkshire, it's going to be pretty difficult.'[80]

This is not to argue that these writers were accurate in downplaying class tensions or to suggest they necessarily obscured the real hardships and problems of the working-class population. Neither is to assume that such novels stilled class conflict and inhibited class consciousness, although some contemporaries believed that they had the capacity to do this. The *Times Literary Supplement's* review of Tommy Thompson's *Lancashire Mettle* (1933), a collection of short stories of Lancashire life, celebrated the doggedness, humour and 'grit of Mr Thompson's characters ... Lancashire may be in the dumps; but it knows how to fight on its stumps indomitably when its legs are cut off. The author has chosen the right title for the book'.[81] Whatever its actual impact, the regional novel of this period clearly did much to keep alive the vision of a pan-class community.

The regional novel was, for all its power, never able and probably never intended to build a wider northern consciousness. Readers were asked to imagine communities that were essentially sub-regional in scale; Bentley, for example, always saw herself as a spokeswoman for Yorkshire or, more specifically, the west Yorkshire textile district. There was nevertheless much slippage there was between local, sub-regional and wider regional terminology, if not in fictional writing, then in the writing that surrounded it. The *Yorkshire Post's* editorial on the 1938 Yorkshire authors' dinner slid continuously between 'Yorkshire', 'the north' and 'the provinces' in its comments, showing the looseness and flexibility of regional allegiance.[82] A 'greater North' can be glimpsed here, never able to emerge fully-fledged, but a powerful ancillary tool when more localised identities seemed a little inadequate.

The specific concerns of the inter war regional writers were not to survive for long. Many of those noted above continued to produce novels into the 1960s and even beyond, and new works such as Thomas Armstrong's *King Cotton* (1947) and *Adam Brunskill* (1952) achieved a lasting popularity. The new trends were unavoidable, however. Phyllis Bentley noted in an honest and poignant section of her autobiography that 'an exceptionally powerful group of young writers [had] burst into public notice' in the late 1950s, pushing her to the margins. 'I had a great many ideas, in whose validity I strongly believed, a great deal of vigour, and if I may say so a good deal of skill still left in me. But from my place towards the centre of the West Riding literary scene, I must now withdraw, with what grace and dignity I could muster, towards the wings.'[83] As already noted, this new group of exclusively *male* writers introduced new themes that made the older fictions seem momentarily tired and dated. Moreover, in some cases they indulged in comic styles that, intentionally or otherwise, satirised the older traditions. Waterhouse's *Billy Liar* was crucial here, providing one of the key moments when it is possible to see tastes shift and old certainties fall. Billy Fisher's endless parodying of set notions of Yorkshire character and its more extreme cultural representation through his imaginary conversations with the *Stadhoughton Echo*'s 'Man o' the Dales', his real ones with Councillor Duxbury and his comic turns with his friend Arthur, provides one of novel's major comic elements. In one sequence, Billy and Arthur walk through Stradhoughton performing their 'trouble at t' mill routine, a kind of serial with Arthur taking the part of Olroyd and I the wayward son.

> 'Ther's allus been an Olroyd at Olroyd's mill, and ther allus will be. Now you come 'ere with your college ways and you want none of it'…
>
> 'Father! The men! They're coming up the drive!'
>
> We turned into Market Street swinging our arms from side to side like men on a lynching spree. Arthur held up an imaginary lantern.
>
> 'Oh. So it's thee, Ned Leather! Ye'd turn against, would ye?'[84]

This was not the first time that the regional novel had been satirised, but coming as it did in a highly acclaimed work by a writer of the new generation, this lampooning reads as an epitaph for an older form. The closeness in nomenclature between Billy and Arthur's Olroyd and Bentley's Oldroyd may not have been a conscious ploy but it adds powerfully to the sense of generational shift. One of the key issues here is the change in attitude to regional 'character'. While the previous generation had explored it, Waterhouse, while not rejecting its existence, satirised the rigidities and the clichés that flowed from too slavish an adherence to stereotypical versions of it. (It seems suitable that in a marvellous antithesis to common representations of bluff northern masculinity, the *Times Literary Supplement* described Billy as 'a hapless Welfare State Yorkshire chap'.)[85] A key text of this period was once again undermining the North's cultural capital. It was also playing a major role in constructing the new version of what one review of *Billy Liar* called 'the humorist's playground, the grim North' that will be examined at greater length in the final chapter.[86]

The literary new wave saw its own moment pass swiftly enough. If any one genre can be said to have dominated the field of northern fiction from that point it was the working-class sagas that were heirs to (and much influenced by) the interpretative regional novel, but which lacked its passion for exploring and explaining region and character. Instead, with its focus on a limited range of themes, locations and historical periods, it provided only Lowryscapes of the most fixed variety. Outside of the saga, although the continued production of 'flight South' narratives has kept the regional condition in focus to an extent, the tendency has been to concentrate on the impact of national and global social processes on communities rather than excavate regional character or debate regional status. By the late 1950s, one of the North's most distinctive voices was clearly exhausted, but its initial energy and sense of purpose has never been fully replicated by any of its successors. That has been much to the region's cost.

Notes

1 W. R. Mitchell, 'The author of "Windyridge"', *Dalesman*, September 1978, pp. 494–6; C. Gordon, *By Gaslight in Winter* (London: Elm Tree Books, 1980), p. 43.
2 V. Williamson, 'Regional identity – a gendered heritage? Reading women in 1990s fiction', paper given at 'Relocating Britishness' Conference, University of Central Lancashire, 2000.
3 D. Pocock and R. Hudson, *Images of the Urban Environment* (London: Macmillan, 1978), pp. 110–27; R. Shields, *Places on the Margin. Alternative Geographies of Modernity* (London: Routledge, 1990), p. 211.
4 *Times Literary Supplement* (from now *TLS*), 26 September 1902; 12 June 1913.
5 K. D. M. Snell (ed.), *The Regional Novel in Britain and Ireland, 1800–1990* (Cambridge: Cambridge University Press, 1998), pp. 27–8.
6 K. D. M. Snell (ed.), *The Bibliography of Regional Fiction in Britain and Ireland, 1800–2000* (Aldershot: Ashgate, 2002), p. 6.
7 R. Colls, 'Cookson, Chaplin and Common: three northern writers in 1951', in Snell, *Regional Novel*, pp. 164–200.
8 *TLS*, 12 May 1961. Sillitoe would obviously be included in a wider definition of 'North'. There were also some titles that made a largely regional impact, such as the novels of Bolton miner John Farrimond.
9 *TLS*, 11 March 1960.
10 Colls, 'Cookson, Chaplin', p. 496; D. Eagle and M. Stephens (eds), *Oxford Illustrated Literary Guide to Great Britain and Ireland* (Oxford: Oxford University Press, 1992 edn). Thanks to Steve Caunce for drawing my attention this work.
11 J. Shattock (ed.), *The Cambridge Bibliography of English Literature*, vol. 4, 1800–1900 (Cambridge: Cambridge University Press, 1999) pp. xx–xxii. Birthplace details from V. Blain, I. Grundy and P. Clements (eds), *The Feminist Companion to Literature in English* (London: Batsford, 1990); S. Kunitz and H. Haycroft (eds), *British Authors of the Nineteenth* Century (New York: H.W. Wilson,

1936); D.C. Browning (ed.), *Everyman's Dictionary of Literary Biography* (London: Pan, 1969). Both regions produced 25 authors.

12 H. Blamires, *A Guide to Twentieth Century Literature in English* (London: Methuen, 1987). Only English-born *novelists* are counted here amongst Blamires' many categories.

13 F. Musgrove, *The North of England. A History from Roman Times* (Oxford: Oxford University Press, 1990), pp. 13–16.

14 For the problems facing poorer authors, see O. Ashton and S. Roberts, *The Victorian Working-Class Writer* (London: Mansell, 1999).

15 Snell in the introduction to his *Regional Novel*, p. 1. For other valuable discussions, P. Bentley, *The English Regional Novel* (London: P.E.N., 1941); L. LeClaire, *A General Analytical Bibliography of the Regional Novelists of the British Isles, 1800–1950* (Paris: Société d'edition 'Les Belles Lettres', 1954); W. J. Keith, *Regions of the Imagination. The Development of British Rural Fiction* (Toronto: Toronto University Press, 1989); R. Draper (ed.), *The Literature of Region and Nation* (London: Macmillan, 1989); I. Bell (ed.), *Peripheral Visions. Images of Nationhood in Contemporary British Fiction* (Cardiff: University of Wales Press, 1995).

16 Snell, *Regional Novel*, pp. 4–5. Keith's treatment of the genre as ultimately rural obviously colours his interpretation and not least in his view that it effectively died from the 1930s. See his conclusions, pp. 173–7.

17 R. Williams, 'Region and class in the novel', in D. Jefferson and G. Martin (eds), *The Uses of Fiction* (Milton Keynes: Open University Press, 1982), p. 60.

18 R. Stevenson, *The British Novel Since the Thirties* (London: Batsford, 1986); J. Carey, *The Intellectuals and the Masses. Pride and Prejudice Among the Literary Intelligentsia, 1880–1939* (London: Faber and Faber, 1992). Keith, *Regions of the Imagination*, p. 10, rightly points out, however, that realism need not be a definitive characteristic.

19 LeClaire, *A General Analytical Bibliography*, pp. 380–4. A number of writers wrote on more than one area.

20 Based on listings in Snell, *Bibliography*.

21 For her limited engagement with local culture, see Colls, 'Cookson, Chaplin', pp. 184–6. She is responsible for 40 per cent of all titles set in County Durham listed by Snell.

22 G. Cavaliero, *The Rural Tradition in the English Novel* (London: MacMillan, 1977), p. ix–x.

23 The hugely popular recent writings of North Yorkshire schools inspector, Gervaise Phinn, are another example.

24 Jameson's Whitby was essentially an industrial one, her 'The Triumph of Time' trilogy (1927–31), for example, concentrating on the town's shipbuilding trade. A number of novels about a thinly disguised Blackpool have also appeared in the twentieth century, including James Hodson's *Carnival at Blackport* (1937), Frank Tilsley's *Pleasure Beach* (1944) and Leonard Gribble's *They Kidnapped Stanley Matthews* (1950), although these are essentially urban/industrial novels at one remove.

25 W. Riley, *Windyridge Revisited* (London: Herbert Jenkins, 1928), p. 312.

26 J. K. Snowden, *The Weaver's Web* (London: Jonathan Cape, 1932), pp. 7, 10. The stories were set around the industrial village of Cowling, near Keighley.

27 J. Belchem '"An accent exceedingly rare": Scouse and the inflexion of class', in his *Merseypride. Essays in Liverpool Exceptionalism* (Liverpool: Liverpool University Press, 2000), pp. 39–40.

28 P. J. Keating, *The Working Class in Victorian Fiction* (London: Routledge and Kegan Paul, 1971); Pocock and Hudson, *Urban Environment*; Shields, *Places on the Margin*, pp. 208–15. Disraeli's *Sybil* (1845), Dicken's *Hard Times* (1854) and Mrs Gaskell's *Mary Barton* (1848) and *North and South* were the most significant.

29 C. Dickens, *Hard Times* (1854, London: Penguin edn, 1994), p. 19.

30 Mrs Gaskell, *North and South* (1855, London: Dent, 1914 edn), pp. 54, 146.

31 Ibid., pp. 6–7, 18–19.

32 J. Barker, *The Brontës* (New York: St. Martin's Press, 1996 edn), p. 92.

33 Keating, *The Working Class*, pp. 8–9. The early stages of Gaskell's *Mary Barton* are perhaps an exception.

34 Gaskell, *North and South*, p. 353.

35 'A Manchester warehouse', *Household Words*, 6 May 1854, pp. 268–72 and 'Our Sister', *Household Words*, 1 July 1854, pp. 471–4.

36 My emphasis. George Bernard Shaw confidently asserted that the 'real' Coketown was Hanley, in the Potteries; presumably he had been reading too much Arnold Bennett. Literary commentators can become very confused about their geography. Walter Sichel, in a 1926 edition of *Sybil*, claimed that 'Mowbray' – actually based on Manchester – was 'really Ripon'. See Shaw in the introduction to the 1912 edition of *Hard Times*, reprinted in G. H. Ford and L. Lane (eds), *The Dickens Critics* (New York: Cornell University Press, 1961), p. 127; Disraeli, *Sybil*, p. xi.

37 P. Dodd, 'Lowryscapes: recent writings about "the North", *Critical Quarterly*, 32, 2, 1990, p. 17.

38 I. Haywood, *Working-class Fiction from Chartism to Trainspotting* (Plymouth: Northcote House, 1997), p. 145.

39 J. B. Priestley, *The Good Companions* (London: Penguin edn, 1980), p. 12.

40 Review of Diana Patrick's *Life is to Seek*, in *Dalesman*, October 1940, p. 18.

41 P. Dudgeon with J. Cox, *Child of the North* (London: Headline, 2001), p. 9.

42 F. H. Burnett, *That Lass O' Lowrie's* (Woodbridge, Suffolk: Boydell Press edn, 1985), p. 47.

43 Dodd, 'Lowryscapes', pp. 22–6. Works by Barry Hines, Pat Barker and Helen Forrester provide his examples.

44 Ibid., p. 27.

45 Ian Haywood, in his excellent *Working-class Fiction*, categorises Billy Fisher as a 'working-class rogue' (p. 113).

46 G. Turner, *The North Country* (London: Eyre and Spottiswood, 1967), p. 399.

47 *TLS* review of *A Kind of Loving*, 5 August 1960.

48 B. Disraeli, *Sybil* (1845; London: The World's Classics edn, 1926), pp. 165, 166–7.

49 Turner, *North Country*, p. 13.

50 'Yorkshire as a novelist's county', *Yorkshire Post*, 19 February 1930.
51 W. Greenwood, *Standing Room Only* (London: Hutchinson, 1935), pp. 111–15, 10–11.
52 M. Joseph, *A Better World Than This* (London: Century, 1986), p. 14.
53 Riley, *Windyridge*, pp. 7, 205, 10, 128.
54 L. Cooper, *National Provincial* (London: Victor Gollancz, 1968 edn), p. 9.
55 J. S. Fletcher, *Memories of a Spectator* (London: Nash, 1912), pp. 222, 8–9.
56 N. Cardus *Autobiography* (London: Collins, 1947), p. 58.
57 A. Bennett, *A Man From the North* (London: Hamish Hamilton edn, 1973), p. 1.
58 Priestley, *The Good Companions*, p. 30; Haywood, *Working-class Fiction*, p. 110.
59 D. Storey, *Flight into Camden* (London: Penguin edn, 1964), p. 148; J. Braine, *Life at the Top* (London: Methuen, 1962, 1983 edn), p. 57.
60 K. Waterhouse, *Billy Liar* (1959, Penguin edn, 1962) p. 145.
61 S. Jameson, *The Lovely Ship* (London: Heinemann, 1929), pp. 58–9.
62 Interviewed by Jim Greenhalf at Bradford Central Library on 17 May 2001, Waterhouse made it clear that *Billy Liar* privileged Liz, the 'doer' over Billy, the 'coward'.
63 F. W. Morgan, 'Three aspects of regional consciousness', *Sociological Review*, 31, 1939, pp. 68–88; E. W. Gilbert, 'The idea of the region', *Geography*, 45, 1960, pp. 157–75.
64 LeClaire, *A General Analytical Bibliography*, pp. 271–360.
65 Author's preface to second edition (London: Richard Bentley and Son, 1886).
66 P. Bentley, *O Dreams, O Destinations. An Autobiography* (London: Victor Gollancz, 1962), p. 82. Most biographical information is derived from this perceptive and self-critical life.
67 Ibid., p. 132.
68 'Novels of the year', *Bookman*, December 1932, p. 171. The other two were Aldous Huxley, *Brave New World* and Charles Morgan, *The Fountain*.
69 Bentley, *English Regional Novel*, p. 7.
70 See her 'Yorkshire' in J. Hadfield (ed.), *The New Shell Guide to England* (London: Michael Joseph, 1981), p. 679. It was first published in 1970.
71 'Yorkshire as a novelist's country', *Yorkshire Post*, 5 February 1930.
72 Bentley, *O Dreams*, pp. 258, 178.
73 Cooper, *National Provincial*, p. 23.
74 *Yorkshire Post*, 10 October 1938.
75 Ibid. On Read and provincial culture, M. Saler, 'Making it new: visual modernism and the "Myth of the North" in Interwar England', *Journal of British Studies* 37, 4, 1998, pp. 437–9.
76 Ibid., 11 Oct 1938.
77 Bentley, *O Dreams*, p. 162.
78 P. Bentley, *Inheritance,* p, 592.
79 J. L. Hodson, *Harvest in the North* (1955 edn, London: author published), pp. 418, 267–8.
80 Cooper, *National Provincial*, p. 195.

81 *TLS*, 6 April 1933.

82 *Yorkshire Post*, 11 October 1938.

83 Bentley, *O Dreams*, pp. 267–8.

84 *Billy Liar*, pp. 41–2. See also, pp. 23–4, 88–93. Waterhouse was quite affectionate toward dialect and had written dialect pieces for the local press while a schoolboy. K, Waterhouse, *City Lights* (London: Hodder and Stoughton, 1994), pp. 173–4.

85 *TLS*, 4 September 1959.

86 *Spectator*, 11 September 1959.

4

Speaking the North

'Ah wish you'd mouth your wods more properer when you're a-talkin' to a gen-tleman'.[1] As this reprimand from an early twentieth-century east-Yorkshire villager to her errant son illustrates, our use of language is a social and cultural indicator of great significance and great difficulty. In P. J. Waller's pithy phrase, it 'is an instrument of communication and excommunication'. Northern dialects and accents have been central in reinforcing and constructing a range of ideas about the North and its role and status in the national culture.[2] They have undoubtedly provided a key vehicle for the stigmatisation of the region and for the parading and embellishment of prejudices about it and yet have also proved a rich source of cultural capital and a major force for the expression of local and regional identities.

This chapter explores these issues through consideration of three interrelated areas. The first deals with spoken dialect, while the second explores dialect *literature* and pays especial attention to the popular mentalities expressed and shaped by it. Here, even more than with the regional novel, is the North on its own territory, being allowed to make sense of itself. From its foundation as the British Broadcasting Company in November 1922, the BBC has been critical to the policing of the English language – 'BBC English' was long a popular alternative term for both 'Standard English' and 'Received Pronunciation' – and in the more general process of trying to define both national and regional cultures. The final section, therefore, considers the role of BBC radio (television is dealt with later) both in structuring ideas about northern speech and wider issues of northern culture. Although this second issue leads into slightly different territory from the rest of the chapter, this seems a helpful place to debate it.

Speaking improperly[3]

'Dialect' is defined here simply as a regional variant of a language that also has a standardised and thus more prestigious form. As writers on northern dialects always stress, dialects are not debased or incorrect versions of 'Standard English' but valid linguistic systems derived from Old English, Norse and Norman roots and possessing their own distinctive accent, vocabulary and grammar. Standard English is itself a dialect but one which, through association with the nation's geographical and social power bases, has come to dominate, first of all in print from the late fifteenth century, and increasingly in spoken form from the late eighteenth. The death knell of dialect has been sounded regularly since the late nineteenth century. There has undeniably been a certain standardisation of accent and grammar and a significant degree of 'lexical erosion', with distinctive local vocabularies proving the most fragile linguistic component in the face of nationalising forces. Nevertheless, it is generally agreed that the predictions of the death of dialect usually 'prove to be premature'. Indeed, signs that since the 1990s girls and young women have been increasingly willing to adopt local dialects formerly 'more characteristic of boys' may even herald new life.[4]

The mixture of dialects within the seven-county North is rich and varied and once again points up intra-regional division. In terms of 'traditional' dialects, those differing substantially from Standard English and virtually confined to older rural dwellers by the mid-twentieth century, the most fundamental division divided not just the North but England itself. It ran from approximately Morecambe Bay on the north Lancashire coast, across North Yorkshire and down to the Humber estuary (see map, p. xii). This line – not so far removed from the boundary of Saxon Northumbria and Mercia – saw a North–South differentiation between such words as lang/long, hoose/house and stane/stone that placed the far North into the same linguistic zone as Scotland. Further sub-division of the North is evident even beyond this basic line with Trudgill identifying seven traditional dialect areas within the region as a whole.[5] It is well known that southern visitors often struggled with the vernacular voices they encountered but many northerners or near neighbours could be equally taxed. A mid-Derbyshire migrant to Sheffield in the 1830s, for example, endured several months of initial social isolation as a result of such problems.[6] If such a relatively modest crossing of dialect boundaries caused serious difficulty, it is probably fortunate that the restricted geographical mobility maintaining linguistic differences also limited the potential for intriguing engagements between South Shields and South Yorkshire or Wigan and Wallsend.

In terms of the 'modern' or 'mainstream' dialects increasingly used by most urban-dwellers from the late nineteenth century, rather than there being one critical boundary, a very loose North–South differentiation can be suggested by a series of isoglosses focused on such pronunciations as passt/pahst and oop/up. The distinction between a short and long 'a' in particular, is seen by many outsiders as a handy device for dividing northerners from southerners, although such a tactic claims much of the midlands for the North. Modern dialect usage still exhibits significant variation, with Trudgill identifying six broad zones within the region as a whole, including those holding the distinctive north-east, central Lancashire and Merseyside versions.[7] Even within a relatively short journey, however, those with a good ear will encounter many changes and the possibility of albeit relatively minor communication breakdown is always present.

The crucial issue in the context of this study is the collision of dialect with Standard English and, more specifically, the supposedly 'accentless' Received Pronunciation (RP). Although even in the late twentieth century perhaps only 12–15 per cent of the population spoke Standard English and only about 3–5 per cent did so without any regional accent, the inferior status conferred upon all other dialects by the emergence of a dominant one has the potential to embarrass those using other linguistic codes.[8] As Patrick Joyce argues, the very word dialect has become

> an unfortunate term, carrying its own silent apology … The emergence of RP as the 'class' dialect of the south of England educated upper-middle class has in turn meant the close association of pronunciation with power, learning and authority, so much so that many have lived with the corrosive illusion that their own speech was somehow 'wrong' or 'ignorant'.[9]

Obviously, this is not an issue for the North alone for all regional accents have always been at risk of ridicule. Moreover, given language's remarkable power to confer social status, this is to a considerable extent a problem of *class* as much as of region. When individuals feel linguistically inadequate, it is their sense of social rather than territorial inferiority that is often most damaging. Nevertheless, the problem has been especially acute for northerners. The North's long association with notions of barbarism and philistinism has often been directly connected to supposedly vulgar or comic modes of speech. A Member of Parliament commenting on the oration to Queen Mary given by the Yorkshire-born Speaker of the House in 1547, claimed that 'I heard not a better ale-house tale told this seven years'.[10] Interestingly, one of the first recorded usages of dialect speech for comic effect was Chaucer's adoption of a northern dialect in the 'Reeve's Tale'.[11] Furthermore, the region has often been closely associated with working-class culture and there has certainly long been a common assumption outside the region that a northern accent is by definition a *working-class* one. Challenges to linguistic competence are thus likely to be registered at two levels. Finally, but vitally, the North simply has a larger range of distinctive accents than any other part of the country and its burden in this regard is consequently increased.

It is understandable that much existing literature focuses on the negative experiences of dialect speakers or those with heavy accents when faced with the demands of the education system, officialdom, the tones of the BBC or whatever representative of 'them' threatened self-image and self-confidence. The encounter with Standard English or RP has probably been at its most problematic for those anyway insecure about their social status: the middle-class entrepreneur moving into metropolitan society; many members of the lower middle-class, the social group always 'most anxious about linguistic usage'; and the working-class scholarship boy or girl or university entrant catapulted into a new environment where nuances of language mattered profoundly.[12] Playwright Alan Bennett, son of a Leeds butcher and Oxford University entrant in 1954, has noted that 'anyone who ventures south of the Trent is likely to catch an incurable disease of the vowels' and claims that his own attempts to lose and then regain his accent meant that '[I] now don't know where I am'.[13] In some situations lives could be genuinely blighted and confidence shattered. Composer William Walton was sufficiently bullied as a result of his Lancashire accent when a choral scholar in Edwardian Oxford that he rapidly set out to lose it. Poet and dramatist Tony Harrison has recorded the anger felt when, as a working-class thirteen-year-old at Leeds Grammar School in the early 1950s, a teacher stopped his reading of Keats' 'Ode to a Nightingale' ('Mi 'art aches') with the words 'That's enough: You Barbarian.' [14] The mountain of self-help and self-improvement language manuals published from the eighteenth century is more than adequate testimony to the tyranny that 'proper' English could impose. It should also be noted that for some younger northerners, local accent and dialects have at times to be rejected not because of pressure to speak Standard English but because they had lost purchase within youth culture. It would be interesting to see how far the North was 'infected' with the Americanisation of speech that so worried inter-war commentators, while a visitor to 1960s Oldham found some Mods cultivating a Liverpool accent and some Rockers a Cockney one, because, according to his informant, 'they thought Cockneys were really tough'.[15]

For all this, it is worth giving greater consideration to other readings of the relationship between dialect and spoken Standard English than is normally the case. It must be said that, for many individuals, the issue of dialect usage over the last two hundred years has not necessarily been problematic. Given the relatively small percentage of the population that has spoken Standard English, let alone RP, once into adulthood 'us' need not meet 'them' very frequently. When this does happen most dialect users have generally had enough bilingual competence to survive. Indeed, it has often been the RP speaker that has felt threatened when faced with groups using dialect as a conscious tool of exclusion and popular empowerment; as Waller has noted 'la-di-da' was often vigorously resisted within the working-class community.[16] The much noted deployment of dialect speech by some northern entrepreneurs as a paternalist managerial strategy is a measure of workers' skills in playing language games as much as that of their employers.[17] It is also the case that regional speech has lost some of its stigma over the period from the 1960s. A national media that has increasingly embraced non-standard dialects, the expansion of youth cultures and the growth of a comprehensive educational system initially unable but also increasingly less willing to dismiss local patterns, have all played major and interlocking roles here. Some northern *accents* have even become fashionable at times. This certainly happened to the Liverpool accent in the 1960s, while a vogue for north-eastern accents was certainly apparent within television advertising, narration and continuity from the late 1990s. From about the same point, northern voices have become more prominent as a result of their increasing ubiquity in telephone call centres. Although labour cost has been a major factor in the location of such centres, there is evidence that employers believe certain voices to be associated with positive character traits in the public mind. If it is true that a Yorkshire accent denotes fiscal probity and a north-eastern one friendliness and helpfulness, it is an indication of how deeply regional stereotypes are rooted in the national culture.

Beyond these usages growing from defensiveness, indifference or market forces, there are also many examples of dialect and accent serving as a source of genuine local, regional and, for some, class pride: the very fact that dialects have survived and adapted in ways that have confounded endless obituarists demonstrates dialect's centrality to notions of social and personal identity. Distinctive speech patterns, or myths built upon them, can be powerful forces for local patriotism. Liverpool's reputation (external as well as internal in this case) for quick-fire repartee is a good case in point.[18] Similarly, many individuals retain at least their accents as a badge of pride or a useful source of idiosyncrasy. Pop musician Paul Heaton certainly found a move from Yorkshire to Surrey in the 1970s, when aged fourteen, a positive experience: 'I became more of a show-off when I moved to Surrey. I was treated differently because I was from up north. My accent set me apart and I enjoyed being the centre of attention.'[19]

Even elocution lessons have not always served the purpose that might be expected. Many undoubtedly used them to lose or modify their accent, but classes could simply be another source of improving popular recreation especially for those with a theatrical or musical interest, and one accompanied or moderated by that old helpmate, bilingualism. The broadcaster and actor Wilfred Pickles, for example, was a keen participant at elocution classes as a youth in Edwardian and wartime Halifax, and yet he remained absolutely dedicated to the West Riding demotic and used the classes largely as an aid to his local amateur dramatic activities.[20] It is easy to imagine the pleasures available to the bilingual as they confounded the expectations of those that sought to make swift linguistic judgments. Charlotte Brontë hinted at this in *Shirley* (1849) through the character of cloth manufacturer Hiram Yorke, whose switches from 'broad Yorkshire' to 'very pure English' were combined with a good knowledge of French and other foreign languages.[21] Finally, and crucially, those mocked for their accent and could also fight back. Tony Harrison's anger at his treatment fired the creativity behind a body of acclaimed poetry and drama. Recalling how his translation of Aeschylus' trilogy of Greek tragedies, *The Oresteia* (1981), was criticised for being 'very northern', he refused to apologise. 'I have my reasons. One is a slow-burning revenge on the teacher who taught me English when I was 13 because he would never allow me to read poetry aloud'.[22]

Critical to all of this has been the degree of loyalty to local speech demonstrated by some of the middle and even upper classes. When asked to be the President of the newly formed Yorkshire Dialect Society in 1897, the Marquis of Ripon deemed it 'my duty not to refuse'.[23] This loyalty was perhaps most clearly sensed by middle-class males whose social position bred self-confidence and whose gender freed them from some of the responsibilities of refinement. Stanley Houghton captured this well in his play *Hindle Wakes* (1912). Industrialist Sir Timothy Farrar proudly speaks broad Lancashire dialect, on one occasion acknowledging his election as Chairman of the local Education Committee with the line 'Ay! Why not? Thou knows I were reet mon for the job'. The satirical point is obvious but it is mellowed by affectionate humour. Farrar's putative son-in-law Alan Jeffcote is far better educated, but remains extremely relaxed about both his accent and his social position.

> He has been to the Manchester Grammar School and Manchester University, but he has not lost the characteristic Hindle burr in his accent, though he speaks correctly as a rule. He does not speak affectedly, so that his speech harmonises with

that of the other characters … He has no feeling that he is provincial, or that the provinces are not the principal assets of England. London he looks upon as a place where rich Lancashire men go for a spree, if they have not time to go to Monte Carlo or Paris.[24]

While there is obviously artistic licence here, Houghton saw himself as enough of a social realist for this to be taken fairly literally. While it might be stretching a point to suggest that a broad populist unity could be built around language usage – class cut across region too often and too fundamentally for this – or that what appertained in 1912 continued to do so from that point onward, there is a sense that local speech patterns could create bonds across class and that middle-class attitudes helped protect non-standard forms as much as they threatened them. As a result, 'speaking improperly' could be a source of empowerment and pleasurable difference as much as a source of embarrassment.[25]

Writing improperly[26]

While spoken dialects proved quite robust in the face of Standard English, written variants were rapidly displaced over the course of the late fifteenth and sixteenth centuries.[27] They were not to re-emerge, and then in a clearly subordinate, almost novelty form, until the late seventeenth century. The first piece of dialect written for a consciously literary purpose under the new order was possibly a 'A Yorkshire dialogue between an awd wife, a lass and a butcher' (1673), with Northallerton lawyer George Meriton's 'In praise of Yorkshire ale' (1684/85), written in the Vale of York variant, another early piece. Edward Chicken's poem 'The Collier's Wedding' (1720) put an albeit rather quaint 'Geordie' into print for probably the first time while the prose works of schoolteacher John Collier (1708–86) of Milnrow, Lancashire, writing from the 1740s as 'Tim Bobbin', were cited by many nineteenth-century writers as a crucial stimulus. Over the late eighteenth century and into the early nineteenth, a growing urban market, increased antiquarian interest in dialect and the inspiration provided by Robert Burns combined to boost dialect writing, with the broadside initially the key mode of dissemination for popular audiences. Indeed, although increasingly marginalised by more sophisticated publications from mid-century, the broadside continued to meet the needs of many in the working-class community until late in the century.[28]

Industrial Northumberland and Durham, the West Riding of Yorkshire, south-east and central Lancashire, and to a lesser degree west Cumberland, were the heartlands of dialect writing, although production in the north-east was more focused on the nascent music-hall song than the literary forms that predominated elsewhere.[29] These areas were indeed the major centres of printed dialect production not simply in the North but in England as a whole.[30] Joyce has speculated that a 'particular blend of change and continuity in the economic and social structure' of these areas explains their predominance, arguing that dialect writing emerged mainly in those areas where a vigorous pre-existing, often oral, popular culture and a relatively stable community structure met especially sharp levels of social and economic dislocation. In essence, communities handled change by drawing from and reworking their existing cultural legacy. The failure of dialect writing to develop in and around Merseyside, which, unlike the dialect heartlands, expanded outward 'in a cultural vacuum, as it were, urbanising an area without previous geographical and occupational identities', adds weight to Joyce's argument.[31] Even within these leading areas there are interesting variations in the scale of production. Of the twenty Lancashire writers born between 1748 and 1890 featured in Brian Hollingworth's anthology *Songs of the People* (1977), no fewer than seven had a strong connection with Rochdale and most others came from either Manchester or from small towns immediately to its south and east.[32] Rochdale's key role may be explained by the inspirational influence of 'Tim Bobbin' in neighbouring Milnrow and of locally born Edwin Waugh (1817–90), the most famous and influential of all northern dialect poets, while the clustering around Manchester must owe much to ease of access to publishing opportunities. A hunt for deeper cultural explanations, however, would be interesting.

There were innumerable ways of reaching audiences. Specialist publication of works by named authors dealing with trademark characters and situations began to appear in significant number in forms beyond the broadside in the 1830s and 1840s. The style of publication, whether of prose or poetry, varied between the major areas of production. In Yorkshire, the major vehicle was the prose-oriented yearly comic almanac which initially part imitated, part parodied the format of *Old Moore's* and other titles, although the calendar element and predictions were increasingly displaced by short stories and dialect sketches. The best known of these titles was John Hartley's *Halifax Original Illustrated Clock Almanack* (1865), edited almost continuously by the Halifax-born writer from 1867 until his death in 1915 and enjoying an annual sale of about 80,000 copies for most of this period.[33] Even some of the shorter-lived and lesser-known publications attained quite reasonable readerships; *T' Nidderdill Olminac an'Ivvery Bodys' Kalinder*, written by Pateley Bridge lead miner, Thomas Blackah, claimed a circulation of 8,000–10,000 in the 1870s. In Lancashire, the monthly journal was the preferred form with one of the most successful, *Ben Brierley's Journal* (1869–91), enjoying a monthly circulation of about 13,000. These publications included poetry and prose of various lengths, and not always in dialect. Leading writers regularly published collections and compilations, while the newspaper served as an particularly important starting point for many; Waugh's 'Come whoam to thi childer an' me' (1856), one of the most popular dialect pieces of the nineteenth century, first appeared in the Manchester press, for example. Novels, children's stories and plays were yet further vital conduits. Yet perhaps its largest audience, at least before 1900, was reached via public performance. Most northern writers both performed their own work and published it for performance by others in a variety of commercial and non-commercial settings. Joseph Wright, then an apprentice woolsorter, but later Professor of Comparative Philology at Oxford and editor of the magisterial *English Dialect Dictionary* (1905), was, for example, much in demand as a dialect reciter in Bradford's chapel-based recreational culture in the 1870s.[34] Through these various routes, dialect literature became more deeply embedded in mid- and later nineteenth-century northern culture than is at first apparent.

The high point of dialect writing was relatively short. In terms of aesthetic quality and within the specific field of poetry, Hollingworth has argued that the greatest flowering lasted only from Waugh's 'Come whoam' in 1856 to about 1870.[35] In terms of output, 1850 to 1880 has often been viewed as the peak period, although Paul Salveson has suggested that production was greater after 1880 than before.[36] Evidence can be produced for both cases. Of the sixteen Yorkshire almanacs in circulation in the 1870s, only four survived into the 1890s. In neighbouring Lancashire, however, Allen Clarke claimed over a million penny pamphlet sales for his *Tum Fowt Sketches* between 1890 and 1930.[37] A reasonable hypothesis would be that production remained high in many areas until the second decade of the twentieth century, although the cultural power of dialect writing probably began to weaken at the end of the nineteenth. Nevertheless, there were still substantial markets at least until the late 1930s. The *Clock Almanack* claimed a circulation of 75,000 in 1931, many local papers continued to offer an outlet at least until the 1950s and, in Yorkshire at least, dialect plays proved popular with amateur dramatic groups in the inter-war period.[38]

The move to the absolute margins took place in the 1950s and 1960s, with the closure in 1956 of the *Clock Almanack* a symbolic moment.[39] A number of

highly skilful practitioners have continued to publish, mainly in county magazines and dialect society journals, and there have been odd flourishes of interest
amongst younger generations and broader publics.[40] However, probably the
best-known 'dialect' publications in contemporary Britain are the essentially
comic works, combining real dialect with mock and with various stereotypical
illustrations and catchphrases. One book, for example, depicts a v-sign in a
roadside warning triangle with the caption 'Lancashire welcomes southern
drivers'.[41] These products, very much an adjunct of the post-1980 heritage
industry, have been heavily criticised by serious scholars for 'exploit[ing] dialect
as something only good for a giggle' and have undoubtedly helped position
dialect writing (and perhaps even dialect in general) as part of the comic, dated
North.[42]

   While dialect literature has long lost its significant within the region's culture, it undoubtedly played an important role in the construction and reflection
of northern mentalities for the century from about 1830. An understanding of
the class origins of both producers and consumers is fundamental to understanding these processes. While not denying Joyce's argument that 'it was from
the culture of the working population that [dialect writing] chiefly drew its
meanings', or ignoring the fact that different classes could interpret the same
item in very different ways, it is argued here that the genre was a far more overtly
cross-class phenomenon than has generally been recognised.[43] Even as subtle a
reading as Joyce's, with its full attention to what he denotes 'higher class dialect
writing' and emphasis on pan-class 'populist' identities, may have not gone far
enough in acknowledging the strength of regional as much as class mentalities
within the form. In terms of authorship, Joyce has argued that the half-dozen
'leading' writers of the nineteenth and early twentieth centuries – his candidates
were Lancastrians Waugh, Brierley, Samuel Laycock and Allen Clarke and
Yorkshiremen Hartley and Ben Preston – were 'decidedly children of toil'.[44]
Although Hartley was briefly a pattern-maker, as the son of a tea merchant and
himself in turn a carpet designer, publican and owner of a Philadelphia carpet
and upholstery business (he continued to edit the Clock Almanack from
America between 1882–94), he does not fit this category well. The others listed
undoubtedly began their lives firmly in the working class and some experienced
real poverty well into adulthood. Many other writers of the period shared this
working-class background, as did leading twentieth-century practitioners,
including colliery surface worker turned engine driver Walter Hampson, who
wrote most of the Clock Almanack from 1918 until his death in 1932.[45]
Arguably of equal importance, however, is the upward socially mobility of

numerous leading writers, with many eventually earning reasonable amounts of money from their writing or from related white-collar posts.[46] This experience of traversing a relatively wide social terrain over their lives was crucial in allowing to them connect with a much wider audience than that provided by the manual working class alone and was possibly as important a factor as their original class position.

At the same time, although full attention has been paid to the role of the middle class as writers in the eighteenth and early nineteenth centuries and as patrons, publishers and dialect scholars from that point, their role as writers even at the Victorian highpoint is less well appreciated.[47] ('Middle class' is defined fairly broadly here to embrace a range from clerks and small shop-keepers through to professionals.) Analysis of an albeit slightly random collective biography of Yorkshire dialect writers in the period to 1945 would suggest that working-class writers only slightly outweighed their middle-class counterparts in the nineteenth century, with just over 50 per cent coming from obviously working-class backgrounds. Most importantly, while some of these middle-class writers were 'gentlemen scholars' working with an antiquarian focus, others made substantial contributions to what Joyce calls 'the dominant popular current'. Isaac Binns, a Batley accountant, was remembered by Ben Turner as a key local writer; James Burnley, a trainee lawyer turned journalist, produced dialect annuals in Bradford in the 1870s and Edmund Hatton, a cashier with a Bradford textile firm, was good enough to produce the *Clock Almanack* in 1873 and 1874 when Hartley first went to America.[48]

In the twentieth century the balance swung away from the working class with well over half and perhaps as many as three quarters of the writers listed in the biography drawn from the middle classes.[49] Many undoubtedly came to genre via the dialect societies that followed the foundation of the English Dialect Society (1873–96). Largely middle- and upper-middle-class in nature these were a clear manifestation of both the long established antiquarian interest in language and a growing concern with 'folk' culture.[50] Middle-class authors were admittedly turning to dialect writing as it lost its wider cultural power and they were possibly drawn more to poetry rather than the comic prose that was ultimately the staple of the popular tradition. Their presence, however, shows that the defence and celebration of dialect had resonance across class. A few had truly ambitious agendas and none more so than Frederic Moorman (1872–1919), educational secretary of the Yorkshire Dialect Society. Born in Devon and eventually Professor of English at Leeds University, he was originally drawn to dialect as a philologist but his attention soon turned 'from dialect speech to dialect speakers. Amongst Yorkshire farmers, farm labourers, fisherman, miners and mill workers I discovered a vitality and an outlook upon life of which I, a bourgeois professor, had no previous knowledge.'[51] Inspired too by his work with the WEA and University Extension, Moorman began to conceive of dialect as a way of bringing poetry to a working class to whom 'Spenser, Milton, Keats' and others spoke 'in a language which they did not understand, and presented to them a world of thought and life in which they had no inheritance'. Viewing dialect as 'the language of freedom' and Standard English as that of 'constraint' he offered his own poems and encouraged others to offer theirs, as a way making the 'men and women of England … partakers in this inheritance of wealth and joy'.[52]

Moorman's premature death in a swimming accident prevented him from taking more than the first steps in implementing this radical programme, although there is little evidence that he would have found a large audience in the popular cultural environment of the inter-war period. Most middle-class writers were less egalitarian and less ambitious than Moorman but they were certainly aware of making a contribution to regional or sub-regional life, if not to the working class specifically. What is indeed being witnessed here is the deployment of a highly specific form of cultural capital that seems utterly suited to the needs of a regional middle class, content to operate within a relatively narrow compass and/or unable to break onto a bigger national stage. Judged or challenged at only a relatively restricted geographical level, individuals could thus operate comfortably but authoritatively in a manageable sphere. Most of this work is obviously a far cry from that of Waugh, Preston, Laycock and others who engaged first hand with the dislocations of the nineteenth century. Nevertheless, albeit at a chronological and social distance and governed by a very different objectives, they shared an affection for their mutual language, history and culture that allowed them to make a modest contribution to the maintenance of a regional outlook in an increasingly nationalised and internationalised culture.

The growth of middle-class writers in the twentieth century was accompanied by, and perhaps helped facilitate, a similar growth of dialect writing amongst women. Only a very small body of women dialect writers existed in the nineteenth century. In the Yorkshire collective biography used earlier, for example, only one writer (Florence Tweddell) is noted. However, no fewer than twelve are listed as active in the period to 1945.[53] Dorothy Una Ratcliffe (1887–1967), yachtswoman, traveller, author of children's books and supporter of many northern cultural institutions, was especially prolific.[54] A few women even gained access to the prized male space of the almanac in the 1930s, albeit at the moment of its rapid loss of purchase within popular culture. John Hartley's third wife had contributed to the *Clock Almanack* immediately following his death, but it was in 1933 and 1934 that women writers including Eleanor Fletcher and Eleanor Gaukroger ('Jenny Wren') began to appear with some regularity. As has been suggested on several occasions in this book, the local and regional once again seem to represent a safe and suitable space in which women could engage with the public sphere.

The core audience for dialect literature was always found in the working and lower-middle classes. The almanacs and journals were cheap, with the *Clock Almanack* costing only 3d in 1880, for example, and the popularity of one-penny broadsides has already been noted. Many public performances were also comfortably within the reach of even the poorer sections of the working class, although the association of such events with Sunday Schools, mutual improvement classes and so forth might have proved a barrier for those concerned with their outward trappings of 'respectability'. As with authors, however, it is worth stressing the social range of both readership for literature and audience for public performance. As Brian Maidment has argued, the 'market was a mixed one, and the literary conventions of dialect writing were closely related to bourgeois taste as well as to the oral and popular traditions of the industrial north'.[55] Expensively bound subscription issues of Waugh's work were produced, evidence for a late Victorian clergyman's claim that 'scores of educated people who would disdain to speak their native dialects, gladly avail themselves of every chance of reading it'. Although the endorsement came from the egalitarian Frederic Moorman, it is surely significant that in 1913 the Yorkshire Dialect Society urged members to buy both the *Clock Almanack* and *Bob Stubbs' Yorksher Awmynack* and enjoy 'a rare intellectual feast'.[56] Yet again, public performances by leading writers were obviously aimed at a fairly respectable audience, with minimum admission prices set above those charged for the cheapest seats in a provincial music hall.[57]

The clear implication of this analysis of dialect literature's social constituency is that while such writing provides an important point of entry into working-class mentalities, the mix of classes involved in both production and consumption has been too broad for the working-class voice to be the only one audible or for any one single class viewpoint to dominate. A further set of commercial and aesthetic factors reinforced this. As Martha Vicinus contends, the marketplace disciplines led even working-class writers to choose 'themes that would offend no one' in preference to writing 'about unique characteristics of their own class'.[58] Again, because dialect writing enjoyed its mid-nineteenth century flowering at the very moment when dialect as a 'living expression' was coming under renewed pressure from nationalising forces, it quickly became rather stylised and tended to resort to what Hollingworth has termed a 'rather nostalgic attempt to conserve a dying culture and language'. This led to the growth of often limiting conventions on the part of writers and certain expectations from their readers.[59] Such tendencies were yet further augmented by the fact that dialect's secondary position in relation to Standard English had always pushed its users towards the comic and the sentimental, modes which can cope with serious issues but often do so obliquely or are simply better and more easily used for other topics. Thoughtful practitioners sometimes commented on the narrow range of vision that resulted and attempted redemption, but favoured ways usually won out.[60]

Dialect literature, then, was clearly well suited to expressing certain cross-class, regional and sub-regional ideologies. Much scholarly writing has noted its lack of sustained political radicalism and class consciousness. It by no means shied away from the realities of poverty and hardship as the careers of Samuel Laycock, Lancashire's Cotton Famine bard, and north-easterners Joe Wilson (1841–75), Ned Corvan (1831–65) and Tommy Armstrong (1848–1920) illustrate, although a number of the latter's powerful strike ballads were in Standard English.[61] Throughout the North from about 1890, there also emerged a number of writers with strong links to both political and industrial labour and whose work captured to varying degrees the increased influence of socialism in working-class political culture. Joseph Burgess (1853–1934) was a pioneer here although Allen Clarke (1863–1935), writing under the pen name of 'Teddy Ashton', was the most influential.[62]

Such voices were not typical, however. There is, indeed, often a sense of the writer disengaging at the very moment when the political moral might be underscored. One example from Hartley's work is instructive here. In his *Clock Almanack* 'Rambling remarks' for March 1880, he discusses the phrase 'as mad as a March hare' and writes of its irrelevance for much of the urban working class.

> but to fowk at live up ginnels [alleyways], amang smook, sooit and stink, an' whose een are seldom made glad wi' th' view o'owt but streets, dusty or sloppy, begrimed, poverty-lukkin' buildins, and factory chimleys spewin' aght ther clads o' black deeath, an shuttin' aght th' blue sky, and makkin' th' heavens seem uninvitin'; it's a sayin 'at signifies varry little.

However, at this point, Hartley sidesteps into a comic tale relating to his dona-tion of a tough and inedible rabbit to a friend.[63] Hartley finished his book-length *Seets I' Lundun* (1876) with the exquisitely downbeat line, 'Blessed is he 'at expects nowt, for he's varry likely to get it'.[64] While on this occasion Hartley's character Sammywell Grimes was bemoaning his family's lack of interest in his travels, this consciously exaggerated lack of expectation arguably captures a key aspect of dialect's political philosophy.

Overall, it is difficult to dissent from Joyce's claim that the dominant polit-ical ideology evident in dialect literature is 'much less a class than a "populist" one'.[65] The working class (usually present as 'working folk' or just 'folk') was cer-tainly absolutely central to this, with dialect providing one of the most positive and empowering repositories of northern working-class imagery that can be found. It portrayed a virtuous population that balanced hard work, dignity and stoicism in adversity and a contempt for hypocrisy, with a sense of justice, a sharp wit, generosity, and a love of hearth and family. Nowhere else was the masculine 'soft heart under a seemingly rough exterior … [the] hard hand that can smooth the pillow of affliction with the gentleness of a mother', more regu-larly exposed.[66] Celebration of domestic pleasure was arguably the single most powerful theme of dialect literature. In Waugh's well known 'Come whoam to thi' childer an' me', after much wifely entreaty, a husband admits that while,

> Aw can do wi' a crack o'er a glass;
> Aw can do wi' a bit of a spree:
> But aw've no gradely comfort, my lass,
> Except wi' yon childer and thi'.[67]

Samuel Laycock's cotton famine work 'Welcome Bonny Brid' (bird) has a poverty stricken father welcome a new baby with the reassurance that 'we'll mak' a bit o'reawm for thee' and the gentle final instruction,

> So hutch up closer to mi breast
> Aw'm thi dad.[68]

Other, more humourous tones, could also be adopted. Ben Brierley's Ab-O'-th'-Yate, *en route* to 'Yankeeland', tells his wife 'When I lost seet o' thee at Liverpool, an after I'd wrung my rag a time or two, I began a-wonderin' what I'd left thee behind for … It had never crossed my mind before at a woman wur a man's best companion, – speshly when he's a bit poorly, as I've bin, goodness knows.'[69] The message, however, was the same.

Working-class culture depicted thus must have been extremely comforting for those within higher social groups. Moreover, such individuals could themselves be embraced for the 'Good North' provided that they conformed to desirable social norms. In Hartley's words, 'Aw've nowt to say agean fowk becoss they're rich; – maybe they've haddled [earned] it. But is it reight for them at's been born fortun's favorits to waste i' one neet's frolic as much as wod keep fifty families for a wick [week]'.[70] The social order was clearly being imagined here far more as a battle between the useful of all classes and the idle, spendthrift rich, than as a matter of capital versus labour. Regardless of the sentiments expressed, the simple act of writing about social elites in dialect could crucial be in this context; the very use of the form, so strongly associated with native wisdom and practical common sense, conferred membership of a common regional culture.

A shared sense of a local and regional identity was fundamental to the building and expression of such a world-view and it is with this that the rest of this section is concerned. It is worth beginning by asking whether all sections of the working-class community were allowed to participate in this process. It is certainly not difficult to find jokes about the Irish in the period before 1914 that, although mild by the standards of the time – Joyce terms the tone 'affectionate' – might be exclusionary in some contexts.[71] There is no evidence of comment on the Jewish migration into Manchester and Leeds after 1880, although an anti-Semitic note was sounded in *The Nidderdill Olminac*'s enthusiastic celebration of Disraeli's electoral defeat in 1880. Noting that 'some say' Britain's economic problems stemmed from the fact that 't' first fiddel's being played by a *Jew*', editor Nattie Nydds calls for 'na marr "Hebrew Melodies" bud sum gud solid English music'.[72] Here, perhaps, are regional discourses working in the name of 'tradition' in order to serve a restrictive function.

Most dialect writing dealt with universal themes such as love, requited or otherwise, stock characters such the hen-pecked husband and his domineering wife and was often rooted in linguistic playfulness. Much of the reader or listener's pleasure came from these familiar situations and devices and it didn't necessarily require dialect to make them work. The conundrum that asked 'Which of Shakespeare's characters wor t'biggest powltry slayer?' and drew the answer, 'Macbeth – he did murder mooast fowl', worked as well (or as badly) in Standard English.[73] However, it was dialect that gave the added dimension, binding groups together in a knowing conspiracy forged by the exclusion of outsiders and in the straightforward pleasure of seeing the world made sense of in their own tongue.

That binding sometimes took place at the purely local level. Almanacs in particular could be extremely parochial, providing local information and advertisements as well as highly specific jokes and references. Interestingly, however, even in the West Riding where *campanilismo* was a notoriously powerful sensibility, dialect writing was never as critical site for the prosecution of local rivalries as might have been expected. They were readily acknowledged but were often used only as building blocks for larger regional identities. The 1906 Barnsley-based *Pogmoor Olmenack*, for example, has editor 'Tom Treddlehoyle' arbitrating over 'a tiff' between Dame Sheffield and Mother Leeds as to which is the leading Yorkshire city. Tom eventually informs them that their rapid urban spread will result in a sinking of differences as they merge to form a great metropolis that will have Manchester, Liverpool and London on their toes.[74] Through gentle fantasies like these, authors both acknowledged and helped articulate a series of regional units. This tendency to privilege sub-regional categories above the purely local may reflect commercial intent: writers had to build audiences not only across class but also across sustainable geographical markets. While Hartley regularly featured his native Halifax and placed his leading characters Sammywell [Samuel] and his wife Mally [Sophia] Grimes in nearby Bradford, other West Riding communities were regularly mentioned. The 1901 *Clock Almanack*, for example, also set stories in Barnsley, Brighouse, Leeds, Ripponden and Sheffield and it is hard to escape the feeling that this was a deliberate marketing ploy.

Whatever the motive, this device helped develop the reader's sense of being part of a family of communities. Other cultural forms could fulfil this function, but dialect writing played an especially significant role, its settled, imaginary functions far less prone to be disrupted by the actual intra-regional tensions that could flow from, for example, sporting or musical contests. The imagined communities that emerged could be broadly recognisable economic and cultural units such as the Yorkshire textile district or the slightly less coherent industrial West Riding. They might even cross county boundaries; linguistic boundaries after all rarely follow administrative boundaries. In certain border areas such as Saddleworth on the Yorkshire/Lancashire border, there were especially rich interchanges between West Riding and Lancashire dialects within local writing. Indeed, Yorkshire and Lancashire were bound as much as they were divided in dialect literature. Jokes were made about each other but they were often knowing and affectionate. Hartley, for example, commenting on Manchester's 'mucky, muggy and suicidal' November weather acknowledged that while Leeds could come close, 'Yorksher cannot expect to be th' fust i' iverything, an Lankysher's entitled to scoor this month'.[75] Similarly, writers influenced each other across the county divide, with Hartley never failing to acknowledge his debt to Edwin Waugh.

It is much harder to assess whether dialect writing generated any sense of their being a wider Northern region. Although writers from across the seven-county North were known to each other and influenced each other's work, the dialect division between far and near North in many ways proved to be precisely that. Nevertheless, while rarely articulated or invoked as an explicit idea, belief in a common belonging to the 'North' was quite possibly generated by the expression of mentalities that could be experienced and recognised right across the region. Absolutely central here was dialect literature's long tradition of intense suspicion of, and, sometimes outright hostility to, the capital. Once again it has been Joyce who has been especially acute to the 'anti-metropolitan tendencies of dialect' that embraced not simply the hard-working labouring classes but could be extended to 'those outside the ranks of workers who also make industrial Britain great'.[76] It is probably in dialect writing more than any other single form that the notion of the North (albeit usually a specific part of it) as producer of wealth and London and its hinterlands as disposer, is at its strongest. One of the clearest statements of this came relatively late, in Allen Clarke's 1923 poem 'In Praise o' Lancashire'. Here, 'England gaffers th' world' because of 'Lanky-made' goods and Lancashire skills: indeed, 'It's Lancashire runs Owd England'. Londoners are put into their decidedly secondary place.

> It weren't yore chirpin' cockneys
> That fit up th' world wi' gear
> Made Lancashire into th' engine-heause
> An Britannia th' engineer;[77]

The 'chirpin', condescending cockney had been a target since at least since Tommy Thompson's 'Canny Newcastle' (1816) and fairly continuously from the 1840s.[78] It is interesting that Londoners of the lower classes aroused the ire of northern writers as much as the idle aristocrat. Ben Brierley was only one writer who appeared to find the London poor work-shy and defeatist.[79] Here was a potential source of division within the working class nationally. There was also a strong sense that London's natural assumption of national leadership had to be challenged. In 1920, in another of those moments where writers tried to subsume narrow local tensions within wider allegiances, Bradford's 'Abe Clegg' (F. J. Newbould) tried to persuade smaller communities faced with absorption into an expanded Bradford that bigger issues were at stake.

> Them fowk i' London can't thoil [abide] t'idee of a metropolis i' t' North, an' its
> pairt o' t' game to play off one agean another an' keep us all dahn as long as they
> can. If that theer point o' view nobbut put afore them dependencies o' ahrs i' a

proper leet, they'd see t' necessity of a ewnited front. It isn't Bradford 'ats ther enemy, it's London.⁸⁰

The relationship between province and metropolis was never entirely biased in favour of the former. Plots focusing on suspicion of London and Londoners could also be used as a tool for the gentle satirisation of northern parochialism, especially in its more remote rural areas. The heroes of Cumberland poet John Richardson's 'The Cockney in Mosedale' meet a bearded stranger lost in a peat bog and, unable to 'mak lal iv his talk' beyond odd references to 'Lunnon and Pell Mell' (depiction of 'cockney' speech was usually thus restricted), they are initially convinced that the interloper must be a monkey.⁸¹ It should also be stressed that it was generally certain types of London*er*/southern*er* rather than London as architectural and cultural entity that raised hackles. This is absolutely evident in John Hartley's highly popular *Seets I' London* (1876) in which Sammywell Grimes visits his friend Smith in the capital. (Hartley briefly lived in London in the 1870s while trying to build a career as a recitalist and popular novelist in the medium of Standard English.)

The tale is replete with standard images of London as snare for the provincial innocent, a role that Sammywell plays to perfection. He assumes St Pancras Station to be St Paul's, asks a policeman if he knows where a man called Smith lives and, on a visit to the Houses of Parliament, wonders which window denotes the bedroom of the Bradford M.P. He expresses his delight in the building in splendidly parochial style; 'Aw'm sorry to have to say it, but its true – ther's nowt like it nawther in Bradford nor Saltaire.' He meets big city immorality in the shape of prostitutes in Cremorne Gardens and despite his determination not be cheated, he is later tricked into buying a drink at 10/-, provoking the response 'Aw want to pay for this drink; aw doan't want to buy th' valliation.' Like so many dialect writers he is struck by the indefensibly wide gap between rich and poor that the metropolis pointed up.⁸² However, he declares London a 'wonderful city' and is enormously impressed by the great tourist sites. Indeed, Smith's habit of feeding him scraps of statistical information about the city give Hartley's book something of the air of an idiosyncratic guidebook. The high point is reached when Sammywell sees Queen Victoria. Convinced that she has nodded at him, he responds – in Standard English – with a celebratory ode to the land 'where virtues dwell' and 'freedom waves her banner high'.⁸³ He is sad to leave but, crucially, must do so. As Vicinus argues, wanderers always return and 'Everything absorbed is put back into the context of life back home, reducing new experience to a selective rejection of the unknown and acceptance of the known.'⁸⁴ Whereas some cultural forms allowed individuals the possibility of escape to the metropolis, dialect writing was, in this context at least, a culture of constraint placing its readers in the warm but tight embrace of an idealised North.

A similarly North-centric viewpoint is visible in engagement with the wider national and international stage and especially in the treatment of monarchy and Empire.[85] The monarch figured surprisingly often and was invariably 'democratised' by being either the recipient or user of dialect and the object of affectionate, respectful but egalitarian treatment. Mally Muffindoaf's annual letter to the Queen in the *Pogmoor Olmenack*, in which Victoria (addressed as both 'Mistress Queen' and 'lass') received advice and local gossip from a Barnsley housewife, was one of the earliest and most entertaining examples.[86] The Empire was brought closer by similar means. In 1901, the same journal took Tom Treddlehoyle to meet a Barnsley-speaking Boer leader Paul Kruger, concerned to have run out of 'bacca' and admitting 'Yis Tom, ah made a mess', and offered a humorous but patriotic letter from a Pogmoorian at Mafeking. In 1907, it celebrated mightily Sheffield's successful Empire day celebrations. 'Nivver sin Owd England sprang inta being az a beacon of liberty for all 't world c all ages, wor owt seen ta eqwal t' bairns Empire Day at Sheffield … A city at can teych its childer ta gie sich a lesson ta an Empire, iz worthy to flourish'.[87] The standard core/periphery model that many outsiders imposed on the North was thus neatly reversed. The region, or specific parts of it, was placed at the centre of a world viewed through local eyes and made to speak in a local voice. Few, if any, other cultural forms had the power to make the world so manageable and to offer so much reassurance. In 1940, the *Clock Almanack* promised not to change its usual mixture of humour, nonsense, pathos and 'a gurt dollop o' homeliness' just because 'a lot o' wrang-heads are stalkin' abroad'.[88]

Dialect literature was an important element of northern culture not merely because of its empowering view of the working class and its ability to express, construct and negotiate a family of regional identities. It also contained some of the roots, in northern guise, of later popular cultural forms including stand up and situation comedy and soap opera. It is hard to read the one-liners that litter the comic almanacs or the terse exchanges between wives and husbands – 'tha' wor born lazy, an' aw wonder tha doesn't engage a chap to draw breath for thi'- without being reminded of twentieth-century voices to come.[89] Stock characters in the form of sharp-tongued women, wise uncles, 'soft lads' and the pompous heading for a fall are also plentiful. Dialect writing was a rich resource for later generations.

Neither has its power entirely evaporated, although it is often now a problematic form for the North. Brian Maidment has noted pamphlets and reprints
of Lancashire writers keeping 'the presence of the Victorian bardic tradition
even into post-industrial Manchester' and several other leading northern figures
have been appropriated to serve various causes in the late twentieth century.[90]
Overt honouring of dialect – spoken as much as written – most typically forms
either part of a tourist strategy or a project to erect a bulwark against mass culture and bureaucratic centralisation. Dialect is seen as bringing 'colour and
vitality to the drab, overall sameness of the modern electronic world' by one
writer, while another hopes it can stem the 'tidal wave of violent American films,
cheap Aussie soaps and junk food for junk minds'.[91] Such sentiments and the
poems, sketches, glossaries and compilations that they stimulate serve what
might be termed the contemporary regionalist movements. Here, linguistic and
cultural traditions along with loyalties to pre-1974 county boundaries help
structure opposition to a 'centre' that, for some, is as increasingly likely to
include Brussels as London. There is a powerful nostalgia here and one that can
appeal right across the political spectrum. In his *Completely Lanky* journalist,
scriptwriter and one time *Coronation Street* actor Dave Dutton, offers an elegy
for the 'parts of Lancashire I love', including the close community of the terrace
house, traditional industries, traditional pubs and 'chunks hacked off the
county by overpaid bureaucrats'. Here is another version of the 'True North' to
be set against the rural-historic confection of the early twentieth-century travel
writers. Dialect allows this version of the past to be recalled and offers hope of
minor cultural victories in the future.

Despite these contemporary practices – and perhaps partly because of them
– the image of dialect *writing* at least, stands as dated and idiosyncratic. The
lighter-hearted works from the 1980s only compound the problem. Once a cultural tool that gave great sustenance to the region it has long removed to the
outer margins of northern life. While work of real skill and value is still produced and older material can provide huge enjoyment, any future linguistic
underpinning for northern identities will surely be rooted in living, spoken language rather than words on a page.

London calling?

For those concerned to protect the local and regional from 'the drab overall
sameness of the modern electronic world', the BBC has always been an easy
target. Although it must not be treated as an unchanging monolith, both its

linguistic and wider cultural policies were clearly much influenced until well into the second half of the twentieth century by the principles of public service broadcasting defined by John Reith during his reign as General Manager and then Director-General from 1922 to 1938. Absolutely central in this context was the role given to the cultural 'establishment' of London and the south-east in the definition of standards of taste, quality and judgment. As Asa Briggs has argued 'the BBC was following all the other mass media of the early twentieth century in bolstering London's supremacy' although no other was perhaps quite so driven by the powerful sense of metropolitan cultural excellence and natural leadership.[92] An internal memo in 1935 defending lower salaries for provincial employees on the grounds that 'the best of the staff tend to gravitate to London' and that 'London's contribution to the National Programme are intrinsically more important than the local contributions of the regions' was fulsome testimony to such thinking.[93] This London-centric mentality has clearly set the tone for BBC radio's treatment of regional culture and language for much of the twentieth century. However, contestation and negotiation of this approach from within and without the Corporation, coupled with shifts in the wider cultural context, have enabled northern voices to enjoy some significant and influential moments. This creative dynamic tension is at the heart of this section.

The BBC's capacity to shape attitudes to language was remarkable and probably unheralded in the modern world. Acutely aware of its responsibilities, it swiftly set up an Advisory Committee on Spoken English under the chairmanship of Robert Bridges, a founder of the Society for Pure English. Waller is undoubtedly correct to warn against simplistic views of the Committee specifically, and BBC language policy in general, when arguing that there was no 'conspiracy of Home Counties or Oxbridge linguistic Tories, designing to overthrow the People's English and to establish a class dialect'.[94] The Committee took advice from a wide circle – northern dialectologist Harold Orton joined it in 1934 – and the development of a uniform tone, voice and accent was driven to an extent by a genuine need to protect announcers from the 'ill-informed criticism' of listeners with particular linguistic axes to grind.[95] There was also common ground across the whole country on such issues as opposition to the 'Americanisation' of English that might have proved more potent than geographically based internal differences. However, the Corporation's Hilda Matheson was equally correct to term the BBC English used by newsreaders, continuity announcers and many of its favoured speakers as 'roughly the educated speech of southern England'. The BBC was clear from the outset that southern English was at the core of a 'narrow band of accents' the users of which 'are recognised as educated speakers throughout the country. They may broadcast without fear of adverse intelligent criticism.'[96] Thus, while there was no conspiracy, cultural assumptions backed up by a recruitment policy that drew key staff from that very group of educated speakers, delivered a similar result.

The BBC did not ignore regional voices, northern or otherwise in its early decades. The problem was that regional and working-class accents – the two were often believed to be synonymous – were seen as comical and lacking weight and dignity. Some were, of course, intended to be associated with humour. Northern comedians appeared from the earliest days, with Yorkshire's 'John Henry' the 'first comedian to become a national [radio] personality', making his debut in May 1923.[97] However, even 'ordinary' northerners appearing as themselves could appear as comic characters and figures of fun. The fact that a lack of recording technology for much of the inter-war period meant that programmes had to go out live was critical in this regard. Fear of unsuitable utterance, whether inappropriate political statement or simple nervous stammering, meant that programmes were tightly and sometimes unsympathetically scripted. For many individuals unused to public reading this could result in stultifying performances that, while probably more comical to twenty-first century ears than those of contemporaries, surely did little to enhance the image and position of regional cultures. As already noted, the North and the northern working class was not alone in receiving this treatment but, given its reputation as a 'comic place', it arguably suffered more than most others in this respect.

The regional response to a language policy that so often marginalised the North, mixed resistance, irritation and gentle amusement in about equal amounts. There is no systematic body of evidence as to the impact of broadcast Standard English on accent and dialect in the period to the 1970s. While it is likely that broadcasting was one of the nationalising forces responsible for lexical erosion within dialects, powerful local attachments and counter-influences probably protected distinctive *accents*. There was certainly considerable hostility at times from the public at large about BBC English with its (masculine) flavour of public school and university.[98] Even when announcers tried hard to acknowledge variation, they sometimes fell foul of local sentiment. S. P. B. Mais (who had spent some of his childhood in Yorkshire) recorded how his apparently 'laboured use' of the short 'a' in Newcastle had angered one Northumbrian recipient of his *This Unknown Island* series (1932). The listener had found it 'snobbish' and 'patronising' and requested the BBC not to ask Mais 'to discourse on our County again'.[99] As has often been the case, southern-based institutions could clearly not be allowed to win whatever the linguistic tactic they used. Nevertheless, despite these patterns of resistance, conscious and otherwise, there can be no doubt that the BBC privileged one particular family of accents above others and made them the benchmark against which all others were measured. Regional voices were to be kept in their place.

No issue better illustrates the possibilities and problems inherent in broadcasting northern accents at this time than the BBC's use of Wilfred Pickles as a newsreader on the National Home Service in late 1941.[100] The idea of using Pickles, a well-established radio figure from the late 1930s, is believed to have come from Minister of Information Brendan Bracken who believed that a northern voice would be both an inclusive and welcome gesture and difficult for German propagandists to impersonate. As will be seen shortly, northern voices (including Pickles's) had actually become slightly more familiar from the late 1930s via programmes originating in the North Region. Again, northern accent had been one of the features deemed to have added to J. B. Priestley's appeal in his famous 'Postscripts' broadcasts of 1940. '[H]is common sense and Yorkshire stoicism' reflected 'the real and everlasting spirit of our race' according to one national paper, happy to allow the North to be fully embraced within wartime Englishness.[101] However, the Pickles broadcasts became controversial because they raised issues about the authority and power that certain voices lend (or otherwise) to the specific and privileged act of news reading.

Passing reference to this affair is a staple of broadcasting history but the scale of the press coverage and public discussion is not always appreciated. It was a major news item for several days and generated large postbags to Pickles, the press and the BBC. At one level, as Pickles acknowledged, the incident provided light-hearted debate at a time when the suspension of normal political culture meant that 'the British public were ready to snatch at any time with a controversial angle'.[102] There was a lot of gentle fun involved at all levels with the continuity announcer following Pickles's first broadcast with a record of 'On Ilkla Moor Baht 'At' and Pickles then famously ending the subsequent midnight bulletin with 'and to all northerners wherever you may be, "good neet"'. Press coverage specialised in standard Yorkshire stereotypes with one cartoonist showing Pickles at the microphone in shirtsleeves, muffler and cap and another suggesting that his opening line might be 'Here is the news and ee bah gum this is Wilfred Pickles reading it.'[103] This is very much the nationally agreed theatre of regional parody and self-parody at work.

However, there were more serious issues. While a majority of the BBC panel of local correspondents (its favoured listener research mechanism) found Pickles to be a less aloof, more homely and thus preferable news reading voice, a significant minority as well as the bulk of those writing directly to the BBC, claimed that his provincial accent and supposedly poor delivery undermined the credibility of the news bulletin. (These claims, made in the North as well as the South, are especially interesting given the extremely understated accent that Pickles adopted.) Clearly, support for Pickles shows that the BBC's standard tone was not always appreciated. However, equally clearly that tone had many admirers and adherence to it within the Corporation was too deeply entrenched for it to be easily cast aside. [104] Before long Pickles was back in Manchester and BBC English remained virtually the sole linguistic currency of announcers and newsreaders for the next thirty years. This short-lived experiment did, interestingly, continue to influence northern versions of the relationship between the BBC and the region for a long time. In 1990, Pickles's hometown newspaper could even claim that until his intervention the Corporation demanded 'that anyone with a Northern accent should be kept off the national airways'. [105]

It was not until the 1970s that regional voices (and those from other parts of Britain) were heard outside of the ghettoes of comedy and 'human interest'. The mimicry of upper-class English accents that became an ever-greater feature of radio comedy from the 1950s was one liberating factor here, but it was the loosening of attitudes towards speech within society in general coupled with the flow of talent unleashed by local radio that finally forced the BBC to appreciate the benefits of speaking in mixed tongues. [106] Brian Redhead, on Radio 4's flagship news programme *Today*, and Patti Coldwell on the same channel's *You and Yours*, were two early northern voices in the 1970s, while the arrival of brother and sister Andy and Liz Kershaw on Radio 1 – in 1984 and 1987 respectively – gave strong regional tones a home in the field of popular music presentation. [107] As late as 2001, however, a senior presenter's faint Merseyside accent could be seen as detrimental to her chances of taking a leading post on *Today*. [108] The very fact that the 'problem' of accent could still be raised in the twenty-first century is indicative of how deeply the BBC has been associated with one particular variant and how sceptical many still are of its willingness to break from it when issues of 'authority' are at stake.

The history of BBC programming illustrates similar patterns of core-periphery relationships, although here the picture was nicely complicated by the Corporation's desire to build regional identities alongside a wider national identity. This became a fully conscious ploy from the late 1920s. Before then, the lack of a fully effective national transmitter rather dictated policy.[109] In order to reach the widest possible audience nine 'main transmitting stations' and ten local relay stations were established to work alongside the London headquarters. In terms of northern provision, main stations were established at Manchester and Newcastle and relay stations at Hull, Leeds/Bradford, Liverpool and Sheffield. Wireless thereby often had an intimate almost parochial tone, with the main and regional stations making much use of local voices, tastes and institutions. Post Office landlines allowed London programmes to reach a national audience, but also facilitated the passage of local and regional programmes around the system. This broad federation was rapidly superseded by the 'regional scheme' first floated in 1925 and fully implemented by 1934, creating a network consisting of seven regional stations operating alongside but subordinate to, the main 'National Programme'.[110] As a result, all relay and some main stations saw their transmitters silenced (their studios were kept open in many cases), although not without a bitter if unsuccessful fight in the case of the Sheffield station, 6LF.[111] The regional stations remained a central plank of the BBC system for almost forty years, enjoying especially fertile periods in the late 1930s and between about 1945 and 1955 (regional broadcasting was suspended during the war). The arrival of BBC local radio in 1967, with Radio Sheffield the first northern station, marked a policy change that saw the closure of the regional networks in 1970. Regional studios were now given the task of feeding distinctive programmes (albeit not necessarily reflective of their region) into the national network.

Many factors prompted the original establishment of the regional structure. It provided at least some degree of listener choice at a time when the expansion of broadcasting throughout Europe made it difficult for the BBC to claim sufficient wavelengths to maintain the old system. It also avoided much of the costly programme duplication that typified the 1920s. For all these attractions, the regional scheme clearly won most favour at HQ because of the increased authority and ease of control that it offered to the centre. There was never any doubt about the nature of the ultimate relationship between Broadcasting House and the regional programmes. The assistant controller's instruction to local stations in 1928 that they should 'take from London what you cannot do better yourself, and do yourself what London cannot give you', captures well the notion that London offered quality, the provinces largely 'difference'. Under the regional scheme from 1930, out stations had to take certain programmes from London deemed to be of national political or cultural importance, were limited in terms of the number of programmes they could make and had to suffer some remarkable condescension. BBC senior management nevertheless took 'difference', especially that between North and South, reasonably seriously and the North Region became for a time both one of the Corporation's most creative outlets and one of the North's most significant cultural institutions.

The BBC's was a generously defined 'North'. Its southern boundary changed on a number of occasions but it absorbed at various times large areas of Derbyshire, Lincolnshire, Nottinghamshire and Staffordshire. It was more a product of technical and administrative convenience than cultural nicety; an acknowledgement that the region was 'already larger than convenient' was the main justification for 'transfer' of the Potteries to the Midlands in 1936.[112] The North Region was based in Manchester – the city's station controller was being referred to as 'North Regional Director' by late 1928 – further evidence that the city was seen by London as capital of the North and a substantial aid to its own claims in that direction.[113] The other major northern centres were less than happy and, as late as 1943, the BBC's John Coatman noted that each 'of the great cities of the north thinks that it should have been chosen for the Regional headquarters, and old passions in respect of this still burn'.[114] The north-east proved especially hard to placate and the Newcastle studio was eventually given greater autonomy from 1938. The fact that the north-east had to share a wavelength with Northern Ireland in the late 1940s and early 1950s, however, caused further resentment.

For all the lack of tight definition, the BBC's public pronouncements would suggest that they genuinely believed that a broadly conceived North formed a distinctive and distinct place. The 1929 *BBC Yearbook* went as far as to argue that it 'may be truly said of the North of England that it is a nation within a nation'.[115] Policy and programme makers made a genuine attempt to build a sense of a shared northern identity that paralleled the Corporation's larger project of identifying and constructing a national culture. In this, it served a unique function within the North's cultural history; no institution before or since has taken on the specific role of binding the region, of giving shape to what have often no more than loose aspirations and assumptions. Given the complexities of the North this was a difficult task, largely attempted by acknowledging difference but at the same time tying 'local idioms and customs in a unifying image of the North as a particular place and people with a distinctive way of life'.[116] Outside broadcasts linking a wide range of communities played a major part here, although technical problems undermined some of the earliest efforts.[117] The very act of opting out of the National network, of course, gave a crucial sense of separateness. The extent of the opt out varied from day-to-day but it could be a powerful tool. On 11 March 1946, the North Regional Home Service offered its own programmes for almost 80 per cent of the time between 5 and 10.45 p.m., the prime period for such switching. Regional listeners were offered their own 'Children's Hour', news bulletin and sport magazine, as well as a concert featuring Kathleen Ferrier and the BBC Northern Orchestra, an early episode of Wilfred Pickles' 'Have a Go, Joe', and 'Sounding Brass and Voices' with Isobel Baillie, Norman Walker and the Bickershaw Colliery Band.[118] This was perhaps an evening of unusually rich northern texture but it shows what could be achieved.

Whether the BBC managed to build and maintain a northern identity is highly debateable. After 1945, many listeners were disappointed to lose national programmes which they had become accustomed to during the war while others objected to the kind of regional evening mix noted above because it assumed an interest in a specific type of northern culture that not all actually shared.[119] Probably the biggest problem was simply that of differentiation *within* the region. The lengths to which the BBC went in stressing the unity of the region – it once felt the need to emphasise that while main offices and studios were in Lancashire the transmitter was in Yorkshire – are strongly suggestive here.[120] The north-east was often dissatisfied, as noted earlier, but there was also the risk that programmes directed at it such as 'Wot Cheor Geordie', featuring comedian Bobby Thomson and the self-explanatory 'Northumbrian Barn Dance', would alienate audiences elsewhere.

At a more modest level, however, there can be no doubting the number of important, some times genuinely groundbreaking, programmes that flowed from the North Region. Most of these tended to define the North in specific and essentially stereotypical ways, making it, if not exclusively working-class, then at least a land of the 'ordinary person' and thus a site of authenticity. The region's association with heavy industry made this inevitable to a considerable extent, but individual aesthetic and ideological positions also exerted influence. Important here was Archie Harding, Director of Programmes at Manchester from 1933–36, and whose eye for talent and encouragement of new thinking shaped much of the station's more interesting output. A southerner educated at public school and Oxford University and a committed Marxist with an accent 'so distinctively Oxford, that he had only to open his mouth [for heads to turn] in astonishment' in central Manchester, he was described by one source as a man 'bitten by that awful bug which gives a man delusions about the north' and makes him see it as 'more full of integrity' than the South.[121] While Harding may have been one of the many whose creativity was fired by this inverted geographical snobbery, there can be no denying his commitment to bring ordinary people to the microphone.

In realising this ambition he was expertly served by Geoffrey Bridson, a young Manchester-born poet whose writing and production was based on left of centre views and a desire to portray the North not as 'not provincial at all [but] an entity standing upon its own'. An early programme satirising the 'more tiresome' side of the Manchester business community was described by one local paper as 'a libel on the people of the north'. This response led Bridson and Harding to view the programme as a success and suggests a nice confusion in the minds of those used to seeing the BBC as 'southern' and unable to contemplate mockery from within.[122] Above all, Bridson brought to the North Region (and from there into the National network) programmes that, by featuring the working-class voice, blended with poetry, especially composed music and sound effects, genuinely developed radio as a medium.[123] Best known among his output were the documentaries *Steel, Cotton, Wool* and *Coal*, the latter deliberately made in Durham because he was anxious to broaden the range of northern accent heard on air, and *Harry Hopeful*, first broadcast in 1935.[124] 'Harry', played by Manchester clock repairer and actor Frank Nicholls, was a fictional glass blower's assistant who tramped around the largely *rural* north – the programme used locations from the Solway Firth to Chester – in search of interesting folk. Although Bridson still had to write the necessary dialogue, he went to great lengths to try and maintain spontaneity and some degree of authenticity. In so doing, he played an important role in beginning the slow shift in attitudes towards the status of regional and working-class voices in the broadcast media. There is little doubt that Bridson romanticised some aspects of northern life and was not above making 'actuality' a little more radio-friendly, as when persuading mill girls to sing at work in a factory that expressly forbad such behaviour.[125] Nevertheless, his contribution to the democratisation and 'regionalisation' of broadcasting remains considerable. Like so many talented northerners in the cultural field, Bridson eventually left for London during the Second World War, becoming a popular member of the Hampstead and Highgate intelligentsia.

Bridson was by no means a force of one. Olive Shapley who worked with him and in her own right, produced a number of influential documentaries and features including *Homeless People* (1938) and *Classic Soil* (1939), often making pioneering use of early mobile recording technology.[126] Discussion

programmes balancing expert and lay opinion and *Burbleton* (1937), an interesting proto-soap opera partially scripted by dialect writer Tommy Thompson,
formed other important elements of North Regional output.[127] Although the
regional frequencies were closed during the war, programmes were still produced for national use, among them the popular *Billy Welcome* (1941–42),
produced by Bridson and with Wilfred Pickles as a 'Harry Hopeful' of the factory canteen. Pickles grew to hate the programme deeming it 'rank propaganda under a cloak of entertainment', but it helped cement his national
reputation and provided part of the inspiration for 'Have a Go!' the single
most popular radio programme from 1946 to 1957 and the vehicle that fully
implanted Pickles and his version of amiable northernness within the national
consciousness. In its distinctive way it did as much to sustain a kind of sub-
political populism as any other northern cultural product in the twentieth
century. First broadcast as 'Have a Go, Joe' on the North Region in March
1946, it transferred to the Light Programme under its revised name that
September and remained in the schedules until 1967.[128] Unscripted and
recorded on location initially in the North but eventually nationwide, it featured light-hearted interviews with members of the audience, quiz questions
for small money prizes and a little community singing. Pickles' catchphrases
"Ow do, 'ow are yer?', 'Now, are yer coortin?' and 'Give him the money,
Barney' (later 'Mabel' after his wife joined the programme) were soon part of
the nation's demotic speech. Pickles was a natural broadcaster with a genuine
flair for connecting with both interviewees and the home audience and it is
interesting that this individual talent was tied by some commentators to
bigger patterns of northern character and culture. A *Radio Times* feature
marking the programme's national debut linked his lack of pretension and
homeliness with his origins in Halifax, a West Riding town representative of
those which had known about 'the intensities and humours of human conflict
for a long time'.[129]

The 1950s was a key decade for the North on air. Pickles' success was
accompanied by the emergence of highly popular comedy shows including the
'Al Read Show' (1951–68), 'The Clitheroe Kid' (1958–72) and Ken Dodd's
'It's Great to be Young' (1958–61).[130] However, by the end of that decade,
outside the field of popular music radio had lost its ability to define the
national culture to television. Moreover, by the late 1960s some of these
classic northern offerings were sounding decidedly dated. 'Have a Go!'
increasingly set the 'old' North against the new brands of Liverpool and the
fictional and cinematic North of the 'Angry Young Men', in an almost elegiac

counterpoint that associated it with the past without ever connecting to the power of that past in the way of ITV's *Coronation Street*. At least the increasing linguistic richness of the national networks and the arrival of BBC local radio in 1970 and local commercial radio in 1974 (four stations began in the North in that year) has given some sense of ownership back to communities within the region. Although many presenters do not have local voices, contributors to the ubiquitous phone-ins usually do, while regular references to known places, characters and institutions can give listeners a sense of being at the core rather than the periphery far more effectively or more straightforwardly than most national programmes. While local radio represents only a relatively minor strand of contemporary cultural life, it is nevertheless one of the arenas in which the North, or at least its constituent parts, has been allowed to define itself to some degree. Any significant power of this type in the broadcasting sphere, however, now lies with television.

Notes

1 Quoted in J. Fairfax-Blakeborough, 'A Yorkshire dialect survey', *Transactions of the Yorkshire Dialect Society* (from now, *TYDS*), 5, 29, 1928, p. 22.

2 P. J. Waller, 'Democracy and dialect, speech and class', in his *Politics and Social Change in Modern Britain* (Brighton: Harvester, 1987), p. 2.

3 This section leans heavily on P. Joyce, *Visions of the People. Industrial England and the Question of Class, 1840–1914* (Cambridge: Cambridge University Press, 1991), chaps 8–12; D. Leith, *A Social History of English* (London: Routledge, 1983); L. Mugglestone, *Talking Proper. The Rise of Accent as Social Symbol* (Oxford: Oxford University Press, 1995); P. Trudgill, *The Dialects of England* (Oxford: Basil Blackwell, 1990); C. Upton and J. D. A. Widdowson, *An Atlas of English Dialects* (Oxford: Oxford University Press, 1996); Waller, 'Democracy and dialect'.

4 J. D. A. Widdowson, 'Sheffield dialect on the eve of the Millennium', *TYDS*, 99, 19, 1999, pp. 10, 16.

5 Ibid., pp. 5–6, 19–49.

6 K. Robbins, *Nineteenth-Century Britain. Integration and Diversity* (Oxford: Clarendon Press, 1988), pp. 45–6; Waller, 'Democracy and dialect', pp. 22–3.

7 Trudgill, *The Dialects of England*, pp. 50–78.

8 Ibid., pp. 2–3. See Leith, *Social History*, pp. 55–6 for RP.

9 Joyce, *Visions*, pp. 195, 200.

10 Quoted in Rev. J. H. Green, 'The Yorkshire dialect and its place in English literature', *TYDS*, 4, 1902, p. 24.

11 H. M. Jewell, *The North–South Divide. The Origins of Northern Consciousness in England* (Manchester: Manchester University Press, 1994), p. 191.

12 Leith, *Social History*, p. 56.

13 A. Bennett, *Writing Home* (London: Faber and Faber, 1994), p. xiii.

14 S. Walton, *William Walton. Behind the Façade* (Oxford: Oxford University Press, 1988), pp. 42–3; B. Garner, 'Tony Harrison: Scholarship boy', *TYDS*, 16, 86, 1986, p. 21.

15 G. Turner, *The North Country* (London: Eyre and Spottiswoode), p. 94.

16 Waller, 'Democracy and dialect', p. 24.

17 Joyce, *Visions*, p. 201; Waller, 'Democracy and dialect', pp. 16–7, 23–4.

18 Turner, *North Country*, pp. 144–50.

19 M. Pattenden, *Last Orders at the Liars' Bar* (London: Gollancz, 1999), p. 45.

20 W. Pickles, *Between You and Me* (London: Werner Laurie, 1949), pp. 47–52.

21 Penguin edn, 1994, p. 41.

22 Garner, 'Tony Harrison', p. 16. See also, T. Harrison, *Selected Poems* (London: Penguin, 1987); C. Rutter, *Tony Harrison. Permanently Bard* (Newcastle-upon-Tyne: Bloodaxe Books, 1995); J. Kelleher, *Tony Harrison* (Plymouth: Northcote House, 1996).

23 *TYDS*, 1, 1898, pp. 3–6 for his inaugural address.

24 *Hindle Wakes*, in G. Rowell (ed.), *Late Victorian Plays, 1890–1914* (Oxford: Oxford University Press, 1972), pp. 469, 480.

25 Hostility to local usage even within the state education system should also not be assumed. For the 1921 Newbolt Report, see B. Doyle, *English and Englishness* (London: Routledge, 1989), pp. 53–4.

26 M. Vicinus, *The Industrial Muse* (Beckenham: Croom Helm, 1974), pp. 185–237; B. Hollingworth, *Songs of the People* (Manchester: Manchester University Press, 1977); B. Maidment, *The Poorhouse Fugitives* (New York: Carcanet, 1987), especially pp. 209–78, 354–70; Joyce, *Visions*, chapters 10–11; P. Salveson, 'Region, Class, Culture: Lancashire Dialect Literature, 1746–1935', Unpublished PhD, University of Salford, 1993.

27 Leith, *Social History*, pp. 41–2.

28 *TYDS*, vol. 32, April 1931, pp. 9–13.

29 Colls, *Collier's Rant*, pp. 14–54; D. Harker, 'Joe Wilson: "comic dialectical singer" or class traitor', in J. Bratton, *Music Hall. Performance and Style* (Milton Keynes: Open University Press, 1986), pp. 111–30; B. Griffirths, *North East Dialect: The Texts* (Newcastle: Centre for Northern Studies, University of Northumbria 2000).

30 Joyce, *Visions*, p. 265 for county-by-county figures.

31 Ibid., pp. 280–1; J. Belchem '"An accent exceedingly rare: Scouse and the inflexion of class', in his *Merseypride. Essays in Liverpool Exceptionalism* (Liverpool: Liverpool University Press, 2000), p. 41.

32 See pp. 151–6.

33 It began as an advertising sheet for a Halifax auctioneer and hatter whose shop under the clock in the town's Cornmarket produced the rather mysterious title.

34 E. M. Wright, *The Life of Joseph Wright. Man and Scholar* (London: Oxford University Press, 1934), p. 26.

35 Hollingworth, *Songs*, p. 2.

36 Salveson, *Lancashire Dialect*, pp. 2–3.

37 B. T. Dyson, 'Notes on the West Riding almanacs', *TYDS*, 13, 75, 1975, pp. 40–1.
38 Many of these were published by Watmough's of Bradford and advertised in the *Clock Almanack* which they took over in 1921. See below, chapter 5.
39 For attitudes to dialect in novels at this time, see below, chapter 3.
40 For the later twentieth-century tradition, see K. E. Smith, *The Dialect Muse* (Wetherby: Ruined Cottage Publications, 1979).
41 D. Dutton, *Completely Lanky* (Bolton: Aurora Publishing, n.d.), p. 13.
42 A. Kellett, *Basic Broad Yorkshire* (Otley: Smith Settle, 1991), p. 3.
43 Joyce, *Visions*, p. 275.
44 Ibid., p. 258.
45 Obituary in *Clock Almanack*, 1933, pp. 46–7.
46 For sketch biographies see Hollingworth, *Songs*, pp. 151–6 and W. J. Halliday and A. S. Umpleby, *A White Rose Garland* (London: Dent, 1949), pp. 290–300.
47 For the 'higher-class' dialect tradition, see Joyce, *Visions*, p. 267–75.
48 Joyce, *Visions*, p. 256; *TYDS*, vol. 32, April 1931, pp. 9–13; Halliday and Umpleby, *Garland*, pp. 292, 295.
49 Halliday and Umpleby, *A White Rose*, pp. 290–300.
50 Some 15–20 per cent of the Yorkshire Dialect Society (1897) were clergymen in its early years. See membership lists in *TYDS*.
51 F. W. Moorman, preface to his self-authored poetry collection *Songs of the Ridings* (London: Elkin Matthews, 1918), pp. 6–7.
52 Ibid., pp. 8–9, 18. His 'A Dalesman's Litany', *Songs*, pp. 23–4, was set to music by folksinger Dave Burland in the 1970s and was assumed by many to be a 'traditional' song. For a biographical sketch, C. Vaughan, 'Memoir', in F.W. Moorman, *Tales, Songs and Plays of the Ridings* (London: Elkin Matthews, 1921), pp. 7–20.
53 For women dialect writers see Salveson, 'Lancashire Dialect', pp. 445–73.
54 See obituary, *Yorkshire Post*, 22 November 1967.
55 Maidment, *Fugitives*, p. 358.
56 Rev. R.V. Taylor, 'On the Yorkshire dialect', *TYDS*, 1, 1898, p. 31; 2, 14, 1913, pp. 10–15. Moorman, however, could not resist finding some inconsistencies and errors in their reproduction of speech.
57 Waugh's concert at Ilkley in 1875 was priced at 6d and 1/-. See Hollingworth, *Songs*, p. x.
58 Vicinus, *Industrial Muse*, p. 225.
59 Hollingworth, *Songs*, p. 4. See also pp. 5–6 and Maidment, *Fugitives*, pp. 355–6, for perceptive discussion of these issues.
60 See Walter Hampson's comments and poem 'On War' in *TYDS*, vol. 32, April 1931, pp. 9–13, 23–4.
61 Several of these, including his 'The Shurat weaver's song', are published in Hollingworth, *Songs*; Harker, 'Joe Wilson', pp. 111–30; A. L. Lloyd, *Folk Song in England* (London: Panther edn, 1969), pp. 377–86.
62 The strongest argument for the radicalism of late Victorian and Edwardian dialect literature is Salveson's 'Lancashire dialect', chapter 4. See, however, Joyce, *Visions*, pp. 290–304. There were also Tory voices, notably that of Charles Rogers, a paper

hanger by trade, editor of *Bairnsla Fowks' Annual and Pogmoor Olmenack* from 1842 to 1875.

63   *Clock Almanack*, March 1880, p. 9.
64   J. Hartley, *Seets I' Lundun. A Yorkshireman's Ten Days Trip* (London: W. Nicholson and Sons, 1876), p. 136.
65   Joyce, *Visions*, p. 290.
66   B. Brierley, *Some Phases of Lancashire Life*, p. 206.
67   Hollingworth, *Songs*, pp. 64–5.
68   Ibid., pp. 141, 73–5.
69   B. Brierley, *Ab-O'-th'-Yate in Yankeeland* (Manchester: Abel Heywood, 1885), p. 15.
70   *Clock Almanack*, 1895, p. 5.
71   For example the *Pogmoor Olmenack* for 1905 records the 'immense thrummaty sweat' experienced by an Irishman when faced with the road sign stating 'Jump 2 miles' (p. 29).
72   *Nidderdill Olminac*, 1880, 'Ta start wi'.
73   *T' Pogmoor Olmenack an Bairnsla Fowks Yearly Jottings*, 1907, p. 20; Joyce, *Visions*, p. 283.
74   *Pogmoor Olmenack*, 1906, 61–2.
75   *Clock Almanack*, 1901, p. 25.
76   Joyce, *Visions*, pp. 293–4.
77   Quoted in ibid., pp. 290–2.
78   Colls, *Collier's Rant*, pp. 41–4.
79   Ibid., pp. 293–4.
80   Quoted in *TYDS*, 3, 81, 1920, p. 32.
81   J. Richardson, *Cummerland Talk* (Carlisle: George Coward, second series 1876), pp. 30–8.
82   Hartley, *Seets*, pp. 9, 27, 21–2, 55, 64–5.
83   Ibid., pp. 118, 43, 45, 80–9,
84   Vicinus, *Industrial*, pp. 200–1.
85   See Salveson, 'Lancashire Dialect', pp. 371–429 on attitudes to war and empire.
86   Mally's jottings first appeared in 1843. For Lancashire examples, see Joyce, *Visions*, pp. 388–92.
87   *Pogmoor Olmenack*, 1901, pp. 2–3, 24–5; 1907, pp. 56–7.
88   *Clock Almanack*, 1940, introduction.
89   Ibid., 1885, p. 36.
90   Maidment, *Fugitives*, p. 23; Harker, 'Joe Wilson', pp. 111–12.
91   A. Kellett, *The Yorkshire Dictionary of Dialect Tradition and Folklore* (Otley: Smith Settle, 1994), p. xi; D. Dutton's *Completely Lanky* (Bolton: Aurora, n.d.), introductory page.
92   A. Briggs, *The History of Broadcasting in the United Kingdom*, vol. 2 (Oxford: Oxford University Press, 1965 edn), p. 308.
93   Quoted in P. Scannell and D. Cardiff, *A Social History of British Broadcasting, vol. 1, 1922–1939* (Oxford: Basil Blackwell, 1991), p. 328.

94   Waller, 'Democracy and dialect', pp. 8–9.

95   *TYDS*, 35, 1934, p. 8. *BBC Yearbook*, 1928, pp. 357–9.

96   Quoted in S. Barnard, *Studying Radio* (London: Arnold, 2000), p. 176; A. Lloyd James, *Broadcast English*, 1926, quoted in Waller, 'Democracy and dialect', p. 8.

97   Denis Gifford, *The Golden Age of Radio* (London: Batsford, 1985), p. 113.

98   M. Pegg, *Broadcasting and Society, 1918–1939* (London: Croom Helm, 1983), pp. 161–2.

99   S. P. B. Mais, *This Unknown Island* (London: Putnam, 1932), p. 113.

100 The issue is well dealt with in Pickles, *Between You and Me*, pp. 130–45.

101 *Daily Mail*, 2 July 1940, quoted in Briggs, *Broadcasting*, vol. 3 (1995 edn), p. 192.

102 Pickles, *Between You and Me*, p. 143.

103 Ibid., pp. 141, 142, 136, 137.

104 Mugglestone, *Talking Proper*, pp. 323–4. BBC written archive, R9/9/5. I am grateful to Wendy Webster for this material.

105 *Halifax Courier*, 4 September 1990.

106 See Barnard, *Studying Radio*, p. 176, on satire and accent. The need to consider race, ethnicity and gender were also issues impacting on the radio voice.

107 P. Donovan, *The Radio Companion* (London: HarperCollins, 1991). John Peel's Liverpudlian tones on Radio 1 from 1967 provided another very early example, but as a late flowering of the 'Mersey Sound' they provided less of a change than the Kershaws' Rochdale. Significantly, Andy Kershaw fronted the documentary 'The Rise of the Common Voice' on Radio 4 on 18 April 1997.

108 'Accentuate the positive', editorial, *Guardian*, 19 February 2001.

109 The relationship between local, regional and national broadcasting is expertly traced in the relevant sections of Briggs, *Broadcasting* (1995 edn), vols 2–5. This section also draws extensively on the equally expert, Scannell and Cardiff, *Social History*, pp. 277–354. The best single-volume introduction is A. Crissell, *An Introductory History of British Broadcasting* (London: Routledge, 1997).

110 There were five regional stations initially, the Midlands, North, South-east, West, Scotland, with Northern Ireland and Wales added shortly after.

111 Scannell and Cardiff, *Social History*, pp. 319–20.

112 Briggs, *Broadcasting*, Vol. 2, pp. 319–20.

113 Briggs, *Broadcasting*, vol. 2 (1965 edn), p. 318. The city's 2ZY was one of the 3 English stations licensed before 1922 and its history and experience made it a very suitable northern HQ.

114 John Coatman quoted in A. Briggs, 'Local and regional: the story of broadcasting in the north of England', in his *The Collected Essays of Asa Briggs, Vol. 3* (London: Harvester Wheatsheaf, 1991), p. 169.

115 *BBC Yearbook 1929*, pp. 99–101.

116 Scannell and Cardiff, *Social History*, p. 336. Their chapter 14 is obligatory reading.

117 Ibid., p. 339.

118 *Radio Times*, 8 March 1946. In contradistinction, the service opted out for only 90 minutes across the whole of the next day.

119 Briggs, 'Local and regional', p. 172.

120 *BBC Yearbook*, 1930, p. 106.
121 D. G. Bridson, *Prospero and Ariel* (London: Victor Gollancz, 1972), pp. 28–31, for an amusing but affectionate portrait; quoted in Scannell and Cardiff, *Social History*, pp. 339–40.
122 Bridson, *Prospero*, pp. 45–6.
123 Ibid., p. 56.
124 Scannell and Cardiff, *Social History*, pp. 342–4.
125 Ibid., pp. 353–4.
126 Ibid., pp. 344–8.
127 Ibid., 351–4. Gifford, *Golden Age*, p. 39.
128 Pickles, *Between You and Me*, pp. 174–95. The programme was attracting some 20 million listeners in the late 1940s. Ibid., p. 198.
129 *Radio Times*, 13 September 1946.
130 A. Foster and S. Furst, *Radio Comedy, 1938–1968* (London: Virgin Publishing, 1996).

5

Staging the North

Although live performance cannot attain the audience levels available to cinema, television and radio, it has nevertheless exerted an important and distinctive influence on popular perceptions of the North. Theatrical perform-ance both helped prepare the way for the mass technological media's representa-tion of northern affairs and provided cinema and television in particular with a rich source of material and personnel. The stage has also played a crucial part constructing the North in its own right. From the early twentieth century a sub-stantial body of northern comedians and a smaller but significant body of plays have heavily influenced the ways in which the region has been imagined. This chapter interprets 'the stage' very widely with the greatest attention given to the so-called 'legitimate theatre' but with space also found for the music hall and variety industries that were so fundamental to popular culture until the mid-twentieth century. Clearly, there have been many differences between the two areas in terms of style, content and audience base: put crudely, theatre has drawn a more middle-class clientele for much of the twentieth century, the period mainly surveyed here. However, there have also been numerous overlaps and the approach adopted here shows both the somewhat artificial nature of boundaries sometimes drawn between cultural forms and the mutually binding body of set characters, situations and locations that make up a recognisable 'North on stage'.

Stage geographies

To a greater extent than any other cultural area surveyed here – save, perhaps, music – the stage has been strikingly metropolitan in terms of its location of provision, personnel and artistic leadership. This was especially the case in regard to legitimate theatre in the century between the later 1860s, when the

London-based touring companies began to dominate the English theatre, and the emergence of 'regional theatre' (a new name for the by then tired concept of 'repertory') in the 1960s. There are certainly many counter-narratives even within this period.[1] The Leeds Grand Theatre, for example, opened in 1878 under the management of Wilson Barrett, gained a national reputation for the excellence of its pantomimes; special excursion trains from all over the North and Midlands drew 200,000 visitors to the 1886 production of *Sinbad*.[2] More fundamentally, the foundation of Miss Annie Horniman's Manchester Company in 1907 was the effective beginning of the British repertory theatre and stimulated a limited but important body of original drama that briefly allowed Manchester to emerge as a key locus for British drama.[3] While 'rep' lost much of its dynamic agenda over the next forty years, the establishment of the Arts Council in 1946 with its brief to stimulate art in the regions and the gradually increasing (although never adequate) funding that it and local authorities made available, saw a major resurgence of regional theatre from the early 1960s.[4] In the north-west alone, theatres such as the Manchester Library Theatre (1947), Liverpool Everyman (1964), Bolton Octagon (1967), Manchester Royal Exchange (1976) and the Oldham Coliseum (taken into local authority control in 1977) greatly increased opportunities for local actors and provided the crucial stimulus for local dramatists. Regional companies including Hull Truck Company (1971) and Halifax-based Northern Broadsides (1992) similarly galvanised British drama. Regional theatre has thus 'provided the decentralising nurturing of artistic strength and individuality and the focus for local cultural growth which has given the British theatre the vitality and variety for which it has become so internationally renowned'.[5] Thereby, it has been an important arena for a northern cultural fight back against the metropolitan core at several moments in the past and continuously since the 1960s, an issue returned to at the end of the chapter.

London has, of course, generally remained the nation's theatrical capital. In 1891, 41 per cent of the 7,321 'actors and actresses' listed in the census were found in London.[6] In the seven-county North, in a situation reminiscent of that explored later in regard to the music profession, Manchester was the best served, although with just 3.7 per cent of English and Welsh performers, closely followed by Liverpool. Even those theatrical figures with the strongest commitment to the North rarely remained there permanently or even for lengthy periods. Horniman maintained a London flat throughout her fourteen years with the Manchester Gaiety and several members of her company – including leading actor Charles Bibby, born and raised in Lancashire – did the same. Similarly, most northern and other provincial critics accepted that leading actors and actresses of the day were infrequent visitors. '[T]he best London acting scarcely concerns us. We are almost reconciled to the knowledge that our chance of making or renewing the company of [leading performers] is small, and that London claims them exclusively.'[7] While more opportunities of building a career in the North existed from the 1950s and 1960s, this long-established pattern remained basically unaltered. It was for good reason that almost 75 per cent of theatrical agencies were based in the capital in the 1990s.[8]

The cultural geography of the playwright suggests a further set of biases toward the South. Of the 116 twentieth-century British writers listed in one standard biographical guide, 34 per cent were born in London (and another 18 per cent in the South and south midlands) in comparison with 31 per cent from the more populous seven-county North.[9] While this is a rather more equal relationship than that already encountered in an earlier consideration of novelists and one to follow of composers, it is still an unbalanced one. Moreover, northern-born dramatists have often migrated to the capital to be closer to the centre of events. His work as a shipping merchant had already taken Harold Brighouse to London in 1902, but the writer of *Hobson's Choice* (1915) and emblem of the 'Manchester School' moved there permanently (and to Hampstead at that) in 1917. Although increased opportunity combined with a sense of obligation to their native region has allowed many recent writers to remain faithful to various provincial locations, even as an avowedly 'northern' figure as Jarrow-born, Hull-based Alan Plater (b. 1935) eventually found himself in London in the 1980s. 'After all that worthy stuff about living in an industrial community, here I am writing this paragraph in downtown N.W.3 … we grow older, we change, we pursue happiness and sometimes we find it.'[10]

These patterns were largely reproduced in the music-hall industry, although to a less pronounced degree.[11] In the nineteenth century, while permanent theatres tended to be found only in towns of approximately 30,000 people and upwards, music hall, which could embrace a remarkably wide range of locations from small pub concert rooms to large 3,000 seat variety palaces, was more widely spread. The constant round of touring that was the lot of all but a small minority of London-based stars meant that some leading northern performers found it just as convenient to live permanently in their native region as to move south. However, for all this and for all the important developments in the industry that were essentially pioneered in the provinces, most notably the emergence of the more self-consciously respectable 'variety' from the 1880s and

1890s, London remained its centre. It was the place that ambitious entrepreneurs, managers, agents and performers ultimately aspired to.

Representations of the North of England and its inhabitants were far less frequent on the nineteenth-century stage than in most other cultural arenas. In the music hall audiences certainly received at least some of their entertainment from representatives of the local and/or regional entertainment profession. Possibly because historians of Tyneside have been more diligent than others, we know most in this regard about the work of mid-Victorian singer/writers such as Ned Corvan, Geordie Ridley, Joe Wilson and others, whose dialect songs reported and constructed the culture of the north-eastern industrial working class with varying degrees of authenticity.[17] It is possible that Liverpool, textile Lancashire and the industrial West Riding had equivalent local traditions, although research is needed here. However, while such artists travelled beyond their immediate localities they do not seem to have established a presence across the whole seven-county North, let alone penetrate national networks. The North offered on the nineteenth-century music hall stage was for very much for local consumption and those northern-born comic singers who went in search of metropolitan success did so disguised as Scotsmen, Irishmen and even Cockneys.

The region probably had an even less of a presence on the legitimate stage. There is little evidence of a strong local or regional dialect drama before the twentieth century, although it certainly existed and systematic research is once again absent here. The nearest thing to a 'northern school' in this period is a thin strand of mainly Lancashire-based factory melodramas, not necessarily written by indigenous writers. This began around 1830 with such works as Douglas Jerrold's *Factory Girl* and John Walker's *The Factory Lad* (both 1832) and carried on throughout the century.[13] Performed both in the North and in London these plays are often interesting in terms of their portrayal of class relationships but typically of the melodrama as genre, they are little concerned with accurate depiction of place or regional character. In the context of this study, they are important only for helping encourage notions of textile Lancashire being co-terminous with the North in general and for some early examples of stock northern characters such as the virtuous mill lass and the 'lumbering Lancashire comic woman' as exemplified by the knockabout comic character Tiddy Dragglethorpe in Watts Phillips's *Lost in London* (1867).[14] Generally, however, London was the Victorian stage's favoured location and northern and other provincial characterisation was under-developed. While Edwardian playwright Stanley Houghton was hardly an impartial observer, it is hard not to concur with his view that what he termed mill girl plays 'were as romantic as *The Prisoner of Zenda* and as far removed from the truth'.[15]

Change occurred in both music hall and theatre in the Edwardian period, thus presenting a chronology rather different from that demonstrated by other cultural forms examined in this book. While this increased presence for the North on the stage might be read as resistance to the increasingly centripetal tug within national culture (the strength of the regional novel at this time was another possible contextual factor), it is more satisfying to see the process as stemming from essentially autonomous factors within the entertainments industry. Within music hall, or variety as it was increasingly termed, the period from about 1902–14 saw the rise to national prominence for a number of male comic singers including Lancastrians George Formby senior, Morny Cash and Tom Foy, and Yorkshiremen Jack Pleasants, Chas Whittle and Whit Cunliffe. Formby, the best known, was certainly gaining national popularity by the early years of the century; his bookings in 1903, albeit still as a middle-of-the-bill act, took him to all corners of the British Isles.[16] He became increasingly popular in London from about the same time, although Morny Cash, 'The Lancashire Lad', may have broken through in the capital before him. This increasingly high profile for northern comedians outside of their native territory most probably stemmed from the legitimisation of 'local' voices made possible by the success of the Cockney costermonger characters of the 1890s, most notably Albert Chevalier, Gus Elen and Joe Elvin, and the triumphal arrival in London in 1900 of Harry Lauder, not the first but certainly the most successful stage Scotsman to have reached London.[17] An industry always alert to new trends and 'fads' could now welcome and promote this latest manifestation of a regional distinctiveness that was obviously popular with audiences. While this first northern group hardly represented a major strand within the industry at this time, it was important both in its own right and in laying the basis for a vigorous future tradition. From the 1920s and 1930s, the variety stage, albeit in an ever less equal relationship with the parallel forms of radio, cinema and TV, produced a string of northern comedians including Billy Bennett, Gracie Fields, George Formby junior, Tommy Handley, Ken Dodd, Norman Evans, Morecambe and Wise and Les Dawson, who took their place at the pinnacle of the British comic tradition.[18]

Although the first flowering of an indigenous legitimate theatre paralleled these breakthroughs in variety, the two processes appear to have been unconnected. The key event in the dramatic field was the opening of Horniman's repertory company in Manchester in 1907, first in the Midland Hotel and then, from the following spring, at the Gaiety. Horniman, the London-born daughter of a tea merchant, had already emerged as a major theatrical patron, with £13,000 of her money making possible the building of Dublin's Abbey Theatre for the Irish Players in 1903. Inspired by its success and by the innovative programmes of London's Grand Theatre from 1904–7, and irritated by the conservative practices of the major West End and travelling companies, she determined to establish a theatre dedicated to the production of short runs of serious drama performed by a resident company of actors.[19] Manchester may have been chosen almost by default; stories have always persisted that Horniman would have sooner set up shop in London. Nevertheless, the Gaiety's first director, ex-Manchester Grammar pupil Ben Iden Payne, gave perfectly sensible reasons for choosing the city, not least its place in the 'centre of a vast population' and its pre-existing cultural reputation. The progressive Manchester Independent Theatre had survived from 1893–97 and this coupled with the city's rich musical tradition, allowed Payne to claim that 'we think there are more righteous men here – more of the faithful – than any place we know of'.[20] Once again, Manchester could claim cultural leadership over the rest of the North, with Horniman's venture providing long-lasting cultural capital in this regard. While the project was far from successful commercially and was essentially dead by 1917, its undoubted artistic successes and the subsequent high profile careers of Gaiety personnel such as Lewis Casson, Dame Sybil Thorndike and Basil Dean has led to generally celebratory treatment in much general literature about the city.

Horniman's policy of encouraging new writing brought into being the so-called 'Manchester School' and thus gave the North its first serious theatrical voice. The best-known writers both to contemporaries and later generations were Harold Brighouse (1882–1958), Stanley Houghton (1881–1913) and Allan Monkhouse (1858–1936), but others, including Gilbert Cannan and J. Sackville Martin, enjoyed some success in the Edwardian period. Houghton, whose *Hindle Wakes* (1912) was the Gaiety Company's first major commercial success, acknowledged his debt to Horniman in the clearest possible terms. 'I started to write expressly and absolutely for you; had the Gaiety not been there, I wouldn't have written a line.'[21] The geographical specificity of the 'Manchester School' should not be exaggerated. Many of Brighouse's plays, for example, were set in decidedly non-Lancastrian locations, while a number of plays set in Manchester and district were actually premiered and even commissioned elsewhere. *Hindle Wakes* opened in London (a probable factor in its initial success) and *Hobson's Choice* was first performed in America before enjoying a long

London season. Nevertheless, its most popular and lasting plays *were* essentially regional in setting and flavour and, as will be argued, these works were to help characterise and define the North in highly specific ways.

Not all writers have been sympathetic to the Manchester 'moment'. The critic James Agate, who had begun his career with the *Manchester Guardian*, argued that 'Houghton's *Hindle Wakes* was a bright flash in what turned out to be a very small pan, and Harold Brighouse never followed up *Hobson's Choice*. The only first-class work … was Allan Monkhouse's *Mary Broome*'.[22] While Agate was right to stress the relatively small scale of the Manchester School, it is difficult to see how the 'regional' play could ever have become a major strand within British theatre. As Harold Brighouse argued in the 1950s, this was partly a matter of prejudice within the London theatrical establishment, the ultimate arbiter of dramatic taste. 'I was essentially a regional author [and] the hard fact is that only exceptional merit, almost by once-in-a-lifetime merit can a regional play overcome London's Mayfair prejudice. Think of Barrie, Bennett, Mr Emlyn Williams – how long did they persist with the drama of Ayrshire, Staffordshire and Wales! … in London the dice are loaded against any but an outstanding regional play.'[23] There are (justifiable) echoes here of arguments aired in an earlier chapter about the inferior status of the regional novel within the literary canon. However, there were also fundamental structural factors deriving from the London-centredness of the theatrical industry that militated against regional projects. While the regional novelist had at least a regional audience to fall back on, without a patron such as the untypical Miss Horniman, the playwright ultimately depended on success in London. Moreover, West End audiences, managements and critics saw regional plays as an interesting addition to a standard theatrical diet rather than a constant ingredient not merely because of the 'Mayfair prejudice', but simply because full enjoyment of such plays sometimes benefited from local knowledge denied to them. As late as 1968, Alan Plater's *Close the Coalhouse Door*, a celebration of north-east mining culture that had enjoyed tremendous acclaim at the Newcastle Playhouse, was well-received at London's Fortune Theatre but left a number of critics feeling that the audience's relative ignorance about the play's context limited both its appeal and impact.[24]

These limiting factors along with the weakening creative power of the repertory movement, help explain why, especially in comparison with the novel, the inter-war period was a relatively thin one for the North in dramatic terms. The 1920s certainly saw a rich supply of rather formulaic one act plays such as *T' Trip to Blackpool*, *Fooils and their Brass* and *Anastasia and Nathaniel go*

Galivantin' to London, mainly aimed at northern amateur groups.[25] There were also further professional products from Manchester and elsewhere such as Walter Greenwood's collaboration with Ronald Gow on *Love on the Dole* (1934) and J.B. Priestley's one major 'Yorkshire play', the comedy *When we are Married* (1938) and his Yorkshire flavoured *Eden East* (1934) but, overall, there was little activity. The late 1940s and 1950s saw a steady trickle of plays including Greenwood's *The Cure for Love* (1945), a gentle comedy set in Salford in which the romance between London factory girl Milly Southern and local soldier Jack Hardacre binds North and South in an harmonious embrace so typical of the 'people's war' mentality. However, it was not until the late 1950s and early 1960s that a culturally significant (if still numerically small) body of northern plays emerged. For the first time, northern drama matched the growth rhythms of the North's other cultural forms, benefiting from and contributing to its new-found status and resonance. These new plays included both works which explored and were very clearly rooted in northern locales, such as Shelagh Delaney's *A Taste of Honey* (1958, Salford), Alun Owen's *Progress to the Park* (1959, Liverpool) and Keith Waterhouse and Willis Hall's dramatisation of *Billy Liar* (1960, the West Riding), and those by northern writers such as David Halliwell and David Storey for whom a northern setting or flavour was helpful but perhaps less central to their dramatic purpose. Perhaps significantly, the initial reinvigoration of northern-set plays came from the margins of British theatrical life, with both *A Taste of Honey* and *Progress to the Park* beginning life at Joan Littlewood's East End based Theatre Workshop, before transferring to the West End.[26] The period also saw a late flowering of the 'Manchester School' style with Bill Naughton's Lancashire family comedies *Spring and Port Wine*, first performed in Bolton in 1959 before becoming a London box-office success in 1965, and *All in Good Time* (1963).

The fact that the region has remained a fairly constant presence on the British stage from that point owes much to the demand from funding agencies that regional theatre serve local audiences and nurture local talent. Following the lead of the Liverpool Everyman's *Mersey Funnel* (1966) which set a trend for a 'local, musical documentary style', northern and provincial theatres began to produce the steady stream of plays exploring local and regional contexts (often with a focus on working-class culture) and that harnessed the talents of aspiring local writers.[27] The best of these broke through into national circulation and from then on, the work of Willy Russell, Alan Bleasdale, John Godber (whose sharply observed social comedies have been amongst the most popular northern-set dramas), James Robson, Andrea Dunbar, Jim Cartwright and others has made the northern play a vital element of the British theatre. Not all of these writers have concentrated solely on the North and few would see themselves as exclusively 'northern writers'. Russell has argued that Liverpool 'is the setting for [my] plays but is never the theme of them. Something like [*Educating*] *Rita* is played all over the world. I would like to think that beneath that veneer of dialect there is a universal truth.'[28] Whatever their views as to locality *versus* universality, the northern writers of the later twentieth century have, like their theatrical and music hall predecessors, contributed to the way in which those both inside and outside the North view the region.

The North on stage

The North seen on stage in the twentieth century has been a limited one with, as in fiction, mill-town Lancashire and Yorkshire providing the setting for most commercially successful plays and music-hall routines and the home of most nationally renowned northern comedians. Githa Sowerby's *Rutherford and Son* (1912), a powerful feminist analysis of relationships within a Tyneside manufacturing family, and Alan Plater's *Close the Coalhouse Door* (1968), are the only plays of national significance set within the north-east.[29] Similarly, north-eastern comedians have usually enjoyed regional rather than national reputations. Bobby Thomson (b. 1909), Tyneside's 'Little Waster', is a prime example here, revered in the north-east but never able to break through in the manner of many 'near northern' counterparts.

The pre-existing tradition of the mill girl drama; the location of Miss Horniman's repertory adventure and the sheer size and importance of Lancashire and Yorkshire both within the North and the national imagination, explain much of this limited stage geography. In terms of north-eastern exceptionalism the issue of accent has presumably added further barriers, although its minor role might also be an index of a more general marginalisation resulting from the region's distance from the centre. Whatever the causes, this narrow base has tended to obscure complex differences within the North and reinforce notions of homogenous urban unity. Some individual towns and cities have admittedly received specific attention as a result of their close association with particular writers and performers. Apart from Manchester and Salford, Liverpool, has been well served by comedians from the 1930s and, since the late 1950s, by playwrights Alun Owen, Willy Russell and Alan Bleasdale. John Godber has to some extent fulfilled a similar role for Hull from the 1970s, although perhaps more by his association with the Hull Truck Company than with any geographical specificity within his plays, and Andrea Dunbar for Bradford in the 1980s.

The North that audiences saw on stage was not only truncated geographically. Stock characters, images, plots and situations have combined to produce a very distinctive version of the region and one which has been surprisingly consistent over a long period. This is not to deny some important changes and especially those in legitimate drama that began in the late 1950s. *A Taste of Honey* is both indicative and formative in this regard, with its story of the relationships between a teenage girl and the black seaman by whom she becomes pregnant, the homosexual student who befriends her and her mother ('a semi-whore', the play script tells us). Here was the new subject matter, language and form which would increasingly mark the 'northern' play (and many others) as changed social and economic contexts, new theatrical styles and, from 1968, the abolition of censorship, allowed new representations to appear. For all of these changes, however, it is hard to escape the sense of a consistent image being generated both within the plays and the critical discourses surrounding them, certainly over the whole period to the 1960s and often beyond.

Put simply, the North on stage has been largely either a site of rich comedy or a place for the exploration of harsh social realities. The two were often present within the same play or comic routine, with the stage providing some of the most enduring contributions to the internal and external myth of northerners as people with an infinite capacity to soften or deflect hardship through laughter. For present purposes, however, the two strands are treated separately. The association of the North with humour is hardly surprising given its rich tradition of comedians and comic actors. While London has probably always been the largest single producer of leading English comedians in the nineteenth and twentieth centuries, the seven-county North, led by Lancashire and Yorkshire, has been only slightly behind.[30] At the same time, comedy has made up much of the best and most popular of the North's legitimate drama from *Hobson's Choice* onward. Equally important has been the willingness of external observers and the indigenous population to celebrate northern humour. Journalistic reference to the 'hard school' of the northern club circuit as a fountainhead of twentieth-century British comedy became a cliché only rivalled by references to the sporting riches that could be summoned up merely by whistling down a Yorkshire pit shaft. Some cities have enthusiastically claimed and often had conceded to them a particular reputation for sharp humour, with Liverpool taking great pride in having 'the best comedians' and the quickest of wits. Liverpool was in fact a relative latecomer to the *national* comic stage. The cluster of stars such as Arthur Askey, Rob Wilton, Deryck Guyler and, above all, Tommy Handley who were made essentially by radio as much as live performance in the 1930s and 1940s, were running three decades behind George Formby senior and his contemporaries.[31]

Whatever the realities of cultural production, the overall strength of the northern comic tradition further heightened and exaggerated by journalistic convention and popular belief rendered the North the place that made the nation smile. One of the most revealing examples of the North's close association with comedy was Londoner Stanley Holloway's adoption of Yorkshire and Lancashire accents respectively for his enormously popular Sam Small (1929–41) and Albert Ramsbottom (1932–40) monologues. While a desire for novelty partly fuelled this decision, Holloway and his Scottish and southern-born writers were clearly tapping into a national consensus around such characteristics as the canniness of northern folk ('I think it's a shame and a sin/for a lion to eat Albert/and after we've paid to come in') and the 'natural' comic potential of the region.[32]

There is clearly no one single style of northern humour. Simply within Lancashire Jeffrey Richards has usefully distinguished between the slow-building, anecdotal, character-based humour associated with comedians and writers in textile Lancashire and the faster, more surreal, patter-based style of Liverpool. This cannot be definitive or binding; Richards is forced to describe Rob Wilton as 'Liverpool-born but Lancashire in delivery, pace and characterisation'.[33] Nevertheless, although there is not space to pursue intra-regional difference at length here, there are fertile ways ahead in this kind of analysis. One of the most persistent comic characters, omni-present until at least the 1970s and glimpsed even beyond that, seems to have been clearly associated with textile Yorkshire and Lancashire and especially the latter. The 'daft' or 'soft' lad, the 'Lancashire loon', was certainly present within dialect literature – John Hartley had a story of young man so embarrassed to admit to his Blackpool landlady that he was on honeymoon that he spent it apart from his wife – but it both matured and reached a far wider audience in the Edwardian period via both music hall and legitimate theatre.[34]

The classic music-hall characterisation of this type was George Formby senior's 'John Willie', developed in the 1890s. Formby entered the stage, coughing mightily (his cough was turned to brilliant comic effect but it was a symptom of a disease that killed him at age 45 in 1922) and dressed in an ill-fitting suit with trousers and arms slightly too short, overlarge boots, a bowler perched on his head and a muffler. His advertising material stressed that, in the words of one of his songs, he was 'Fair Gawmless'; one publicity still shows him with a luggage label attached to his jacket.[35] Various publicity slogans forged a unbreakable link between his peculiarities and his adopted home town of Wigan (he was born in Ashton-under-Lyne), variously describing himself as 'a quaint comedian, all the way from Wigan'; George Formby, better known as 'Wigan' and, most famously and most ironically, 'the Wigan Nightingale'. Outside of Lancashire, his act often opened with the line 'Good evening, I'm Formby from Wigan … I've not been in England long.'[36] His songs and patter, delivered absolutely deadpan irrespective of audience response, dealt mainly with the adventures of a Lancastrian innocent on the loose. The delights of London provided the setting for some of his best known songs such as 'John Willie Come on', and 'Playing the Game in the West', which concluded with the memorable line, 'And I'm not going home 'til a quarter to ten, 'cause it's my night out'.[37] Importantly, however, George invariably won out, accident or design showing him not to be 'the biggest mug in town' that many Londoners took 'The Man from Lancashire' to be.[38]

While Formby was possibly the most overtly and relentlessly 'northern' comedian, several came close. Morny Cash, billed as the 'Lancashire Lad', used similarly ill-fitting stage attire and performed such songs as 'You Must Hear All and You Must say Nowt', and 'Stick to my hand, Penelope' which dealt with provincial ingénues in similar situation to John Willie. Yorkshire's Chas W. Whittle had as his signature song 'Billy Muggins (commonly known as a juggins)', while Jack Pleasants developed the character of the bashful Yorkshire lover, most famously paraded in 'I'm shy Mary Ellen, I'm shy' (1911).[39] Although these and later comedians used many different comic styles, 'daftness' clearly proved enormously popular with audiences and became a stock-in-trade for a line of northern comedians from George Formby junior, who borrowed large chunks of his father's act and personae and added the ingredient of sexual innuendo, through in the 1950s to Ken Platt ('I won't take me coat off, I'm not stopping'), some of Al Read's characters ('Ha-Ha-Ha- Hallo') and Danny Ross's portrayal of the hapless Alfie Hall in BBC radio's *Clitheroe Kid*. It died out in stand up comedy only in the 1970s and 1980s, too dated for the new generation of comedians, although it continued to surface in film and situation comedy.

In the theatre, the comic adumbrations of Formby and others received a more developed treatment. The key figure here was Harold Brighouse, who produced a line of memorable 'soft' lads between 1911 and 1916. Like their music-hall counterparts they were puny or physically rather ill formed, child-like, shy and inarticulate but, with the help of an observant and good woman, capable of triumph. Brighouse's first such product was Sam Horrocks, 'a hulking young man of rather vacant expression', who appeared in the one-act play *Lonesome-Like*, premiered by the Glasgow Repertory Company in 1911.[40] (The play remained popular well into the 1950s when it was televised with Wilfred Pickles as Sam.) Sam begins with a pitifully inadequate wooing of sharp-tongued mill lass Emma Brierley.

> Emma: What's tha' getting' at Sam Horrocks? Tha's got a tongue in thy faice, hasn't tha'?
> Sam: A suppose so. A doan't use it much though.

Unsurprisingly jilted by Emma, the lonesome Sam eventually accepts that talking to young women makes me 'ot' and cowld all over' and instead 'adopts' the aged and workhouse-threatened Sarah Ormerod, whose nagging reminds him affectionately of the verbal abuse he received from his deceased mother; 'by gum, she could sling it at a feller if 'er tea weren't brewed to taste'.[41]

Sam was in many ways a dry run for Will Mossop, the boothand in *Hobson's Choice*, 'a lanky fellow, about thirty, not naturally stupid but stunted mentally by a brutalised childhood. He is raw material of a charming man, but, at present, it requires a very keen eye to detect his potentialities'.[42] That eye is provided by Maggie, eldest daughter of domineering boss Horatio Hobson, under whose firm but loving guidance he gains in self-respect and confidence, rising to be master of his own shop with the defeated Hobson as the most somnolent of sleeping partners. Brighouse to a degree reprised Will Mossop in *Zack* (1916), the story of Zachariah Munning, a joiner much put upon by his immediate family and perilously close to having to marry a girl he has courted out of pure sympathy.

> Zack: I know I kissed her, but it wasn't a meaning kiss. She was blubbing and she wouldn't hush and so I kissed her like I'd kiss a baby to console it.
> Mr Wrigley: You kissed her. That's enough.
> Zack: But it weren't for pleasure, Mr Wrigley. She was too wet.[43]

Zack's true worth is eventually realised and the marriage averted by the arrival and love of Virginia, his distant cousin.

Brighouse's creations of the 1910s represent the soft Lancashire lad at his apotheosis but as with the music-hall variant, the character remained strong well into the twentieth century. The nervous Arthur, would-be husband of Florence Crompton in Bill Naughton's *Spring and Port Wine* (1959) who eventually gains the confidence both to win the hand of the apparently half-hearted

Florence and stand up to her bullying father, has clear echoes of Will Mossop. Perhaps more surprisingly, so too does Billy the phone repair man in Jim Cartwright's *The Rise and Fall of Little Voice* (1992). One reviewer shrewdly saw this play as at times 'oddly reminiscent of the north-country comedy of an earlier era' and there is little doubt that versions of the shy youngster, whose love for Little Voice allows her to stop living through the voices of the singers she has learnt to impersonate via her dead father's record collection and find her own, had been on stage before. 'I should be up a telegraph pole three streets away, but I came here. I don't know what to say now. I'm like it at work. Then when I do speak they all jump like I've dropped a brick in a bucket.'[44]

These gentle, sometimes slightly foolish yet lovable and attractive characters have been by no means the only northern comic males on offer. The eccentric, the self-opinionated (Al Read's 'Johnny Know-all') and the cheeky (Jimmy Clitheroe) are all easy to find along. So too is the soft lad's anthithesis, the curmudgeonly patriarch embittered or bemused by life. Here, Horatio Hobson bemoans his daughters' spiritedness: 'I felt grateful for the quiet when my Mary fell on rest, but I can see my mistake now. I used to think I was hard put to fend her off when she wanted summat out of me, but the dominion of one woman is Paradise to the dominion of three.'[45] Nevertheless, the soft lad is worthy of particular attention, and not least because he compares so strikingly with the angry young men of post-war literature, the 'hard men' of sporting legend and similar tougher, harder personages that inhabit other areas of the imagined northern landscape. There is a gentler North here and these characterisations of it perhaps owed some of their popularity to the appeal they had for women. Unthreatening, loyal and increasingly confident and competent characters such as Will Mossop, exaggerated versions of the 'ordinary chap' that many women might hope to settle down with, were in their own way oddly romantic, offering emotional security and certainty. While a universal comic character undoubtedly lurked behind the regional accent, it is certainly tempting to see reflections of the realities of life in the textile communities that were so often the setting for these stage representations. In the relationship between a guiding hand like Maggie Hobson's and the struggling Will Mossop, there was arguably recognition of a society that provided women with relatively high opportunities for wage-earning and very considerable domestic power. This issue of Lancastrian matriarchy will returned to shortly.

Women themselves were afforded comic status in various guises. Women music hall and variety comedians have been fewer than their male equivalents – exceptions such as Gracie Fields or Hylda Baker tended to come to national prominence in other arenas – but the theatre provided many rich characterisations. 'Low-life' characters, usually servants or neighbours with a penchant for alcohol and a permanent shortage of cash feature in many plays, providing comic colour in their own right but also functioning as either a counterpoise to a more virtuous individual or as commentator on the morés of social betters. Mrs Northrop the cook in Priestley's *When we are Married,* a comedy centring on the shockwaves that flow from the discovery that three eminent Cleckleywyke couples might not be legally married, exemplifies the genre. Enjoying mightily the opportunity to deflate the pretensions of the three wives 'trying to look like duchesses…trying to swank', she reminds them of their humble origins. 'I remember when you were Maria Fawcett an' you were nobbut a burler and mender at Barkinson's … And as for you [Clara Soppitt] – I remember time when you were weighin' out apples and potatoes in your father's greengrocer's shop … an' a mucky little shop it were an' all.'[46]

Perhaps more explicitly northern (usually Lancastrian) were two closely related characters, the strong mother and the independent, determined young woman often conveniently labelled the 'Lancashire lass'. The long-suffering 'stout, cheerful little Lancashire woman, with a rough edge to her tongue when wanted', as Ronald Gow described his Mrs Lovejoy in *Ma's Bit of Brass* (1938), was present almost from the earliest days of 'northern' drama until the 1950s and 1960s.[47] Her function was to hold families together at difficult times and to work hard to encourage suitable marriages and prevent unsuitable ones.

> Mrs Metherall; How did you bring her up?
> Edmund Whitworth: As a lady.
> Mrs Metherall: Then she's handicapped for life. But I've seen some grow out of it.

Thus the mother of football star Jack Metherall begins to test the suitability of a candidate for her son's hand in Harold Brighouse's sporting comedy, *The Game* (1913).[48] Gow's Mrs Lovejoy wins £500 on the pools and rearranges her family's life much to the consternation of husband George who can only offer the plaintiff, 'Here hold on! I haven't been consulted, you know'. Inevitably, her plans to open a rural café prove highly successful with happy consequences all round. Interestingly, this empowering characterisation was commonplace in the interwar period one-act plays aimed at amateurs, suggesting some local affinity for such representations. Although examples of the powerful mother figure can still be found in the later twentieth, changed sexual politics altered the character somewhat. While Mrs Gow's power comes from her skilful deployment of a traditional, family-centred role that she happily accepts, Willy Russell's eponymous

Shirley Valentine (1986), for example, gains hers from an increasingly confident challenge to the position her family has assigned to her.

The witty, shrewd 'Lancashire lass' (often the sharp-tongued mother in training) was both a necessary romantic counterpoise to the Willie Mossops of the world and a dynamic character in her own right. Probably the finest dramatic creation of this type was Brighouse's Maggie Hobson, whose forceful personality is the engine that drives *Hobson's Choice*.

> Maggie: I've watched you for a long time and everything I've seen, I've liked. I
>   think you'll do for me.
> Willie: What way, Miss Maggie?
> Maggie: Will Mossop, you're my man. Six months I've counted on you, and it's got
>   to come out some time.
> Wille: But I never …
> Maggie: I know you never, or it 'ud not be left to me to do the job like this.
> Willie: I'll- I'll sit down. *(sits)* I'm feeling queer like. What dost thou want me for?
> Maggie: To invest in. You're a business idea in the shape of a man.
> Willie: I've got no head for business.
> Maggie: But I have. My brain and your hands 'ull make a working partnership.
> Willie: *(getting up relieved)* Partnership! Oh, that's a different thing. I thought you
>   were axing me to wed you.
> Maggie: I am.[49]

This character, well suited to modern sensibilities, lasted far longer than many stock figures. Willy Russell's Rita, for all her nervousness and awkwardness at the start of her Open University education, has a sharpness and an ability to draw strength from her own culture that echoes some of her earlier stage sisters.

Central to both figures was a great stoicism, with their humour helping to alleviate personal difficulties while simultaneously shining through them. Forbearance, unflappability, lack of 'fuss', these words have been frequently cited in lists of the northern (especially the Yorkshire and Lancashire) stereotype, and it is interesting that in fictional and dramatic representations, much of the burden here is carried by women. The 'Lancashire lass' is also marked out by an appetite for hard work and a refusal to be deterred by setbacks. One of the earliest and most characteristic statements of this type is that uttered by Houghton's Fanny Hawthorn, the young woman whose willing sexual dalliance with a mill owner's son forms the dramatic and at the time highly controversial context to *Hindle Wakes*. Rejecting the young man's offer of help after the disgrace leaves her homeless, she tells him, 'I'm not without a trade at my finger tips, thou knows. I'm a Lancashire lass, and so long as there's weaving sheds in Lancashire I shall earn enough brass to keep me going.'[50] Echoes of Fanny's sentiment and character could still be heard in the late 1950s in the form of Jo's proud boast in *A Taste of Honey* that her flat is 'mine. All mine' despite having 'to work all day in a shoe shop and all night in a bar to pay for it'; and in 1980, through the hard work in the background of *Educating Rita* that funds the eponymous heroine's academic efforts.[51] A shop assistant and a hairdresser respectively, these two characters lack Fanny's closely rooted occupational specificity but they are northern/Lancashire lasses of their day, attitude and demeanour keeping an important tradition alive.

The strong women and the matriarchal structures suggested here were obviously not universal. Sowerby's *Rutherford and Son* powerfully evokes a patriarch who crushes the life and spirit out of the women (and men) around him. Although ultimately realising and repenting his sins, Rafe Crompton in Bill Naughton's *Spring and Port Wine* (1966) dominates and bullies his 'Lancashire lass' daughter Hilda, his wife Daisy and the rest of the family to the point where it almost breaks apart. Nevertheless, they are a constant and significant presence. Jeffrey Richards has argued with some conviction that their presence in the popular culture of Lancashire (and the North and Lancashire are often coterminous in the theatrical context) is a reflection of the matriarchal nature of the north west, brought about by the social ramifications of the relatively high level of female employment in the textile industry.[52] Whatever the exact link between culture and context, they clearly became highly effective stock figures, able to carry a great deal of dramatic weight in terms of plot development and to serve as a positive, at times almost utopian model of women with power in the household and in their own lives.

At one level, the wide-ranging celebration of the North as a place of laughter resulted in a most pleasing and positive public image. The North in the national imagination could be warm and witty as well as grim, even if the grimness and the laughter were sometimes intimately connected. However, there was always the risk that the region would become not just a place from which comics and comedy came, but, of itself, a comic place. This is literally what happened to Wigan. In the late twentieth century when the town was trying to reinvent itself, most of the blame for its long established reputation as a national joke was laid at the feet of Orwell's *The Road to Wigan Pier* (1937). In fact, Wigan's status was established long before Orwell arrived to find a full chamber pot under the lodging house breakfast table. Formby senior was probably initially the most culpable. His endless references to the town and his tales of 'Wigan Pier' – a tip-up mechanism for coal trucks on the canal side thus ironically nicknamed by locals in the 1890s – were amusing to a local population which could share the joke, but outsiders were always likely to take such humour at a far more superficial and damaging level.

Wiganisms subsequently became a minor sub-genre of British writing. It is no coincidence that Wigan was chosen by H. V. Morton as the site for his brief foray into 'Black England' in his *In Search of England* (1927) and he was clearly well aware that the 'words "Wigan Pier" spoken by a comedian on a music-hall stage are sufficient to make an audience howl with laughter'. In the same year, the sporting comic *Football Favourite* included in one of its tales one Aubrey Nott, 'the ugliest full back in the world' and who is introduced to his colleagues with the words 'he may not be an art plate, and it's true he comes from Wigan'. Two years later, when Wigan Rugby League Club set off to London for the first Challenge Cup Final to be held at Wembley, the captain expressed a determination to show that something more than a joke could came out of the town. As late as 1949, a football manager could introduce into his autobiography, *a propos* of not very much, a gag in which a railway passenger stating that he wants to go to the town is told by the booking clerk, 'you're a liar – you've got to go'.[53] This is an extreme and specific case, but it is a salutary one. The North's comic writing, comic actors and comedians were amongst its greatest products and its most valued emissaries but they carried a double-edged sword.

The association of the northern stage with social issues has also brought mixed blessings, particularly in the legitimate theatre. Although there were exceptions, most northern plays have been informed by some degree of social realism. As a result, one of the more positive virtues claimed for them has been a supposed honesty and authenticity. Patterns of speech have been important here. Most writers have admittedly eschewed full-scale dialect writing, preferring instead a demotic speech that captures the essence of the regional voice without demanding too much of 'external' audiences and, indeed, of some actors. The accents offered to audiences have often been approximations rather than genuine articles or closely observed reproductions. Until Barrie Rutter founded Northern Broadsides in 1992 in order to perform drama (mainly Shakespeare) in northern voice, no company had a policy of recruiting actors solely from the North; even Horniman's Gaiety Company was sometimes linguistically embarrassed. Its production of J. Sackville West's *A Question of Property* (1908), consciously a dialect piece, led one local paper to note with obvious pleasure that 'there were flaws in the pronunciation of the patois, bits of Cockney creeping in, and the "yons", "tha's", "aw's" and "i's", "mecks" and "macks" not always squaring with the canons of Waugh and Brierley.' Sixty years later, Alan Plater still had to plead with would-be performers of his *Close the Coalhouse Door* that certain characters '*must* have convincing Geordie accents'.[54]

Nevertheless, the sound of these plays added much to their sense of fidelity and became central to journalistic and critical discourses celebrating the region's energy, rawness and power to stimulate. As has been frequently argued in this book, the North has periodically been celebrated as a purifying and cleansing force whose function is to rejuvenate and refresh the tired metropolis specifically, and the national culture more generally. One of the earliest and most striking examples of this can be seen in the reaction to the initial London run of *Hindle Wakes* in 1912. In a revealing notice, *The Times* saw the play as 'the real, rugged article' that was much needed on the London stage.

> Despite its cynicism and occasional grossness, the play won favour by the truthfulness of its homely detail and the sincerity of its players. Change of air is a tonic inside, no less than outside, the theatre; and it is refreshing to get away from the familiar stage morality and stage-language. By and by, no doubt, these angular, rough-tongued Lancashire ways will become conventions like another; but for the moment in London, at any rate, they are an agreeable novelty[55]

A reviewer in *The Lady* saw not just the play but the nature and style of the acting as providing a much-needed lesson to London companies.

> It is doubtful if any London company could give so perfect a performance as these people with their queer, raw dialect, their ugly clothes, and their prim manners. A West End company would want to 'act' in *Hindle Wakes*. Miss Horniman's company do not give the impression of 'acting': they seem to be living their parts, truest of all true art.[56]

Notions of the region as 'genuine' and lacking artifice, so important to regional self-image, were here accepted, almost cherished, in the wider arena. This is an important reminder that even at the moment when a southern-centred Englishness was increasingly powerful within the national culture, the North could find a space and serve an important function. That space would be only be briefly occupied and inhabiting it involved carrying labels ('homely', 'rough-tongued', 'queer') that reinforced long-standing notions about the region. This move of the periphery toward the core is nevertheless significant.

Northern drama fulfilled this rejuvenating role at other moments across the twentieth century. In the late 1950s and 1980s respectively, Salford's Shelagh Delaney and Bradford's Andrea Dunbar, both young, working-class women writers with no formal experience of the theatre, were acknowledged for bringing a kind of raw energy to the stage. Here was the dramatist as insider turned anthropologist, Delaney offering 'tribal rites interpreted by a genuine

cannibal', Dunbar serving as 'the bard of the West Riding council estate jungle'.
[57] While their class and gender was probably of more interest than their geographical origin, the North was once again associated with new trends and currents. In the 1990s, Northern Broadsides's highly successful Shakespeare
productions were celebrated in their turn in a language remarkably close to that
used of the Manchester School. *Richard III*, for example, was seen variously as
'earthy', 'harsh,' and pervaded by 'a gritty industrial atmosphere' while the company was complimented for pulling Shakespeare 'out of the grasp of the
Islington luvvies back into the real world'.[58] The fact that the company regularly
performed in industrial spaces, used discarded industrial equipment for props
and spoke exclusively in northern accents obviously makes these statements
understandable and to a substantial degree accurate. The continuity of a very
particular discourse across the century is, however, revealing.

The moments when the regional connected with the national were, of
course, sporadic and short-lived. The 'North' was a place to whistle up when
certain aspects of English (or British culture) needed stiffening or jolting, but at
most times it occupied a less exalted and privileged position. It could be just too
foreign. Harold Brighouse claimed that he once heard a member of London
audience greet a comment that Edyth Goodall, then playing Maggie in *Hobson's
Choice*, was from Lancashire, with the rejoinder 'Oh no! She is really quite
English.'[59] Moreover, the very features found within northern plays that sometimes excited critics were also those that ran the risk of reinforcing more negative representations of the region. As in other cultural areas, the theatre had the
capacity to make the North unattractive because 'real life' tended to take place
there.

Initially, this stemmed partly from the simple fact that the Manchester
School brought working-class characters on to the serious stage in larger numbers than hitherto. Moreover, although most Gaiety plays were not in any significant sense concerned with 'social problems', the controversy that
surrounded the sexual politics of *Hindle Wakes* in particular (Allan Monkhouse's
Mary Broome (1911) also dealt with sexual relationships between a middle-class
male and a working-class woman of independent spirit), may well have had the
effect of linking 'northern' drama with a realism that was uncomfortable for
many. This became more problematic from the late 1950s as a body of plays
emerged which consciously engaged with contemporary social issues and daily
life. As ever, critical discourses and plot descriptions were crucial here, with far
more people reading about plays than actually going to watch them. *A Taste of
Honey* was 'tough, humourous and close to the ground', it's dialogue 'redolent

of the Lancashire back streets'. Alun Owen's *Progress to the Park* was, according to one headline, a 'Slice of Liverpudlian Religious Bigotry'. In the 1980s, Jim Cartwright's *Road* (1986) was a 'nightmare reworking of *Coronation Street*' and 'a northern *Under Milk Wood*, high on booze and pills'.[60] The plays themselves, of course, provided plentiful evidence of a quintessential northern coarseness for those who sought it. A good example is provided by the character of Mari, mother of Little Voice, in Cartwright's 1992 eponymous play. Played originally by Alison Steadman as 'a nightmare in glittering nylon tat', she marks her entry to one scene by drunkenly vomiting in the sink and in another, shows an marvellously inelegant gift for sensing and expressing romantic attraction. When describing her initial reaction to theatrical impresario Ray Say she observes, 'when I first spied him, I knew there was summat down for us. I just had that twat-bone feeling, and you know me, I can predict rain with that.' Later, she and Ray enjoy the following exchange.

> Mari: You have a wisdom, Ray. Also, you know what to say in many situations, also you know how to have a laugh, dress and drive. Also you have a fair sized dong. I'm glad I made your acquaintance.
> Ray: I'm going for a slash.[61]

The North's close association with harsher realities was enhanced in the 1980s by a number of works dramatising the social group increasingly termed the 'underclass'. The poor had always been with us, usually in somewhat beery, tragic-comic form and in fairly minor roles. From the early 1980s, however, as the impact of mass unemployment became obvious, the dispossessed became a key feature of some contemporary drama. This was prefigured in 1980, when Willy Russell's Rita observed to her Open University tutor that, 'I've read about [working-class culture]. I've never seen it though … I just see everyone pissed, or on the valium, tryin' to get from one day to the next.'[62] Over the next decade, in the hands of Jim Cartwright, Andrea Dunbar (*The Arbor* (1980), *Rita, Sue and Bob Too* (1982) and *Shirley* (1986)), Alan Bleasdale *On the Ledge* (1993) and others, they moved from noises off to centre stage. Representation of these 'victims of monetarism' as one reviewer termed the characters in *Road*, were obviously to be found in many other cultural arenas, most notably in fiction, film and television, which reached far greater audiences.[63] Perhaps the specific function of these stage representations was to bring a version of northern life to audiences that gained power from the intimacy that is the special ingredient of live performance. This analysis not intended to serve as moral criticism or to deny the theatrical craft and often mordant humour of Cartwright and others.

Neither is it suggested here that the North was the only part of Britain that saw its characters being projected in this way. However, given the long established image of the region as rough, untutored and uncouth, as with the case of comedy discussed earlier, such representations had the potential to reinforce existing external stereotypes of the region in ways that were ultimately unhelpful. Moreover, the plays themselves were always likely to be naturalised within pre-existing discourses surrounding the North, thus risking the denial of the very considerable body of imaginative achievement that they represented.

Theatres of identity

The stage provided one more important place in which northerners could set or compare themselves against other parts of the country. These processes usually took place at the level of the 'imaginary' in the sense of the consideration and contemplation of plot and character, rather than through any direct engagement with actual representatives of other regions. Some histories of music hall have certainly implied an intrinsic hostility to 'Cockney' stars amongst northern audiences. Marie Lloyd, for example, was supposedly 'never loved outside of London', apparently received the 'bird' for the first time in Sheffield and reputedly had rivets thrown at her in one northern location.[64] These isolated incidents may have happened (hard evidence is never presented) but press reports suggest that Lloyd was actually generally well received in the North. During a provincial tour in 1904 she received a 'hearty reception' in Bradford, a 'phenomenal' one in Liverpool and drew 'enormous houses' in Oldham.[65] While some southern performers clearly failed to reproduce their popularity in the North – Max Miller in the 1930s and 1940s is a case in point – there was no blanket rejection or set response.

The stage in all its guises certainly provided a number of possibilities for the negotiation of North-South rivalries and tensions. The provincial innocent on the loose in the metropolis discussed above was (in terms of northern consumption) a generally empowering music-hall figure in the Edwardian period and many other performers have since found ways of putting the capital in its place. Comedian Chubby Brown's observation that 'It's an exciting place, London. I mean, we've all got sewers but who thinks to put fucking trains in them', perhaps captures something of the bitterness that could edge in to such activity during the 1980s and early 1990s. In the dramatic field, while some plays such as *Hobson's Choice* work so well partly because they occupy an entirely closed geographical space and many others have been little concerned with metropolitan issues,

London is often waiting in the wings, sending new arrivals onto the stage and drawing other characters back from it.

Because action is so rarely set in the capital, plays about the North and northerners cannot give quite the depth to discussion of provincial-metropolitan relationships that can be found in novels but it is nevertheless present. Given that many playwrights have experienced the contradictory pulls of region and capital, it is no surprise that the problems and possibilities of 'going south' have been central in this regard. In the plays of the earlier twentieth century when provincial culture was still relatively confident of its ability to match that of the metropolis, drama provided determined statements of regional self-sufficiency. Stanley Houghton's character sketch of millowner's son Allan Jeffcote in his *Hindle Wakes* clearly articulates this complexly layered self-confidence.

> London he looks upon as a place where rich Lancashire men go for a spree if they have not time to go to Monte Carlo or Paris. Manchester he looks upon as the centre or headquarters for Lancashire manufacturers, and therefore more important than London. But after all he thinks that Manchester is merely the office for Hindle and the other Lancashire towns which are the source of wealth. Therefore Hindle, Blackburn, Bolton, Oldham and the rest are far more important in his eyes than London and Manchester, and perhaps he is right.[66]

Again, while Brighouse's football comedy *The Game* (1913) compresses a quite complex debate about northern culture into a brief and humorous exchange between youthful would-be poet Leo Whitworth and his émigré uncle, it is the latter's gentle refusal to concede to the young man's assumption of London's supremacy that has arguably the greatest resonance.

> Leo: You will speak to them [his family] for me uncle? They'll listen to you ... At least you come from London, where people are civilised.
> Edmund: Are they? In London I hold a brief for the culture of the provinces.
> Leo: You took jolly good care to get away from the provinces, yourself. And you mustn't tell me you think Blackton is cultured.
> Edmund: I heard my first Max Reger sonata in Blackton long before London had found him.
> Leo: Music's another matter.
> Edmund: Yes, your father played it to me.
> Leo: Well, there you are again. Music and football are the only things he cares about. That's just what I complain of. I've tried to raise his tastes, but I find generally a lack of seriousness in men of his age.[67]

The relatively limited body of northern-based drama in the inter-war period neither kept this kind of defence alive or indulged in the regional advocacy that was so prominent within the field of literature. A broadly comic note was the one more likely to be sounded, as in Priestley's *When we are Married*, an affectionately nostalgic evocation of 'various aspects of West Riding life and manners known to my boyhood'.[68] Joe Helliwell and Albert Parker's attack on their southern-born chapel organist was beautifully crafted but certainly had little of the bite that can sometimes be seen in other contemporaneous fields.

> Helliwell: Young Forbes is a southerner an' all.
> Parker: *(with grim triumph)* Ah – I was coming to that…No, as soon as they told
>   me he's a southerner and his name's Gerald, I said: 'We don't want him'. I said:
>   'La-di-dah. That's what you're going to get from him' I said. 'La-di-dah. What
>   we want at Lane End – biggest chapel for miles – wi' any amount o' money in
>   the congregation – what we want is a bit o' good old Yorkshire organ-playing
>   and choir training', I said. 'We don't want la-di-dah'…
> Helliwell: Mind you, he'd good qualifications, an' he seemed a nice quiet lad. But
>   I must say, after old Sam Fawcett, chapel didn't seem right with an organist
>   who goes round wearing one o' those pink shirts and knitted ties and creases in
>   his trousers.[69]

From about 1960, the provincial-metropolitan conflict once again became a serious issue in drama precisely because it was becoming a personal one for many young dramatists. As in literature, London was disruptive hinting at new opportunities and fuller, supposedly richer lives elsewhere although only rarely was it portrayed as uncomplicated cornucopia and then usually only for purposes of plot or character development. In *Educating Rita*, for example, Rita's trip to a summer school in London provides a short (and off stage) but important acceleration in her move to a more independent and self-confident state. Her comment to her tutor Frank that it was 'fantastic. Honest it was – ugh!', captures a necessary moment of personal excitement rather than a common view of the capital. More typically it was a place of confusion where the balance sheet measuring gain and loss was hard to draw. In Owen's *Progress to the Park* bright, working-class scholarship-boy Teifion, back home in Liverpool for a visit, depicts the capital as a place where provincial identity (in this case, a hugely exaggerated north Walian identity) can help find work as a TV scriptwriter, where working-class roots attracts a supply of sexually available middle-class women and where there is at last respite from the excessive passion and religious division of his native city. At the same time, when there he misses Liverpool's level of caring about things 'mad things, wicked things silly things … Everyone down there is so tolerant and withdrawn to the point of religious excess but if a fella's a pacifist up here, he'll beat the living beejesus out of anyone to prove it.' Ultimately he is torn between the city he has left and the one he has adopted. 'Yesterday I was walking down Fleet Street, I had me ticket but I had serious doubts if Liverpool even existed … and now I'm beginning to wonder if London's still there.'[70]

By the 1990s, notes of bitter disappointment and even betrayal can be found. London is enemy territory for young Liverpudlian character 'Upright' in Bleasdale's *On the Ledge*, a place 'where y' fuckin' accent stands up in court and pleads guilty on y' behalf. No wonder the bastard cockneys call it y' North and South.'[71] The trajectory from a self-confident provincial culture alternately irritated and fascinated by London, to one in which the capital can in some instances be genuinely despised that this account suggests, is probably too neat. Nevertheless, it captures and perhaps helped define a major late twentieth-century relationship between core and periphery.

The stage has undoubtedly contributed to a sense of northern pride and self-consciousness, although probably rather more at the local and sub-regional level than across the North as a whole. When Formby senior performed before the King at a private concert in 1913, he declared himself proud 'to represent Lancashire, as a Lancashire comedian' and there is little doubt that many in the county were delighted to have him as their representative. Leading variety artists and stand up comedians have been amongst the most widely celebrated champions of northern culture, clear evidence of the claims made within the region, or its constituent parts, for the special gift of humour.[72] The legitimate stage largely lacked sufficient popular base to operate in quite such a way, although key episodes such as the success of the Manchester Gaiety have become embedded in local historical consciousness and many who never stepped inside a theatre have been aware of the achievements of local playwrights and actors. Those who did venture inside have often had the double pleasure of hearing local references that not only put their town (literally) on the national stage but which, as with dialect literature, were fully comprehensible only to them. In Willy Russell's *Blood Brothers* only those intimate with the story of Merseyside's new towns could appreciate the fatally misplaced optimism behind Mrs Johnstone's musical celebration of her family's re-housing:

> We're starting all over again,
> We're leaving this mess,
> For our new address,
> 'Sixty five Skelmersdale Lane'.

Rita's strictures on the tediousness of the Liverpool dormitory town of Formby in *Educating Rita* and a passionate discourse on the emotional deficiencies of

Southport in Bleasdale's *On the Ledge* ('I wanna have beliefs, I wanna be decent, I wanna care, you can't fuckin' well care in Southport') served a similar function.[73] Local references or stylistic idiosyncrasies were not always appreciated by critics, with Michael Billington claiming that *Blood Brothers* took a while to recover from its opening 'harvest of Liverpudlian corn'.[74] Local audiences, however, were generally appreciative. Problems arose only when, as happened with Delaney's *A Taste of Honey*, some sections of local society objected to the image projected and argued that this was not a suitable version for national consumption.[75]

Perhaps the closest approximation to a theatrical manifestation of northern identity has been provided not by a play but by a theatre company. Founded by Hull-born actor Barrie Rutter in 1992 to mount a touring version of *Richard III*, by the later 1990s Northern Broadsides had become internationally recognised for its interpretation of Shakespeare.[76] Although the company has never sought to speak for the North or to have an agenda beyond the cultural field, there have clearly been many ways in which its work could be seen to have contributed more widely to the region's collective sense of self. Most obvious here is the company's stipulation that 'All of its work will be in the Northern voice and performed by Northern born actors'.[77] This was partly an artistic ploy designed to release the rich potential that flows from placing Shakespeare's words in (theatrically) unfamiliar voices but it was also one that reclaimed the classics for people in a region where many had been told, as Rutter had been at school, 'that [Shakespeare] wasn't for people like us'. He was much influenced here by the poet Tony Harrison, whose strictures on the straightjacket of RP were noted in the previous chapter and who had written for the actor in the early 1990s.[78] Crucially, the full range of northern accents has been utilised, giving the company a more inclusive feel than many 'northern' institutions. At the same time, the company has commissioned or been presented with work by a number of northern (in this case mainly Yorkshire) writers, including Harrison, Blake Morrison, Ian McMillan and Ted Hughes and thus served as a creative force in its own right. In a very different but important contribution, the company has been closely associated with the regeneration of the urban North by virtue of being based in Dean Clough, a Halifax carpet mill turned business and arts complex, and its use of such places as Salts Mill near Bradford for touring productions.

Clearly, too heavy an interpretive weight clearly cannot be laid upon an institution that has only relatively limited purchase within the wider society. It is also the case that coverage of the company's performances has sometimes brought with it versions of the disabling clichés that have always clustered around the industrial North. When Rutter won a Creative Briton of the Year

Award in 2000, one journalist referred to the company's 'earthy touring productions making up in blood, sweat and tears what they might lack in subtlety'.[79]
Here, established notions of the North as authentic and hard-working risk
obscuring the possibility – claimed by the company – that northern accents in
fact lends subtlety by allowing the expression of nuances of class and status far
better than the standard 'uniform' theatrical voice. Nevertheless, Northern
Broadsides has played at least some role in providing a positive self-image for
the North by placing its accents and intonation at the absolute heart of the
national culture. Audiences, nationally as well as locally, have been reminded
that Shakespeare's audiences would have listened to actors speaking with
regional tongues and an unsettling message has been sent to those who thought
that 'Romeo was an Italian, wasn't he? He spoke perfect Oxford/BBC English,
didn't he – as did all the other Shakespearean Italians ... and Danes, and
Romans, and Scotsmen?'[80] If the success of Northern Broadsides helps bring a
long-term shift in the soundscape of the 'serious' theatre – and there are plentiful signs that it is – then at least one element of the English stage will have been
partially freed from the constraints that have allowed representation of the
North and the regions to flourish only in certain circumstances and on decidedly restrictive terms.

Notes

1   See M. Booth, *Theatre in the Victorian Age* (Cambridge: Cambridge University
     Press, 1991) pp. 18–21, on touring.
2   Booth, *Victorian Age*, pp. 36–7. See also *Yorkshire Post*, 22 December 1882.
3   G. Rowell and A. Jackson, *The Repertory Movement. A History of Regional Theatre in
     Britain* (Cambridge: Cambridge University Press, 1984), p. 1, pp. 36–53.
4   D. Rubin, *The World Encyclopedia of Contemporary Theatre, vol. 1* (London:
     Routledge, 1994), pp. 896–903; Rowell and Jackson, *Repertory Movement*,
     pp. 89–190.
5   Rowell and Jackson, *Repertory Movement*, p. 190.
6   The Census does provide a conservative estimate of the profession. M. Baker, *The
     Rise of the Victorian Actor* (London: Croom Helm, 1978), pp. 83–4, 225.
7   Catalogue to Horniman Collection, John Rylands Library, Manchester, p. 4; *Who's
     Who in the Theatre, 1912* (London: Pitman, 1912); *Manchester Guardian*, 31
     December 1907.
8   D. McGillivray, *Theatre Guide, 1996–7* (London: Rebecca Books, 1996),
     pp. 75–104. Manchester, with some 5 per cent, had the next highest concentration.
9   D. L. Kirkpatrick, *Contemporary Dramatists* (London: St. James Press, 1988).
     'Contemporary' meant 'biologically alive' at the time of compilation.
10 Ibid., p. 432.

11 For histories, P. Bailey (ed.), *Music Hall. The Business of Pleasure* (Milton Keynes: Open University Press, 1986); D. Kift, *The Victorian Music Hall. Culture, Class and Conflict* (Cambridge: Cambridge University Press, 1996); D. Russell, *Popular Music in England, 1840–1914. A Social History* (Manchester: Manchester University Press, 1997), pp. 83–167.

12 D. Harker, 'The making of the Tyneside Concert Hall', in R. Middleton and D. Horn (eds), *Popular Music*, 1 (Cambridge: Cambridge University Press, 1981) pp. 27–56 and D. Harker, 'Joe Wilson: "comic dialetical singer" or class traitor', in J. S. Bratton (ed.), *Music Hall. Performance and Style* (Milton Keynes, Open University Press, 1986), pp. 111–30.

13 S. Vernon, 'Trouble up at t'mill: the rise and decline of the factory play in the 1830s and 1840s', *Victorian Studies*, 20, 1977, pp. 117–39; M. Booth, *English Melodrama* (London: Herbert Jenkins, 1965), pp. 136–8, 151–4. *The Factory Lad* is included in M. Booth (ed.), *The Magistrate and Other Nineteenth Century Plays* (Oxford: Oxford University Press, 1974), pp. 121–50.

14 Booth, *Melodrama*, p. 154.

15 *London Evening News*, 20 August 1912.

16 His 'cards' in the *Era* show him visiting at least twenty-three towns including Belfast, Dublin, Glasgow, Southampton, Cardiff, Bristol and Plymouth. Foy was born in Manchester but became best known for his Yorkshire sketches.

17 D. Russell, 'Varieties of life: the making of the Edwardian music hall', in M. Booth and J. Kaplan (eds.), *The Edwardian Theatre. Essays on Performance and the Stage* (Cambridge: Cambridge University Press), pp. 75–8; S. Featherstone, "E Dunno where 'E are: coster comedy and the politics of music hall', *Nineteenth Century Theatre*, 24, 1, 1996.

18 J. Richards, *Stars in our Eyes. Lancashire Stars of Stage, Screen and Radio* (Preston: Lancashire County Books, 1994).

19 R. Pogson, *Miss Horniman and the Gaiety Theatre Manchester* (London: Rockliff, 1952). S. Gooddie, *Annie Horniman: A Pioneer in the Theatre* (London: Methuen, 1990).

20 *Manchester Guardian*, 11 July 1907.

21 Letter to Horniman quoted in Horniman Catalogue, p. 40.

22 Quoted in T. Wyke and N. Rudyard, *Manchester Theatres* (Manchester: North Western Regional Library System, 1994), p. 34.

23 H. Brighouse, *What I have had. Chapters in Autobiography* (London: Harrap, 1953), p. 9.

24 See Simon Trussler's review, *The Times*, 23 October 1968 and Rowell and Jackson, *Repertory Movement*, p. 125.

25 See the set of twenty-nine mainly Yorkshire plays published by Watmoughs of Bradford, in Bradford Central Library.

26 For History Workshop, originally a Manchester-based socialist theatre which moved to London in 1953, see H. Goorney and E. MacColl (eds), *Agit-Prop to Theatre Workshop* (Manchester: Manchester University Press, 1986).

27 Rowell and Jackson, *Repertory Movement*, pp. 157–65.

28 *Independent*, 23 January 1988.

29 *Rutherford and Son* was revived at the National Theatre in 1994.

30 Although both biographical directories and records of birthplace serve as only the roughest guides, Roy Busby's *British Music Hall. An Illustrated Who's Who from 1850 to the Present Day* (London: Paul Elek, 1976) records 40 per cent of English comedians as having a London birthplace and 38 per cent as having been born in the North.

31 Alderman John Braddock in *Liverpool Echo*, 4 November 1963. Also Councillor Cyril Carr, in *Liverpool Echo*, 7 November 1963. For its late arrival, see E. Midwinter, *Make 'em Laugh* (London: George Allen and Unwin, 1979), pp. 199–200.

32 M. Marshall (ed.), *The Stanley Holloway Monologues* (London: Elm Tree Books, 1979).

33 Richards, *Stars*, pp. 8–9, 35.

34 'A Siddal Honeymoon', *Clock Almanack*, 1886, pp. 39–42.

35 Richards, *Stars*, p. 13.

36 *Era*, 24 October 1903; 12 November 1903; *Wigan Observer*, 3 December 1912; Richards, *Stars*, p. 14.

37 British Library, H3983 rr. 31 (1909); MacInnes, *Sweet Saturday* (London: MacGibbon & Kee, 1967), pp. 62–3.

38 British Library, H3986 tt. 51 (1904).

39 British Library, H. 3986 K. 49 and K. 10 (1909); MacInnes, *Sweet Saturday*, p. 101.

40 H. Brighouse, *Lonesome-Like* (London: Samuel French, revised edn, 1955), p. 10.

41 Ibid., pp. 10, 18.

42 H. Brighouse, *Hobson's Choice* (London; Constable, 1916), p. 30.

43 *Zack. A Character Comedy*, in H. Brighouse, *Three Lancashire Plays* (London; Samuel French, 1920), p. 259.

44 Benedict Nightingale in *The Times*, 18 June 1992; *The Rise and Fall of Little Voice*, in J. Cartwright, *Jim Cartwright, Plays: 1* (London: Methuen, 1996), p. 203.

45 *Hobson's Choice*, p. 12.

46 J. B. Priestley, 'When we are Married', in *The Plays of J.B. Priestley, vol. 2* (London: Heinemann, 1949), pp. 181–2.

47 R. Gow, *Ma's Bit O' Brass* (London: Deane, 1938), p. 19. This had first appeared as a film, *Lancashire Luck*, in the previous year.

48 Brighouse, *Three Lancashire Plays*, p. 86.

49 Heinemann edn (1992), p. 16.

50 S. Houghton, 'Hindle Wakes', in G. Rowell, ed., *Later Victorian Plays, 1890–1914* (Oxford: Oxford University Press, 1972), p. 506.

51 S. Delaney, *A Taste of Honey* (London: Eyre Methuen, second 1959 edn), p. 47.

52 Richards, *Stars*, p. 12.

53 *Football Favourite*, 1 January 1927; H. V. Morton, *In Search of England* (London: Methuen, 1949 edn), pp. 181–5. He was pleasantly surprised given he had 'shared the common idea of Wigan'. G. Allison, *Allison Calling* (London: Staples Press, 1948), p. 52.

54 *Manchester Courier*, 28 January 1908; A. Plater, *Close the Coalhouse Door* (London: Methuen, 1969), p. xi.

55 *The Times*, 18 June 1912.

56 *The Lady*, 24 July 1912.

57 *Theatre Arts*, May 1959. Alan Brien was interpreting the play for an American readership but similar sentiments were voiced in Britain. *New Statesman*, 9 May 1986.

58 *Observer*, quoted in programme for *Richard III* tour, 1998.

59 Quoted in *Hobson's Choice* (York Notes, 1988), p. 10.

60 *The Times*, 28 May 1958, 11 February 1959, 4 May 1961, 14 June 1986; *Sunday Times*, 30 March 1986.

61 *The Times*, 22 October 1992; *Little Voice*, pp. 201, 214–15.

62 W. Russell, *Educating Rita* (London: Longman, 1991 edn), pp. 29–30.

63 *The Times, 29 March 1986.*

64 MacInnes, *Sweet Saturday Night*, pp. 23–4.

65 *Era*, 27 February 1904, 5 March 1904, 20 February 1904.

66 In Rowell, *Late Victorian Plays*, p. 469.

67 Brighouse, *The Game*, pp. 25–6.

68 *Plays of J.B. Priestley, vol. 2*, p. x.

69 Priestley, 'When we are Married', p. 166.

70 Owen, *Progress*, pp. 143–4.

71 A. Bleasdale, *On the Ledge* (London: Faber and Faber, 1993), p. 3.

72 *Wigan Observer*, 17 May 1913.

73 *Blood Brothers*, p. 35; *Rita*, p. 12; *On the Ledge*, pp. 37–8.

74 *Guardian*, 17 June 1980.

75 D. Haslam, *Manchester, England* (London: Fourth Estate, 1999), p. xxix.

76 For a history-cum-interview see 'Northern light', *Guardian*, 18 September 2000.

77 Programme note, *The Merry Wives* tour, June to August 1993.

78 *Guardian*, 18 September 2000.

79 *Guardian*, 29 June 2000.

80 Programme note by Mike Poulton, *Romeo and Juliet* tour, October–November 1996.

6

Screening the North

No other cultural forms considered in this study can rival the reach and cultural power of cinema and television. Cinema's greatest years as a cross-class, cross-generational popular art came between about 1930 and the early 1950s, with annual admissions peaking at 1,635 million in 1946.[1] Even though its popularity fell thereafter and it became ever more noticeably a medium appealing to the under-35 age group, it still had (and has) the potential to draw vast numbers to specific films. Television in its turn moved from novelty in 1950, when only 350,000 licences were issued, to a standard household appliance by 1961 when 75 per cent of families owned a set; the figure had risen to 91 per cent by 1971.[2] Under no circumstances could such potent forces be excluded from this book.

Feature film and the North

Cinema and television are grouped together here because they share so much in terms of style, personnel, production and influence. However, their very different histories demand independent treatment. In the context of this book, perhaps the biggest single difference concerns the relative degree of control they have given to northern communities in the domain of regional representation. While northerners have often been able to exert some influence over television's depiction of their region, feature film (other genres are excluded from this analysis) has offered remarkably little scope in this regard. Even more than tourist literature, cinema's gaze seems in Shield's words 'south-centred', the product of 'external, London-centred, political authority and economic power'.[3] A major factor here has been the industry's need to appeal to audiences already armed with well-conditioned expectations of what to expect from the 'North'. The industry's remarkably narrow geographical base has also proved significant. While the North has produced key directors, producers and actors, the British studio system was almost exclusively focused on London and its immediate hinterland by 1914.[4] Provincial locations, stories and accents were thus never integrated into the daily work of the leading studios, which only looked north during the intermittent moments when regional themes became fashionable. Only John Blakeley's Mancunian Films, active from 1933–53, succeeded in working outside the tiny south-eastern golden triangle for any sustained period.[5] Initially using spare capacity in minor southern studios before eventually moving to Manchester in 1947, the company produced twenty-five low-budget films featuring leading Lancashire comics such as Frank Randle and Norman Evans. Significantly, these films were largely produced for northern (especially near northern) audiences rather than national distribution. It is no coincidence that the demise of the studio system and the concomitant growth of the independent sector in the last decades of the twentieth century opened up one of the richer periods for the cinematic representation of the North.

These various constraints have dictated that northern films, defined here as those set in the region and/or extensively featuring northern characters, make up only a small proportion of the total output of the British film industry, albeit one that includes some works of genuine artistic and cultural importance.[6] While films with a northern theme appeared throughout the period, the region attracted particular interest in the 1930s, between 1959 and 1963, in the 1980s and again in the mid and later 1990s. This more or less repeats the by now familiar pattern of enhanced northern penetration of the wider culture and, indeed, often took the form of a second level response to activity in other cultural fields. This was especially the case in the 1950s and 1960s when the northern film was almost exclusively rooted in contemporary literature and drama. While broader social and cultural currents were therefore probably responsible for these moments of northern exposure, autonomous factors within the industry have also exerted some influence. The relative power of independent production companies was crucial to the region's cinematic moment in the early 1960s, while the substantial body of northern films appearing in the late 1990s owed much to both a desire to chase the box-office success of *Brassed Off* (1996) and *The Full Monty* (1997) and the lower production costs offered by many northern locations.[7]

The North that has emerged on screen has been extremely restricted geographically, focusing perhaps more than any area save drama on the urban and the industrial. Richards is surely correct to argue that Lancashire has been its key location, becoming 'within England and outside London … the county

with the most sustained and influential cinematic image'.[8] There clearly have
been northern films that stood outside the urban-industrial milieu including J.
Arthur Rank's first ever production, *Turn of the Tide* (1935), based on Leo
Walmsley's stories of north Yorkshire fishing communities; Victor Saville's version of Winifred Holtby's east Yorkshire novel *South Riding* (1938) and Bryan
Forbes' directorial debut *Whistle Down the Wind* (1961), set in rural north
Lancashire. These, however, have been exceptions. Film critics and historians
have added to this sense of the North's urban-industrial quintessence by their
manner of constructing film cycles. *Whistle Down the Wind*, for example, is
invariably ignored in discussions of 'northern' cinema between 1959–63 despite
its northern location, unusually self-conscious use of genuinely northern voices
and the fact that the setting of the original 1958 children's novel was moved
from the South to the North in order to profit from the region's fashionable cultural status.[9] While it makes sense to construct a northern cycle of this period
around the images and motifs of working-class and industrial society that
undoubtedly predominated, ignoring exceptions helps create a feeling that the
northern film can only refer to highly specific landscapes and communities.

Central to this reductive process has been the tendency to locate films not in
definite, knowable places but in carefully chosen, often stereotypical terrain providing an easily recognisable and swiftly assimilated version of the region.
Certainly, some northern locations have such well-established iconographies
that they can be utilised fairly unproblematically. Blackpool almost rivals Gracie
Fields as the central character in *Sing as we Go* (1934), Newcastle's waterfront provides a striking backdrop for *Get Carter* (1971) and Liverpool's defines a number
of 1980s movies. Generally, however, films have been shot in specific places only
knowable to local audiences – *Billy Liar*'s 1963 Bradford, for example – or in a
series of locations then moulded into a suitable composite. John Scheslinger's *A
Kind of Loving* (1962), based on a novel with a clear West Riding setting but shot
in Lancashire, is an interesting example here. *Sight and Sound*'s Eric Rhode
believed it to depict Burnley while the *Daily Telegraph*'s Patrick Gibbs saw the film
enlivened by its setting in a 'northern industrial city which I took to be Burnley or
Bolton'. More recently historian Robert Murphy has placed it in Stockport.[10]
The film in fact used a number of Lancashire locations, including some of those
cited as well Preston and Manchester, where Schlesinger apparently alighted with
enthusiasm on St Mary's Church, Beswick Street after scouring the North for a
suitable setting for the wedding that so memorably opens the film.[11] The North
on offer here is literally an invented one, a collection of suitable images. There has
been greater attention to specificity of place in recent decades but landscapes that

reflect cinematic desirability rather than actuality are still easily identifiable. *When Saturday Comes* (1995) includes shots of pithead winding gear in a city (Sheffield) that has no pits.[12] A local review of *Billy Elliott* (2000) noted that 'the accents are all over the place. So is the geography. The pit is open cast one minute and deep mined the next.'[13] Carelessness in critical notices, as when two writers claimed that *Brassed Off* was set in north rather than south Yorkshire, can also help create an impression that the North matters more to the film community as an idea than as reality.[14]

The use and abuse of accent has been similarly potent in this process. Performers such as Gracie Fields and George Formby obviously brought a linguistic authenticity to many productions, as did those recruited locally to star in films such as *Whistle Down the Wind* and *Kes* (1969). There have always been non-northern actors willing to make strenuous attempts to master local speech (John Mills in *Hobson's Choice* (1954) is a notable example) and this willingness has been far more apparent from the 1980s. For much of the period, however, directors were happy either to mix different northern accents even more loosely than they might mix locations and/or to use stars not always able or willing to rise to the challenge. Penelope Houston noted 'complaints of lack of verisimilitude in accent and setting' in *Room at the Top* (1959) amongst Yorkshire audiences, although she gave the cast credit for trying harder than normal.[15] It is ironic that probably the most extreme example of such deficiency occurs in *Get Carter*, a film that is tied unusually closely to a specific and recognisable location. Only one obviously north-eastern actor (Alun Armstrong) was cast and Michael Caine, as Geordie returnee Jack Carter, is not the only one who chooses to solve the problem of accent by not bothering at all.[16] (Caine's image as a Cockney Jack-the-lad would, in fairness, have rendered any such efforts worthless.) This is not to offer some linguistically correct condemnation of past cinematic practice and neither is it to ignore the genuine problems that authenticity could bring. Ken Loach had to re-dub sections of *Kes* when the supposed impenetrability of the Barnsley accent became one factor threatening the film's release.[17] Rather, it is to stress that invention and approximation once again often ironed out the North's internal complexities and reduced it to a undifferentiated whole largely constructed and viewed from outside.

Putting the North on screen

The distinctive and partial northern geography generated by cinema has necessarily restricted the ways in which the region and its people can be depicted.

While film set in the South is just 'film' and can be about any and everything, northern film always arouses certain expectations. As with the North on stage (from where, after all, it derived a significant amount of its material), the North on screen has tended to be either a comic place where daily hardship was softened by humour, or a site for debating serious moral, economic and social issues. It is broadly possible to see films made before the late 1950s (and certainly before 1939) as falling more obviously into the first category and those after that point into the second. Such a categorisation admittedly does not do justice to the realism that flickers even in some of the early Formby and Fields films and more obviously in a work like *The Stars Look Down* (1939), Carol Reed's realisation of A. J. Cronin's novel of the north-eastern mining industry (and one of the very few films to engage with the far North). Similarly, it downplays the rich humour that underlay even some of the bleakest underclass films of the 1980s such as *Rita, Sue and Bob Too* (1987) and the more obviously Ealingesque qualities of *Brassed Off* and *The Full Monty*. The case is nevertheless broadly sustainable. The conservatism of 1930s film censorship certainly prevented the cinematic North from engaging with social and political issues in the manner of its literary equivalents. The British Board of Film Censors' refusal to countenance a version of Walter Greenwood's novel *Love on the Dole* is the best-known example here. Only in the radically different climate of the Second World War when inter-war unemployment and its attendant consequences could be safely decanted to the 'past' and its eradication incorporated in visions of a future that made the war worth fighting, could the book be tackled.[18]

The eventual release of John Baxter's film version in 1941, however, in no sense began a major reconsideration of northern themes and it was not until *Room at the Top* in 1959, a cinematic breakthrough for far more than just the North of England, that social realism became more common currency. There were undoubtedly considerable differences in the tone and register of that realism even between films made in the same period – the films of late 1950s and early 1960s were differentiated as much as they were unified by style and content – and there were broad changes in terms of subject matter across the period as a whole.[19] In general terms, the largely male-centred dramas of 1959–63, focusing on social mobility and sexual morality within the borderlands between working and lower middle class, were supplanted in the 1980s by far more women-centred narratives of poor working-class/underclass life, before a concern with the impact of de-industrialisation on masculine identities moved to the foreground in the mid-1990s. The later twentieth-century concern with the North as a particularly 'real' world is nevertheless clear.

In certain cultural contexts, northern films of whatever genre have placed the region (or parts of it) in a highly positive light. The enormous success of Lancashire's Gracie Fields and George Formby junior in the 1930s and early 1940s provides one of the most significant examples. Making their screen debuts in 1931 and 1934 (as an adult performer) respectively, Fields was the most popular British attraction at the box office in 1936 and 1937, with Formby following suit in the next three years.[20] Fields' success was rooted in her genuinely open and unpretentious personality, comic talent, energy, vocal dexterity and overt 'Lancashireness'. Her resolute refusal to soften her Rochdale tones pleased northern audiences and gave an added dimension to her work, sharpening the many exchanges with well-spoken middle-class characters that punctuated her films. Although always in character as a 'Lancashire lass', few of her films were actually set in the county. Both her debut *Sally in Our Alley* (1931) and *Looking on the Bright Side* (1932) used the long-established device of the provincial in London, although Gracie's strong characters are long way from the comic naïves so often associated with this role. It was not until her fifth film, *Sing as We Go* (1934), that Fields was placed in the setting of industrial Lancashire. The film, scripted by one of her greatest fans, J. B. Priestley, records mill girl Grace Platt's adventures in Blackpool where she seeks work following the closure of Greybeck Mill. Inevitably, the mill is saved after Grace and the millowner's son combine to find a new owner whose 'miracle' process offers the workers a long-term future. This upbeat story with its cheerful eponymous theme tune, sharing and solving of difficulties across class barriers and central message of faith in the resilience of the economic system, is one of the finest examples of the promotion of 'consensus, co-operation and national unity' that Richards sees as her major ideological contribution to 1930s Britain.[21]

Formby's films served a very similar purpose, depicting a Lancashire 'Everyman' figure for whom it always 'turned out nice again' despite the humiliations and struggles passed through on the way to winning the hand of a good woman. Although his earliest pictures for Mancunian Films were set in the North and the Walter Greenwood scripted *No Limit* (1935) took him to the Isle of Man T-T races, his films usually placed him in a generalised and rather genteel South where he could play the more traditional provincial innocent to perfection. As with Fields, his accent helped highlight and deflate the southern pretension that he sometimes encountered there. Both performers gave a tremendously positive image of the North at a time when so many other representations, external ones in particular, were essentially problematic and negative. (So, too, were some internal ones; it is interesting commentary on the nature of writing for a living that Greenwood could write pieces as distinct as *Love on the Dole* and *No Limit* within four years.) Moreover, there is a sense in which they made the North, or Lancashire at least, a key part and a fully paid up member of the nation. Richards' stress on their role in building a cross-class consensus works just as well in a spatial sense. By making the two so obviously of the North but placing them so often outside of it, their films allow the region to infuse the national culture with the characteristic virtues of ebullience, spirit, wit, decency and warmth that were so often seen as its distinctive gift.

Changes in public taste in Formby's case and Fields' effective retirement ended their box-office hegemony and, after the early 1940s, no other northern film stars were ever able to reprise such sustained levels of success. Northern film's function of showing the region's spirit and fortitude has nevertheless remained intact. As noted earlier, an engaging humour, albeit of a type radically different from that of the 1930s, enlivens even some of the bleakest films of the 1980s. It would be straining too far to see the leading women of *Letter to Brezhnev* (1985) or *Rita, Sue and Bob Too* as the Gracies of their day – Rita in *Educating Rita* (1983) gets closer – but they do share the same refusal to buckle. Similarly, it is hard to consider Claire Monk's plausible reading of *The Full Monty* as broadcasting an 'optimistic message … that even a de-industrialised community – or country – with few apparent resources or natural markets can put itself back on its feet' without hearing more than faint echoes of Gracie and George.[22]

The portrayal of the North and northerners in the region's greatest cinematic 'moment' between 1959 and 1963 could not have differed more dramatically from that witnessed in the 1930s comedies. No one label neatly describes the cycle of films that began with Jack Clayton's *Room at the Top* in January 1959 and ended with Lindsay Anderson's *This Sporting Life* in January 1963. 'New Wave', 'kitchen sink', 'angry young man' and 'northern realist' (used most frequently here for convenience rather than conviction) all summon up such common elements as the use of black and white photography, desolate urban/industrial settings and jazz influenced scores as well as a concentration on sex, class and generational conflict, without capturing the many differences between the individual films. Whatever the nomenclature, their success in both critical and box office terms placed the region at the core of a significant moment of cultural change and creativity.[23] Admittedly, cinema was a pace behind literature and drama in this regard and drew its subject matter for these films entirely from their stocks. The cycle was small, usually seen as including just seven titles, and could easily have never materialised.[24] Tony Richardson's *A*

Taste of Honey (1961) was initially postponed due to a failure to find adequate funding and only went ahead after the success of *Saturday and Sunday Morning* (1960), itself only released because of the cancellation of a showing for another picture.[25] Some critics were unconvinced and others soon got slightly bored, with the *Guardian* telling its readers in September 1962 that these films were in danger of becoming formulaic and that any formula was 'likely to be tedious'; with fitting irony, the paper failed to spot that it had voiced virtually identical sentiments and in virtually identical words just five months before.[26] Nevertheless, even those not enamoured admitted that something important was taking place.

Whereas the Lancashire comedies of the 1930s had essentially celebrated northern character, the realist films made the North itself the object of interest and perhaps even fascination. Part of the cultural value imparted by these films was their obvious association with notions of artistic quality and originality. A region long stigmatised as philistine and most likely to be celebrated for its achievements in lower status cultural arenas such as comedy and mass sport, found itself placed at the forefront of a serious cinematic trend. Above all, the films allowed the North to fulfil its ascribed role as cleanser and purifier. Its otherness became a virtue as those very aspects often at the heart of its stigmatisation became attractive, especially to those born outside the region and outside of the working class. Of the five directors involved in the northern realist cycle – Lindsay Anderson, Jack Clayton, Karel Reisz, Tony Richardson and John Schlesinger – only West Riding-born Richardson came from the North and even he had left to study at Oxford and work mainly in London. Lindsay Anderson, born in Bangalore to a military family and educated at Cheltenham College and Oxford, was perhaps the most excited by a region that he had first encountered while making a series of documentaries around Wakefield between 1948 and 1952. Although he stressed the universal nature of the themes addressed in *This Sporting Life*, the film at least gave him the chance to challenge a mainstream cinema that he had characterised in 1957 as 'Southern English … metropolitan in attitude, and entirely middle-class'.[27] Here in the North lay the 'authentic' England, for once privileged over the comfortable South, where cinematic traditions could be refreshed and post-war class relations and the rigidity of moral codes probed and sometimes challenged. Many reviewers also captured this link between the region and new cinematic and social forces, albeit in ways that drew on existing comic discourses. *Picturegoer's* review of *Room at the Top* described it as by far 'the sexiest film to come out of a British – or almost any other – studio. And, by gum, this scorching analysis of bed and brass in a

Yorkshire town rates its X certificate'; the *Daily Herald* captioned a still of the film 'Whoever heard of such goings on in Yorkshire?' Nevertheless, as Neil Sinyard has argued, the sense of a new world being opened up before them is apparent in the response of many reviewers.[28]

The North's periods of cinematic centrality were, however, decidedly provisional and tightly rationed. The highpoint of 1959–63 was followed by a rapid shift of interest to 'Swinging London', albeit a London sometimes gently satirised and where northerners and other provincials were often encountered. The North itself had only the thinnest of attention for the next twenty years and when it returned it did so in the far more pessimistic guise of the 'duty' or 'state of the nation' films charting the decay of the industrial heartlands in Thatcher's Britain.[29] Moreover, believers in a more geographically inclusive cinema had once again to call for more attention to the provinces, with *The Guardian's* Derek Malcolm celebrating the Liverpool settings of *Letter to Brezhnev* and claiming it to be one of at least six cities deserving far more screen exposure.[30] The next decade saw such a call answered to some degree but it was a depressed North of England that drew the film industry's attention.

This is hardly surprising. For all the positive images of the North on film, even at its moments of triumph the region has ultimately been depicted in ways that reflected and reinforced long-established and often prejudicial external views. Indeed, feature film has generally produced a far more negative, limited and stereotypical view of the North than any other form of popular culture. In its comic heyday in the 1930s, the northern film helped add to a sense noted elsewhere in this study of the North as a comic place. Moreover, probably more than any other medium it encouraged the notion that innate northern wit and resilience would see the region through troubled times, an idea hardly likely, then or later, to encourage the framing of practical measures by external agencies. From the late 1950s, the region has undeniably often been presented as a site of special anthropological interest. The focus on industrial locations noted above has proved important here, as has the 'southern gaze' that organises the consumption of these locations. Higson and Shields have drawn attention to the way in which the audience was given a sense of 'spatial power and authority' by such standard devices as the long shot from the hill top or the sequences following characters through urban industrial landscapes, that so typified the iconography of the realist films of the 1960s.[31] The documentary influence was also obviously crucial here. For all the genuinely exciting images of the region generated by what Raphael Samuel termed an 'urban pastoral' aesthetic, these films and their successors did little to challenge the standard space myth.[32]

There were exceptions, as in the demolition scenes scattered across *Billy Liar* showing the Victorian past making way for a modern cityscape. Even these, however, did more to symbolise the generational conflict between Billy and the adult world than to establish regional regeneration.

Many films of the 1990s added a distinctive contribution to the weight of clichéd representation. In her analysis of the decade's working-class films, Julia Hallam has noted how they commodify 'the cultural identities of economically marginalised communities, re-packaging their experiences for sale in the global marketplace'.[33] One element of this has been the conscious use of standard, albeit often increasingly outmoded (or inappropriate) signifiers of working-class culture. *The Full Monty* featured, albeit briefly, a brass band in its opening scene, despite being set in an area where banding has never held a central place in working-class culture. The sequence does little for the film beyond perhaps placing a symbol of community amidst Sheffield's economic disintegration. (It also, of course, linked the film it to its successful precursor *Brassed Off.*) *Little Voice*, the 1998 film version of Jim Cartwright's 1992 play, makes Billy, the young telephone repairman and saviour (literally and metaphorically) of the eponymous heroine, a pigeon fancier. This move into the stereotypical perhaps works better, allowing the film to end with an image of Little Voice letting a pigeon fly free in a gesture that directly reflects her own release from emotional entrapment. It nevertheless risks taking the audience into the land of Andy Capp.

These views of the North have often been embellished by cinema's close attention to the narrowness of region's emotional, intellectual and moral register. Patrick Gibbs in the *Daily Telegraph*, for example, congratulated Jack Clayton on capturing the atmosphere of a 'stuffy provincial town' in *Room at the Top*, noting that monochrome was perfect 'for this background and subject'.[34] Although recognising the novelty of the film, readings such as this hardly reconfigured the North as exciting and modern. As 'stuffy' places, northern towns were clearly to be escaped from at an early opportunity. While Fields and Formby were often found dispensing northern virtues well beyond their native heaths, their leave taking was largely unexplained and thus unproblematic. From the 1960s, and obviously taking a lead from their literary originals, the issue became more insistent and more troubling. Although *Billy Liar* was the only northern film of that decade that addressed this issue head on – Billy stays while girlfriend Liz makes the journey that prefigures the cinematic turn to 'Swinging London' – most of the others are pervaded by a strong sense of frustration, restlessness and confinement. The parodying of Yorkshire dialect that forms such an important part of the novel is also prominent in the film of *Billy Liar* and adds another element to the region's antique flavour. As in literature, the North's apparent artistic apogee proved a mixed blessing in many ways.

The exodus to London became more substantial from the mid-1960s when a number of films including *The Knack* (1965) and *Smashing Time* (1967) followed young northerners and other provincials to the capital in search of financial, social and sexual liberation.[35] When the North returned to cinema screens in the 1980s, escape was again on the agenda in *Letter to Brezhnev* and *Dancin' Thru the Dark* (1990), in both cases from Liverpool. As late as 2000, *Billy Elliot*, a film that paid some degree of homage to the realist films of the early 1960s, suggests that north-eastern teenager Billy's dreams of dancing can only be fulfilled in London. Many characters hang on to their return tickets and use them, but the general pattern is clear. London as ever is the arena for the pursuit of excitement and personal ambition and one set against a restricted North/provinces that was only to be returned to as sanctuary, consolation or after a suitably life-enhancing experience.

Beyond the issues of imagery and plotline, it is also worth reiterating earlier comments on the limited generic range. Joyce Woolridge has argued this point well in respect of the 1990s, noting that the region largely missed out on three of the main movements within British cinema of the period, the youth film, gangster cycle, and romantic comedy. Instead of these largely 'aspirational' genres, most northern films of the decade were either realist dramas or comedies that were nevertheless still rooted in serious social issues, with both tending to feature what she terms the 'ossified mythic north'.[36] Although the 1990s did at last see a section of the North's Asian community reach the commercial cinema (albeit in a 1970s setting) in *East is East* (1999), in a decade of significant change for the region in terms of urban renewal, the North was to remain troubled, insular and backward looking. By then, the cinematic North had become an obvious source of knowing humour, as exemplified by Chris Peachment's *Daily Mirror* review of *Brassed Off*:

> It's trouble down at t' pit time again in *Brassed Off*. Blokes with names like Clegg and Barrowclough are going 'By 'eck, if they close down t'colliery, we'll have to eat the whippet'. Actually, there aren't any whippets in the film, and the comedy is all very sweet-natured, but too much northern grimness does bring on the urge to send it up a bit.

In an informative but similarly comic piece, the *Guardian* offered a 'brief history of the grim north' that worked through films from *The Man in the White Suit* (1951) to Ken Loach's *Raining Stones* (1993) and their depiction of a world where 'even the rainbows are in black and white'. [37] Such post-modern humorous tropes, however, themselves run the risk of reinforcing traditional stereotype as much as they draw attention to undeniable artistic tendencies and tired clichés.

It is not easy to gauge internal reaction to cinematic depiction of the North. From the late 1950s, civic leaders have certainly been highly sensitive to supposed sleights and such concern intensified from the 1980s with the growth of urban tourism. Whereas Bradford's civic dignatories merely kept a diplomatic silence in regard to locally filmed *Room at the Top* in 1959, *Rita, Sue and Bob Too*, dealing with the sexual adventures of two Bradford schoolgirls and the collapse of community within their local council estate, was far more obviously a cause for concern some thirty years later. A number of Sheffield councillors and members of the business community were critical of the city's representation in *The Full Monty*, with one revealingly referring to the '*Room at the Top*' image that it conjured up; realist iconography, or a remembered version of it, had clearly penetrated deep.[38] 'Ordinary' cinemagoers could also be irritated, with one north-eastern writer remembering the annoyance felt when locals discovered that the cast of the Newcastle-set thriller, *Payroll* (1961), spoke largely in southern accents. The residents of the Bradford council estate depicted in *Rita, Sue and Bob Too* were apparently much exercised by reports of the commentary the film it passed on their lives, although in this instance, a private showing rapidly assuaged fears.[39] Overall, while the pleasurable recognition of familiar sights doubtless added much to the enjoyment of films shot locally there is little evidence of communities experiencing a genuine ownership of them. The North on screen has generally been constructed too far south for that.

Smaller screen, bigger North[40]

Although the BBC began its service in 1936, it was not until the early 1950s that television really emerged as a major cultural medium in Britain. The North inevitably featured in BBC programming but the Corporation was not particularly active in serving the regions. Indeed, the Beveridge Committee of 1951 criticised its excessive 'Londonisation' and it was criticism of this type that helped lay the regional basis of ITV when the battle for commercial television was finally won in Parliament in 1954.[41] The initial arrangements created franchises for three loosely defined regions; London, the Midlands and the North, with different companies being allotted weekday and weekend output. The northern weekday franchise was awarded to Manchester-based Granada, thereby substantially enhancing the city's role as northern media capital (Leeds and Liverpool had also been considered for the company's headquarters), while ABC Television gained the weekend schedule.[42] ITV transmissions began in September 1955, although Lancashire and Yorkshire were not connected to the system until the following May, the north-east (through Tyne-Tees Television) until January 1959 and the English–Scottish border regions (via Border Television) until September 1961. The opening of Yorkshire Television in Leeds in July 1968 and the eventual ending of the weekday/weekend split, effectively completed the initial process of northern provision.

The franchise arrangements demanded that companies produced material substantially reflecting the culture of their regions and John Corner has captured well the consequences.

> However loosely the companies chose to interpret their declared commitments to their regions, a stronger sense of different voices, of previously unaccessed experience, came through the filter of their programme formats than had hitherto managed to penetrate through the sieve of metropolitan-centredness which habitually, if unconsciously, was used by the BBC in fashioning its images of the nation.[43]

Although new programmes and ideas were of the greatest importance here, companies were quick to realise the benefits of drawing on the pre-existing stock of iconic cultural products and cultural icons. In September 1958, Granada celebrated the fiftieth anniversary of the opening of the Manchester Gaiety by broadcasting an adaptation of Allen Monkhouse's *Mary Broome* and followed this with five other Gaiety plays over the next fifteen months.[44] Yorkshire Television produced *The Brontës of Haworth* series in 1973 and, in the following year, commissioned a much-acclaimed thirteen-part adaptation of Winifred Holtby's *South Riding* from West Riding writer Stan Barstow.[45]

The crucial 'northern' event, however, was Granada's first broadcast of *Coronation Street* on Friday 9 December 1960. Industry insiders were extremely uncertain about the programme – both ATC Midland and Tyne Tees initially refused to take it – but within twelve months it had become the nation's most popular programme. The BBC could hardly ignore its success and the regional dimension to it or the fact that ITV was maintaining a two-to-one lead in its share of audience viewing time. One vital response was the launching of police series *Z Cars* in January 1962, set in locations loosely based on Liverpool and its overspill satellite, Kirkby.[46] Other programmes soon followed, including Dick Clement and Ian La Frenais' groundbreaking *The Likely Lads*, produced by the newly created BBC2 in December 1964 and the first major situation comedy clearly located outside of London.[47]

The arrival of the North on television both reflected and continued the wider process of northern penetration of the national culture so prominent from the late 1950s. The desire to portray northern working-class life so strongly felt by Tony Warren, the twenty-three-year-old originator of *Coronation Street*, was certainly inspired by the success of contemporary northern-based fiction and film. Similarly, the North provided the largely southern-based creative team behind *Z Cars* with the sense of excitement they craved. Scriptwriter Troy Kennedy Martin was attracted and 'frightened' by the North, claiming that in its new towns 'one felt the rawness of the "Wild West"', and he made one of his characters repeat these sentiments in the first episode.[48] Moreover, the North's heightened cultural profile undoubtedly made it easier for executives to countenance programmes set in the region and for external audiences to engage with them.[49] The crucial difference between television and other cultural fields, however, was that it continued to utilise northern locations after their relative fall from fashionable grace in the mid-1960s. Although the output of material set in the North or featuring northern characters has fluctuated in accordance with wider cultural patterns it has remained a constant and prominent feature from the 1960s. The expectations placed upon regional franchise holders and the genuine local and regional commitment of many of their leading executives; the BBC's need to counter commercial television's threat and to offer some form of regional remit of its own; the popularity of the first generation of 'northern' programmes and the discipline imposed on planners by the simple facts of audience population distribution, have combined to keep the North somewhere near the forefront of the viewing experience and to prevent the erratic, fashion-led trajectories experienced in so many other arenas. In the late 1990s, thereby, *Heartbeat* (Yorkshire Television, 1992), *Coronation Street* and *Emmerdale* (Yorkshire Television, 1972) formed three of the nation's favourite twelve programmes, attaining peak viewing figures of 18.3 million, 18.0 million and 14.2 million respectively.[50]

As a corollary of the forces shaping television's regional remit, the North it has constructed has been a far wider and more embracive one than that encountered in most other cultural forms. There was certainly a lack of specificity about many early northern settings. Dramatist Alan Plater, the only northern-based (although not north-western) writer on the early *Z Cars* series, noted the tendency within TV and film to set the '"non-metropolitan piece" ... in an ill-defined, generalised lump of the good earth called "The North"' and to accept that, in terms of accent, 'near enough was, generally speaking, near enough'.[51] This generalising tendency was partly the simple result of having to make the best use of those actors available. *Z Cars*, although ever more associated with Merseyside as it developed, was always a fairly loosely northern confection, especially in its early days. Of the leading characters – amongst whom were anyway numbered an Irishman and a Scotsman – only Sergeant Twentyman (Leonard Williams) had a clear Liverpool accent and very few of the bit players and minor characters that can give much local flavour had obviously scouse tones. Indeed, the first episode made a point of placing characters' origins in very specific non- Liverpudlian locales, as if to broaden the programme's appeal, with much comic mileage being made of P.C. 'Fancy' Smith's (Brian Blessed) belief that his home town of Leigh was 'the centre of the universe'. However, no effort was made to substitute Blessed's native West Riding for any approxima-tion to Leigh's highly distinctive accent. Similarly, although the game had the thinnest of roots in Liverpool, a generalised sense of northern-ness was invoked by an extended sequence based around a Rugby League match in Wigan.

Nevertheless, attention to distinguishing physical, linguistic and cultural features became far more marked in the decades ahead. Yorkshire and Lancashire have, as ever, featured more prominently than any locations, but there has been a move beyond the standard mill-and-mine version of the near North. Such settings have obviously featured on occasions. So too have modern urban environments such as the Quarry Hill Flats in Leeds, which served as the backdrop for *Queenie's Castle* (1970–72), a Keith Waterhouse/Willis Hall sitcom headed by Diana Dors with impressive Yorkshire accent, or inner-city Bradford, the focus of Kay Mellor's successful crime thriller *Band of Gold* (1995–97). However, the Yorkshire shown on screen is equally likely to be rural, as in *Emmerdale Farm/Emmerdale* and *All Creatures Great and Small* (1978–90), both set in the Yorkshire Dales, or *Heartbeat*, filmed in the North Yorkshire Moors.[52] Yet again, the small industrial towns ringed by countryside that so typify the West Riding have also featured regularly. *Oh No! It's Selwyn Froggitt* (1976–78), shot largely around Skelmanthorpe between Barnsley and Huddersfield and *Last of the Summer Wine* (1973–), filmed to the south of Huddersfield at Holmfirth, are key examples here.

The near North's – and, indeed, the North's – most frequently portrayed location has been Liverpool, ironically the least 'typical' northern city in terms of history, economy and culture. Although BBC police story documentaries *Tearaway* (1957), *Who Me?* (1959), *Jacks and Knaves* (1961) and, above all, *Z Cars* (for all its infelicities) began the trend, it was Carla Lane and Myra Taylor's BBC1 sitcom *The Liver Birds* (1969–79, 1996) that really established it.[53] Beginning life like so many successful series as a single *Comedy Playhouse* and concerned with the trials and tribulations of two young female flatmates from different social backgrounds, it was to some extent a late manifestation of Liverpool's fashionable 1960s status. Although the accents of some leading characters were decidedly 'near enough', a strong supporting cast of local actors was utilised and the programme's locations and iconography were rooted absolutely in the city where the two scriptwriters had grown up. The original title sequence was important here with its rapid succession of classic Liverpool sites including the Liver Building (the sculpted birds on which provided the punning title), the docks, Lime Street Station and Penny Lane, and its theme tune by Liverpool pop group The Scaffold. One of the most popular programmes of the 1970s, it ran for nine series between 1969–79, with a short series updating the lives of Beryl (Polly James) and Sandra (Nerys Hughes) screened in 1996.

The series sealed Carla Lane's reputation and her remarkably successful *Bread* (1986–91), which chronicled the struggles of the Boswell family to gain the most from life in general and the Department of Health and Social Security in particular, was one of the programmes that made the 1980s the highpoint of Liverpool's TV presence. One episode in December 1988 attracted 21 million viewers, extraordinary for a sitcom and testament to Lane's ability to test the boundaries of that genre.[54] Jim Hitchmough's *Watching* (1987–93) provided another rich exploration of Liverpool life in sitcom form. Developments in the fields of soap opera and drama were also critical in establishing the city's high profile. *Brookside* (1982–), one of the first offerings of the newly opened Channel 4, although never a serious challenge to the existing northern soaps in terms of ratings – in the late 1990s, its audience ran at about 5.5 million – featured a variety of challenging plotlines that kept it and Liverpool in the news.

Perhaps the most crucial television moment for the city, however, came in October 1982 with the launch on BBC2 of Alan Bleasdale's five part series, *Boys From the Black Stuff.* The follow up to a 1980 drama entitled *The Black Stuff,* chronicling the disastrous adventures of an asphalting gang, the series followed their attempts to cope with the disintegration of the Liverpool economy in the early 1980s. Repeated almost immediately on BBC1 it became 'the TV drama event of the 1980s' and probably one of the key TV events of any type in the decade.[55] It was Bleasdale's series that effectively defined the city's future representation. As Bob Millington has argued, 'Through the influence of *Blackstuff,* the prospect of a Liverpool screen fiction automatically arouses expectations about unemployment, working-class resilience to social hardship and, above all, comedy in the face of adversity'.[56] Although one episode contains a ferocious attack by one character on the Liverpudlian tendency to use the symbolic weapon of laughter in preference to concrete forms of struggle, the dark humour chimed in with local self-perception. Billy Butler, an influential Radio City DJ, claimed that, 'Scouse people are quick thinkers and our humour is unique … [*Blackstuff*] said things I don't think anybody but a Liverpool writer would have said. I don't think they could have summed up the despair and also the humour that's connected with today's situation as well as we can'.[57] Bleasdale added to Liverpool's screen presence with *Scully* (1984), a Channel 4 series based on the writer's own novels about a problematic teenager, and *GBH* (1991), a drama serial exploring the city's tangled left-wing politics. In all three programmes, extensive use of local actors, locations and culture – football featured heavily in *Scully* in both the storyline and the extended title sequence – provided an unusual degree of authenticity.

A number of plays and serials by Jimmy McGovern, once a writer for *Brookside*, including *Hillsborough* (1996) and *The Lakes* (1997–99), and the police series *Liverpool One* (1998–) and *Merseybeat* (2001–) are among more recent programmes keeping the city at the heart of the small screen North. Liverpool's centrality as a TV location stems from a variety of factors including its crucial popular cultural role in the 1960s, the sheer quality of its leading television writers and the performers that interpret their work and a certain audience expectation that the city, having featured so regularly, will continue to do so. The simple fact that Merseyside was at the epicentre of so much of the economic and political change of the 1980s, is obviously also crucial here. Underpinning it all is a sense that the city really has exerted a fascination in modern times, its distinctive history, accent and culture (the latter albeit sometimes asserted rather than demonstrated) making it 'other' in a way that few other northern locations have managed to be. 'Textile' Yorkshire and Lancashire had long lost the capacity to shock by the 1970s and Liverpool, although soon wrapped in clichés and often the recipient of extremely hostile representation within the wider culture, took centre stage.

The north-east, especially Tyneside, also began to exert something of a similar fascination, and for some of the same reasons, from the 1970s. It certainly represented a fresh version of the North. As Jarrow-born writer Alan Plater has noted, during the 1950s and early 1960s, the region was still 'a largely unexplored patch within the larger landscape of the fictional "North"'.[58] Although Newcastle United Football Club's three FA Cup successes between 1951–55 had raised the region's profile, the north-east had largely missed out on the earlier moments of northern cultural discovery. While literature was crucial to the imaginative construction of textile Yorkshire and Lancashire in the mid-nine-teenth century and radio to that of Merseyside in the 1930s and 1940s, it was popular TV in the 1960s and 1970s that finally placed the north-east firmly within the national imagination. The driving forces here were locally born scriptwriters working through the BBC rather than regional TV companies. *The Likely Lads* (1964–66), scripted by Dick Clement (actually from Essex) and Whitley Bay's Ian La Frenais, began the process, although the programme nodded only generally at locality; only Sunderland-born James Bolam as Jack-the-lad character Terry Collier had an authentic north-eastern accent, with Rodney Bewes playing his friend Bob Ferris without ever deviating from his native west Yorkshire. The even more successful *Whatever Happened to the Likely Lads* (1973–74) was more clearly set on Tyneside, although even here Brigit Forsyth, who played Bob's wife Thelma, admitted later to playing the first nine episodes in 'a posh Manchester accent' before 'Jimmy Bolam told me I was supposed to be doing a Geordie'.[59]

A foundation had been laid, however, and it was again to be Bolam who fea-tured in the first programme to be firmly built upon it, the BBC historical drama series *When the Boat Comes In* (1976–1981). Set in working-class South Shields and tracing aspects of inter-war history through the life of Bolam's Jack Ford character from 1918 until his death in the Spanish Civil War, it was the creation of James Mitchell, better known at that point as the writer of detective series *Callan*. Mitchell was born and educated in South Shields (his father, a shipyard fitter, had served as Mayor) and he worked hard to create authenticity through close attention to accent and dialect and by using local actors; Bolam was indeed the only non-Tynesider amongst the leading characters. Moreover, although Mitchell wrote most of the material, local writers Sid Chaplin, Tom Hadaway and Alex Glasgow also contributed, with Glasgow performing the nineteenth-century dialect children's song that introduced the programme and provided its title. The discourses surrounding the programme were almost as important as the programme itself in generating ideas about the area. In a *Radio Times* profile H. R. F. Keating described the north-east as 'that little nation-state that has kept its separate existence for centuries', as a place with a 'tough and vital lifestyle' and a humour that could be 'brutal' and yet offered 'abundant friendliness' and a rich communal spirit.[60] Although stressing the separateness of north-eastern culture and thus allowing the region a distinctive, almost exotic place within English culture, such writing also helped pull it toward the mainstream as an exhibitor of a classic northern/working-class virtues. In this its representation differed from Liverpool's, which was always harder edged and more focused on a culture of individual survival. Moreover, while Geordies were, like their Merseyside counterparts, invariably portrayed as plucky under-dogs, they were not tainted by the kind of wider cultural critique that surrounded Liverpool and caricatured it as a place of self-pity and complaint, a city that lay in a mess of its own making. North-easterners remained lovable angels of the North.

The discovery of the area continued through the 1980s with Clement and La Frenais' hugely successful *Auf Wiedersehen Pet* (1983–86, 2002) for ITV Central, placing three unemployed Geordie bricklayers at the centre of a comedy-drama about British workers forced to seek employment in Germany.[61] BBC1's *Byker Grove* (1989–), aimed at children and teenagers, added Newcastle to the list of English soap locations, while a rash of Catherine Cookson adaptations from Tyne Tees Television beginning in the same year and locally-born writer Peter Flannery's extensively debated political drama *Our Friends in the North* (1996) in their different ways demonstrated that the urban north-east was no longer marginal in imaginative terms. Indeed, as a site of popular hardship mitigated by humour, it had become central.

'Flat-vowelled vulgarity in curlers'?

While TV has clearly given increased exposure to the North and enlarged the nation's vision of what it actually encompasses, it is less certain whether it has offered any fundamentally new representations or altered external attitudes. In many crucial senses it has, in fact, continued to carry much traditional ideological freight and distribute it to very large audiences. The sheer number and success of comedies set in the region, ranging from the stand up/sketch shows featuring such stars as Norman Evans (1956), Ken Dodd (1960–), Jimmy Clitheroe (1964–68), Les Dawson (1969) and Morecambe and Wise to the sitcoms so popular from the 1960s, raises the now familiar issue of whether being funny was always good for the region. Certain types of comedy and comedian have clearly had a greater capacity to reinforce stereotypes than others. Strong accents and/or dialect usage and the adoption of exaggeratedly northern Christian and surnames have doubtless played a part here, particularly when allied to a certain cheerful vulgarity which could allow the region to appear not merely as a fount of humour but also as lacking sophistication, even crude. This became more of an issue from the late 1960s as writers pushed a little further at the boundaries of popular taste. Granada's *Nearest and Dearest* (1968–73), with variety artists Hylda Baker and Jimmy Jewell as pickle factory-owning brother and sister Nellie and Eli Pledge, embraced many of the classic features of regional language and nomenclature and tested attitudes to swearing on TV at a very gentle level, although Baker's brilliant malapropisms ('I could have been electroplated') were probably as effective in popularising the programme as Jewell's many 'bloodies' and frequent *double entendres*. Jack Rosenthal's harder edged Granada series *The Dustbinmen* (1969–70), a richly inventive, ratings-topping comedy set around the crew of the dustcart 'Thunderbird 3', was an early target for clean-up TV campaigners. The vigorous 'bloodies' of foreman 'Cheese and Egg', delivered by actor Bryan Pringle in firm Lancashire tones and sometimes embellished by 'V'-signs, were the main problem here.[62]

Two Granada variety shows carried especial weight in this difficult area. *The Comedians*, which enjoyed eleven series between 1971–92, was essentially a vehicle for long-established northern club circuit artists previously relatively unknown on a national level. It made stars of black Yorkshireman and ex-professional footballer Charlie Williams, who brought probably the strongest south Yorkshire accent until then ever heard into the mainstream media, Lancastrians Duggie Brown and Bernard Manning, north-easterners Alan Fox and Mike Burton and many others.[63] *The Wheeltappers and Shunters Social Club* (1974–77) was effectively a spin-off from the earlier show set in the concert room of a fictional working men's club. Both shows did much to cement the notion of the 'club' as a core institution of northern comedy but they also tended to foreground a style of humour that, while undoubtedly popular in the North (and elsewhere), alienated many and gave a less than positive image of the region it emanated from. In particular, although not always as offensive as sometimes painted by the practitioners and fans of the 'alternative comedy' that grew up in conscious opposition in the 1980s, some performers (*Wheeltappers* compère Manning was singled out by many later critics) used a high quotient of jokes about the Irish, Pakistanis and Jews and physical disability. *Wheeltappers*, moreover, often came dangerously close to self-parody and sometimes tipped over into it. While northern viewers might see as affectionate satire a club chairman constantly interrupting proceedings with announcements 'on behalf of the committee', cries of 'now give order' and introducing a bingo sessions where all cards carried the same numbers, there was always a danger that the non-initiated viewed it more literally. At the same time, the show's accent on middle-of-the-road entertainment gave the northern working men's club scene a very dated feel.

The burden of comedy has continued through to the present day in various guises. The late 1990s and early 2000s saw a particularly rich crop of critically and commercially successful programmes including *The Royle Family* (1998), Victoria Wood's *Dinnerladies* (1999) and *Peter Kay's Phoenix Nights* (2001), in which the working men's club returned to its place at the centre of the comic North. Its assortment of worryingly believable characters and ill-fated acts including a racist folk group singing 'Send the Buggers Back', a drunken circus horse that tries to mate with a slot machine and the hopeless auditionnees who ended each episode, took TV club land a long way from the *Wheeltappers*. Not all of these programmes have been to taste, however. The groundbreaking *The Royle Family* (1998), created by Caroline Aherne, Craig Cash and Henry Normal and featuring a family that, according to one early reviewer, just 'sit in front of the television saying "my arse" and bickering', alienated some viewers because of what they believed to be its patronising portrayal of the northern working class.[64]

It is perhaps because the labels 'northern comedian' and 'northern comedy' carry so many problematic inflections that some have refused to accept their embrace. The four northern-born creators of The *League of Gentlemen* (1999), a richly imaginative comedy set in the fictional northern town of Royston Vasey, expressed annoyance that 'we always get "four northern lads" … If we were from somewhere else, no one would say "four southern lads"'. Their irritation stemmed from general issue of northern stereotyping and a particular marketing ploy – a trailer featuring a brass band – that risked restricting comic creativity by structuring audience expectations in a specific way.[65] It would obviously be misleading to imply that the North has been the only region to feature extensively in comedy programmes or that its comic representations have been the only ones to receive critical comment. No programme received more hostile attention as a result of its language and content than Johnny Speight's *Til Death Us Do Part* (1965–75), which introduced East End bigot Alf Garnett to the world. Nevertheless, there is no denying that television has played a key role in continuing the work begun in earnest by George Formby Senior in the 1890s of placing the North at the centre of the nation's comic culture, with all that that has entailed, for both good and bad.

Running alongside the comic motif, and, indeed, often woven into it, has been television's contribution to one of the North's other and ingrained role as the fundamental site for the examination of the class system and the panoply of social, political and economic issues associated with it. Almost all genres set in the North are rooted to some degree in issues relating to class and status. In the field of comedy, *The Likely Lads*, and even more so its 1970s follow up *Whatever Happened to the Likely Lads*, explored this skilfully, dealing in lighter vein with the very issues of working-class upward social mobility that was so central to the 'New Wave' novels and films of the period. Much of the programme's humour stemmed from the gentle conflicts between James Bolam's Terry, happy (at least in the 1960s) with his working-class lot, and Rodney Bewes' Bob, ever aspiring after modest social and self-improvement. Bewes to some extent reprised this role as toffee bar salesman Albert Courtney (footballer Tom Finney had already bagged the snappier New Wave name) in *Dear Mother, Love Albert* (1969–72). This had the useful additional element of being set in London, thus allowing exchanges with the southern middle class to fuse social with spatial tensions. Thus, one episode saw him constantly trying to pronounce 'class' with a long 'a' and having a misunderstanding with his upper-class girlfriend who assumed his father's rowing triumphs were for Oxford or Cambridge rather than, as in actuality, the Co-op.[66]

The comic potential of working-class aspiration has remained a strong theme, as has the variant that follows the issue of social mobility further up the social scale. In an early example, *Meet the Wife* (1964), a BBC vehicle for Freddie Frinton and Thora Hird as Freddie and Thora Blacklock, made much comic capital of the tensions between a contented master plumber and his socially ambitious wife. Most famously, this lead to her attempts to refine his name to 'Fray-d' being met with his sarcastic response of 'Yayss?'. A more recent contribution was the David Nobbs comedy series *A Bit of a Do* (1989), which took the issue further up the social hierarchy. Here, the middle-class *arriviste* Simcock family, headed by David Jason (working hard on a Yorkshire accent) as father Ted, becomes entwined at all manner of personal levels with the upper-middle class Rodenhursts. The opening episode which saw the families united by both marriage and Ted Simcock and Liz Rodenhurst's adultery, included endless moments of social embarrassment, as when Mrs Simcock's father informs aloof dentist Laurence Rodenhurst that 'Eh by 'eck, your daughter's a belter.' Rodenhurst exacts a certain revenge later in proceedings when assuming that 'Spragg' was a 'charming old dialect term' rather than, as it was, the father's surname.[67]

As might be expected, drama and soap opera have ultimately played the largest role in exploring these themes. The plays of Alan Bennett (b. 1934) are important here not only for their quality and impact but because his distinctive output and the dryly comic, resigned manner with which he writes and speaks about his life and work (a style often affectionately parodied and impersonated) have made him emblematic of a gentle, elegiac strand of contemporary northern-ness, almost as if one of the uncertain 'soft' heroes of earlier stage and

dialect comedy had been given a typewriter. In a ten-year series of plays beginning with *A Day Out* in 1972 as well as in certain of the *Talking Heads* monologues (1987) and some documentaries in the 1990s, he has defined an area of
northern life so distinctive as to be 'widely known as Alan Bennett Territory'.[68]
Skilfully rooted in West Riding speech patterns and recognisable locations
(Leeds, Halifax, Morecambe), that territory is inhabited by ordinary, excessively
respectable but often profoundly disappointed and marginalised individuals,
people like Mr and Mrs Palmer whose literally fatal decision to retire from the
demolished terraces of Leeds to Morecambe forms the substance of the aptly
titled *Sunset Across the Bay* (1975). Nobody has captured better, through character and silent, solitary imagery as much as by narrative or direct depiction, the
decline of a settled working- and lower middle-class northern way of life.[69]

No programme has been more central to the representation of the daily life
of 'ordinary' northern folk, however, than *Coronation Street*, the first programme to portray the North on a regular basis and consistently one of the
nation's most popular programmes for over forty years[70]. Of especial importance here, was the extent to which the programme initially stressed its realist
ambition, arriving as it did at (and rapidly becoming a part of) the very
moment of the wider 'discovery' of the region in literature and film. A memo by
creator Tony Warren outlining the programme's aims made its quasi-documen-
tary purpose clear.

> A fascinating freemasonry, a volume of unwritten rules. These are the driving
> forces behind life in a working-class street in the north of England. To the uniniti-
> ated outsider, all this would be completely incomprehensible. The purpose of
> *Florizel Street* [its working title] is to entertain by examining a community of this
> kind and initiating the viewer into the ways of the people who live there.[71]

Whatever its actual content, the programme has constantly generated debate at
various levels of seriousness about the North and its external representation and
these discourses have at times done as much as the programme itself to keep
ideas of northern 'difference' alive. Much early critical reaction focused on
Warren's agenda. A slightly doubtful Maurice Richardson told readers of the
Observer that 'Where it does score over its rivals is in its effect of realism. It
eschews glamour and sensational curtains and concentrates instead on trapping
the rugged ambience of North-country working and lower middle class life'.[72]
Many others, both within and without the region, found it wanting. One
Liverpool paper noted in 1967 that while 'you can love it for its warmth and its
comradeship and for its real-life joys and sorrows' you could also dislike it
'because it has inevitably spread around the picture of the North as being all

back alleys and booze'. A *Daily Mirror* reviewer of the same period claimed 'that many southerners think this knuckleheaded series depicts the sum total of the intelligence of the average northerner. Oh! What Granada has to answer for'. In 1974, an Oldham councillor even called for the series to be dropped in the interest of the North's image. 'People who see *Coronation Street* think we are all married to Hilda Ogdens, wear clogs and have outside loos'.[73] The programme's initial claims for realism also laid it open to criticism when it appeared to be failing to adapt to changing times. As early as 1967 critics were asking 'where are the Pakistani family, the beaten wife and the woman with eight children?' and by 1970s the claim that the programme was little more than nostalgia for a 'golden age' of lost community was a commonplace.[74]

Whether the programme ever become quite the potent 'symbol for the undefined nastiness north of Watford ... [a] shorthand for coarse, flat-vowelled vulgarity in curlers' that some claimed, is unlikely.[75] Nevertheless, it is possible to see how the programme might have 'become' the North for many external viewers, especially in the 1960s and earlier 1970s when televisual versions of the region were neither as frequent nor varied as they later became and the version on offer chimed in with so many pre-existing representations of the region. Later audiences were perhaps more knowing and alert to the programme's history and function. Its nostalgic power has become more obvious and it is surely likely that viewers inside and outside the North have been attracted by the sense of stability offered by the *Street*'s slow pace of change, long-lasting cast and rich fund of memory. Its long parade of women characters has also added much to the programme's popularity with an audience that generally exhibits a 60:40 ratio of women to men. While the production of strong and resourceful women has always been a major feature of the soap as genre, northern soaps in general and *Coronation Street* in particular have been notably rich in this context. In so doing, they have done much to continue and to hone the wise matriarchs, sharp 'Lancashire lasses' and other classic fictional characterisations developed in literature, drama and film.[76]

The North's televisual image had become so settled by the 1970s that it became subject to a degree of parody from within the medium. Some of the earliest and most affectionate examples were generated by Liverpool-born writer Peter Tinniswood. His early 1970s north-country novels featuring the Brandon family formed the basis of BBC1's *I Didn't Know You Cared* (1975–79). The key figure here was Uncle Mort (Robin Bailey), a heroically dour, *über*northerner, through whom Tinniswood managed to catch much of the essence of Lancastrian speech pattern and flavour while also guying many of the standard elements (and representations) of northern-based culture. The flavour is well caught by Uncle Mort's strictures on the North as source for the heritage industry.

> 'I wonder where that back kitchen table is now?' said Uncle Mort. 'It's probably in some poncey-arsed antique shop. It'll be in some swanky house in London all polished and done-up, and they'll be sat round it talking about poetry and eating Italian food in fishermen's smocks and open-toed sandals ... Do you know, if I were to go to the taxidermists and get myself stuffed, I'd make a fortune being an ornament in some arty farty Hampstead parlour.'[77]

Interestingly, Tinniswood's later reworking of the northern archetype theme, *South of the Border* (1985) for Yorkshire Television, was a failure. Starring Brian Glover as a Yorkshireman forced to take his family to London to find work, it was described by one northern reviewer as 'a so-called northern comedy which perpetuates the outdated cloth cap image of Northerners ... so far over the top it is as high as a kite'. Another Yorkshire paper trailed it as a 'Disappointingly duff Peter Tinniswood comedy starring Brian Glover as a displaced cardboard cut out northerner'.[78] The boundary between parody and caricature was clearly a hard one to police. The most consummate and most commercially successful parody was Granada's *Brass* (1983–84, 1990). Set in the inter-war period in the fictional Lancashire town of Utterley it focused on the relationships between the capitalist Hardacres and the working-class Fairchilds, it played brilliantly with every known device and cliché of industrial fiction and drama. In an early episode, Matthew Fairchild explains how his father's injury in a factory explosion and his brother's entombment in a mining disaster will prevent him accompanying the rampantly homosexual Morris Hardacre to Cambridge as his manservant.

> Like me Uncle Lawrence sez, our rough working-class ethic demands that I mun shoulder th' hod that me fayther and brother has laid down and I mun put away me little pencil in top drawer o't dresser where me mother keeps family treasures and the postage stamp we keep for emergencies.

Later in this episode, self-made man and master of Utterly, Bradley Hardacre (Timothy West) plots to demolish a local cottage hospital by placing the rescue tunnel to trapped miners under it. When his daughter manages to reach the miners before he can do this, the men refuse to be rescued until their shift allowances are increased.[79] Parody is a highly complex mode. In many cases it pays the highest of compliments, affectionately recognising the popularity of the original. However, despite the obvious wit and warmth underlying many of these works, their reinforcement of long-standing attitudes towards the North meant that, as in so many cases, they ran the risk of perpetuating old mentalities rather than simply having fun with them.

The emphasis in this section has largely been upon television's general failure to match its wider and more inclusive view of the North in physical and linguistic terms with new and challenging views of the region and its people. However, it would be misleading not to sound some positive notes. It has certainly provided a host of new cultural heroes, even icons, for northern audiences to cherish. Actors such as Thora Hird, Ricky Tomlinson, Sue Johnston and many others have appeared across a range of programmes over their careers in ways that have effectively welded them in a kind of extended northern family; a review of *The Royle Family* captured something of this when referring to its cast as 'the premier northern league'.[80] There have been other less likely additions and none more so than Dales farmer Hannah Hauxwell, whose struggles against isolation, poverty and climate captured in Barry Cockcroft's 1973 Yorkshire TV documentary *Too Long a Winter* launched her into unexpected (and sustained) celebrity. The medium gave yet another (and especially high profile) outlet for northern commentary on the South. Few observations were as pithy as Victoria Wood's satire of metropolitan mentalities that completed the oft heard 'we would like to apologise to viewers in the North' with the unexpected 'it must be awful for them'.[81] It was, however, perhaps Alan Plater's mock-Chaucerian lay at the beginning of *Trinity Tales* (1975), an updating of *The Canterbury Tales* following the progress of a group of rugby league fans en route to Wembley, that captured traditionally expressed enmities as cleverly and knowingly as any writer has managed.

> When the sweet showers of April fade away,
> Bedazzled by the darling buds of May,
> In grey-faced northern towns the world grows sick.
> As workers leave the factory, pit and mill,
> The message, swiftly born by word of mouth,
> Once more my friends unto the decadent South,
> Where merchant bankers rule the land,
> And only the stray dustman soils his hand.[82]

It must also be stressed that TV brought a bigger view of the North to a larger audience than any other medium. While many traditional views were on offer and many of the new versions of the region will have been interpreted through pre-existing mentalities, the possibility of outsiders, and indeed, insiders, gaining a fuller understanding of their culture as a result of exposure to TV was at least always present. While almost any northern-set drama is likely to be viewed through the long-established languages of 'gritty' realism, television does allow for the possibility that 'normal' life can exist in the North, that ordinary things just happen there just as they might do anywhere else.

In all this, the rewards, especially for northerners, have been particularly rich. The opening episodes of *Coronation Street* are often remembered as an exciting time when 'the telly, instead of piping their culture into our homes was showing ordinary people doing ordinary things in ordinary accents'.[83] A shrewd observer of Alan Bennett's work has noted how the intimacy made possible by TV allowed him to use his native idiom 'to make central what was normally on the sidelines' and to show that 'disappointed lives in Leeds could be given a dramatic life that came fully up to scratch'. (Bennett significantly terms his provincial voice 'being yourself' and the metropolitan one he uses in many stage plays 'speaking properly'.)[84] Admittedly, northern audiences did not always like what was offered to them in their name and image. Sometimes, as with Carla Lane's *Bread*, initially unpopular with many Liverpudlians because of its apparent perpetuation of the dole-queue-scrounger image, attitudes shifted. On other occasions, as with *South of the Border*, they did not.[85] Nevertheless, at least some of the texture of daily life was being received. Above all, largely as a result of the 1954 Television Act, the North became something like an equal partner in the process of mass cultural production for the first time. Indeed, the success of Granada and Yorkshire Television made it an exporter. Whatever the image received elsewhere, these were real gains.

Notes

1 P. Corrigan, 'Film entertainment as ideology and pleasure', in J. Curran and V. Porter (eds), B*ritish Cinema History* (London: Weidenfeld and Nicholson, 1983), p. 30.

2 A. Marwick, *British Society Since 1945* (London: Penguin, 1982), p. 121; A. Crissell, *An Introductory History of British Broadcasting* (London: Routledge, 1997), p. 120.

3 R. Shields, *Places on the Margin* (London: Routledge, 1990), pp. 220, 219.

4 P. Warren, *British Film Studios. An Illustrated History* (London: Batsford, 1995) lists just six northern studios, four of which had ceased production by the early 1920s. For northern non-fiction film, see V. Toulmin, '"Local films for local people": travelling showmen and the commissioning of local films in Great Britain, 1900–1902', *Film History*, 13, 2001, pp. 118–37.

5 See J. Richards, *Film and British National Identity* (Manchester: Manchester University Press), pp. 267–72.

6 The seven-county definition of the North excludes *Saturday Night and Sunday Morning* (1960) and *The Loneliness of the Long Distance Runner* (1962), both based

on the literary work of Nottingham's Alan Sillitoe and key elements of the so-called 'kitchen sink' cycle of 1959–63. Although most contemporary critics placed these films in the 'Midlands', writers such as Shields treat them as 'northern'. I have avoided doing so purely for reasons of consistency across the book.

7 J. Hill, *Sex, Class and Realism. British Cinema 1956–1963* (London: BFI, 1986), chapter 2; J. Hill, *British Cinema in the 1980s* (Oxford: Clarendon, 1999), chapter 1; 'North swaps clichés for starring role on film revival', *Observer*, 7 November 1999.

8 Richards, *Film and British*, p. 252.

9 The book was certainly inspired by the Sussex countryside. M. Hayley Bell, *Whistle Down the Wind* (London: Hodder Children's, 1997 edn), p. 153. I am grateful to Jeffrey Richards for this point.

10 *Sight and Sound*, 31, 3, Summer 1962, pp. 143–4; *Daily Telegraph*, 14 April 1962; R. Murphy, *Sixties British Cinema* (London: BFI, 1992), p. 143.

11 D. Haslam, *Manchester, England* (London: Fourth Estate, 1999), p. x.

12 J. Woolridge, 'Living in the past: the imagined north of England in contemporary British films of the 1990s', *Film and Film Culture*, 2, 2003, pp. 25–32.

13 *Northern Review*, 9 and 10, 2001, p. 205.

14 *Sight and Sound*, 11, 1996, p. 44; *Guardian*, 1 November 1996.

15 *Sight and Sound*, 28, 2, 1959, p. 58. For such a criticism, see the *Daily Telegraph*, 24 January 1959.

16 Carter/Caine's Geordie credentials are surely sunk irredeemably when, with a broad sweep of hand along the Tyne, he refers to Newcastle as 'this craphouse'.

17 J. Hacker and D. Price, *Take 10. Contemporary British Film Directors* (Oxford: Clarendon, 1999), p. 282.

18 J. Richards, *The Age of the Dream Palace. Cinema and Society in Britain, 1930–1939* (London: Routledge and Kegan Paul, 1984), pp. 119–20; also R. Murphy, *Realism and Tinsel. Cinema and Society in Britain, 1939–1948* (London: Routledge, 1989), pp. 23–5.

19 There is no space to rehearse debates on 'realism', but John Hill's view that it should be seen as 'a discursive construction rather than an unmediated reflection' is subscribed to here. Hill, *Sex, Class*, p. 127.

20 Richards, *Dream Palace*, p. 160. Richards' treatment of the two in *Dream Palace*, pp. 169–206 is the basis for the ideas here. Also A. Higson, *Waving the Flag. Constructing a National Cinema* (Oxford: Clarendon Press, 1997 edn), pp. 98–175.

21 Richards, *Dream Palace*, p. 172.

22 C. Monk, 'Underbelly UK: the 1990s underclass film, masculinity and the ideologies of "new" Britain', in J. Ashby and A. Higson (eds), *British Cinema, Past and Present* (London: Routledge, 2000), p. 285.

23 *Room at the Top* was the third biggest box office success of 1959 and *A Kind of Loving* the sixth of 1962. Hill, *Sex, Class*, pp. 50–1.

24 The seven are *Room at the Top*, *Saturday Night and Sunday Morning* (1960), *A Taste of Honey*, *A Kind of Loving* (1962), *The Loneliness of the Long Distance Runner* (1962), *Billy Liar* (1963) and *This Sporting Life*.

25 P. Cook and M. Bernink, *The Cinema Book* (London: BFI, 1999), p. 90.

26 Review of *The Loneliness of the Long Distance Runner*, *Guardian*, 26 September 1962; review of *A Kind of Loving*, *Guardian*, 12 April 1962.

27 Quoted in S. Laing, *Representations of Working-Class Life* (London: Macmillan, 1986), p. 116. Biographical data is based on J. Wakeman (ed.), *World Film Directors*, vol. 2, 1945–1985 (New York: Wilson, 1988); Hacker and Price, *Take 10*.

28 N. Sinyard, *Jack Clayton* (Manchester: Manchester University Press, 2000), pp. 56–8. Also A. Aldgate and J. Richards, 'New waves, old ways and the censors: *The Loneliness of the Long Distance Runner*', in their *Best of British. Cinema and Society from 1930 to the Present* (London: I.B. Tauris, 1999), pp. 182–200, and A. Marwick, '*Room at the Top*, *Saturday Night and Sunday Morning*, and the "Cultural Revolution" in Britain', *Journal of Contemporary History*, 19, 1984, pp. 127–52.

29 Hill, *British Cinema*, pp. 133–91.

30 *Guardian*, 7 November 1985.

31 Shields, *Places*, p. 217; Hill, *Sex and Class*, pp. 131–2.

32 R. Samuel, 'North and South', in his *Island Stories: Unravelling Britain* (London: Verso, 1998), p. 165.

33 J. Hallam, 'Film, class and national identity: re-imagining communities in the age of devolution', in Ashby and Higson, *British Cinema*, pp. 270–1.

34 *Daily Telegraph*, 24 January 1959.

35 M. Luckett, 'Travel and mobility: femininity and national identity in Swinging London films', Ashby and Higson, *British Cinema*, pp. 233–45.

36 Woolridge, 'Living in the past', p. 25.

37 *Daily Mirror*, 1 November 1996; 'Friday Review', *Guardian*, 1 November 1996.

38 *Bradford Telegraph and Argus*, 24 January 1959, 8 September 1987; Hallam, 'Film, class and national identity', p. 270.

39 B. Lancaster, 'Newcastle – Capital of what?', in R. Colls and B. Lancaster, *Geordies* (Edinburgh: Edinburgh University Press, 1992), p. 58; *Bradford Telegraph and Argus*, 5 January 1991.

40 Individual programme histories are drawn from the following invaluable works of reference. P. Cornell, M. Day and K. Topping, *The Guinness Book of Classic British TV* (London: Granada, 2nd edn, 1996); M. Lewisohn, *Radio Times Guide to TV Comedy* (London: BBC, 1998); J. Evans, *The Penguin TV Companion* (London: Penguin, 2001). Individual programmes have been watched either in commercially available video or in the 'TV Heaven' facility at the National Museum of Film, Photography and Television, Bradford.

41 Crissell, *An Introductory History*, pp. 76–87.

42 D. Forman, *Persona Granada* (London: Andre Deutsch, 1997), p. 53.

43 J. Corner, 'Television and British society in the 1950s', in his *Popular Television in Britain. Studies in Cultural History* (London: BFI, 1991), p. 9.

44 *Granada's Manchester Plays* (Manchester: Manchester University Press, 1962).

45 The programme won four separate awards.

46 S. Laing, 'Banging in some reality: the original *Z Cars*', in Corner, *Popular Television*, pp. 125–44; S. Sydney-Smith, *Beyond Dixon of Dock Green. Early British Police Series* (London: I.B. Tauris, 2002), pp. 152–79.

47 Limited audience access to BBC2 meant a national following only after transfer to BBC1 in March 1965.

48 Quoted in Laing, 'Banging in some reality', p. 140.

49 There were also good practical reasons for looking outside of London, including the time the Met. was taking to vet scripts. See Sydney-Smith, *Beyond Dixon*, p. 124.

50 *Taris UK Television Yearbook*, 1998 (London: Taylor Nelson AGB), p. 49. Figures are based on the highest figures for a single episode in 1997. Excluding the exceptional case of Princess Diana's funeral, *Heartbeat* was the most popular programme of the year.

51 A. Plater, 'The drama of the north-east', in Colls and Lancaster, *Geordies*, p. 73.

52 *Emmerdale Farm* changed title in November 1989. It was originally shot in the village of Arncliffe in Littondale but moved to Esholt, just outside Bradford.

53 Sydney-Smith, *Beyond Dixon*, pp. 119–51.

54 Lewisohn, *TV Comedy*, p. 101.

55 B. Millington, '*Boys From the Blackstuff*', in G. W. Brandt (ed.), *British Television Drama in the 1980s* (Cambridge: Cambridge University Press, 1993), p. 119.

56 Ibid., p. 126.

57 'This stupid soddin' city's full of it … why don't you fight back, you bastard'. The attack comes in episode 4, and was delivered by Angie (Julie Walters), wife of the unemployed Chrissie (Michael Angelis). D. Self (ed.), *Boys from the Blackstuff* (Cheltenham: Stanley Thornes, 1990), p 177. For Butler, pp. 12–14.

58 Plater, 'The drama of the north-east', pp. 74–5.

59 R. Webber, *Whatever Happened to the Likely Lads* (London: Orion, 1999), pp. 40–51; *Radio Times*, 21–7 January 1984, p. 17.

60 Ibid., 3–9 January 1976, pp. 6–7.

61 The second series split their time between England and Spain and a third, largely set in Arizona, brought the main characters together again in April 2002. The fact that other key characters came from London, the Midlands and Bristol allowed the programme a national flavour while making the north-east the signifier of a particular way of life under pressure.

62 Lewisohn, *TV Comedy*, p. 213; see episode 5, 21 October 1969.

63 Londoner Mike Reid and Northern Irish comedian Frank Carson were the main non-northern beneficiaries.

64 *Sunday Times*, 20 September 1998.

65 'Odd men out', *Guardian Weekend*, 10 February 2001, p. 11.

66 Series 2, episode 1, 25 April 1970.

67 Series 1, episode 1, 13 January 1989.

68 D. Turner, *Alan Bennett. In a Manner of Speaking* (London: Faber and Faber, 1997), p. ix.

69 Ibid., pp. 3–15, 67–75.

70 D. Little, *The Coronation Street Story* (London: Boxtree, 1995). For *Coronation Street* and representation of the North, see especially Shields, *Places on the Margin*, pp. 222–9. I am especially grateful to Steve Sandwell whose '"Coarse, Flat-Vowelled Vulgarity in Curlers". *Coronation Street* and the Representation of the North of England' (Unpublished MA dissertation, University of Central Lancashire, 1998) contains much valuable information and who provided me with much of the newspaper material drawn upon here and the sub-title.

71 Little, *Street*, p. 8.

72 *Observer*, 2 December 1962.

73 *Liverpool Daily Post*, 19 December 1967; *Daily Mirror*, 13 March 1969; *Sun*, 13 December 1974.

74 *Sun*, 21 June 1967. On nostalgia, see the *Daily Telegraph*, 15 May 1972; *Guardian*, 16 December 1974.

75 *Guardian*, 16 December 1974.

76 C. Geraghty, *Women and Soap Opera* (Cambridge: Polity, 1991); D. Little, *Women of Coronation Street* (London: Boxtree, 1999).

77 P. Tinniswood, *Uncle Mort's North Country* (London: Pavilion, 1986), pp. 40–1.

78 *Yorkshire Post*, 31 August 1985; *Bradford Telegraph and Argus*, 30 August 1985.

79 Episode 5, 20 March 1983.

80 *Daily Express*, 15 September 1998.

81 Quoted in P. Taylor, 'The meaning of the North: England's "foreign country" within?', *Political Geography*, 12, 1993, pp. 146–7.

82 Episode 1, 'The Driver's Tale'.

83 *Guardian*, 16 December 1974.

84 Turner, *Bennett*, pp. 149–50; Bennett, *Writing Home*, p. xi.

85 Lewisohn, *TV Comedy*, p. 101. For an intelligent 'insider's' critique of Tyneside's representation, see S. Figgis, 'Old Tyneside revisited: *Our Friends in the North*', *Northern Review*, 3, 1996, pp. 45–57.

7

Singing the North

In spring 1903, Edward Elgar adjudicated at the Morecambe Music Festival and was deeply impressed by the mainly working- and lower middle-class choirs from the North and Midlands that he encountered there. His experiences led to one of the best-known observations on the geography of English music.

> It is rather a shock to find Brahms's part-songs appreciated and among the daily fare of a district apparently unknown to the sleepy London press: people who talk of the spread of music in England and the increasing love of it rarely seem to know where the growth of the art is really strong and properly fostered. Some day the press will awake to the fact, already known abroad and to some few of us, that the living centre of music in Great Britain is not London, but somewhere further north.[1]

While the composer was undoubtedly accurate in his judgment of the comparative strengths of amateur musical culture, his strictures on the press were perhaps less so. Although much ignorance still surrounded provincial (especially working-class) musical life, there had been growing acknowledgment of the standard of and appetite for music making, especially in industrial Yorkshire and Lancashire, from at least the late eighteenth century. By the 1950s, when a biographer of singer Kathleen Ferrier told readers that 'All over the north … thousands of ordinary people take an enormous interest in making music, listening to it, and discussing and criticising it far more than in the south', such sentiments had long become clichéd, albeit one rooted in a very substantial core of truth.[2]

Consideration of music and place is, then, absolutely central to this study. While the North has ultimately never been able to wrest free of London's power and influence and while some of its key musical institutions have lost their cultural purchase over the twentieth century, music has nevertheless provided the region with some of its most potent cultural, symbolic and psychic capital and earned some of the most positive and least grudgingly given external respect.

This chapter deals with the broadest possible range of musical activity, juxta-posing artists and genres rarely, if ever, considered together. Any disadvantages that might arise from such aggregation will hopefully be offset by the demon-stration of common themes and issues across the musical field as a whole.

Musical geographies

As ever, it is essential to start with the realities structuring the cultural politics of regional identity. Initial attention is directed to the music profession and, as with the other culture industries surveyed in this study, the most striking feature is the dominance of London. This is nothing new: the profession's leading his-torian has estimated that while there were perhaps 1,500 musicians in the metropolis in the mid-eighteenth century, no other town ever managed to sup-port more than about 50.[3] As provincial opportunities grew, the proportion of musicians and music teachers in England and Wales living in the capital cer-tainly fell from 36 per cent in 1861 to 22 per cent in 1911 and Victorian London was never quite able to match the ratio of musicians and teachers to head of population attained by some southern leisure and dormitory towns (see Table 3). Nevertheless, even by the latter date, its rich opportunities in terms of concert life, theatre, teaching and much else still supported a professional musical community some ten times larger than that of its nearest rivals.[4]

Over the twentieth century, London maintained its dominant position and, indeed, enhanced it from the 1920s as the establishment of the BBC, the largely south-eastern-based recording and film industries and a plethora of new dance halls and cafes added to its advantages. The imbalance may have been redressed slightly from the 1960s as a result of growing opportunities in provincial uni-versity music departments, the foundation of new orchestras and, within the popular music industry, the growth of independent record labels.[5] Nevertheless, London could be described in 2000 as one of the three 'main centres of the global recording and music publishing industries' and was home to over 75 per cent of the UK's recording companies, 40 per cent of its full-time musicians and over half of those 'whose main professional [musical] activity is composition'.[6] Inevitably, therefore, it has always been a magnet for the most ambitious musi-cians in virtually all fields. It has drawn to it both established provincial figures such as Hallé leader John Tiplady Carrodus, lured to Covent Garden in 1869, and brass band virtuoso Jack Mackintosh, recruited in 1930 as principal trumpet in that most centripetal of institutions, the BBC Symphony Orchestra, as well as aspiring hopefuls such as guitarists Hank Marvin and Bruce Welch who gravitated from the Newcastle skiffle scene in the late 1950s.[7] Even Sir Charles Hallé, associated with the cause of provincial music more thoroughly than most, insisted on being allowed to spend each summer in the capital as a condition of his going to Manchester in 1848 and maintained a house there throughout his career.[8]

The supply of professional musicians within the North itself has always varied according to the economic structure of specific communities. Our most solid data stems from nineteenth- and early twentieth-century censuses, which, until 1901, enumerated the profession in all towns with a population of over 50,000; discussion of this issue will not stray beyond that date.[9] Although resorts such as Blackpool, Harrogate and Scarborough were too small to receive detailed attention in the census, it is probable that in the summer season at least, they housed the heaviest concentrations.[10] As the table below illustrates, the hierarchy of supply then descended through commercial and commercial-industrial cities, to large industrial and finally medium-sized industrial towns.

Industrial centres were not inherently less 'musical' than commercial ones: poorly served Barrow, for example, produced the Barrow Madrigal Society, one of Edwardian Britain's finest mixed voice choirs. Many smaller towns also had extensive networks of *part-time* teachers, often manual workers. Simply, the larger centres were blessed with a higher proportion of middle-class and lower

Table 3 Supply of musicians and music teachers to population in ten selected English Towns, 1891

Town	Numbers	Ratio to population
Brighton	476	1:243
Bath	187	1:277
Croydon	258	1:398
London	10,425	1:404
Liverpool	1,160	1:447
Manchester	1,043	1:485
Newcastle	356	1:523
Sheffield	444	1:730
Oldham	115	1:1,143
Barrow	35	1:1,477

Note: Only towns with populations above 50,000 included.
Source: Census, 1891.

middle-class families with the level of disposable income that could sustain a significant professional musical community.

Manchester and Liverpool clearly had the highest level of provision in the North and probably in the provinces in general. Large population bases (the hinterlands were vital here), the presence of German merchant communities, buoyant local entertainment industries and the proximity of numerous coastal and inland resorts to provide summer employment were the crucial factors. Pure numbers aside, Manchester's musical culture was of a qualitatively higher level than that of any other northern or provincial city, with one leading Edwardian musical writer deeming it 'next in importance to London in musical activity'.[11] It was indeed a genuinely major European art music centre from the 1850s until the early decades of the twentieth century. The establishment of the Hallé Orchestra in 1857 was absolutely fundamental here, holding some local and regional talent in the area for far longer than might otherwise have been the case while also drawing in some of the finest performers in the western world for stays of varying lengths. The establishment of the Royal Manchester College of Music in 1893, with Hallé's influence again crucial, played a similarly important role.[12] Although even Manchester was ultimately unable to stop the southern 'drift', the city's rich musical life was hugely important to the negotiation of its self-image and self-representation. Once again, the city was able to claim provincial leadership and sometimes more.

Whatever the situation within the North, standard North–South/ provinces–London divisions are easily apparent. Most professional and trade organisations, including those originating in the North, have eventually followed the wider trend within business and commerce and situated their headquarters in London. The Incorporated Society of Musicians (1882) and the Amalgamated Musicians Union (1893), both founded in Manchester, were just two of the bodies that went in search of the largest concentration of potential members. Even the National Operatic and Dramatic Society (1899), founded by northern enthusiasts to serve their burgeoning amateur operatic movement, rapidly moved to the capital.[13] The service industries of music publishing and instrument-making remained largely London-based, long-established craft traditions, business networks and markets preventing a major shift to the provinces.[14] Certainly there were always exceptions to this and, in keeping with the North's generally stronger cultural position from the 1960s, the later twentieth century saw various successful niche ventures in the region, such as the establishment of one of Britain's leading early music instrument shops and manufactures by Bradford-based firm Woods in 1970.

Patterns of musical consumption have also often been typified by clear spatial inequalities. In the field of art music, audiences in larger northern towns could enjoy a reasonable range of events, with Manchester unsurprisingly the best served throughout the period. However, even there the diet was modest indeed when compared with the capital: while Manchester might enjoy 15–20 public concerts a month during the winter season in the 1890s when such activity was at its zenith, London offered about 50 a week.[15] Within popular music in the same period, provincial audiences could expect to see leading music-hall stars far less frequently than their metropolitan counterparts. This imbalance was probably adjusted a little in some areas of pop music from the 1950s, as major London venues became fewer and as some northern ones, such as the Cavern in Liverpool (1957–73) and the Hacienda in Manchester (1982–97), attained mythical status; the (relocated) Cavern was indeed reopened as a heritage site in 1984.[16] The overall metropolitan dominance, however, is unmistakable.

A final but important issue of musical geography concerns the over-representation of London and the South within the ranks of English art music composers. The only major northern-born composers in the nineteenth century were Sheffield's William Sterndale Bennett (1816–75) and Bradford's Frederick Delius (1862–34), whose relationship with his German merchant father was so dire that he left Yorkshire and Britain for good in the 1880s.[17] The twentieth century saw a slightly improved position with the North producing amongst others, such internationally significant figures as Harrison Birtwistle (b. Accrington, 1934), Peter Maxwell Davies (b. Manchester, 1934) and William Walton (b. Oldham, 1902). Nevertheless, an analysis of 62 English composers active between 1890 and 1960 and deemed worthy of inclusion in a standard dictionary of musical biography shows that London, with approximately 12 per cent of the population of England and Wales, produced some 40 per cent of them while the North, with 33 per cent of the population, provided only 20 per cent.[18]

Such a pattern is broadly similar to that identified in the preceding analysis of English authors and, as in that context, could be offered as evidence of Frank Musgrove's claims for the North as largely exhibiting a 'practical and pragmatic character' and possessed of a political and economic heritage 'disastrous for intellectual life'.[19] Musgrove would have found an ally in Delius, whose dislike for elements of Bradford's middle-class led, albeit in a stressful moment, to the claim that he 'really could see these sort of people wiped out by the thousands with the greatest equanimity'.[20] However, and again in congruence with the earlier chapter, a more compelling explanation for London's dominance might be provided by the relative levels of opportunity. London dominated British art music and it is predictable that those living closest to its rich resources, in terms of concert life, tuition and the plethora of informal opportunities and contacts, provided a disproportionate share of successful composers. It is equally significant that as opportunities for provincial musical higher education grew over the twentieth century, so the northern (and wider provincial) contribution has become greater. As the careers of Birtwistle and Maxwell Davies testify, the Royal Manchester College of Music played an important role here, although the general opening up of educational opportunity from the mid-century has probably mattered more than any 'internal' factors of this type. Probably as a result of this, there is evidence that the North's improved representation amongst the ranks of English composers noted above continued after 1960.[21]

This emphasis on the North's secondary position must not be allowed to obscure its role as a major centre for the wider production and nourishment of musical life. At certain times and in certain places, it has been a major force within what will be referred to here rather loosely as popular music. Its contribution to the national picture broadly parallels that noted for other cultural products, although with interesting variations. The previous chapter chronicled the rise of northern (especially Lancashire) singers from the late nineteenth century and noted the success of George Formby and Gracie Fields in the 1930s, one of the region's most visible decades. The 1950s certainly saw no immediately apparent musical equivalent of the strongly northern-tinged 'new wave' in literature, cinema and, to a lesser degree, theatre. The arrival of rock 'n' roll in 1956 focused attention firmly on America and where the form did become in anyway anglicised, it did so with either mid-Atlantic tones (favoured by early northern rock star Billy Fury) or the decidedly Cockney tinge provided by such performers as Tommy Steele and Joe Brown and the Bruvvers. Nevertheless, a strong beat culture was growing in a number of northern locations. The eventual arrival of the 'Merseysound', generating fifteen British number one hits between April 1963 and July 1964 by Liverpool-based bands and singers (including five by the Beatles), transformed the situation and represents perhaps the North's greatest single cultural 'putsch'.[22] The extraordinary talent and success of the Beatles has inevitably drawn attention to Liverpool in this period, but Manchester was also extremely fertile, at least in commercial terms, producing the Hollies, Freddie and the Dreamers, Herman's Hermits and Wayne Fontana and the Mindbenders, while the Animals gave Newcastle its first nationally prominent pop music stars.

It is hard to plot clean lines between either Merseybeat specifically or northern pop in general and the wider cultural rise of the North in the 1950s and 1960s; indeed, in the 'leading sectors' of literature and film, the North's moment was effectively over by 1963. While the general popularity of northern themes and locations probably helped facilitate the musical successes of the 1960s, the crucial factors, which included the industry's need for novelty, the sheer talent of the Beatles and the persistence of their manager Brian Epstein in pursuing their cause, were probably largely peculiar to the music industry. Some commentators have argued that the successes of 1963–65 served to challenge London's pre-eminence and to make the North an established force within popular music.[23] However, this is unconvincing. As in most other areas of cultural life, music was heavily influenced by the turn to 'swinging London' from the mid-1960s, a phenomenon which both drew much northern and provincial talent to the capital and placed southern bands such as the Rolling Stones, The Who, the Small Faces and the Kinks in the foreground. A firmer, more continuous place for northern bands did not really begin until the late 1970s and, again, industry politics and economics were important here in the shape of the rise of independent record labels, many of which were based outside London. Throughout the 1980s – once again in consonance with wider trends – and still fairly steadily from that point, Manchester and Liverpool in particular have produced a substantial number of the nation's commercially successful and/or musically significant bands, with important contributions too from Sheffield, Leeds, Hull and other cities.[24] In the last two decades of the twentieth century popular music has thus played a key role in representing and defining the North for younger generations.

Folk music, although a minority strand within popular musical culture, has also enjoyed moments of prominence and served as an important source of northern imagery and self-expression.[25] Northumberland most particularly has enjoyed a highly distinctive musical culture with the intensely rural nature of much of the county, its proximity to Scotland and thus a strong tradition of country dance bands and, arguably most importantly, the survival of the Northumbrian small pipe, giving it a continuous, indigenous folk tradition second only to that of the west of Ireland within the British Isles.[26] With full regard to this history and for the popularity of younger performers such as Northumbrian piper and fiddle player Kathyrn Tickell (b. 1967) and other northerners prominent in the 'roots' phenomenon from the mid-1980s, it was the burgeoning folk club movement in the 1960s and 1970s that saw folk music reach its widest audience in recent times. A significant number of performers in this period featured a repertoire with a decidedly regional tinge and Liverpool's Spinners and textile Lancashire's Oldham Tinkers, Fivepenny Piece, Houghton Weavers and singer/songwriter and playwright Mike Harding gained considerable national media coverage, including regular spots on peak-time television.[27] Some retained substantial followings long after this period.

For all the importance of pop and folk music from the 1960s, for most of the period under review the North's most distinctive and defining musical traditions were those stemming from its rich culture of amateur music-making. It was the North's contribution in this area, described by one commentator as 'the backbone of our national musical life', that earned its reputation as England's 'true' musical centre.[28] Paramount here have been the brass bands that began to emerge from the 1830s and 1840s and the choral societies that grew out of local clubs and household gatherings at roughly the same time, although the North has also been a major forcing ground for amateur orchestras, operatic societies, concertina bands and handbell teams.[29] This rich musical culture reached its zenith in the 1890s and early 1900s and was effectively in decline from that point (with the exception of the buoyant amateur operatic sector), enduring particular periods of difficulty in the 1930s and the later 1950s and 1960s.[30] However, the quality of much that remained and the weight of historical reputation kept the North's peculiar status largely intact. The endless favourable comparison of northern amateurs with their southern counterparts that accompanied this was a substantial boon to local and regional pride.[31]

The North's reputation in these fields is so strong that the brass band movement is often regarded as specifically northern and, although the popular imagination tends to associate singing most firmly with Wales, the choral movement is similarly overlain with northern associations. The reality is a little more complex, with bands and choirs both national phenomena and the North itself providing a far from uniform picture. Nevertheless, while what follows tries to identify some subtleties, there can be no denying the overall centrality of the industrial North to these areas of musical life.

In the brass band field, analysis of national competition results provides compelling evidence of northern strength, especially in Lancashire and Yorkshire, with bands from the two counties taking almost 50 per cent of the leading positions at the two major English contests between 1853 and 1914 and around 40 per cent between 1918 and the early 1960s.[32] Exclusive focus on national contesting can admittedly mislead given that some bands chose not to contest or did so only within their own geographical confines. The figures above certainly downplay the role of the north-east in band history at least before 1914. Although north-eastern bands contested vigorously amongst themselves – in 1895, there were as many contests in Northumberland and Durham as in the more populous counties of Yorkshire and Lancashire – there was a marked reluctance to travel further afield, even to major events. Monetary considerations may have been a factor but it is more likely than a localism deeming competition between local villages as far more significant than 'foreign' campaigns, mattered most here. Similar patterns have been identified in regard to competitive sport and suggest once again important fault lines between the 'near' and 'far' Norths.[33] Differences within these broad sub-regions can also be identified. Industrial south Yorkshire, especially in the immediate vicinity of Sheffield, has, for example, produced far fewer bands of contesting repute than the West Yorkshire coal and textile belts.[34] Even within the latter area, there have been particular banding 'hotspots' and most notably in the Huddersfield area, focus in the nineteenth and earlier twentieth centuries of one of the most dynamic centres of popular music-making in the whole of Britain.[35] Explanation for these patterns of differentiation awaits the work of patient local historians.

The later emergence and less developed nature of choral competition makes it is far harder to offer the kind of data provided for bands.[36] Nevertheless, a wealth of qualitative evidence testifies to the strength of the northern choral tradition and especially that of Yorkshire (the textile district was once again most strongly celebrated). From Charles Dibdin's comment in 1788 that the poorer classes of the West Riding 'are, so to speak, born musicians'; the *Musical Times*' observation in 1877 that the Leeds Festival Chorus 'proved to be the best in the kingdom if not the first in the world' and the PEP *Arts Enquiry* claim in 1949 that 'Yorkshire may be justifiably singled out for its popular [choral] tradition', the county has been widely celebrated within musical writing.[37]

While amateur music (especially the larger choral societies) could and did flourish in cities and larger towns, this was ultimately a culture of small industrial towns and villages, communities with a population range of about 3,000–15,000. Too small to sustain a strong commercial entertainments industry they were nevertheless large enough to generate finance and audiences. Common work hours and shift patterns often added a further benefit, as did the relative ease of communication and the sometimes intense local rivalries that existed between neighbouring villages and fuelled their representatives to greater effort. Some of the nation's highest levels of adherence to nonconformity in general, and Methodism in particular, was a further crucial ingredient in many areas. Here were a set of advantages that big cities, and London above all, simply could not match.

Hymning the North

Music has proved a rich resource for the imagining of both the North and its relationship to the rest of the country. There are at least four major ways it can operate in this context: ideas can be carried or encoded within the musical language itself; in the lyrics or the manner of delivery of those lyrics; by the actions and personae of performers and within the discourses that surround music, musicians and performance. The remainder of the chapter concentrates on the last three areas for the simple reason that even cursory consideration of socio-musical linguistics is beyond the competence of this writer. It should be noted, however, that certain types of sound have long been associated with the North and much used as locational cues. Brass band music provides the most obvious case, although certain choral works, notably *Messiah*, have served similar purpose and the popularity of guitar, banjo and whistle in a number of northern folk groups from the 1960s can create a supposedly authentic northern soundscape. Certainly, since the 1960s most advertising soundtracks attempting to depict a northern context have adopted at least one of these ingredients. In the 1970s, Lancashire-born singer-songwriter Peter Skellern took these stereotypical formulae to a more sophisticated level and combined dialect-inflected lyrics with musical arrangements much embellished by brass bands and choirs to create something close to a specifically northern popular song. This was obviously a route that few could travel down, however, and Skellern's work stands as an interesting idiosyncrasy rather than a genuine new direction.[38]

Northern musical life of all types allowed for the parading, polishing and subtle embellishment of a wide range of ideas and images connected to the region and its constituent parts. Although there might be variations as to exact significance and emphasis, these were largely 'agreed' between insiders and outsiders to a far greater extent than was the case in most other cultural arenas. One of the most interesting set of ideas gathered around the familiar conception of the North as a place of unfussy, unpretentious hard work, a site of authenticity. The sacrifices involved in brass banding or choral work in terms of finance, time and emotional energy has (with much justification) been regularly celebrated from the early nineteenth century. Moreover, involvement and investment in such activity has generally been viewed as an organic growth from local social conditions, cultural practices that northern people adopt out of real commitment and not fashionable dilettantism. An Edwardian contributor to the *Musical Home Journal* captured this well:

> in an unpretentious way, the people of Huddersfield give probably more time to music than do those of any town of a similar size in England. One of the striking ways in which the musical spirit shows itself is in glee singing. It is no uncommon thing in the local public-houses to see several young fellows suddenly rise and give a lust rendering of 'When evening's twilight' or 'Here's health and life to England's king' or 'Who will o'er the downs with me?'. And that, be it duly set down, long before 11 p.m. In the mills and the workshops, the same kind of thing is heard.[39]

Elgar's claim noted at the outset that part songs were part of the 'daily fare' of northern communities added a powerful voice to such notions. Exaggerated or not, such narratives carried much cultural weight. Equally important was the common emphasis on 'ordinary people' as the backbone of music-making in the North, with the *Daily Express* describing the Huddersfield Choral Society in 1932 as 'drawn from offices, factories, shops and warehouses. They are all working people.' Without in any way seeking to diminish the deep and genuine popular contribution to northern musical life, such neat characterisations were sometimes more the product of journalistic convention and/or popular belief than close knowledge. In 1889, the Leeds Festival Choral choirmaster told the *Musical Herald* that 'he has seen remarks by London critics to the effect that the "Yorkshire mill girls" sing wonderfully … [but] he doubts if there is a single mill girl in it'.[40] Nevertheless, even such erroneous variants of the North as 'land of the working class' story served a most useful purpose by rooting musical excellence in the natural patterns of ordinary northern lives.

A similar set of representations grew around certain northern musical stars, stressing their propensity for hard work and their ordinariness, modesty and lack of pretension. It is instructive to consider in tandem the careers of variety artist Gracie Fields (1898–1979) and concert hall and operatic contralto Kathleen Ferrier (1912–53), two 'Lancashire lasses' usually looked at separately but whose lives were often interpreted in extremely similar ways. *Lancashire Life* told readers in 1949 how Ferrier missed Lancashire (true to standard migratory patterns she had moved to London in 1942) but that 'she looks back with affection at the bleak hills, grey streets and warm-hearted people of the North Country'. Some years after her death, a local newspaper remembered her as someone 'who never forgot she was a Lancashire lass even after she had moved from Blackburn and the North Country to New York and Vienna'.[41] The

Rochdale Observer struck a similar tone when reporting a charity concert in Fields' native town (she had left in 1914) in 1933.

> When the town as whole, with the mayoress as spokeswomen, tried to tender adequate thanks, the Lancashire girl broke down. For few moments she was unable to speak ... In that moment she was indeed 'our Gracie' – never have the hearts of an audience gone out to her more than they did then. Rochdale was deeply touched by the love of a great daughter who, in her immense success, refuses to forget her humble home.[42]

There must be no denial of the genuine character traits in both women that allowed such pictures to be constructed. Ferrier's comment to the secretary of a Macclesfield choral society – 'Ee lad, it'll cost thee tuppence to speak to me now. I've just come from singing with Barbirolli and the Hallé' – captures the air of surprise at her own success that shines through all accounts of her life. Nevertheless, the characteristics selected for civic celebration are highly significant. Here are two stars depicted in ways richly illustrative of how the North would most like itself to be seen.

In yet another version of this celebration of northern authenticity, many writers have enjoyed exploring the juxtaposition of artistic creativity and unlovely physical surroundings. Rock musicians and commentators have tended to stress a causal relationship between the two, seeing urban bleakness and poverty as a creative spur. Noel Gallagher of Oasis argued in an interview in 1995 that 'when my generation left school [in the mid-1980s] they had only three choices offered them: football, music or the dole. That's why there are so many big rock groups from the north.' Pop music historian Dave Haslam has been somewhat pithier. 'Maybe if Manchester was less of shit-hole then creativity in the city would die.'[43] Those concerned with art music have focused less on harshness as the spur for creativity, although such ideas can be found in discussions of the band movement, and rather more on the incongruity between physical environment and artistic achievement. One Huddersfield resident recalled visits to his music teacher, the highly regarded Lewis Eagland, in the 1930s.

> Lewis lived in Slaithwaite ... in the sprawling industrial conurbation of the Colne Valley. His house, one of a small group of blackened stone terrace dwellings, was quite overshadowed by the high walls of a huge textile mill of truly satanic aspect, from which you could hear the muffled throb of the engine powering the clattering looms as soon as you turned the corner.[44]

There is obvious pleasure in this account in the fact that the North is not always what it seems, that beauty can be found in surprising places and artistic achievement occur without unnecessary trappings. In 1900 a Manchester magazine noted the apparent contradiction between Manchester's physical appearance and received reputation and the arrival in the city of Hans Richter, then Europe's most celebrated conductor, to take over the Hallé.

> To the ordinary person it may seem strange that 'foggy Manchester' should be preferred to the gay and sunny Austrian capital 'the metropolis of modern music'. Dr Richter lets us, however, into the secret of this preference. After conducting Tchaikovsky's *Symphonie Pathetique* in Manchester, a few days subsequent to the death of Sir Charles Hallé, he said to a friend, 'I never knew anything like the responsive character of the audience'. Our city may be dull to ordinary observers, as they come and go, but we are proud of the fact that there is a world behind the dullness which responds to the appeal of genius, and gives back inspiration in return.[45]

Here, pleasure in incongruity is joined by another central notion, that the North formed a repository of unusually acute knowledge and wisdom, an idea also encountered in the sporting arena. Manchester played on this idea particularly forcefully, using the success of the Hallé and other local cultural institutions to challenge long-held claims of local and more general northern philistinism.[46]

Powerful as traditional views about northern hard work, integrity and so forth were in the musical context as in all others, as the explanation of Richter's arrival suggests, they could be effectively counterbalanced by a willingness to acknowledge rather more sensitive, delicate sensibilities. This can be glimpsed in the *Huddersfield Examiner*'s delight in the 'well nigh perfect' *pianissimo* achieved by the women members of the Huddersfield Glee and Madrigal Society in a rendition of Vaughan Williams's *Five Tudor Pieces* in 1937. The choir in general 'brought us beautifully graded tone and a complete answer to some southern critics who seem to think that Yorkshire choirs sing resonant *fortes* all the time'.[47] Here, the received image of the industrial North is recast in much softer tones, stressing delicacy, subtlety and lightness of touch – all characteristics far more valuable in many workplaces than sheer physical strength – to open up much richer notions of northern character. Representations of the brass band from inside the movement have in their turn often skilfully balanced celebration of 'traditional' masculinity, with much emphasis on the sheer physical effort involved and on the prevalence of boisterous forms of behaviour, with acknowledgement of the deeper emotional significance of the music made. One bandsman recalled that cornet player Harry Mortimer 'could strike a note so beautifully it would make you cry'.[48] While such sentiments could be appropriated for all manner of well-worn northern narratives, not least those emphasising warm hearts behind hard exteriors, music was one of the foremost sites for the enrichment as well as merely the reinforcement of standard views of the North.

Representing the North

Musical life has contributed extensively to the construction of numerous layers of territorial loyalty and identification. As is so often the case, probably the dominant sensibility has been allegiance to locality, with music creating at the very least a sense of civic pride and sometimes much deeper feelings of belonging. For smaller towns and villages the success of local amateur bodies in the competitive arena has been the most potent vehicle for most of the period. Although bands and choirs rarely matched sporting bodies in their power to mobilise communities on a regular basis, their function has not been dissimilar. At least until the 1930s, and beyond in some cases, leading musical personalities, especially brass bandsmen, were often local heroes. Supporters would follow bands and choirs to contests – local mills closed for the day to allow for the scale of the exodus in support of Lancashire's Cornholme Band at Belle Vue in 1893 – and victories could result in public celebrations mirroring those enjoyed by conquering football teams.[49] Once again, as in sport, formulaic press coverage of these often featured imagery that, while undoubtedly capturing genuine cross-class sentiment 'suggested a magical resolution of the many internal tensions and conflicts that in fact beset the communities … offering an idealized vision of society.[50]

Some towns also had successful individual professionals or institutions to celebrate. In the field of art music, the Hallé's importance to Manchester has already been noted while Bradford's belated discovery of long-departed composer Frederick Delius resulted in a street on a new council estate being named in his honour in 1930 and his receipt of the freedom of the city in 1932. From the 1960s, although events such as the annual Huddersfield Contemporary Music Festival (1978) have brought considerable kudos within a specialist context, it has been pop and rock that have played the major musical role in the construction of local patriotism and self-image. This has sometimes involved little more than the vicarious pleasure of association with local performers, particularly as popular music was largely devoid of local references and contexts for much of the twentieth century. That began to change with Merseysound of the early and mid-1960s, although even this was initially largely restricted to the (albeit very important) matters of showing demonstrable pride in an English regional identity and utilising the local accent when singing. With the exception of Gerry and the Pacemakers' 'Ferry Across the Mersey' (1964) and occasional lines in Beatles's songs, local references were still rare and in terms of musical language there was, in Charlie Gillett's words, eventually 'little to distinguish [Liverpool acts] from the rest of the country's pop groups'.[51] Only from the 1980s did the habit of using local references in lyrics became an increasingly common practice, with Manchester's The Smiths, for whom lyricist Morrissey produced such titles as 'Rusholme Ruffians' and 'Strangeways here we come', a particularly important case in point.[52] Until the late twentieth century, folk singers had been those more prone to give audiences the 'shock of the familiar', in songs like The Oldham Tinkers' 'Owdham Edge', Fivepenny Piece's 'King Cotton' and, above all, folk-rock band Lindisfarne's 'Fog on the Tyne' (1971). Re-recorded with vocals from Gateshead-born footballer Paul Gascoigne in 1990 and reaching number two in the British charts, the song has become something of a Tyneside anthem.

In exceptional moments, pop music has generated similarly exceptional levels of local pride, most notably in Liverpool in the mid-1960s when the city came close to establishing hegemony in Western popular music, and in Manchester during the 'Madchester' moment of 1989–90. The latter saw T-shirts proclaiming 'On the Seventh Day God Created Manchester' and, with one of those interesting slippages from the local to the regional, 'Born in the North, Live in the North, Die in the North'.[53] The success of Michael Winterbottom's film *24 Hour Party People* (2002), focusing on the career of Factory Records boss Tony Wilson, has added to the city's sense of being at the true core of British popular music from the 1970s. More modestly, Wigan gained a boost to its self-image and external credibility through the reputation of the Wigan Casino (1973–81) as the capital of the 'northern soul' dance scene.[54] Despite, or perhaps even because of, the intense local pride that pop music has generated, even the most successful performers such as the Beatles have been 'frequently criticised or treated as deserters' if they chose to move elsewhere. The desire to pull local stars back to their roots and keep them under the influence of 'democratic' sensibilities remained a powerful force.[55]

Local pride can be essentially parochial and inward-looking, pitting one community against others within a wider region. Rivalries between brass bands have often been quite fierce with specialist band press proving a powerful vehicle for the airing of petty grievances well into the 1950s. Long-established tensions could be re-activated or re-focused by musical issues. There was a strong feeling in Manchester in the 1960s that local groups had been undeservedly overshadowed by the publicity surrounding the Merseysound. As late as 1992, a book on 1960s Manchester pop music entitled *It Happened in Manchester* featured a cover design with 'Manchester' written in above a scrawled out 'Liverpool'.[56] Nevertheless, local pride can be a building block for wider regional identities, albeit those expressed without compromising a sense of local patriotism and experienced ultimately through attachment to, and knowledge of, the immediate environment. County loyalty has certainly been in evidence in various guises. Yorkshire's rich choral culture was often explained well into the twentieth century by reference to local dialects, especially the long vowels which, it was claimed, 'kept the throat open'.[57] Two key foci of county pride are married here in a not altogether scientific but nevertheless satisfying manner. More visceral evidence of contemporary county loyalty comes from the football/cricket chants of 'Yorkshire, Yorkshire' that sometimes greet Hull-based band The Beautiful South elsewhere in the county.[58] Music has effectively reinforced other sub-regional alliances. A civic reception given to South Shields brass band St Hilda Colliery in Newcastle in 1920 following the band's success in the National Championship was in conscious recognition of the band's service to the larger Tyneside region.[59] Similarly, Northumbrian folk music has often carried a cultural burden for a wider north-east.

It is much harder to identify an obvious sense of a greater 'northern' identity. Some forms of musical activity possibly helped build such a feeling simply by bringing musicians from different areas into contact. With allowance for the parochialism of some north-eastern brass bands noted earlier, travelling to competitions allowed bandsmen to get to know areas of the North beyond their immediate locality and to feel part of a musical community which, while always proudly celebrated as a national movement, was also seen as northern at its core.

More generally, the family of anti-metropolitan mentalities noted throughout this book and already pointed to earlier in this chapter was clearly present. Hostility to London in the musical context carried especial resonance because of the North's reputation and expertise. Although clearly visible in nineteenth-century northern musical life, it is probable that anti-metropolitan sensibilities were strongest from the early twentieth century. This partly reflects the declining position and status of the North's voluntary musical culture, an issue returned to below, but also the growth of the BBC from the 1920s and more general southward shift in so many areas of the national culture. As ever, it would be misleading to see attitudes to London as entirely negative. Northerners were obviously aware of its status as national and imperial capital and enjoyed the chance to appear centre stage. Invitations for northern bands and choirs to appear at concerts in London were much cherished and, while participation in events such as the National Brass Band Championship at the Crystal Palace was always flavoured by a sense of cultural 'missionary work', there is little evidence that the metropolitan location was in any way resented. There was, indeed, a weary acceptance of London's dominant position and a certain pleasure at recognition by its leading figures. When Malcolm Sargent took over the conductorship of the Huddersfield Choral Society in 1932, the local newspaper claimed that 'it is also something of a compliment to the reputation of the Huddersfield Choral Society that a young conductor with so many avenues of employment open to him, with an established place in London, should have consented to have come to another provincial society'.[60] What *was* disliked was any southern/metropolitan presumption of cultural leadership, an attitude guaranteed to transmute reluctant acceptance into hostility.

Concern with London's position and attitude could be expressed from almost any part of the musical world, although amateur musicians were one of the most vociferous groups and supply many of the following examples, and in many tones. The vice-chancellor of Manchester University's claim in 1903 that 'the musical metropolis of England was Manchester' and the shouts of 'hear, hear' voiced by his audience, could have carried any number of meanings from real anger to mild and slightly self-deprecating rebuke. The *South Shields Daily Gazette*'s strictures in 1920, following the success of the St Hilda Band noted above, were really not much more than a forceful if slightly over-defensive reminder of the northern reputation for music-making.

> The southerner is apt to regard the northman – especially if the latter hails from an industrial or coal-mining area – as a somewhat grim and hard being, who has little use for the refining graces and arts of life. As a matter of fact, the North is, we believe more musical than the South: that is musical inclination and aptitude are commoner possessions of the people.[61]

Four years later, however, the *Huddersfield Examiner* struck a more aggressive note, reporting a local concert featuring the works of William Byrd and Thomas Weelkes.

> Coinciding with the tercentenary of those two composers there comes a marked revival of interest in the works of Tudor composers. But perhaps one should say a marked revival of interest in London and the South, for in Huddersfield it did not need a tercentenary to draw attention to the madrigals of Byrd and Weelkes. The Huddersfield Glee and Madrigal Society has been singing Byrd and Weelkes ever since the society was formed and there are few choirs better qualified to interpret the Tudor madrigalists than they. Whilst the South has neglected the Tudor composers, the smaller choirs of the West Riding have not.[62]

On occasion, comments on London bias and ignorance teetered dangerously into territory that could allow outsiders to claim a sort of northern paranoia. From the late 1920s, for example, northern brass bandsmen (and many of their counterparts in other regions) had been critical of the BBC's thin coverage of banding. Yet in 1946 one Yorkshire paper managed to turn to the BBC's disadvantage the fact that the 'first four placings [at Crystal Palace] were announced by Stuart Hibberd, Frank Phillips and others nearly a dozen times in the space of six hours', by arguing that the equally important Open Contest at Manchester's Belle Vue received no such headline treatment.[63] Any action of the BBC, even well-intentioned ones, had, it appeared, to be placed in the context of London's sense of superiority.

As banding and many other aspects of flagship northern amateur culture have passed to the margins, leadership in the battle against London pretension and dominance has passed largely to pop and rock musicians and their interpreters. Unsurprisingly, the emergence of the Merseysound generated the first major North–South (or, more accurately, Liverpool–London) pop music conflict. Although this owed much to media adoption of obvious and well-tried strategies, with *Melody Maker* exhorting readers to 'join in the Big North–South Beat War', it was a letter to the paper asking 'how many more Northern beat groups must we endure?' that sparked the debate, and both camps found many willing correspondents.[64] While an Essex-based reader complained that 'it seems you have to come from the north' and that top London bands 'can't get a hit in edgeways', Liverpudlians wrote of the 'nasty jealous criticism … we have to endure' and complained of carping from the 'musically over-privileged south'.[65] 1994–95 saw something of a reprise when 'Britpop' was enlivened by the rivalry between Blur (London) and Oasis (Manchester).

From the late 1970s, the growth of independent record labels and the emergence of (sometimes) faster and more varied road, rail and air links, allowing for easier movement to and from a provincial base, has led to a number of groups minimising the time spent in London and in some cases developing a consciously regionalist position. Certainly, in the 1980s, when pop music sometimes exhibited an explicit anti-Thatcherite political perspective, the marriage of class and regional politics so typical of the period could emerge within popular musical culture. In 1987, after the Conservative's third election victory in succession, the Hull-based Housemartins produced an album entitled 'London 0 Hull 4', a gesture seen by the group's biographer as 'a perfect rejoinder from the underdog, a reminder of northern pride'. Rebuked by the Independent Broadcasting Authority for obscenity after making comments about Margaret and Denis Thatcher, they invited the couple to visit 'some of the housing estates in Hull, that's what I call obscene'.[66] In his *Manchester, England* (1999) Manchester-based (although not born) DJ Dave Haslam constructed a narrative which, if not explicitly anti-metropolitan, places Manchester at the heart of a new popular musical culture that grew up in the spaces left by the loss of the city's traditional industries and the ever increasing migration of political power to the capital. Where once the city's wealth financed empire,

> now the city dominates English pop culture, trading in music, the sounds from the city's streets resonating around the globe … Away from the centres of political power – and you can't get much further away than a bedroom in Burnage or a dance floor in Ancoats – Manchester's mavericks and misfits have created a magnificent, unofficial underground culture.[67]

Here, the North, or at least one of its major cities, is once again cast as the site of innovation, of challenge and alternative to an old order.

Muting the trumpets

For all its positive connotations, there were nevertheless still many ways in which northern musical culture, or representations of it, chimed with some of the more disabling versions of the region's image. The sheer strength and longevity of London's dominance of so many aspects of the musical sphere has been examined in depth above and needs no reiteration here, but the fact of that power provides a crucial context that has always limited the North's scope for sustained cultural leadership. Beyond that key constraint a number of other factors have played a role in ultimately holding the North at the margins.

The decline in scale and status of the voluntary associational culture so central to the North's musical reputation has been one of the most decisive. For all the success and celebration of the northern amateur tradition noted above, there had always been a degree of critical ambivalence and ignorance. This was particularly so in regard to brass bands and male voice choirs where a combination of social and aesthetic factors kept them in a subsidiary position within the overall musical field. Their largely working-class membership, their roots in small towns and villages that lacked status within the national geographical hierarchy and the tendency, despite all protestation to the contrary, for many cultural commentators to value commercial, high-status musical events above the voluntary and the communal, were all key factors here. There was also the issue of artistic distance from the musical establishment. While the larger choral societies were rooted in the sacred art music repertory of Handel, Mendelssohn and Elgar, and the smaller mixed-voice choirs stimulated much new art music composition during the late Victorian and Edwardian 'English musical renaissance', bands and male voice choirs enjoyed repertoires that were often shaped by values, attitudes and audience expectations peculiar to their sub-cultures.[68] Outsiders did not always grasp this, as when Peter Warlock claimed in 1930 that, all allowance for the high technical standards reached, 'the quality of the average brass band programme leaves much to be desired … operatic potpourris and showy Victorian concert solos still predominate in their brass band catalogues'.[69] Similarly, a far from unsympathetic survey of amateur music published in 1949 argued that the 'high standard of performance common to male voice choirs rarely goes with a high standard in repertoire … Most choirs are led by musicians whose enthusiasm is greater than their musical knowledge'.[70] Whatever the validity of such comments, they showed that those institutions responsible for earning the North important cultural capital were not sufficiently well anchored in the national culture to survive the much harsher critical and cultural climate of the later twentieth century.

Once they began to fall victim to changing social and economic circumstance, it was easy for them to be represented as still interesting and worthy but essentially outdated. Brass bands suffered as expanding consumer choices and shifting patterns of youth culture meant that their half-century journey from somewhere near the centre of northern working-class culture to marginal, special interest group was virtually completed in the 1950s.[71] This is nowhere better captured than in the text and subsequent film of Stan Barstow's novel *A Kind of Loving* (1960/62). The father of central figure Vic Brown is a keen bandsman but, although suitably proud of him, Vic succumbs to pressure from his mother-in-law and new wife and takes his seat not at his father's concert but in front of the newly acquired television set. This episode symbolises many social and sexual issues explored by the book including the emasculatory power of women, the move to consumerism, changes in taste within working-class society and generational conflict. However, the regional dimension is also crucial. Barstow's text, central in the rediscovery of the North in this period, both records and reinforces the brass band's trajectory of decline, placing it firmly in the 'old North' that was being unpicked in the post-war period. Raphael Samuel's observation that jazz was the favoured musical mode when 'making a cobbled walkway lyrical' in the northern new wave movies takes on added significance in the context of this particular episode.[72]

Bands struggled to find a new image from the 1950s and 1960s but still often found themselves associated more firmly in the public mind with a set of traditional northern stereotypes. The use of a brass band playing Dvorak's 'New World Symphony' as soundtrack for an exaggeratedly 'northern' Hovis commercial in the 1970s was a definitive moment here. (The fact that a parody of the advert and its version of northern-ness by folksinger Tony Capstick enjoyed chart success in 1981 probably added to the power of the original.)[73] On the few occasions when the brass band has penetrated the national culture in the late twentieth century, it has in both fact (during the 1984–85 miners' strike and the pit closures of the early 1990s) and fiction (in the 1996 hit film *Brassed Off*) generally symbolised the decline of a collective way of industrial life. Significant artistic moments, such as Grimethorpe Colliery Band's work with composer Harrison Birtwhistle in the 1970s, their appearance (with Black Dyke Mills Band) in the 1974 Proms and much else of interest since, have tended to have been lost within this wider picture.[74] The claim by one local paper that such moments as the 1974 Proms performance have dispelled the 'cloth cap image many southerners have of brass bands' has been no more than wishful thinking.[75] The choral movement ultimately fared little better, secularisation rendering the once great northern Christmas *Messiah* tradition, for example, little more than a rather interesting element of museum culture. From the 1960s, celebratory quotes of the type that opened this chapter became ever less frequent.

Issues within the field of art music, potentially a cultural symbol of much weight for the region, have also played a part in the production of northern stereotypes in the twentieth century. Neville Cardus' 1954 essay on Ferrier, 'The girl from Blackburn', is interesting here. One of the most influential music critics of his generation, Cardus was both a passionate devotee of Ferrier's and a loving chronicler of Lancashire life. In this essay, his penchant for knowing exaggeration and highly embellished versions of northern-ness lead to a narrative that comes close to denying the region's capacity for musicality and creativity. For example, there erupts at times a sense almost of surprise and certainly of incongruity as he traces Ferrier's progress 'from Blackburn to Vienna, from gold medal in Lytham to "*Das Lied von der erde*" in Salzburg, from "number engaged" to the heartbreaking, isolated tones of "Blow the wind southerly"'. In another passage he asks

> By what alchemy in her mind and bloodstream did a woman of Blackburn, of Lancashire goodness of heart and humour, a women exuding from her north-country nature a loving kindness that was communal, inspiring friendship, brotherhood and sisterhood – how did she come to sing Mahler, sing his song of loneliness in the world as few Austrian singers have done, and no English singer ever?[76]

For northern audiences such comments are interesting, unthreatening and not without gentle comic possibilities. For external audiences, however, they point up old notions setting northern bluffness against southern sensitivity and almost invite readers to agree to the unlikelihood of the North producing such a genius.

Sometimes, as with Bradford's relationship with reluctant son Frederick Delius, the North just seemed to be trying too hard. This is well demonstrated by the 1962 Delius Festival, a ten-day event in honour of the centenary of the composer's birth that brought some of the leading international talent of the day to the city. Although in many ways successful, the festival generated a series of debates that reinforced precisely the image of the city that it was intended to dispel. Some critics queried its artistic value, suggesting that Delius simply did not deserve such sustained attention. There were occasional hiccups in the performances, with the much-celebrated local sopranos producing top notes 'as white as their dresses' according to *The Times*.[77] Most problematic of all was the intervention of Richard Hoggart, keynote speaker at a conference on the issue of public culture organised in parallel with the festival. In a short and deliberately provocative lecture, Hoggart characterised the festival as the high-profile pulling of a cultural 'Christmas cracker' which did little to connect with the daily needs and lives of ordinary Bradfordians. No journalists actually attended his session and no definitive version of the speech was ever circulated but the local and then national press seized on his purported remarks and elevated this minor event into a brief *cause célèbre*. The defensive tone of the organisers and some local councillors was far from helpful, with the Festival Chairman noting that 'Education is a wonderful thing. Now I know there is a man named Hoggart'.[78] Such studied anti-intellectualism did little to dispel the feeling that in trying to establish its artistic credentials the city was in fact in danger of parading the very *parvenu* tendencies it sought to cast off. For several years, *Daily Telegraph* columnist 'Peter Simple' had chronicled the adventures of one Alderman Jabez Foodbotham, the 'perpetual Chairman of the Bradford City Tramways and Fine Arts Committee', and suddenly he appeared to have come to life.[79]

Ironically, contemporary critical comment and subsequent analysis of the rock bands of the post-punk period, the North's newest and in many ways most dynamic musical ambassadors, have sometimes provided another set of images that tie the region to long-established narratives. In April 1979, for example, the *New Musical Express* described the music of Manchester's Joy Division's as 'sketch[ing] grey abstractions of industrial malaise ... Unfortunately, as anyone who has ever lived in the low-rent squalor of a northern industrial city will know, the vision is deadly accurate'. Some fifteen years later, writer Jon Savage described the band's singer/lyricist Ian Curtis as exploring musically 'an environment systematically degraded by the industrial revolution, confined by lowering moors with oblivion as the only escape'. It is difficult for newcomers to read Curtis' intensely personal and non-place-specific lyrics in this way, but critical discourses certainly encourage them to.[80] Comments made by rock stars about their neighbourhoods can also be less than positive in terms of image management, as when Happy Mondays' singer Shaun Ryder described his native Manchester to *Q* magazine in 1996 as 'a Disneyland for drugs'.[81] Indeed, as implied earlier, there is a sense in which some northern bands and their interpreters have made a conscious attempt to emphasis various hard, tough and bleak images of the North, in order to convey both a regional and personal 'authenticity' and distinctiveness. Thus, while Ryder objected to the mimicry of his street Mancunian in music press interviews – 'I always come over double thick, I sound brainless … If they're interviewing a black guy they don't start writing in patois, do they?' – he has also been accused of playing up to this image.[82] Haslam's notion of Manchester as creative 'shithole' quoted above provides another example of such thinking while members of Elbow, a band from nearby Bury, have been taken to task for exaggerating the town's social and economic plight.[83]

For younger generations, however, the negative reading of popular music's impact offered above would probably seem unsympathetic and partial. If written in the mid-1970s, this chapter would have been almost elegiac, an obituary suggesting that the cultural capital flowing from northern music of all types was now close to exhaustion. However, the North's place in the national culture always fluctuates and the last two decades of the twentieth century witnessed the recovery of much ground. For all the importance of activity within art music and its supporting infrastructure, popular music has been the crucial force. Whereas the North's association with popular culture was seen as potentially problematic until as recently as the 1960s, the increasingly elevated status of popular culture and the 'taken as read' importance attached to it by those born since that period has given parts of the North, even the grim, de-industrialised North of the The Fall and Joy Division, a cultural cachet. It was claimed that the 'Madchester' moment had led to a 30 per cent increase in applications to Manchester's institutions of higher education in 1990, while the quality of Leeds' club life has been seen as a factor increasing the city's popularity as a higher education location from the 1990s.[84] Whether the region can remain powerful within the notoriously fickle field of popular music is unknown but it remains likely to be the most potent musical force in the cultural politics of the North–South divide. The once important voluntary musical can now do little more than mobilise a residual local and regional pride and is too easily appropriated in the service of old-fashioned images of the region. While rock music and musicians can make it feel grim up north, as with the novelists and film directors of the late 1950s and 1960s, they have also sometimes made it seem exciting as well.

Notes

1 Letter to the organiser, Canon Gorton, quoted in *Musical Times*, July 1903.

2 P. Lethbridge, *Kathleen Ferrier* (London: Cassell, 1959), pp. 3–4.

3 C. Ehrlich, *The Music Profession in Britain since the Eighteenth Century. A Social History* (Oxford: Clarendon Press, 1985), p. 3.

4 D. Russell, 'Musicians in the English provincial city: Manchester, *c*.1860–1914', in C. Bashford and L. Langley (eds), *Music and British Culture, 1785–1914. Essays in Honour of Cyril Ehrlich* (Oxford: Oxford University Press, 2000), pp. 234–7.

5 The best known was Manchester's 'Factory' label (1978–92) but there were numerous others in the city as well as in Liverpool, Sheffield, Newcastle and elsewhere. For the independent labels through a London example, see D. Hesmondhalgh, 'Post-punk's attempt to democratise the music industry: the success and failure of Rough Trade', *Popular Music*, 16, 3, 1997.

6 D. Laing and N. Yorke, 'The value of music in London', *Cultural Trends*, 38, 2000, pp. 7, 4, 5.

7 *Musical Times*, August 1895; N. Kenyon, *The BBC Symphony Orchestra* (London: BBC, 1981), pp. 50–3; P. Doncaster and T. Jasper, *Cliff* (London: Sidgwick and Jackson, 1981), p. 60.

8 M. Kennedy, *The Hallé Tradition. A Century of Music* (Manchester: Manchester University Press, 1960), p. 19.

9 For census material, see Ehrlich, *Music Profession*, pp. 51–2.

10 On resorts, see Russell, 'Musicians', p. 235.

11 W. J. Galloway, *Musical England* (London: Christophers, 1910), p. 139.

12 Kennedy, *The Hallé Tradition*; Russell, 'Musicians', pp. 239–42.

13 J. Lowerson, 'An outbreak of allodoxia? Operatic amateurs and middle-class musical taste between the wars', in A. Kidd and D. Nicholls (eds), *Gender, Civic Culture and Consumerism. Middle-Class Identity in Britain, 1800–1940* (Manchester: Manchester University Press, 1999), p. 200.

14 C. Ehrlich, *The Piano. A Social History* (London: Dent, 1976), pp. 34, 39, 203–10; D. Russell, *Popular Music in England, 1840–1914. A Social History* (Manchester: Manchester University Press, 2nd edn, 1997), pp. 178–9.

15 Russell, 'Musicians', pp. 236–7: Ehrlich, *Music Profession*, p. 61.

16 P. Thompson, *The Best of Cellars* (Liverpool: Bluecoat Press, 1994).

17 Biographies include C. Delius, *Frederick Delius. Memories of My Brother* (London: Nicholson, 1936); E. Fenby, *Delius as I Knew Him* (Cambridge: Cambridge University Press, 1981 edn) and C. Palmer, *Portrait of a Cosmopolitan* (London: Duckworth, 1976). His relationship with Bradford is touched on later in this chapter and in D. Russell, 'Music and northern identity, *c.*1890–1965', in N. Kirk (ed.), *Northern Identities. Historical Interpretations of the 'The North' and 'Northernness'* (Aldershot: Ashgate, 2000), pp. 29, 31–2, 38.

18 The sixty-two are those deemed important enough to be included in Eric Gilder, *Dictionary of Composers and their Music* (Newton Abbot: David & Charles, 1985). For further details, Russell, 'Music and northern identity', pp. 25–6. The strictures offered in chapter 2, on birthplace as a guide to an individual's actual place of formative experience and the limitations of biographical dictionaries, are acknowledged again here.

19 F. Musgrove, *The North of England. A History from Roman Times* (Oxford: Oxford University Press, 1990), pp. 13–16.

20 Letter to Jelka Rosen, written at the time of his father's funeral, in L. Carley (ed.), *Delius. A Life in Letters* (London: Scolar Press: 1983), pp. 194–5.

21 For example, of thirty-four composers of contemporary music (an admittedly narrower field than that considered by Gilder) born after 1940 and listed in B. Morton and P. Collins, *Contemporary Composers* (London: St James's Press, 1992), eight were born in London and nine in the North.

22 The other successful artists were Gerry and the Pacemakers (three number ones, including the first, 'How do you do it?'), The Searchers (three), Billy J. Kramer and the Dakotas (two) and Cilla Black (two). On 20 June 1963, four of the top-five best-selling singles were by Liverpool acts, with the fifth by Manchester's Freddie and the Dreamers.

23 D. Haslam, *Manchester, England. The Story of the Pop Cult City* (London: Fourth Estate, 1999), p. 92.

24 Leading performers include The Buzzcocks, Joy Division, The Fall, The Smiths, The Stone Roses, The Happy Mondays, Oasis, MPeople and Simply Red from Manchester and its surrounds; Teardrop Explodes, Frankie Goes to Hollywood, Elvis Costello, Echo and the Bunnymen from Liverpool; Embrace from Huddersfield, The Housemartins/The Beautiful South from Hull and Pulp from Sheffield.

25 There is absolutely no attempt here to enter the swampy grounds of definining 'folk'.

26 Colin Irwin provides a good introduction in *Rough Guide to World Music* (London: Rough Guides, 1999), pp. 67–70.

27 D. Stuckey, *The Spinners. Fried Bread and Brandy-o!* (London: Robson, 1983). For biographies of leading northern performers, see *The Guinness Who's Who of Folk Music* (London: Guinness Publishing, 1993).

28 PEP, *The Arts Enquiry. Music. A Report on Musical Life in England* (London: PEP, 1949), p. 98.

29 Russell, *Popular Music*, pp. 186–200.

30 D. Russell, 'Amateur musicians and their repertoire', in S. Banfield, *The Blackwell History of Music in Britain: The Twentieth Century* (Oxford: Blackwell, 1995), pp. 145–50.

31 For example, *Brass Band News*, July 1895; *Radio Times*, 30 June 1944; PEP, *The Arts Enquiry*, pp. 100, 102.

32 The 'Open' at Belle Vue, Manchester began in 1853, the 'National' at Crystal Palace in 1900.

33 *Brass Band Annual* (Sibsey: Lincs, 1895), pp. 49–70; A. Metcalfe 'Organised sport in the mining communities of south Northumberland, 1800–99', *Victorian Studies*, 25, 4, 1982, pp. 469–95.

34 Of the twenty-one Yorkshire bands taking a prize in the Belle Vue Open Championship between 1853 and 1914, only two came from south Yorkshire.

35 Russell, *Popular Music*, p. 209.

36 For an outline history at least of the nineteenth century, see ibid., pp. 248–71.

37 E. Mackerness, *A Social History of English Music* (London: Routledge and Kegan Paul, 1964), p. 113; quoted in F.R. Spark and J. Bennett, *History of the Leeds Music Festivals, 1858–1889* (Leeds: F.R. Spark and Son, 1892), pp. 136–7; *Arts Enquiry. Music*, p. 99. The report identified Lancashire, Tyneside and Durham as other 'famed areas' within the North.

38 His only major hit was 'You're a lady' in 1972. The most commercially successful pop song with a northern flavour was Brian and Michael's celebration of L. S. Lowry, 'Matchstick Men and Matchstick Cats and Dogs', a number one hit for three weeks in 1978. For an art music composer strongly influenced by northern landscape, see entry on Arthur Butterworth (b. Manchester 1923) in *New Grove Dictionary of Music and Musicians* (2nd edn, Basingstoke: Macmillan, 2001).

39 *Musical Home Journal*, 10 March 1908.

40 *Daily Express*, 19 May 1932; *Musical Herald*, March 1889.

41 *Lancashire Life*, January–March 1949, p. 227; *Lancashire Evening Telegraph*, 7 October 1968.

42 Quoted in J. Moules, *Our Gracie. The Life of Dame Gracie Fields* (London: Robert Hale, 1983), pp. 71–2. Fields' marriage to an Italian during the Second World War and her eventual move to Capri led her to being branded a 'deserter' by some locals, but her reputation survived basically intact.

43 Haslam, *Manchester, England*, pp. xxvii, xxx.

44 H. R. Clark, *Music's G.P. A Memoir* (Peterborough: author published, 1992), p. 7.

45 *Manchester Faces and Places*, January 1900, pp. 166–7.

46 Russell, 'Musicians', pp. 251–2.

47 *Huddersfield Examiner*, 13 November 1937.

48 A. Taylor, *Labour and Love. An Oral History of the Brass Band Movement* (London: Elm Tree Books, 1983), p. 59.

49 *Cornet*, October 1893.

50 J. Hill, 'Rites of spring: cup finals and community in the north of England', in J. Hill and J. Williams (eds), *Sport and Identity in the North of England* (Keele: Keele University Press, 1996), pp. 106, 108.

51 C. Gillett, *The Sound of the City* (New York: Pantheon, 1983 edn), p. 267. See also Sarah Cohen's important 'Identity, place and the "Liverpool Sound"', in M. Stokes, (ed.), *Ethnicity, Identity and Place. The Musical Construction of Place* (Oxford: Oxford University Press, 1994), pp. 117–34.

52 J. Rogan, *Morrissey and Marr. The Severed Alliance* (London: Omnibus Press, 1992), pp. 218–19, 308.

53 M. Collin, *Altered States. The Story of Ecstasy Culture and Acid House* (London: Serpent's Tail, 1998), p. 159.

54 R. Winstanley and D. Nowell, *Soul Survivors. The Wigan Casino Story* (London: Robson, 1996).

55 S. Cohen, *Rock Culture in Liverpool. Popular Music in the Making* (Oxford: Clarendon, 1991), p. 11.

56 The (excellent) book is by Alan Lawson. *It Happened in Manchester* (Unsworth, Lancs: Multimedia, n.d.).

57 See, for example, E. C. Bairstow, 'Music in Yorkshire', *Music and Letters*, October 1920.

58 M. Pattenden, *Last Orders at the Liars' Bar. The Official History of the Beautiful South* (London: Victor Gollancz, 1999), p. 19.

59 *British Bandsman*, 9 October 1920.

60 *Huddersfield Examiner*, 22 February 1932.

61 Quoted in *British Bandsman*, 23 Oct. 1920.

62 *Huddersfield Examiner* [n.d], in *Huddersfield Glee and Madrigal Society correspondence book, 1920–29*, Kirklees Central Library, Huddersfield.

63 *Brighouse Echo*, 25 October 1946.

64 *Melody Maker*, 29 June 1963.

65 *Melody Maker*, 15 June, 29 June, 22 June 1963. EMI producer Norrie Paramor signed up six Birmingham bands in July 1963 in an attempt to cash in on the 'regional' moment. *Melody Maker*, 20 July 1963.

66 Pattenden, *Last Orders*, pp. 76–7.

67 Haslam, *Manchester, England*, p. xxvii.

68 See Russell, *Popular Music*, pp. 228–38, 258–69 for pre-1914 repertory.

69 Quoted in K. Cook (ed.), *Oh, Listen to the Band* (London: Hinrichen, 1950), pp. 36–7. 'Warlock' was the *nom-de-plume* of composer, Philip Heseltine.

70 PEP, *The Arts Enquiry*, p. 108.

71 D. Russell, 'What's wrong with brass bands? Cultural change and the band movement, 1918–c.1964', in T. Herbert (ed.), *The British Brass Band. A Musical and Cultural History* (Oxford: Oxford University Press, 2000), pp. 96–110.

72 S. Laing, *Representations of Working-Class Life* (London: MacMillan, 1986), pp. 130–4. R. Samuel, 'North and south', in his *Island Stories: Unravelling Britain* (London: Verso, 1998), p. 165. 'Jazz inflected' might be better.

73 'Capstick Comes Home', backed by Carlton Main Frickley Colliery Band.

74 For the Proms, see *The Times*, 5 August 1974. For comments on contemporary banding image and culture, see W. Johnstone, 'The brass band movement', *The Conductor*, January 1974; Taylor, *Labour And Love*; E. and P. Howarth, *What a Performance. The Brass Band Plays* (London: Robson, 1988); Herbert, *British Brass Band*, 'Introduction'.

75 *Bradford Telegraph and Argus*, 5 August 1974.

76 N. Cardus (ed.), *Kathleen Ferrier, 1912–1953. A Memoir* (London: Hamish Hamilton, 1955), pp. 214, 220.

77 *Sunday Observer*, 1 April 1962; *The Times*, 2 April 1962.

78 *Yorkshire Evening Post*, 2 April 1962.

79 See his creator's autobiography. Michael Wharton, *A Dubious Codicil* (London: Chatto and Windus, 1991), p. 18.

80 Quoted in Haslam, *Manchester, England*, pp. 124–5. Haslam adds his own version of this, p. 126. Savage in foreword to D. Curtis, *Touching From a Distance. Ian Curtis and Joy Division* (London: Faber and Faber, 1995), p. xi. For Curtis' lyrics, see pp. 145–201. He was a policeman's son and spent most of his short life in the Cheshire town of Macclesfield.

81 Haslam, *Manchester, England*, p. xxix.

82 Collin, *Altered States*, p. 168.

83 *Melody Maker*, 22 September and 6 October 2001.

84 S. Champion, *And God Created Manchester* (Manchester: Wordsmith, 1990), p. 11.

8

Playing the North

Long ignored by historians whose sense of professional dignity too often outweighed their grasp of the significant, sport has finally gained the attention it demands in the last two decades. A cultural practice that has engaged the time, money and emotional commitment of so many people (albeit mainly but not exclusively men) must be at the heart of any project seeking to understand the construction and operation of popular political and social ideologies. It takes on a particular import in this study because of its extraordinary capacity to dramatise and symbolise the supposed aspirations, characteristics and values of one particular territorial unit as it comes into literal and metaphorical conflict with another. As Eric Hobsbawm has so neatly said of football's role in the construction of national identity, 'The imagined community of millions seems more real as a team of eleven named people' and what is true of football and the nation is equally so of sport and the region.[1]

Sports of the North

Patterns of sporting diffusion and development are rarely neat and the frequently encountered divide between 'near' and 'far' Norths and the many differences within these two broad sub-regions are as apparent in the field of sport as in all others. This was especially the case in the late nineteenth and early twentieth centuries when patterns of sporting preference were still being established. Until the late 1890s, for example, association football was the dominant code in the Sheffield area but was virtually unknown elsewhere in the West Riding where rugby ruled. In neighbouring Lancashire, the 'dribbling code' had swiftly superseded rugby in the east and centre by this date but had made poor progress elsewhere.[2] As ever, the North was no monolith.

The region has no significant claims to paternity in terms of the nation's major sports. Essentially individualistic activities such as athletics, boxing and rowing were very much part of its culture but in no significant sense originated there, while many team sports had, if not southern roots, then at least strong southern inflections. Cricket's growth from the later eighteenth century was concentrated most notably in Kent, Hampshire and London. While pre-codified versions of folk and street football were certainly played throughout the country and some of the earliest clubs were founded in the North, both rugby and association football emerged between 1860–80 as games with an increasingly national spread but with most leading sides and key organisational structures firmly rooted in London and the home counties. For all the importance of Sheffield as a footballing centre, both kicking and handling variants of the game were codified in London by the Football Association in 1863 and the Rugby Football Union in 1871.[3] However, as Tony Mason points out, if association football 'as a game was not invented in the North ... football as a spectator sport certainly was' and it is here that the region's characteristic contribution can be found.[4] As sport emerged as a mass phenomenon in the last quarter of the nineteenth century, it was the urban communities of the North above all others that nourished and sustained it. Equally important, their representatives have subsequently dominated many major competitions.

The histories of association football and cricket clearly illustrate these two processes. From the late 1870s, particularly in the textile towns of Lancashire where above-average family incomes and the relatively widespread availability of the Saturday half-holiday facilitated rapid sporting development, the willingness of a growing body of spectators to pay at the 'gate' led to the swift development of professional football. By 1888 its economic infrastructure was sufficiently robust to necessitate the establishment of a properly regulated and financially viable competition and Lancashire provided no fewer than six of the twelve founder members of the resultant Football League. The League (88 strong by the 1920s) remained very much dominated by northern and midland clubs until the 1920s, although even from this point northern clubs were of considerable importance. The seven-county North provided at least 50 per cent of Football League clubs at all times before 1920 and usually 40–45 per cent from that point until the later 1970s when the figure fell to about 35 per cent, where it currently remains.

Northern clubs have also competed successfully at the game's pinnacle. At least one northern side appeared in all but 20 of the 105 FA Cup Finals from 1889 to 2003. From the earliest period until about 1970, the region's teams comprised between about 45 per cent and 75 per cent of the Football League's First Division membership; in 2002–3 50 per cent of clubs in its modern equivalent, the Premiership, were northern. Only in the 1980s did the North ever really come close to losing its position as effective heartland of the English game. Although Liverpool and Everton dominated the domestic game, overall northern representation in the First Division fell to under 20 per cent in the early and mid-1980s. Moreover, a number of once-important clubs such as Preston, Bolton and Burnley slithered down the divisions and thus provided a small but potent contribution to the decline of the North narratives that were a hallmark of the decade. Overall, however, footballing success, whether as proud memory, current triumph or future expectation, has fostered a sense in the North that it has a special place in a key arena of public life.

Although cricket's growth was geographically far more uniform across the country, northern and near-northern counties were again heavily involved in its emergence as a spectator sport, with the 'border' city of Nottingham an important early centre. In 1838, William Clarke, landlord of the Trentbridge Inn, laid out a cricket ground on adjacent land which was to become of the country's leading cricketing venues and from where, in 1846, Clarke organised the All-England X1 whose tours were crucial in helping establish professional cricket in England. One of his associates, batsman George Parr, was nicknamed 'the Lion of the North', indicative that in the cricketing context at least, Nottingham could be regarded as northern.[5] When the County Championship, cricket's premier tournament, was founded with nine members in 1873 (it was placed on an official basis in 1890) Lancashire and Yorkshire were the North's representatives and both were to enjoy much success. Yorkshire in particular had an exceptional playing record, winning 21 of the 46 championships between 1890 and 1939 and another 9 titles between 1946 and 1968. With the exception of Westmorland, simply too small to sustain a county side, the other northern counties eventually joined the Minor Counties tournament established in 1895, with Durham finally graduating to the County Championship in 1992.[6] The lower status accorded to first class County Cricket in the far North can be attributed to both the thinner population base and the less hospitable climate, but this issue would repay further investigation.[7] So too would the extent to which cricket fans from the neighbouring 'minor counties' in both the far North and the north midlands have attached themselves to Yorkshire and Lancashire. This has interesting implications in terms of the construction of cross-county sporting identities and the possible existence of 'northern'

cricketing communities that embrace, for example, Lincolnshire and
Staffordshire. Finally, league cricket, a Saturday afternoon variant designed to
fit the work patterns of the industrial working and lower middle classes,
although not peculiar to the North was most highly developed there, especially
in Lancashire and the West Riding, and provided further distinctive flavour to
northern sporting geography.[8]

While football and cricket are best seen as national sports significantly
coloured and shaped by the North, beneath them in the national sporting hierarchy stand a cluster of sports that might more genuinely be seen as essentially
'northern', either because they were founded in the region or have been particularly closely associated with it. The most significant on both counts is Rugby
League. Known until 1922 as Northern Union, it originated in battles over the
desirability or otherwise of giving working-class players 'broken-time' payments to compensate them for money lost while playing in and travelling to
matches.[9] Recompense was favoured by an alliance of working-class players and
many of the industrial and commercial middle classes who generally ran
northern clubs, and opposed by the administrators in the London-based Rugby
Football Union and their northern counterparts, often drawn from the professional middle classes and wedded to a strict amateur ethos. After several years of
increasing antagonism over this and other issues, representatives of twenty
Yorkshire and Lancashire sides (two others swiftly followed) established the
Northern Rugby Football Union at the George Hotel, Huddersfield on 29
August 1895. From the early 1900s, and particularly 1906 when sides were
reduced from fifteen to thirteen players, Northern Union began to emerge as a
separate sporting code. The dramatic growth of association football from the
1890s to 1915 effectively prevented the game from breaking out of its northern
confines, although it periodically tried to do so. Six Welsh clubs joined the
Northern Union in the early 1900s, but none survived beyond 1914, and there
have been several attempts to plant the game in London, most notably in the
1930s, and again from the 1980s. Even in the North, Rugby League has only
really established itself in south-west Lancashire, west Cumbria, 'textile' West
Yorkshire and Humberside. Indeed, a 1994 survey showed that 60 per cent of
those regularly attending rugby league matches came from 'just four postal districts in the M62 corridor'.[10] However, as will be seen, where the game has taken
root, it has become a powerful source of local pride and a northern signifier of
real potency.

A number of other, lesser-known sports have similarly strong northern
roots and connotations. Crown green bowling has a considerably lower profile

than rugby league, even in its heartlands, but one informed insider estimated that 250,000 people were playing in the 1970s.[11] Although played as far south as Worcestershire, its core territory lies between the River Trent and north Yorkshire and many in this area regard it as a strongly northern activity. (The rarity of the game in the north-east where its flat green equivalent prevails, underlines yet again a broad cultural division between 'far and 'near' Norths.) Both its major tournaments, the Talbot (1873) and the Waterloo (1907), originated on the greens of eponymous Blackpool hotels and the association of the game's key events with the North's greatest symbol of mass leisure further reinforces its northern flavour. Knur and spell, a game between two individuals involving the striking of a small wooden or porcelain ball (the knur) fired from a trap (the spell) with a stick or mallet, had a strong following in south and west Yorkshire and east Lancashire from the early nineteenth century (the game dates from at least the fourteenth century) until the 1930s. The so-called 'World Championship' was revived briefly in the 1970s, with sponsorship provided by Yorkshire Television, but the game is now really only a heritage curiosity.[12] The list of northern sports can be further extended by reference to quoits and potshare bowling, both the subject of intense interest amongst Northumberland miners at least until the early twentieth century; Cumberland wrestling; hunting (on foot) with beagle packs, a popular activity in the industrial margins of west Yorkshire and other areas; whippet racing and fell-running.[13]

Being northern

Sport has served at least three crucial cultural functions in the context of this study: it has provided a powerful means of expressing a body of supposed northern values; acted as a site for the definition and symbolic resolution of differences between North and South and facilitated the expression and construction of a range of personal and collective northern identities. It is difficult to disentangle these roles but for the sake of organisational convenience, this section considers northern values and the next focuses on issues of North–South rivalry and northern identity. To say that 'sport' of itself has served these functions is, of course, somewhat misleading. Although actual sporting activity must engage the historian, what is mainly at issue here are the meanings generated by the written and verbal discourses surrounding sport in the press (always the most important element) and other media sources, and by the oral traditions so central to sporting culture.

The analysis here and for the remainder of the chapter concentrates on team sport, especially association football, cricket and rugby league as played by professionals, and has a decidedly masculine flavour. Team sports are generally the most potent agents of community identification if only because the participants invariably carry the name of a particular town or region and because it is usually possible to find at least one member who displays the characteristics demanded by local mythology. Individual sports can also bear these cultural burdens especially when local or regional stars are pitted against metropolitan opposition – the nineteenth-century Tyneside rowers who competed against their Thameside equivalents are good examples – or if they express clear loyalty to place, as with later twentieth-century north-eastern athletes Brendan Foster and Steve Cram.[14] However, individuals cannot always be trusted to observe the myths; indeed, in the 1970s and 1980s, rival middle distance runners northerner Sebastian Coe and southerner Steve Ovett effectively reversed patterns of expectation. In terms of gender, as Richard Holt has argued, for much of the period 'animals were more readily accepted than women as the objects of sporting admiration', and this chapter reflects that.[15] This is not to deny exceptions to this rule and analyses of such stars as Yorkshire cyclist Beryl Burton, paying close attention to regionally-based gender stereotypes, would be invaluable.

Central to northern celebration of its sporting culture was a belief that it was infused with an acutely developed competitiveness simply unmatched elsewhere in the country. This was expressed in any number of sporting contexts, but was perhaps most fervently articulated in relation to Yorkshire cricket. J. M. Kilburn, the *Yorkshire Post*'s cricket correspondent, claimed that 'Yorkshire eyes were fixed upon victory from the first ball of every match ... The "will to win" was more pronounced than in any other county', while Wilfred Rhodes, Yorkshire's great all-rounder from 1898 to 1930, reputedly made the pithier observation, 'we doan't play cricket in Yorkshire for foon'.[16] Here was the determination and purpose so central to the Yorkshire, and, to a lesser degree, the wider northern self-image. Although, as will be seen, the county's matches against some southern opponents were invested with much importance, the competitive edge was most frequently to be found in the twice-yearly 'roses' matches against Lancashire. From the 1890s, when a talented Lancashire side emerged to displace Nottinghamshire as Yorkshire's premier rival, until the 1980s, when the decline of both counties and the wider decline of the county game reduced the fixture's significance, these games produced a level of intensity and commitment unknown outside of Test cricket. It found its most important delineator in Neville Cardus, cricket (and music) correspondent of the *Manchester Guardian* from 1919 and one of the twentieth century's most influential inventors of northern mythology. Taking basic elements of roses cricket and its social and geographical context, he elevated them into an affectionate, mock-heroic search for the essence of northern life. His report of the 1919 roses match at Sheffield's Bramall Lane typifies his style.

> The squat chimneys outside the ground loomed black against a lowering sky, and Bank Holiday or no Bank Holiday, there was a suggestion of smoke about and steel smelters. All these things told eloquently of the stiff-energy of North-country life, making the proper accompaniment to a battle between ancient hosts whose informing spirit is the dour combativeness of hardy northmen.

In a telling comparison, he once described the game at Lords, the St John's Wood home of the MCC and Middlesex County Cricket Club, as cricket played 'as in the drawing-room of civilised men and women'.[17]

Closely allied to this emphasis on competitiveness was the placing of a high premium upon a certain physical hardness, a highly prized virtue in a culture where hard physical labour was the daily context in which sport was set. What Holt has termed 'a self-conscious cult of northern aggression' took on many forms.[18] Press reports proudly recorded feats of hard work and bravery, while fans were apparently happy to see a fairly high level of strategically directed foul play in certain contexts. In the 1912 FA Cup semi-final, for example, Barnsley players dealt so severely with Swindon Town forward Harold Fleming that he did not play again for almost a year. When he was carried off injured, the Barnsley fans jeered.[19] Unsurprisingly, rugby league has been the game most heavily freighted in this regard: it is significant that David Storey's novel *This Sporting Life* (1960), set within the game, begins with central character Arthur Machin losing both teeth and consciousness via contact with an opponent's shoulder. The game's fans have been proud of its fierceness, one terming it 'arguably the most demanding contact sport there is'.[20] Delicate sporting skills were obviously also hugely prized but were appreciated even more if combined with an ability to absorb physical punishment. Although Tom Finney, the Preston North End and England footballer from 1946 to 1960, was admired ultimately for his levels of skill, his equable temperament and bravery elevated him yet further in popular affection.

All this is not to suggest that – perhaps rugby league aside – physical toughness was objectively more apparent in northern sport than elsewhere. Virtually all soccer teams, for example, have always employed at least one 'hard man' and southern and London clubs have been no exception. Indeed, Fulham's Bobby

Keetch in the 1960s, Chelsea's Ron 'Chopper' Harris in the 1960s and 1970s and Wimbledon's Vinnie Jones in the 1980s were, albeit in the last case partly due to assiduous media cultivation, as infamous as any of their northern equivalents.[21] A valuable study of local reaction to the decidedly hard playing style of Portsmouth F.C. in the late 1940s and 1950s demonstrates this point well, arguing that 'regional aspects of the culture of football production and consumption may amount to only subtle variations on [a] more powerful national or British theme'.[22] The key point, however, is that northern fans have appropriated this particular national theme for their own locality or region. The bunch of flowers supposedly presented to England and West Ham captain Bobby Moore in 1964 by a group of northern fans speaks volumes here, his blonde good looks and lucrative contract advertising a hair care product doubtless only adding to his suitability as a target for the 'daffodils and dainty hand gestures' proffered by his detractors.[23]

Alongside the passion, hard work and physical commitment on the field, a unique combination of expertise and devotion was believed to exist around it. North-eastern soccer fans have been particularly convinced of their special status in this context, and there may indeed be substance in their claims. London-born Charlie Buchan, who played for Sunderland from 1911–25 before returning south to Arsenal, certainly supported such a view, claiming north-eastern fans to be the most knowledgeable he had ever encountered. A particularly determined loyalty is suggested by the fact that Newcastle and Sunderland lost fewer spectators proportionate to local levels of unemployment than almost any other English clubs during the early 1930s.[24] Yorkshire cricket-lovers, most notably those in Sheffield, have been similarly convinced of their especial knowledge and wit. The *Athletic News* noted in 1896 that 'the average Sheffielder considers it his own particular privilege to captain the team from his position outside the ropes, and never omits to issue commands to put so-and-so on or take so-and so off'.[25] The annual 'invasion' of London for cup finals was often viewed as a valuable opportunity for missionary work amongst its residents, whose fickleness and undemonstrative manner was commented on at every opportunity. On the day of the 1966 World Cup final a Liverpool newspaper recorded rather tartly that that even 'normally undemonstrative Londoners were wearing England favors last night'.[26]

As has already been noted in earlier chapters, many northerners placed great stress on lack of pretension, on retaining 'roots' even after national or international success, and this cult of 'ordinariness' forms another key ingredient of supposed northern sporting distinctiveness. At least until the 1950s and 1960s it was often possible for reality to match aspiration. The conditions under which sportsmen worked were important here. In soccer, the maximum wage that appertained until 1961 helped hold players in, or reasonably close to, the manual working class that most had been born into, while the retain and transfer system much restricted players' geographical mobility. Obviously, these were features of the game nationally, but the dominance of northern clubs in League football for most of the period meant that the successful local boy staying loyal to his home-town club seemed, if not peculiar to the North, then quintessentially a part of the northern landscape. Stars of the 1940s and 1950s such as Nat Lofthouse at Bolton, Jackie Milburn at Newcastle and Tom Finney at Preston, were sporting heroes almost as much for their normality off the pitch as their extraordinariness on it. Lofthouse and Milburn had been miners in the early stages of their careers and were respected for it. Tales were and still are told of Milburn queuing at a bus stop with fans on match days and being ushered forward by those worried that he might miss the kick off. Alan Hardaker, one-time secretary of the Football League, recounts how Finney, who ran a plumbing business, arrived to repair his sink on the morning of a match in the 1950s.[27] Such stories may be exaggerated or even apocryphal but it is their existence rather than their veracity that matters. As a study of Jackie Milburn points out, those who continued to live locally after their careers ended added yet another layer to their exemplary lives; avoiding the road south was especially important.[28]

From the 1960s, it became ever harder for leading footballers to retain local roots and modest lifestyles and it is against this context that rugby league has been seen to fulfill a special function by many of its fans. This is apparent in Simon Kelner's 1996 study of the game in which he approvingly quotes a line of Frank Machin's in the film version of *This Sporting Life*.

> 'Stars? There are no stars in this game. Just men like me.' Machin's words still ring true more than thirty years later. Rugby league players can earn enough to escape the hardships of those around them, but do not betray the fact that they are products of the same background ... this is an environment in which vanity does not flourish. Traditionally, the rugby league player works and lives among the people he represents when he pulls on the jersey at the weekend. No other professional sportsmen have such intimate dealings with their public. During the miners' strike of 1984, their own supporters jeered players who were blacklegs, while those who seek privileged treatment are firmly rebuffed.[29]

Rugby league, the 'people's game', so it is argued, as football moves inexorably upmarket, remains therefore in such analyses, the true sport of the North 'linked to our community, to our industry, to our attitudes'.[30]

Northern identities

What of the particular identities generated by northern sport? Interpreting patterns and consequences of sporting allegiance is not a straightforward activity. Most obviously, different sports can generate different levels of identification. While soccer and rugby league have always ultimately tended to structure local patriotisms, first-class cricket generates loyalties at the larger county level. Individuals can thus quite easily express and enjoy multiple identities, supporting footballing representatives of a specific town at one moment while uniting with bitter local rivals in the support of a county cricket side at another. Local and county rivalries can in their turn be suspended and subsumed in shared support for national teams.

The fluidity and flexibility of collective identities is made even more explicit if attention is paid to changes over time. This is well exemplified by a brief consideration of soccer in Lancashire. While the game has undeniably been most effective in building local attachments, the balance between local and regional or, more accurately, sub-regional identities, has varied according to historical context. From the 1880s to about 1914, for example, local rivalries could be deep indeed. In 1888, Preston North End actually refused to play a Lancashire Cup tie against Blackburn Rovers as a result of 'the offensive way in which North End players have beforetimes been received in Blackburn … [by] a limited number of uncouth and unmannerly onlookers'.[31] This is not to deny the possibility of sympathy for neighbouring clubs and a willingness to claim their triumphs as a regional success, especially if obtained at the expense of southern opposition. As the *Blackburn Telegraph* argued in 1883, 'local rivalry fades when that of the favoured London men comes to the fore'.[32] However, this more generous, inclusive spirit was probably not as prevalent as it was to become in the period from about 1920 to the early 1960s. By then, many fans could enjoy at least some sense of belonging to a regional or, specifically, countywide 'family' of clubs. One supporter recalled how 'When Blackpool played Newcastle in the Cup Final [1951] we wanted Blackpool to win 'cause they were from Lancashire, and Burnley [in 1947], we wanted Burnley to win because they were from Lancashire'.[33] Some fans would watch more than one side with a genuine commitment to both, others simply out of a desire to watch particular players. Even in Liverpool, which at times seemed decidedly not of the county, celebration of the Lancashire sporting family could be very strong. After success across a number of sports in 1928, the *Liverpool Echo* proclaimed 'Hail Lancashire! Never have the honours descended upon the county with quite such plenitude as now ... a gradely place to live in any time, Lancashire, but the Red Rose blooms wondrous well just now'.[34]

From the late 1960s the increasingly bitter rivalries that reached their most advanced form in the tensions between Liverpool and Manchester United, Blackburn and Burnley and Preston and Blackpool effectively destroyed this more broadly based style of regional fandom.[35] These patterns – admittedly presented here a little too schematically – are easier to describe than explain. The unifying experiences of the two world war wars and the impact of shared national cultural forms such as broadcasting and the popular press might explain the emergence of more inclusive mentalities from the 1920s to the 1960s. In turn, their erosion probably owes much to the disintegration of shared regional economies that turned neighbouring towns into rivals for precious economic resources. The emergence of a popular culture placing a high value on ridicule and mockery is another possible candidate. Whatever the causes, it is the very existence of these shifts in mentality that needs stressing here, generating a need for caution but providing rich opportunity for future research.[36]

While sensitivity to subject matter and period is, then, essential, the rest of this section attempts some broad generalisations rooted in exploration of the relationship between the local, sub-regional and wider northern or quasi-northern mentalities. Local identity, defined as an intense identification with a city, town or village where an individual has been born or has long residence or connection, has been the strongest of all the personal and collective territorial loyalties expressed by English sport. The simple fact that local sporting communities can usually watch their local representatives more frequently than any others makes this inevitable. It appears to have mattered but little that, in football at least, local aspirations were so often vested in rootless professional mercenaries who might soon be playing for a rival. The best-known manifestations of this identification have been the rich pattern of community ritual so well captured in his study of football and rugby league cup finals by Jeff Hill.[37] The 'invasion' of London by northern fans proudly displaying attachments through team colours, local symbols and a sometimes exaggerated accent and dialect has been a central mechanism for both celebrating local attachment and placing often little-known towns on the national map. Similarly, in the civic homecomings that follow and which have invariably ended with the players taking their bows on the balcony of the local town hall, the disparate parts and communities of a town or city briefly appear to be made whole.

In certain contexts, this type of activity can take on an extraordinary importance. Perhaps the best example is provided by the 1984 Milk Cup Final at

Wembley when Merseyside rivals Liverpool and Everton faced each other at a time when both extreme economic problems and a much publicised political crisis stemming from divisions within the city's ruling Labour Party had pushed the city's reputation to an extraordinarily low point. In a period of great concern over football hooliganism, endless appeals for good behaviour by fans travelling to London were made before the match. This, so one fan argued 'would enrich us all and go along way to restoring some of our lost pride in the eyes of the watching Londoners'.[38] In the event, the opportunity to display local unity was seized enthusiastically, with rival fans watching the game together in extremely good order and joining together at the end in chants of 'Merseyside, Merseyside' intended to demonstrate the region's unbroken spirit.

In sports, and especially association football, where professional clubs are based in larger cities and towns, many fans find it hard to express what we might call a 'first level' local sporting identity by simple fact of living in a community too small to possess a major club. While some attain that identity by attaching themselves to a local amateur or semi-professional team, many more have adopted a club within the wider region or sub-region. Sport thus provides a kind of local identity by proxy that can build eventually into sub-regional loyalty focused on a major town or city but transcending simple administrative boundaries. In an illuminating piece, Alan Metcalfe has shown how support for Newcastle United Football Club in the late 1890s and early 1900s helped the miners of East Northumberland begin 'to perceive themselves as Northeasterners rather than as members of isolated mining villages ... for the first time the miners did not look on Newcastle as the arch enemy but rather as carrying the pride and hopes of the northeast'.[39] Metcalfe's attention to sub-regional identity is extremely welcome for it is not a subject that has not drawn much attention either in the sporting or wider contexts. Such 'places' as the north-east, north-west, South Yorkshire or wherever often either have no fixed administrative boundaries or, when they do, rarely keep them for any length of time. It would be valuable, therefore, to try to construct versions of them that accord with the experiences of particular interest groups. In regard to sport, this might best be achieved by mapping the vast network of leagues (amateur as well as professional) that grew up from the late nineteenth century and to see whether they fit neatly onto either standard political and administrative units or the various territories defined by historians focusing on non-sporting topics. It is perfectly possible that autonomous 'sporting' regions or sub-regions have provided quite distinctive personal or collective geographies that await academic exploration.

Until such work is done, sub-regional identity is most likely to focus on the county, a topic approached here through analysis of first class cricket in Yorkshire. The role of Yorkshire County Cricket Club in helping the county's four million or so inhabitants hone a distinctive self-image and conduct battles with the outside world has already been raised here in discussion of northern competitiveness. This, however, is only one aspect of a wider process. [40] From about 1890 when cricket's County Championship was placed on a firm basis until the decline of the Yorkshire side in the 1970s, the game has been the single most important mechanism through which England's largest and most geographically complex county has become known, both objectively and metaphorically, to those within and without its boundaries. For five months of the year the team moved around the county playing in anything up to seven or eight different locations, thus drawing disparate communities together in a shared sporting embrace. The West Riding dominated in terms of venues and in other ways (Sheffield and then, from 1902, Leeds acted as headquarters), but visits to Middlesbrough, Hull and Scarborough helped make Yorkshire a little more a sum of its parts. Played largely during weekdays and in working hours, county cricket only rarely attracted large crowds but detailed coverage in the local and regional press kept supporters informed and served as the major vehicle for the construction and reinforcement of the county's self-image.

Two aspects of Yorkshire's cricketing culture were central here. First, from the late 1880s until as recently as 1992, the county insisted that players be born within the county boundary. Kent and Nottinghamshire had also originally adopted this policy but swiftly abandoned it in favour of finding a wider pool of talent. For Yorkshire, it became a point of honour that the county's successes were earned by native talent, something admittedly made much easier by the sheer size of its population. Significantly, exceptions were made in order to allow for the eligibility of suitable gentleman-amateur captains (believed essential for the maintenance of good order); Lord Hawke Yorkshire's most influential captain (1883–1910) was born in Lincolnshire and his successor, Everard Ratcliffe, was a Devonian. Such fine points were rarely publicised, however, and a sense of moral worth was much enhanced through the qualification clause. Similar capital was generated by the team's social structure in the period up to 1939. The Yorkshire side was at this time effectively a professional one, usually taking the field with nine or ten professionals led by an amateur captain. Until the 1930s, when the amateur cricketer became far less a feature of the county game, only Nottingham and to a lesser extent Lancashire – this shared sporting 'northern-ness' in this matter is interesting – exhibited such a profile, with most sides playing four or five amateurs. In 1896, no fewer than nine appeared in the Hampshire side that played Yorkshire at Harrogate, tempted no doubt by the spa town's social delights and thus robbing several professionals of their match fees in the process. While a number of Yorkshire's amateur captains were extremely modest players owing their place only to social position, claims that the composition of the county side reflected the essentially meritocratic nature of Yorkshire society had sufficient substance to engender a strong sense of sporting and wider cultural superiority.

The symbolic power of Yorkshire cricket perhaps attained its maximum purchase at moments of rivalry with southern sides, especially with Middlesex and most notably during in the inter-war period when the two counties were often well-matched rivals for the County Championship. This fixture effectively encapsulated starkly drawn worldviews ascribed to North and South within the northern imagination. Middlesex represented the metropolitan world at its most unenchanting. The club played at Lords, headquarters of the MCC, the game's governing body and generally viewed as a bastion of southern privilege. A leading member of the Yorkshire committee revealingly compared the popular nature of the patronage at Yorkshire grounds with Lords where provision was made mainly 'for people who wanted to be in the pukka seats'.[41] Most important of all, as the *Yorkshire Telegraph and Star* noted before a fateful encounter in 1924, the Middlesex team 'as usual contain[ed] more amateurs than professionals', and was thus representative of a morally inferior sporting culture.[42] Yet further spice was added by the fact that the Middlesex amateurs played as seriously as any professionals, helping the club to consecutive county championships in 1920 and 1921. This refusal to act out the role that northern mythology allotted to them was not appreciated.

Tensions were most marked during their game at Sheffield in July 1924 when a section of the crowd, allegedly encouraged by a Yorkshire player, jeered and booed the umpires following controversial decisions. The fall-out from this relatively trivial affair was considerable. Middlesex were rumoured to be boycotting future Yorkshire fixtures, the Yorkshire committee suspended the errant player and were forced into extensive backstage diplomacy, while the Yorkshire press fought a rearguard action against what one paper called the 'scandalous … unwanted tirade' of the southern press, and its 'pitiless and scurrilous attack … on [Yorkshire's] sportsmanship and honesty'.[43] When Surrey players then accused the Yorkshire side of verbally intimidating opponents and scuffing up pitches to help their bowlers, the county's press sensed a conspiracy. Sheffield's

Yorkshire Telegraph and Star told its readers on 28 August that it 'seems obvious that there is someone in London bent on attacking the Yorkshire players out of sheer spleen. It is scandalous that such an unwarranted tirade should be kept up ... jealousy of Yorkshire is prevalent to a big extent in the south'.

These county or other sub-regional sporting loyalties have often run alongside or even transmuted into something closer to a wider 'northern consciousness'. This may admittedly be a rather grandiose description for what has often been a vigorous anti-metropolitanism as much as a fully inclusive embrace of the North as region. Moreover, the issue of division within the North immediately becomes an issue even when seeking commonality of experience and attitude. As Mike Huggins has pointed out in an astute study, different parts of the North experienced these tensions with the centre in different ways at different times.[44] For the late Victorian and Edwardian north-east, for example, London was far less a sporting enemy than it was for Yorkshire and Lancashire. Without a first-class cricket team, lacking a sufficiently developed football culture to be worried by battles over professionalism in the 1880s (explored below) and unaffected by the 'Great Split' in rugby in 1895, north-eastern sport quite simply had little practical or emotional investment in the major battles between North and South. Indeed, for north-easterners, the 'south' was often Yorkshire and Lancashire, defeat of whose representatives (along with Scotland's) represented a crucial yardstick of athletic progress. Rivalry with the 'true' South, largely dormant after the 1870s when professional rowing matches pitting Tyne against Thames declined in importance, did not really resurface until the 1920s and 1930s with football now the battleground. With all due acknowledgement of such important provisos, however, the overall extent of opposition to an over weaning London and its hinterlands was considerable and was expressed more forcibly than in any other cultural field surveyed in this study.

Key to these antagonisms between North and South has been sport's tendency to replicate larger core-periphery tensions within the national culture. Just as many northerners saw the South in general and London in particular as a place that consumed, paraded and organised the wealth generated by the hard physical work and business acumen of the North, so they also saw the capital as the over-powerful administrative centre of a sporting world with its 'real' core two hundred miles to the north. While the Football League and the Northern Union were based in the North and clearly saw themselves as provincial counterweights to metropolitan ambition – one eminent Football League official opposed the organisation's national expansion in 1909 on the grounds that 'the idea of London coming to dominate the League and becoming the "heart" of the Association game' worried him – the Football Association, Rugby Football Union and most other governing bodies were, as already noted, London-based.[45]

Although most governing bodies had extensive provincial representation and were never exclusively mouthpieces for London and the South, arguments within sports were inevitably overlain with a powerful spatial dimension. This was certainly present in the conflicts surrounding the legalisation of professionalism in football and rugby in the late nineteenth century.[46] In the former the issue came to a head in a suitably symbolic way in January 1884 when, after an FA Cup tie between Preston North End and London-based Upton Park F.C., the Upton Park secretary reported the Lancashire club for making illegal payments. North End were subsequently ejected from the tournament and, in the eighteen months of wrangling that preceded the legalisation of a closely defined professionalism in July 1885, there was a real chance of northern and midland clubs breaking away from the FA to form a new governing body. Throughout the period of dispute, the northern press consistently emphasised the North–South dimension, with the *Preston Herald* talking of a breakaway as a way of reducing 'the London tyranny to a minimum'. Similarly, rugby's crisis in 1895 was portrayed very much as a conflict between a purposeful, egalitarian and fair-minded North and an elitist and hypocritical South. Herbert Fallas, a town clerk and one time leading Wakefield Trinity player, drew on traditional pictures of northern virtue and southern vice when noting how 'one club in Yorkshire alone has paid more for champagne dinners and shilling cigars for southern gentlemen having their holiday in the North in the shape of tours, than would trebly pay all that is asked for in broken time'. The *Wigan Observer* in its turn celebrated 'freedom from the thralldom of the southern gentry'.[47]

In objective terms, although the North–South issue was important, it actually represented only one essentially secondary element of a wider set of social and cultural tensions. In both football and rugby, professionalism also had it opponents in the North and, at least in soccer, was rapidly to gain supporters in the South. Even the apparent neatness of the argument between Preston and Upton Park is complicated by the fact that some of the Upton Park committee were unhappy about reporting the Lancashire club, even offering to pay its expenses when it faced the FA in London, and because there is suggestive evidence that the Londoners were encouraged to lay the charges by Blackburn Olympic, one of Preston's greatest (and similarly quasi-professional) rivals.[48] At the risk of simplifying, the arguments in both games are best seen as emanating from divisions within the middle class, with the commercial and industrial sector tending to favour payment for pay, while the professional, often public-school educated element, defended the amateur ideal. Obviously, the differing social structures of North and South flavoured this intra-class conflict, but class and status rather than regional affiliation were ultimately the key ingredients. Nevertheless, it is instructive that the language of 'northern-ness', or at least, of 'anti-metropolitan-ness' emerged so strongly, illustrating the ease with which it could surface and be adopted by a wide variety of social groups. Moreover, especially in popular sporting histories and in the stories that fans weave around the development of the game, the North–South narrative still looms large in discussion of these incidents.

Conflicts stemming from the capital's key role in sporting administration and politics can be seen in a variety of other contexts, with the selection of English international sides particularly revealing. In January 1884, an England-Scotland rugby match at Leeds was enlivened by the crowd bestowing the names of favourite Yorkshire players upon the English team, in wry protest at the selectors' failure to choose a single Yorkshire representative.[49] This is one of the earliest manifestations of the northern belief that southern-based players have a much enhanced chance of representing their country. In its coverage of test cricket, the northern press was invariably alert to quirks of selectorial geography, with the *Bradford Daily Telegraph* leading an article on the 1924 touring team with the headline 'All But Three Players From the South', although the wound was softened with the secondary line 'Two Yorkshiremen'. At the Leeds test against Australia in 1968 Essex's Keith Fletcher, chosen instead of Yorkshire batsman and outstanding fielder Phil Sharpe, had a disastrous start, dropping a number of (difficult) catches. As *The Times* reported, 'The Yorkshire crowd of 20,000 let it be known that they thought "Sharpey" would have caught them'. Mischievously, the *Yorkshire Post* carried a front page photo of Fletcher dropping a catch, with an inset illustration of a thoughtful Sharpe gazing out from the pavilion.[50]

The northern football world has been no less suspicious of the English selection procedure. Until the decision was taken in the 1960s to give the England manager complete control over the process, it was certainly idiosyncratic. At least until the 1930s, when international games began to be taken far more seriously, selection was sometimes little more than a reward for good club service granted at the whim of sympathetic individuals. There is little evidence of actual systematic bias against the North. Southern players dominated the England side in the 1870s and early 1880s just as they dominated the game in general, but as the game spread and as the selection process became slightly more scientific, opportunities equalised: some 47 per cent of players selected from Football League clubs between 1888 and 1988 came from clubs in the seven-county North, a figure more or less congruent with the number of northern sides in the First Division from which most internationals were drawn.

Sections of the northern press were nevertheless certain that some southern players were the beneficiaries of favouritism. The most extreme victim was Johnny Haynes, an inside-forward with London-based Fulham who was capped 56 times between 1955 and 1962, and served as England captain from 1960–62. Haynes received particular criticism in the Manchester press; indeed, most other northern regional papers were relatively neutral in their coverage. Throughout his England career, the *Manchester Evening News* regularly accompanied mention of his name with such loaded descriptions as 'golden boy', 'wonder boy', 'London glamour boy' or 'the pride of London'.[51] Sometimes this was accompanied by a more overt attack. On the eve of the 1958 World Cup, Eric Thornton, a particular critic of Haynes, argued that

> I really think it is about time someone said their piece on London's glamour boy. He's had more chances of winning his spurs than any other player that I can remember in post-war soccer. And he's disappointed time and again. I am told they are still intent on building an England attack around the Fulham inside man. I think it's [a] mistake.[52]

Two years later, David Meek hinted, with little if any suggestion of irony, that Haynes and his London colleague Jimmy Greaves had shown an uncanny sense of geography during the previous night's England *versus* Young England game.

> Although he had an overall fine game [Haynes] hardly gave outside left Charlton a pass. Little of the ball came from Jimmy Greaves either. Perhaps it's just coincidence that right winger Peter Brabrook, of Chelsea, got all the service from Londoners Haynes and Greaves.[53]

This supposed 'starving' of Manchester United's Bobby Charlton is especially significant here, as the *Manchester Evening News*, like most local papers, saw the international career enhancement of locally-based players as a civic duty of some importance.

Both Haynes and Fulham colleague Jimmy Hill saw what Hill referred to as 'the great tendency in the north of England to belittle his ability' as a product of press manipulation (fuelled, according to Hill, by Manchester United manager Matt Busby) rather than genuine popular sentiment.[54] Whatever the case, the journalists responsible clearly sensed a deep resentment they felt they could tap into. While Haynes' rapid rise through the professional game (his England debut came less than three years after his League debut and while a Second Division player) and his adoption of a body language on the pitch that could be construed as denoting arrogance, probably made Haynes a particular target for accusations of special treatment and southern pretension, long-held antipathies toward the capital were clearly being called upon and reinforced.

Similar mentalities can be seen in regard to Wembley Stadium and its relationship with other major association football grounds. Built in 1923, its use as an international football stadium was restricted for some time to hosting the biennial England–Scotland game, with other internationals played around the country, and often at northern venues including Anfield and Goodison Park in Liverpool and Maine Road in Manchester. Argentina became the first opponents apart from Scotland to play at the stadium in 1951 and, from the following November, the Football Association chose Wembley as the venue for all but a handful of matches.[55] Although Wembley's place as the home of the FA Cup Final gave it a special status amongst football fans, its privileged position in this context could cause antagonism. The fact that many northerners thought Londoners unworthy of the games played there only fuelled such attitudes. Many of these tensions and attitudes surfaced during the 1966 World Cup when other major grounds enjoyed the opportunity to show their qualities and those of their fans. The Yorkshire-based President of the Football League, for example, talked of the 'cold' and 'aloof' atmosphere at the stadium and claimed that it was 'time [England players] got encouragement from the Wembley crowd'.[56] The Mayor of Middlesbrough, whose Ayresome Park was a World Cup venue, made the revealing remark that local people 'now feel that they are part of the country' as a result of the town's inclusion in the event.[57] The most significant moment followed the Football Association's decision that England should play their semi-final against Portugal at Wembley instead of Everton's Goodison Park where all previous plans suggested it was to have been played. There was much anger in the city with four men trying to get onto the pitch before the West Germany v. Russia game that was eventually staged there, to unfurl a thirty-foot banner reading 'England Fix, Insult to Liverpool'. The lengthy debate in the late 1990s over the location of the proposed National Stadium and the eventual decision to place it in a reconstituted Wembley kept this subject very much alive.[58]

It is possible that the close identification of English international football with the metropolis may even have had the effect of distancing some northern fans from the national side that played there. Clearly, many northerners have been passionate England supporters but interesting hints of alienation are discernable. John Williams certainly argued for such a distancing in Liverpool in the 1980s, although, as he suggested, other factors also played a part here.

> The national football team – resolutely tied to its southern base of Wembley – is identified by many young fans in areas like Liverpool as representative, less of a united nation, than of a discredited national government ... young football followers in Liverpool, a city ravaged by the effects of recent government policies, exhibit a scathing lack of concern for the national football enterprise, for the performance of 'their' team.[59]

Even more intriguing is the oral testimony gathered from Cheshire-based fan who claimed that she did not support the national team because it was 'too far away' and that, if she was to support a national side, it would be Wales because it was 'nearer'.[60] Such apparently tortured logic is actually highly suggestive of a substantial sense of separateness from the capital and its activities.

North–South rivalries and antipathies could also be profound at club level. In association football, the relatively modest contribution initially made by southern clubs to the professional game limited such tensions in the early period. However, the remarkable success of Arsenal, League champions five times between 1931 and 1938, FA Cup winners in 1930 and 1936 and consistently the best-supported side in the country, achievements that coincided precisely with the onset of mass unemployment in many parts of the North of England, altered the situation radically. The strong northern antipathy toward the London side was openly acknowledged in the media. When seven Arsenal players were selected to play for England against Italy in 1934, the *Daily Mail* joked that it would be 'a pretty sight at the game to see northern onlookers as patriotic Englishmen, sinking their feelings and shouting "come on Arsenal"'.[61] To a degree, the club's unpopularity was simply rooted in resentment at its success, and a success based on a counter-attacking style earning them the nickname 'Lucky Arsenal'. At the heart, however, lay a symbolic role ascribed to the club whereby southern footballing achievement was held to mirror a (much simplified) wider socio-economic picture. Writing in 1956, George Scott remembered how, in his native Middlesbrough, Arsenal were disliked for coming from the 'soft south, from London, from the city of government, where, it was imagined, all social evil was plotted and directed against places like Teesside'.[62] Here was a club with celebrity supporters such as film producer Herbert Wilcox and film star wife Anna Neagle, a high media profile and, above all, financial resources that apparently allowed it to replicate wider processes by which industrial change forced workers to move south in search of new opportunities. Arsenal broke the English transfer record when paying Bolton

Wanderers a fee variously reported as between £10,340 and £10, 890 for David Jack in 1928, with Jack's initial reluctance overcome by the offer of a weekly column on the *Evening Standard*. Alex James was attracted from Preston in the next year, his passage similarly smoothed by a lucrative additional engagement with a sport's outfitters. Preston's leading football correspondent claimed that 'to me and to thousands of others his going is a sort of football tragedy'. As so often, London seemed to be absorbing talent honed elsewhere.[63]

A long spell of mediocrity in the 1950s and 1960s somewhat diminished the club's unpopularity and it is interesting that the team's renewed success from the late 1990s has not generated anything resembling previous levels of hostility, although this may have resulted more from Manchester United becoming the team to despise than any decline in anti-metropolitan sentiment. Arsenal replica shirts are indeed a far from unknown sight in the modern North as television and new football economics reconfigure sporting loyalties. No other London or southern-based side has ever again generated such antipathy although Chelsea, with its 'fashionable London' status in the 1960s and 1970s and its trend-setting influx of foreign players into the club from the mid-1990s, both of which groups were believed not to 'fancy it' on wet afternoons in Sunderland or wherever, has perhaps come the closest. Generalised anti-southern sentiment has always simmered, however, with a local paper blaming Gateshead's failure to secure re-election to the Football League in 1960 on a conspiracy by 'a cosy clique of southern clubs' who believed that the north-east of England was 'up in the wilds'.[64] Northern fans have also been both offended and amused by the stereotyping they have received at the hands of their southern counterparts. Liverpool fans could still be greeted with chants of 'does the social know you're here?' when visiting West Ham's ground as late as November 1999.[65] In a moment of gentle, if still slightly exasperated revenge, a Preston fan recounted (doubtless with some exaggeration) for the local paper, southern conversations overheard during a recent visit by the club to Arsenal.

> 'There's a fair few down from Preston.'
> 'Yeah, the town must be empty tonight.'
> 'Must be a big occasion for them to come "oop T'London"' (this last in an accent that only an American having seen a trailer for *Coronation Street* would recognise).
> 'Where is Preston any way?'
> 'Dunno, somewhere up north'
> 'How is it you know everything there is to know about NT workstation but don't know where Preston is?'
> 'Need to know basis'.[66]

On occasions it is possible to glimpse a level of northern consciousness that goes beyond the powerful but to some degree emotionally limited register of anti-metropolitanism. An, at first sight, extremely unlikely example is offered by the sporting relationship that grew up around Yorkshire and Lancashire county cricket. While the roses rivalry was certainly intense, a shared sense of 'northern-ness' surfaced beneath it. Indeed, the fierceness of the rivalry actually fed this kinship; here was tough, competitive cricket, played as only these two counties could play it, a sporting fixture unique within the county game and thus a distinctive gift from the North to the national culture. The fact that the Lancashire club shared a somewhat similar image to Yorkshire's outside of the North – the players boycotted a civic lunch at Eastbourne in 1931 after the Mayor accused them of negative play – only served to tighten the bond. It is surely significant that at the end of the troubled 1924 season, with Yorkshire finally triumphant in the County Championship, a *Yorkshire Observer* cartoon satirising responses to that success around the country, included a depiction of the Lancashire captain declaiming that 'I'm real glad a rose won it. Red, or white, it doesn't matter.' The true nature of these sibling rivalries was again symbolised by the holding of a joint dinner in 1949 at which Yorkshire presented Lancashire with a flag showing their respective rose emblems entwined, to be flown at all future fixtures between them.[67]

Rugby league offers an even more striking version of northern unity. As seen, the game was specifically a northern invention and it has remained very much a northern phenomenon. As well as being rooted in a struggle that contained considerable elements of north–south rivalry its whole history has been punctuated by battles against southern-based sporting and media interests. As recently as the 1990s, a London newspaper columnist described the southern view of Rugby League, and one with which he fully concurred, as a game 'for ape-like creatures watched by gloomy men in cloth caps'.[68] More than a little of the much-vaunted post-modern irony probably lurks behind this statement but the fact that the writer chose to call upon such imagery is revealing of long standing prejudices.

Against this background, rugby league does appear to have generated a sense of family membership amongst its adherents, a unity based on the shared love of a game they feel is undervalued by others. By definition, this is largely a northern construct. Although issues of class and status also impinge strongly on a game often seen as the property of the 'working class', 'ordinary folk', 'the people' and so on, the tendency by many in and outside the north to elide 'north' and 'working class' in no way weakens this regional sense. The fusing of the two can indeed be seen in Simon Kelner's recent version of the game's history. 'Just before the end of the nineteenth century, the oppressed labourers created something that would engage their desire for independence from the bosses, and that would help them forge an identity outside their working environment … The sport of Rugby League was born of rebellion and has been, for a century, a source of pride for the people of the north.'[69] Although the self-consciously modern, Americanised image imposed on the game by the introduction of the Super League in 1996 has complicated the situation (Bradford Northern became the Bradford Bulls), for most of its history, insiders have represented the game in a self-consciously northern way. An excellent oral history of the game published in 1993 used grainy, black and white photographs often depicting classic industrial landscapes (cost as much as aesthetics may have militated against use of colour) and sought to define the game as notably authentic. It was, one of the editors claimed, an activity 'in opposition to an increasingly systemized world where everything is pigeon-holed and organised like a day at the local theme park'.[70] Such ideas have been encountered in other contexts in this book. The crucial point is that this sense of shared history and distinctiveness has helped create a community out of disparate elements of the North not normally united in other ways. This is especially important for Rugby League strongholds in more isolated areas that are rarely 'imagined' as part of the North, such as the West Cumbrian towns of Barrow, Workington and Whitehaven, and even Hull in east Yorkshire, a large city somewhat out of the mainstream. Even if these places are rarely visited, their presence on the rugby league map has rendered them visible and visibly northern.

In the final analysis, there are clear limits to the extent of such northern consciousness. The examples of genuinely embracive identities discussed above are still quite limited in their scope. Yorkshire and Lancashire cricket has generated only a sub-regional bond and while Yorkshiremen and Lancastrians denounced the machinations of 'an abstract South' in the early years of the struggle within rugby union, they did not 'sing the praise of an abstract North'.[71] Even in later years when rugby league has allowed for the communion of territories from a wider area, the game's geographical limitations means that it can never mobilise the full seven-county North. Yet again, while anti-metropolitanism often literally speaks the North by using the phrase as a convenient term, there is often a sense that it is the locality or at best, a sub-region, that writers and speakers have in mind. While those in, say, Manchester might recognise and sympathise with some wrong done to Newcastle, their own sense of northernness probably stems more from a region imagined in local terms than any wider vision. To repeat an earlier point, local allegiances are the strongest of all geographical ties as well as being the crucial building blocks for wider identities, the core belief in a complex web of territorial allegiances. For all this, however, the fact that ideas and discourses about northern sporting superiority and southern perfidy were shared across the region as a whole, recognisable and identifiable by individuals in any part of it, formed a unifying bond that must remain in sight amidst the chaotic jumble of internal rivalries and conflicts.

Sport and the image of the North

Although perhaps not as markedly as in the field of music, northern sporting excellence has often been happily acknowledged and celebrated within the national culture. Nevertheless, it is not necessarily the case that its sporting reputation has actually benefited the region's overall standing. Not for the first time in this study it is hard to avoid a sense that, for all its achievements, northern culture has been filtered through a set of preconceptions that can generate less than helpful readings elsewhere. Many opportunities for this were provided by the annual cup final pilgrimages to the capital. Although much celebrated in the local and regional press, its metropolitan counterpart was often able to give these activities a rather different gloss by tying the behaviour of northern fans into existing stereotypes, admittedly with varying degrees of acerbity and seriousness. The most frequently quoted and most extreme example of such comic treatment occurred in the *Pall Mall Gazette* in 1884 where a columnist referred to Blackburn Rovers followers as 'a Northern horde [of] hot-bloodied Lancastrians, sharp of tongue, of uncouth garb and speech'. The local response to these slurs was swift and furious but, in this instance, there is some evidence that the attack came not from one of the 'milk and water' Cockneys targeted by the *Blackburn Standard* but the son of Blackburn Rovers committee member, Dr Edward Morley. Quite what his motives were are unclear, but, if he was the culprit, he produced a template that was utilised in many different ways over the next decades.[72] In recent decades, rather darker versions of northern 'otherness', as in the stigmatisation of Liverpudlian football fans as dole queue scroungers noted earlier, have surfaced although the latter has been as common inside the North as outside of it.

As has so often been noted in this book, some of the most powerful reinforcement of existing stereotypes came not from Londoners or from mischievous spirits like the young Morley, but from squarely within the North. Neville Cardus' self-conscious 'northernism' has already been touched on. Ultimately aimed at a northern audience that was privy to his modes of thinking and that could laugh with him and at itself, his work nevertheless ran the risk of taking on less positive meaning when read in other settings. From the late 1950s and 1960s, such problems have been exacerbated by the fact that satirising northern character has become a major part of the national comic grammar.[73]

It is in this context that the BBC's renowned rugby league commentator, Eddie Waring, should be placed.[74] Originally a local sports journalist, Waring enjoyed an extremely successful spell in rugby league management in the 1930s and 1940s, before returning to journalism. His first rugby league commentary came in 1951 and, with a weekly showcase on *Grandstand* from 1958, he remained 'the voice of rugby league' until his retirement in 1981. Although Waring was a skilled broadcaster, some northern fans eventually grew extremely tired of his voice. During a televised game in the late 1960s, fans chanted 'send Waring to Vietnam', while in 1976 10,000 people dissatisfied with television coverage of the sport signed a petition to the BBC that included some criticism of his style.[75] This opposition stemmed from what was seen as his increasingly clichéd and simplistic commentary on the game and from his pantomime portrayal of northern life. Waring became famous for a series of catchphrases ('it's an up-and-under', 'it's an early bath for him', 'never mind the ball, get on with the game') and idiosyncratic observations ('this lad's a window cleaner, so he'll kick this') all delivered in a distinctive accent that became part of the stock-in-trade of innumerable impersonators. Graeme Garden began the Waring cult in the radio show 'I am Sorry I'll Read that Again' in the 1960s but it was television impressionist Mike Yarwood who made it a national phenomenon.[76]

According to some critics, the fact that the BBC allowed this style of comic presentation 'only served to fuel the feeling that there was anti-northern bias in establishment circles, a view that has had currency ever since 1895'.[77] The defence offered for Waring was that he had 'transformed the game from one only vaguely understood outside the northern counties to a popular national entertainment' and this was undoubtedly true.[78] However, the cost was surely considerable. In an age when the idea of the comic North was taking on a new intensity, Waring placed himself, rugby league and the North at the heart of the national culture but in problematic and stereotypical ways. Similar outcomes might also be claimed in other sports, especially cricket, where the utterances of Yorkshiremen Freddie Trueman and Geoffrey Boycott have sometimes tended to self-parody.

There is also a more general point to be made. The North's celebration of sport represented another dimension of its tendency, albeit not always self-conscious, to make a virtue of the demotic and to place popular culture at the heart of its cultural distinctiveness. This has become troublesome on occasions when the region has attempted to shed the old tag of 'philistinism' and project a more sophisticated image. This problem was well understood in Liverpool in the early 1960s when the Merseysound and success of the city's football clubs placed the city at the very heart of British and, indeed, western popular culture. A *Liverpool Daily Post* editorial entitled 'Beatles and Boots' wondered anxiously whether 'the fame brought to Merseyside by fringes and football may be something of an embarrassment', adding to a popular stereotype of Liverpool as a place of drunkenness and delinquency. 'Into this false image, those who want to bolster it can crush without too much distortion the Beatles fans and the soccer fans indiscriminately. That they do so is evident from the quite disproportionate brouhaha that any sort of hooliganism in Clacton or Margate occasions if only it can be linked, however tenuously, with Merseyside.' In a city desperate to attract new economic investment, halt migration and recruit new workers – Ford's Halewood plant made extensive attempts to 'sell' the area to southern-based staff at this time – popular cultural success did not necessarily appear to offer the way forward.[79]

As popular culture has taken on an ever more central role in the national culture in the late twentieth century, this problem may have diminished with the North perhaps even gaining status from its popular cultural past and buoyant present. In regard to football, television has certainly allowed leading northern clubs effectively to become 'national' sides attracting fans throughout England, including the South. Liverpool F.C. has been a major beneficiary but it was Manchester United that began the trend in the 1960s and that has taken it to its highest level.[80] By the end of the 1990s, an incredibly successful decade for the club, 18 per cent of all English football fans claimed allegiance to it. However, whether support for Manchester United in Basingstoke or Bethnal Green implies a sudden reappraisal of southern attitudes to Manchester specifically (even with the strong music and club culture discussed in chapter 6) or the North more generally, is unlikely. United has in some senses become a world brand, dislocated from any precise geographical moorings and with many fans attached to a club they may never visit and based in a city that they might not be able to locate on a map. Nevertheless, in post-modern times, sport perhaps represents a less problematic route to the heart of the national culture than previously and certainly offers a considerably safer one than many selected by (or, more normally, *for*) the region in the past.

Whatever the future possibilities and despite any comic or unsavory associations that it might have generated, many northerners have seen sport as one of their region's most distinct and richest gifts to the nation. This contribution to Englishness via sport has, as in other contexts, been complementary rather than alternative. While there has been anger directed at 'them' down in London, there has never been any sustained desire for separation, that the North should stand alone. While rugby league was born in the North it has spent much of its subsequent history trying to build a national presence, a process that even involved the adoption of Wembley Stadium as the home for the Rugby League Challenge Cup Final from 1929. For all its rhetoric, the sport has always wanted to be loved. Furthermore, as Jeff Hill has shown, trips by northern sports fans to London have shown a desire not only to enrich but also to be enriched by their experience on the national stage and in the capital.[81] The very claim of bias against northern players in national selection processes reflects a similar desire for inclusion, a wish to have the distinctive qualities of Yorkshire, Cumbria, Tyneside or wherever made available for the national good. Even suspicion of the southern establishment could be overcome in the pursuit of that good. When Surrey captain Douglas Jardine came out to bat at Sheffield in 1933 after leading the England cricket team in Australia during the previous winter's controversial 'body-line' tour, the crowd gave him, according to one Yorkshire player, a welcome exceeding 'anything I have known given to a Yorkshire player there. The crowd – it was a big crowd – stood to cheer and show what Yorkshiremen thought about the way he had fought in Australia.'[82] Here, the Winchester and Oxford-educated son of the Advocate-General of Bombay, the very model of the southern, patrician amateur, was forgiven the sins of his birth and personal geography. The northern desire has simply been for its distinctive admixture of passion, competitiveness and hardness (always, of course, mitigated by a basic sense of fair play), administrative efficiency and commercial sense to be on hand to stiffen a national resolve otherwise too open to the detrimental influence of gentlemanly values and a carelessness about results. Play was too serious to be left to others.

Notes

1 E. Hobsbawm, *Nations and Nationalism Since 1780. Programme, Myth, Reality* (Cambridge: Cambridge University Press, 1989), p. 143.

2 D. Russell, '"Sporadic and curious": the development of rugby and soccer zones in Lancashire and Yorkshire, *c.*1860–1914', *International Journal of the History of Sport*, 5, 5, 1988, pp. 185–205.

3 For Sheffield, see A. Harvey, 'Football in Sheffield and the creation of modern soccer and rugby', *International Journal of the History of Sport*, 18, 4, 2001,

pp. 53–87. For football in the 1840s and 1850s, see J. Goulstone, 'The working-class origins of modern football', *International Journal of the History of Sport*, 17, 1, 2000.

4   T. Mason, 'Football, sport of the north?', in J. Hill and J. Williams (eds), *Sport and Identity in the North of England* (Keele: Keele University Press, 1996), p. 45.

5   R. Holt, 'Sporting heroes', in Hill and Williams (eds), *Sport and Identity*, p. 144.

6   Durham were founder members, with Northumberland joining in 1896, Cheshire in 1909 and Cumberland in 1948.

7   M. Huggins, 'Sport and the construction of identity in north-east England, 1800–1914', in N. Kirk (ed.), *Northern Identities* (Aldershot: Ashgate, 2000), p. 135.

8   J. Hill, 'League cricket in the North and Midlands', in R. Holt (ed.), *Sport and the Working Class in Modern Britain* (Manchester: Manchester University Press); R. Light, 'The Other Face of Cricket' (Unpublished MA thesis, De Montfort University, 2002).

9   See the outstanding T. Collins, *Rugby's Great Split. Class, Culture and the Origins of Rugby League Football* (London: Frank Cass, 1998).

10   S. Kelner, *To Jerusalem and Back* (London: Macmillan, 1996), p. 99.

11   K. Hawkes and G. Lindley, *Encyclopaedia of Bowls* (London: Robert Hale, 1974), p. 47.

12   J. Arlott (ed.), *The Oxford Companion to Sports and Games* (Oxford: Oxford University Press, 1975), pp. 578–81; *Halifax Courier*, 7 December 1982.

13   A. Metcalfe, 'Resistance to change: potshare bowling in the mining communities of East Northumberland, 1800–1914', in Holt (ed.), *Sport and the Working* Class, pp. 29–44 and 'Sport and the community: a case study of the mining villages of East Northumberland, 1800–1914', in Hill and Williams (eds), *Sport and Identity*, pp. 221–2, 27–9; 'A Fine Hunting day: Songs of the Holme Valley Beagles', Leader Records, Lee 4056, accompanying booklet.

14   Huggins, 'Identity in north-east England', pp. 141–5.

15   Holt, 'Heroes', p. 139.

16   J. M. Kilburn, *History of Yorkshire County Cricket Club* (Leeds: Yorkshire County Cricket Club, 1950), p. 123; Holt, 'Heroes', p. 147.

17   J. Arlott, ed., *Neville Cardus. The Roses Matches, 1919–1939* (London: Souvenir Press, 1982), p. 30; quoted in R. Hart-Davis, *Cardus on Cricket* (London: Souvenir Press, 1977), p. 43.

18   Holt, 'Heroes', p. 154.

19   R. Holt, *Sport and the British. A Modern History* (Oxford: Clarendon Press, 1989), p. 175.

20   Kelner, *Jerusalem*, p. 12.

21   Jones did play for Leeds United from 1989–90 and Sheffield United from 1990–91, but is absolutely associated with the South.

22   N. A. Phelps, 'The southern football hero and the shaping of regional and local identity in the south of England', *Soccer and Society*, 2, 3, 2001, p. 55.

23   *Daily Mirror*, 25 February 1993.

24 D. Russell, *Football and the English* (Preston: Carnegie Publishing, 1997), pp. 69, 83.

25 *Athletic News*, 1 June 1896.

26 *Liverpool Daily Post*, 30 July 1966.

27 R. Holt, 'Heroes', pp. 150–7; A. Hardaker with B. Butler, *Hardaker of the League* (London: Pelham, 1977), p. 185.

28 R. Holt, 'Football and regional identity in the North of England: the legend of Jackie Milburn', in S. Gehrmann (ed.), *Football and Regional Identity in Europe* (Munster: LIT VERLAG, 1997), p. 60.

29 Kelner, *Jerusalem*, pp. 11–12. 'Arthur' Machin became 'Frank' in the journey from novel to film to prevent confusion with Arthur Seaton in *Saturday Night and Sunday Morning*.

30 I. Clayton and M. Steele, *'When Push Comes to Shove.' Rugby League the People's Game* (Castleford: Yorkshire Arts Circus, 1993), pp. 123–4.

31 R. Lewis, 'Professional football and identity in Lancashire, 1870–1899', in F. Caspistegui and J. K. Walton (eds), *Guerras Danzadas. Fútbol e Identidades Locales y Regionales en Europa* (Pamplona: Ediciones Universidad de Navarra, 2001), pp. 162–3.

32 Quoted in ibid., p. 167.

33 'Football crowds in the north-west of England, 1946–1962', *The Sports Historian*, 19, 2, pp. 36–7.

34 *Liverpool Football Echo*, 5 May 1928. I am grateful to Christopher Beesley for this reference.

35 Significantly, the broad chronology offered here is also applicable to levels of football hooliganism and crowd disorder.

36 My thinking here owes much to Gavin Mellor, 'Football and its Supporters in the North West of England, 1945–1985' (Unpublished PhD thesis, University of Central Lancashire, 2003).

37 J. Hill, 'Rite of spring: cup finals and community in the North of England', in Hill and Williams (eds), *Sport and Identity*, pp. 85–111.

38 *Liverpool Echo*, 20 March 1984.

39 A. Metcalfe, 'Sport and community: a case study of the mining villages of East Northumberland, 1800–1914', in Hill and Williams (eds), *Sport and Identity*, p. 30.

40 D. Russell, 'Sport and Identity: the case of Yorkshire County Cricket Club, 1890–1939', *20th Century British History*, 7, 2, 1996, pp. 206–30 and 'Amateurs, professionals and the construction of social identity', *The Sports Historian*, 16 May 1996, pp. 64–80.

41 *Yorkshire Observer*, 21 August 1931.

42 *Yorkshire Telegraph and Star*, 5 July 1924.

43 Ibid., 28 August and 2 September 1924.

44 Huggins, 'Identity in north-east England', pp. 134–5.

45 M. Taylor, 'Little Englanders: tradition, identity and professional football in Lancashire, 1880–1930', in Gehrmann (ed.), *Football and Regional Identity*, p. 44.

46 T. Mason, *Association Football and English Society, 1863–1915* (Brighton: Harvester Press, 1981); Collins, *Great Split*, pp. 112–53.

47 *Preston Herald*, 23 January 1884; *Bradford Observer* 7 September 1895; quoted in Collins, *Great Split*, p. 157.

48 *Preston Herald*, 30 January, 6 February 1884; *Preston Guardian*, 30 January 1884.

49 *Yorkshireman*, 12 January 1884.

50 Both 26 July 1968.

51 *Manchester Evening News*, 14 June 1958, 24 May 1960, 25 May 1960, 27 October 1960.

52 Ibid., 19 May 1958.

53 Ibid., 7 May 1960.

54 J. Haynes, *It's all in the Game* (London: Arthur Baker, 1962), pp. 136–9: J. Hill, *Striking for Soccer* (London: Peter Davies, 1961), pp. 207–9.

55 Provincial stadia have again been used recently, but only as a result of the closure of Wembley for refurbishment.

56 *Yorkshire Post*, 6 July 1966.

57 *Middlesbrough Evening Gazette*, 13 July 1966.

58 *Liverpool Daily Post*, 26 July 1966. As so often, this was matter of provinces rather than simply the North against the centre, with Birmingham especially aggrieved about the national stadium.

59 J. Williams, 'White riots: the English football team abroad', in A. Tomlinson and G. Whannel (eds), *Off the Ball* (London: Pluto Press, 1986), p. 13.

60 Evidence provided by Gavin Mellor.

61 *Daily Mail*, 13 November 1934.

62 Quoted in D. Read, *The English Provinces, c.1760. A Study in Influence* (London: Edwin Arnold, 1964), pp. 231–2.

63 G. Allison, *Allison Calling* (London: Staples Press, 1948), pp. 79–182; *Bolton Evening News*, 12 and 15 October 1928; *Lancashire Daily Post*, 8 June 1929. James's talents had admittedly been honed in Scotland, with Preston the initial predator.

64 Russell, *Football and the English*, pp. 152–3.

65 *Mail on Sunday*, 28 November 1999.

66 'Talking rubbish is a capital offence', *Lancashire Evening Post*, 20 October 1999.

67 *Yorkshire Observer*, 3 September 1924; Kilburn, *Yorkshire County*, p. 15.

68 Kelner, *Jerusalem*, p. 14.

69 Ibid., p. 1.

70 Clayton and Steele, *When Push Comes*, p. 11.

71 Collins, *Great Split*, pp. 70–1.

72 Lewis, 'Professional football and identity', pp. 170–1. For the Morley family connection, see F. Wall, *Fifty Years of Football* (London: Cassell, 1935), p. 38. For further examples of the comic approach, see Mason, 'Football, sport of the north?', pp. 46–7.

73 This is explored in the concluding chapter.

74 See J. Williams, '"Up and under". Eddie Waring, television and the image of rugby league', *The Sports Historian*, 22, 1, 2002, pp. 115–37 for a perceptive analysis. Also, *The Times*, 29 October 1986; *Yorkshire Post*, 29 October 1986.

75 Clayton and Steele, *When Push Comes*, p. 105; *Yorkshire Post*, 29 October 1986.

76 Williams '"Up and under"', pp. 118–19.

77 S. Kelner, *Jerusalem*, pp. 61, 80–1.

78 *The Times*, 29 October 1986.

79 *Liverpool Daily Post*, 20 April 1964, 11 November 1963.

80 G. Mellor, 'The Genesis of Manchester United as a National and International "Super-Club", 1958–68', *Soccer and Society*, 1, 2, 200, pp. 151–66; Russell, *Football and the English*, pp. 183–4.

81 Hill, 'Rite of spring', pp. 87–93.

82 H. Sutcliffe, *For England and Yorkshire* (London: Arnold, 1935), pp. 104–5.

9

The North in the national imagination

This book has had four central concerns: the image of the North within the English imagination; the major functions served by the North within the national culture; northern identity and the relationships between regional and other forms of collective identity; and the measurement of the northern contribution to English cultural life. With the exception of the latter, excluded to avoid undue repetition, this final chapter reflects on these, building on ideas and material already raised and introducing new aspects where appropriate in order to offer some broad conclusions about the place of the North within English culture from the early Victorian period. It concludes with a necessarily speculative consideration of the region's future prospects.

Images and function

It has been argued throughout that the North of England has ultimately held a marginal and often problematic place within the national culture. Nevertheless, this has been accompanied by an insistent counter-narrative stressing that its institutions, people and landscapes have often been cast in a far more positive light and given far greater significance within notions of 'Englishness' than has often been appreciated and it is important to give this aspect full weight. It has certainly been clear that many elements of the pre-industrial and scenic North have been as happily and enthusiastically claimed for 'Deep England' as any of the supposedly more favoured regions to the south and west. That process has equally certainly been detrimental to the urban/industrial North, but it must still be acknowledged. Even these urban regions, what was once called 'Black England', have at times served a crucial purpose. National leadership has often been ceded to them in the fields of music, sport and popular entertainment for much of the period under study and in other specific arenas (including politics and economics) at other albeit briefer moments. There is indeed a case to be made for 'Englishness' taking on a far more definitely northern flavour from the late 1950s, with the terraced street and its residents, as imagined particularly in popular fiction and television, coming to stand for the ordinary English community at its most virtuous and self-sustaining.

At the core of most these positive versions of the North has been its construction as the place where necessary balances and correctives are erected against the bourgeois, complacent, softer, perhaps even effete aspects of national culture and character, often associated with the South. Its status as the 'land of the working class' with the implications of authenticity and moral worth that this generates in the eyes of many external enthusiasts for the region has been vital here. Related to this, although not deriving exclusively from it, has been a widespread belief in its capacity to cleanse and rejuvenate. Just as its bracing climate and rugged hillsides have been invested with the power to refresh the bodies and souls of jaded visitors, so its supposed quick humour, communal warmth, lack of pretension and consequent capacity to prick metropolitan condescension, have been seen as central to the resuscitation of tired cultural practices. As quoted in chapter 5, an enthusiastic Edwardian reviewer of *Hindle Wakes* argued that 'change of air is a tonic inside, no less than outside, the theatre' and it has been in this role as, both literally and metaphorically, a breath of fresh air that the North has found its major role within English culture.[1] In a variant of such thinking the region has been imagined in the twentieth century as a powerful bulwark against the general threat of mass culture and the specific one of Americanisation. In 1930, for example, praise for the brass band movement by composer Hubert Bath led him to claim that the 'breath of our good, honest, fresh brass air from the north was, and always will be, an invigorating tonic to the jaded, Americanised southerner'.[2] The North is by no means the only terrain to have been empowered by place myths of this type. Cornwall has considerable power as a signifier of intellectual and artistic replenishment and the cheerful Cockney has been a rival source of working-class vibrancy and initiative.[3] Overall, however, only the North, with its large ensemble of supposed characteristics and associations, has been imagined on a grand and complex enough scale to generate something close to an alternative or, probably more accurately, a complementary Englishness.

The 'flexible positional superiority' of the dominant culture driven from London and the South has clearly then allowed the North the space to enjoy a considerable degree of influence and strength. Superiority, nevertheless, must remain the key word. For all of the positive notes and the subtly varying and contending images that have emerged according to the dictates of specific cultural forms, the ultimate position of the North has been secondary, a powerful imaginary space to be called up when needed but only then, and one never able to shed its accretion of negative images. While the region's complexity has been acknowledged in certain cultural forms, its core, stereotypical imagery has basically survived in all its pared down simplicity. The North as urban and industrial, grim and bleak, harsh and uncultured has been encountered in many guises in preceding chapters and it is not helpful to parade yet more examples here. What must be stressed is the constancy of these representations, with the external image of the north over much of the 150 years covered by this book remaining in some ways remarkably similar to the pattern that was in place by about 1840 and changing little over the period. It is striking that forty years after the PR-driven recruitment campaigns which in many senses began the 're-branding' of the North and more than twenty years after the emergence of the 'new' urban tourism, northern agencies still have had to repeat so insistently their message that the North has changed.

This is partly because many outsiders simply do not want to believe that it has. Neither, perhaps, do all insiders. Much of the power of the northern, working-class variant of Englishness is that it harks back to a supposedly safer, more certain, less complex world and an unchanging North has its attractions. Unfortunately, unlike those strands of English identity that hark back to organic roots laid down well before the emergence of cobbled streets and corner shops, this northern version offers a deeply sombre past. It deals with the loss and decline of industrial communities that can all too easily pervade ideas about the present and it is unsurprising that historical fiction and autobiography are two of its major vehicles.[4] It is also a troublingly recent past and it may be some time before it can be used to galvanise the present.

The North's problems have been further compounded by cultural formations of a very different type. The region's short but significant spell of cultural importance from the late 1950s and its winning of a more deeply rooted and consistent place within the national culture from that point, have been paralleled by the revival or reworking of stereotypical and comic versions of the region's history and culture. This process has been mentioned episodically in individual chapters but is sufficiently important to demand sustained treatment here. It emerged from a number of disparate sources and is easier to identify in hindsight than it was at the time. Crucially, its major protagonists were mainly born in the North but had moved south in pursuit of media careers, generating a valuable critical distance that allowed for both affection and wry mockery. At the very moment when the North was gaining some control over its own representation, the latter mode proved a decidedly mixed blessing. 1957 saw the birth not only of John Braine's Joe Lampton but also of cartoon character Andy Capp in (initially) the northern edition of the *Daily Mirror*, a crucial moment in the emergence of this newly minted comic North. Drawn by Hartlepool-born Reg Smythe, the indolent, cloth-capped Andy, cigarette permanently on lip, pint glass never far away and perpetually in trouble with long-suffering wife Flo, was to become one of the great universal figures of amiably dissolute working-class masculinity. The cartoon was eventually syndicated in fifty countries and translated into fourteen languages. In Britain, however, its northern roots and references were obvious and Andy became a potent signifier for the region, often indeed subsequently referred to 'the land of Andy Capp' or similar.[5]

The late 1950s also saw the appearance of another less influential but still significant northern archetype in the form of the '18-stone-indigo-waist-coated-iron-watch-chained monolith' Alderman Jabez Foodbotham, created by Michael Wharton for Peter Simple's 'Way of the World' column in the *Daily Telegraph*.[6] An amalgam of civic worthies remembered from his West Riding childhood and the (southerner) Sir Stanley Rous for whom Wharton had worked at the Football Association, Foodbotham was a bygone Chairman of the Bradford City Tramways and Fine Arts Committee whose utterances skilfully parodied one style of northern civic patriotism. Rejecting a peerage in 1924 for services to the catering and bottling industries, he thundered that he 'would rather be an alderman of Bradford than Emperor of Byzantium and would sooner don my long black worsted overcoat than the purple of Imperial Rome'. In his parody of the 'Angry Young Man' novels, featuring, for example, Len Drearclough, an expletive-inserter at the West Riding Proleterian Novel and Television Play Factory, Wharton then placed one of the North's highest earners of cultural capital firmly in the firing line.[7] The comic treatment of traditional northern cultural life by Billy Fisher and his friend Arthur in both the novel and film versions of Keith Waterhouse's *Billy Liar*, discussed in earlier chapters, was also important in implicating the new northern novel in the parodic process.

By the mid-1960s, the comic North was becoming a comic staple. Monty Python's 'Four Yorkshiremen' sketch is perhaps the best remembered of all the resultant pieces, a brilliantly constructed affair in which four tuxedoed businessmen relax with post-prandial cigars and drinks by outdoing each other's tales of childhood poverty and deprivation.

'We had nothing, used to live in a tiny old tumbled down house, with great holes
   in the floor.'
[Pause]
'A house? You were lucky to have a house! We used to live in one room, 26 of us,
   no furniture and half the floor was missing.'

While the Pythons' sketch originated with comedians from outside the North,
most other contributions continued to be insiders. Michael Parkinson's *Sunday
Times* sports column offered cleverly exaggerated youthful memories of the (real)
Barnsley footballer 'Skinner' Normanton. In Parkinson's version Normanton
became a fierce tackling, steel-toe-cap wearing defender whose premature retirement was blamed in one column for the 'sad closure of Barnsley Hospital
Casualty Department'.[8] Liverpool cartoonist Bill Tidy produced a string of
memorable northern characters including the flat-capped Sam Hinchliffe who
first appeared in *Punch* in 1969, the folk-dancing *Cloggies* in *Private Eye* from
1971–81 and the *Daily Mirror's Fosdyke Saga* (1971–85), the story of family of
tripe producers.[9] Rochdale singer-songwriter Mike Harding, novelist and TV
writer Peter Tinniswood and the TV series *Brass* (1983–84,1990) were also
important contributors. A coarser but hugely popular humorous note was
sounded in the *The Fat Slags* ('Can I have a shag?'; 'Yeh, if you give us a chip') and
Sid the Sexist strips in the Newcastle-based scatological comic *Viz* from 1980s.

   At one level, much of this simply extended the work of the many from
comedian George Formby senior to cricket and music writer Neville Cardus
who had produced consciously exaggerated versions of northern folk from
'within'. Such modes had always been problematic in that writers laughing
affectionately *with* local and regional cultures always ran the risk of encouraging those from outside to laugh *at* these cultures; internal and external representations were invariably superficially close enough to allow for this. In the
context of the later twentieth century such writing, whether based on nostalgic affection or simple a desire to have fun with clichés, became increasingly
troublesome. While Formby and others were part-celebrating, part-guying a
living culture and often doing so from a known and visible base within the
North, their successors were targeting (often from the capital) forms of
northern working-class culture at the moment when that culture was
changing irrevocably. As the North's economic and political position within
the national culture weakened, comic representations that were often intended
to satirise commonplace assumptions about the region ran the risk of reinforcing the very stereotypes that were being satirised and which were ever less
appropriate to the North as it sought a post-industrial future.

As a result, the North has been claimed for and associated with a distinct version of the past. Furthermore, symbols that were once signifiers for the working-class nationally, or that had some but by no means exclusive links with the region have become entirely associated with it as emblems of conservatism. This process has increasingly occurred throughout the culture and not just in the work of comedians and novelists. When, in 1970, footballer Bobby Moore's newspaper ghost referred to Leeds United as the most unpopular team to 'leave the country of cloth caps and racing pigeons to come south', he was adopting one of the most popular of such symbols, although on another day he might have chosen whippets ahead of pigeons.[10] John Belchem's penetrative study of the cultural impact of modern 'scouse' identities, suggests that Liverpool provided an extreme example of this general case. Recent largely humorous writing within the city from a variety different perspectives has happily repeated some of the city's most disabling stereotypes, often rooted in crude and ahistorical readings of the city's nineteenth century Irish community. As a result, the 'unadulterated image of the lowly Irish "slummy", reckless and feckless, has been adopted as the foundation stone, a symbolic figure of inverse snobbery and pride in the evolution of the true Scottie Road Scouser' and one easily appropriated by those outside the city.[11]

By the 1990s, this comic grammar was so strongly ingrained that it had become a standard device, albeit heavily overlain with ironic tones. A London *Evening Standard* piece by Kate Battersby on the failure of foreign footballers to settle in northern cities is indicative.[12] Although anxious to avoid suggesting that 'northern England is a right dump or anything' the article does, of course, precisely that via her analysis of 'Armpit United'. She admits that 'cosmopolitan urban pockets exist in the provinces' where foreigners might feel at home and offers 'Newcastle, Manchester, Newcastle, Manchester' as 'just a few of these'. London, however, is the only place where players have 'no problem'. The piece is extremely well written and rooted in a genuine problem: as Battersby reports, the wife of one Brazilian player really had termed Middlesbrough 'a strange and terrible place'. It is obviously intended as light comedy and everyone is expected to recognise the knowing overstatement about the North. Nevertheless, not everyone gets or enjoys the joke; such writing, especially when found in a London source, often fails to amuse northerners. At the same time, there is always a danger that those from outside the region will not fully comprehend it either and will simply add it, consciously or not, to their store of northern imagery. Indeed, even if external readers are fully attuned to post-modern ways, there is no reason to believe that even such gentle jibes might not reinforce preconceived notions. Irony does not necessarily provide an excuse.

Being serious about comedy is a funny business and perhaps this line of argument is simply too earnest and joyless while also overstating even the collective impact of such small popular cultural moments. Moreover, it is possible that the northern urban renaissance of the 1990s and the general 'greening' of so much of the North that has taking place in the post-industrial phase, really is beginning to generate a new image that allows the long lineage of jokes about the region to be neutralised, to be sources of knowing laughter both within and without, but no more than that. Whatever the interpretation, all cultures need stories to tell about their fellow inhabitants and the North has served a useful comic purpose for a long time. There is no obvious reason why old habits should not continue and for the capacity of humour to damage as well as amuse to continue with them.

Northern identity

The question as to whether it has ever been possible to speak of a 'northern identity' in the sense of a shared consciousness of a defined community and culture has not been extensively discussed within academic literature. Where it has, a consensus emerges that northern consciousness is both extremely fragile and generally secondary to other systems of identification. Tony Mason's comment that 'in the complex world of individual loyalties to wider groups, family, street, town and nation will usually come before region' captures such thinking effectively.[13] In many senses it is hard to disagree with this position. In terms of Mason's first three alternatives, this study is replete with examples of the narrowness of many individual worlds and the internal tensions and rivalries that have punctuated the region's history. Far less has been said here about nation but although there are good arguments for seeing English or British identity as something constructed in and experienced through the *locality*, it would be foolish to downplay the power of national and imperial sensibilities within the North as in every other region. Thus, while Melvyn Bragg's celebrated oral history of his native Wigton inverts the normal spatial hierarchy by placing a supposedly 'marginal' place at the centre, there is nothing remotely incongruous about asking a small Cumbrian town to 'Speak for England'.[14] Mason might also have added class to his list of more significant loyalties. While again often most intensely experienced as a local phenomenon and prone to be disrupted by local and regional conflicts, some sense of, in particular, an embracing national working-class identity will have been a powerful element for many northerners.

Although there may be signs of change, returned to in the final section, the North (and other English regions) has certainly not exhibited the kind of politically attuned regional consciousness typical of some European countries.[15] This is explained to a considerable extent by the factors just discussed. The North was clearly fractured by the physical and cultural geographies of localism and sub-regionalism. While town and city had probably the strongest emotional pull, the county was also a highly charged unit. Indeed, some of the most unexpectedly determined political battles of the late twentieth century were those fought to prevent the loss of county identity as a result of boundary changes stemming from the 1972 Local Government Act.[16] Sport and various forms of voluntary organisation played a role in building these identities from the later nineteenth century, as did the county regiments that emerged from the 1870s.[17] At national level, the working class, especially its radical and socialist leaders, knew that fellow workers in other places had similar problems and sought solutions at the national centre. The upper middle class, in its turn, increasingly although not exclusively educated in public schools by the late nineteenth century, felt itself to be part of a national network.

In terms of national identity, the fact that England really is an old country has been absolutely key in retarding regionalism, rendering it difficult for its inhabitants to imagine alternative arrangements. Even the memories of the kingdom of Northumbria absorbed by the English state in the tenth century are so distant that (with all respect for the symbolic power that exerts in some contemporary north-eastern regional politics) they have never been able to generate the 'sufficiently shared origin myths, differentiating shared experiences and distinctive historical memories' that are essential to separatist regional politics.[18] As England and then Britain emerged as a centralised state, albeit one usually able to devolve sufficient power to local elites to maintain their allegiance, and one at the core of an extraordinarily powerful empire, 'regionalism' could hardly hope to mount a major challenge to patriotic and imperial sentiment. It was indeed often seen as a weakness in other cultures ('unfortunate' was the word used by one late Victorian commentator on Italy), a solvent that could only have dangerous implications for an imperial power. As late as 1991, a Conservative government minister could term political regionalism 'un-English'.[19] In England then, regions have become 'an exemplar of national culture and not an alternative to it' with regional cultures acting as safety valves for the expression of any repressed regional political ideology.[20]

As a result, individuals have rarely if ever been asked to think 'northern' in terms of any concrete project or set of institutions. As will be discussed below, supporters of regional devolution have only infrequently been able to find space upon the political agenda and most calls have anyway been for assemblies that acknowledge divisions within the North. David Robins' recent call for representation for a Single North Region rather than a system based on 'little cliques in big cities mapping out their vision of a north divided – and crippled – by parochial perspectives' reflects what has always been a minority strand.[21] There have been occasional attempts to stimulate northern self-awareness, most normally within the cultural arena, through magazines such as the *County Monthly* (1902) and the *Northern Review* (1924). However, such projects were short-lived and enjoyed only low circulations.[22] Significantly few books in any subject sphere, even travel literature, are written about 'The North', with writers invariably focusing on its component parts. Even sport has failed to generate much sense of popular communion in its occasional North *v* South or similar fixtures in football, rugby and cricket. Such games were admittedly usually arranged as trials for international sides or as exhibition matches and thus lacked competitive edge, but it was ultimately the loss of the *local* element that was so important: the 'North' was far better sensed through attachment to a specific place than through an, in this context, abstract concept.

The ideological underpinning of 'northernness' is similarly weak with its greatest single component taking the form of a dislike for another imagined community rather than a clear sense of its own. Anti-metropolitanism and northern self-consciousness have in fact become effectively inter-changeable concepts and northerners have perhaps been most likely to 'recognise each other in what they would regard as often uncomfortable company, with people from "down south", people who talk posh'.[23]

While ultimately accepting both the standard placing of northern identity within the hierarchy of English allegiances and its limitations as an intellectual construct, it remains vitally important to acknowledge the undoubted power and potential that it has possessed. The sheer extent and continuity of hostility to 'London', the 'South', the 'south-east', or whatever label its opponents choose has been apparent in every cultural form investigated in this study and at every point in time, and with the strong likelihood that it has intensified over the course of the twentieth century as the provincial–metropolitan relationship has become ever more imbalanced. One 1960s commentator talked of northern 'defiance' turning 'to resentment' over the century and that does capture something of the mood.[24] Many northerners have, like John Hartley's fictional tourist Sammywell Grimes, certainly found it a 'wonderful city' and embraced with enthusiasm its cultural richness, opportunities for advancement and potential for anonymity or personal reinvention. Ironically, a significant number of the metropolitan elite, the 'them' who do endless harm to 'us', has therefore been drawn from the North. That, however, is perhaps the ultimate problem. Behind all the varieties of hostility to the centre from the gentle humour of Liverpool fans singing 'London Bridge is Falling Down' as their team beat Arsenal in 1964, through the considered deliberations of regional novelists bemoaning the capital's power and on to the emotional charged condemnations recorded by Graham Turner in his travels in the 1960s – 'well, damn them! We don't need the south any more' – lay irritation at the capital's centripetal pull and the implications of it for those left behind.[25] The competition between loyalty to region and ambition has been troublesome for many. Yorkshire-born art critic Herbert Read argued for artists turning 'our backs on London' in the 1920s but later went to live there, fully appreciative of the ambitious provincial's ambition to be '"at the centre of things"'. Yet he was eventually to return North 'tired of London and its committees and sophistication'.[26] Interestingly, one of the most articulate recent criticisms of metropolitan power has come from (Lord) Melvyn Bragg who has been more successful than most at maintaining a balance between his Cumbrian roots, much celebrated and explored in his fiction and other work, and a place at the very heart of the national media. Yet, when interviewed in 1996, he was able to argue that

> I think the enemy of the rest of England is London, and it always has been. It's quite right to recognise it as an enemy … At present, people *have* to go to London to work in this job or that job. The centralised newspapers come from London, centralised television comes from London, and the city just gathers everything into itself which drains the rest of the country dry … [There is a sense that] if you don't live in or make it in London you are somehow second-rate.[27]

Not everybody who leaves for London has viewed things thus and doubtless many amongst the majority who have never left the North think only rarely thought about such issues; they simply lived what was to them a normal life. Overall, however, the these frustrations and resentments combined with the awareness of the North holding 'a questionable place within the larger social and political geography of England' has been too powerful for too long for it to be downplayed here.[28] It has been both unusual and discomfiting for a segment of the English people to find themselves 'other'. While the central ideological plank of northern-ness is formed by a negative and therefore provides little platform for restorative political action, it is nevertheless an extremely potent one and the basis for a far more powerful individual (if not necessarily collective) identity than has sometimes been allowed for.

The obvious but often neglected point that the words 'north', 'northerner', 'northern' have regularly been used by people of their region and of themselves, is crucial in this context. While it is undeniable that the North within the national imagination has been largely constructed within the South, to go on to argue that 'this external scripting means that no coherent "North Country" has been invented in its own right' or that the North 'has no meaning except with respect to the rest of England; it is compass point not a people' pushes an Orientalist perspective too far and refuses an equally undeniable northern agency.[29] It clearly had meaning for the BBC's John Coatman when a young soldier on the North West Frontier in the early twentieth century. 'The words "North Country" had touched a much deeper layer of feeling than even the word "England" because they referred to my England.'[30] It has not proved possible to provide a detailed history of the usage of these terms, and it may be that the nineteenth century saw a preference for sub-regional or more localised terminology; the large contemporary literature on 'Yorkshireness' is suggestive here. Yet, whatever the exact timings and processes, these are clearly terms that have passed into everyday use and therefore possess considerable emotional resonance. At one level, adoption of such terminology might simply be a convenient way for individual communities to find allies in situations where standing alone limits authority. It is interesting that the *South Shields Daily Gazette*'s celebration of the local St Hilda Colliery Band noted in an earlier chapter, moved beyond civic pride to offer endorsement of a wider northern cultural vitality. It denied that the 'northman' lacked 'the refining graces and arts of life' and argued that the 'North, is we believe more musical than the South'. Here, perhaps, was a move, conscious or otherwise, to conjure up a more potent territorial signifier and to avoid the bathetic embarrassment that might flow from the over extended claims of one small community.

Even this is a somewhat negative way of looking at northern self-consciousness. Being northern imbues individuals with valuable cultural associations implying a capacity for hard work, a lack of pretension, a certain generosity and warmth and much else. While the notion of the North as 'breath of fresh air' enters the national culture largely on the terms laid down elsewhere, *within* the North that idea has enjoyed deep and continuous existence. Here is the region that provides the competitiveness, resolve, wit and community spirit that the nation needs in all spheres. Northerners have been aware that they are to some degree 'in England but never quite of it' and this has clearly generated anger and disappointment.[31] Nevertheless, they have ultimately been a race apart in order to serve the national cause, not just English men and women but the very best of the breed. Many might have disliked some of the accompanying cultural trappings – the 'professional' northerner is not always appreciated – many have left the region and some discarded their accents on going. In general, however, a pride in being northern that rises does seem to rise easily to the surface. This slightly edgy sensibility clearly has attraction for some outsiders and for some on the region's southern margins. For all the negative imagery associated with the North (indeed, perhaps precisely because of it), the region has clearly attracted many who find in it a supposed authenticity believed to be lacking elsewhere in English culture. Similarly, while we still know little of the territorial mentalities of those living on its borders, many who live there clearly feel themselves to be northern and are anxious to be taken as such, seeking to share in what, for all its problems, is still the nation's most powerful regional identity. Although northern identity might support a very weak political project and in some contexts a weak cultural one as well, it can clearly provide individuals and sometimes larger communities with a valuable extra resource in their search for identity, recognition and self-respect.

Northern identities and the social order

To this point in the chapter (and at a number of points throughout the book) the emphasis has necessarily fallen upon on the unifying, embracive role of northern identity and it would be easy to thus infer that it acts as a simple populism binding disparate groups, if not in a close common bond, then at least in hostility to outside forces. In reality, populist mentalities are extremely flexible and experienced and deployed by different groups in a variety of ways in battles over power and status. It is this theatre of exchange that receives attention here with especial reference to the issues of class and race and ethnicity. The focus is upon northern 'identities' rather than a single 'identity' as some of the issues considered relate as much to sub-regional and even local allegiances as much as to a wider sense of a single North.

Genuine pride in place can undoubtedly be experienced across the whole social spectrum. This has probably been most easily realised through sport where social and to some degree, gender mixes, have usually been wide enough to allow for a real sharing in the pleasures of success. However, as Jeffrey Hill has demonstrated in an important study of the role of sport, the local press and civic ritual, media representation stressing the apparent unity of whole communities in support for their local team often obscured 'the actual disharmonies present in the every-day life of northern towns'.[32] A similar point might be made about the depiction of larger northern regional and sub-regional territories and about other cultural arenas. Hidden within the broader unifying narratives generated by the press or dialect literature, music-hall comedy or whatever the form may be, there were both powerful forces pulling against regional coherence and/or using it, consciously or otherwise, to maintain social advantage.

Regional identities can service political and social ideologies of almost any type, but it is argued here that northern identities have more frequently and more effectively operated as conservative rather than radical forces. Ironically, this flows to a considerable extent from the North's close association in both reality and in the popular imagination with the working class generally and its radical political and industrial culture in particular. In some narratives, this association becomes so close that 'North' and 'working class' become indivisible. It has been claimed that twentieth-century analysis of the metropolitan versus the provincial is too easily dominated by such an elision of class conflict and regionalism, with regionalism offering 'a new way to restate social identity, alienation and defiance'.[33] Whatever the merits of this particular argument, there can be denying either the close linkages between the two or the fact that regional symbols can be skilfully manipulated so as to serve class or broadly popular interests. Sir Harold Wilson's Yorkshire accent, much advertised fondness for Huddersfield Town F.C. and what the press referred to in his 'homely' manner, were vital tools in his bid to persuade the electorate of the fundamental differences between his Labour Party and its patrician, privileged Conservative opponents in the 1960s. More obviously and more aggressively, the 1984–85 miners' strike in which Yorkshire was a key centre of the conflict and which saw the National Union of Mineworkers leave its London headquarters for Sheffield, was easily seen as a battle between a radical, almost colonised North and an oppressive South.

The problem for a radical northern identity, however, is that the cultural value flowing from the region's standard association with 'ordinary folk' has been quite easily and effectively appropriated by dominant social groups, or appropriated on their behalf. A particularly fertile topic in this regard concerns the use, wittingly or not, of various modes of northernness by the northern middle and upper classes in their attempts to manage the field of class relationships. Of the wide 'family' of populisms or pan-class identities on offer in the last two centuries, a shared regionalism has more power than most to serve middle-class interests.[34] Its special gift was to enable the local realities of class conflict and power to be displaced to the South, that potent mythic landscape in which social inequality reigned. (Wilson's political language in the 1960s was a Labourist attempt to do precisely the same.)

Some of the clearest examples can be seen in the sporting arena, with Yorkshire county cricket in the period to the 1950s providing arguably the richest. It was argued in chapter 8 that the unusually large predominance of professionals over amateurs in the county side was matter of great pride, demonstrating the supposedly meritocratic nature of Yorkshire society. Many of these amateurs were drawn from the highest realms of British society, with those captaining the side between the 1880s and 1930s, for example, including the Eton and Cambridge-educated aristocrat Lord Hawke, successful stockbroker and wartime MI5 agent Everard Ratcliffe and William Worsley, eventually to serve as Lord Lieutenant of North Yorkshire from 1951–65 and father of the future Duchess of Kent. Some, although most certainly not all, of these players were decidedly modest cricketers, chosen purely for their social position in a period when professionals were expected to be governed by their social superiors. In a skilful display of populist discourse, sections of the press worked hard to 'democratise' these individuals in ways that both disguised their cricketing shortcomings and recast their social origins in a manner that better suited the county stereotype. In 1908, in celebration of Hawke's twenty-fifth year as captain, a Leeds newspaper published a tribute in dialect claiming that 'Iverybody knaws as 'ow his Lordship 'as done more fer Yorkshire nor any Prime Minister could dew'. Thus a landowner with substantial business interests in South America (and, in fairness, a far more competent cricketer than many of his counterparts) was embraced within the common culture of the Yorkshire people. On his death in 1938, many obituaries downplayed some of his notoriously conservative and autocratic dimensions, with one remembering him as 'a counsellor and friend of the professionals, in a way that was quite new to county cricket, and that did an immense amount of good to the game'.[35] While there was undeniably much substance in this narrative, it was a highly selective one seeking to turn the amateurism derided in a southerner into a vocation, almost a quasi-profession. The local realities of class power were thereby disguised and perhaps partially defused. Similar outcomes could be seen in rugby league, a game intensely associated in the popular imagination with northern working-class culture and its battles with the privileged South, and thus a powerful symbol of personal egalitarianism for middle-class supporters and sponsors of the game.

This displacement function has also been visible in areas besides sport. The use of dialect by some employers in conversation with their workforce could also serve a similar function. Indeed, virtually any celebration of distinctive northern virtue made in almost any cultural form or public context could operate in this way. One of the most skilful manipulators of this cultural tool was Sir Marcus Fox, Chairman of the Conservative Party 1922 Committee from 1992–97. Very much the self-made man who rose from a terrace house in Dewsbury to company directorships and a frontline political career he was fond of blunting the thrust of interviewers with the mantra 'look, I am a Yorkshireman' and regular mentions of 'good common sense'. Such observations were delivered in an accent that a rival claimed became stronger 'the nearer he gets to the metropolis' and which helped relieve his party of the image 'of the Yorkshire grouse moors' and replaced it with a much needed 'breath of the Yorkshire mill towns'.[36] In these ways, claims of Conservative privilege and lack of sympathy for 'ordinary' people were countered by reference to some of the most powerful signifiers of that very ordinariness.

The use of regional strategies by Fox and others was sometimes more than simple artifice. Such ploys could be fuelled by both a genuine sense of regional pride (Fox reputedly rejected an army career because he had 'never heard a general with a Yorkshire accent') and the closely related feelings of inferiority and resentment often experienced by the northern middle class and those on their way into its ranks when faced by their southern counterparts.[37] When interviewing Manchester Grammar School pupils in the 1960s Graham Turner noted their 'wide-ranging resentment against the South and all its works … a corrupt society where ability did not matter and where people who could pull the right strings commanded the positions of power and profit'.[38] The northern middle class has often felt unloved and insecure on the national stage. At the local and regional level, however, that insecurity has been put to good use.

Regional and sub-regional identities must not be seen as a form of false consciousness imposed upon a pliant working class. There is a danger that the kind of cultural history being practised here renders crucial histories of popular struggle invisible, but in fact, class consciousness, or perhaps more accurately, consciousness of class, made many northern workers fully aware of the contradictions between protestations of shared northern culture and the facts of daily economic life. Joint sympathy for a sports team or a cheerful address in 'deep Lanky' were never enough of themselves to avert industrial conflict or to rein in the independent cultural institutions of the working class. Nevertheless, in a culture that had always accepted some degree of class collaboration, whether out of reluctant necessity or genuine belief, and in which the discourse of North–South division was so much a part of the mental apparatus, the language of region undoubtedly had the capacity to act as a social cement and smooth some of the rougher edges of class conflict. Regional and sub-regional allegiances have also had the potential to divide the working class and thus dilute class consciousness; the North's widely noted scepticism about 'Lunnon' and its 'chirpin' Cockneys' has been crucial here. Whether this actually hindered the effective mobilisation of political and industrial movements or proved to be expendable in the interests of a wider cause is impossible to judge from the current state of knowledge. A reasonable guess might be that North–South tensions have tended to place limits on institutional developments but are capable of being over-ridden in a crisis. The same, of course, might also be suggested in terms of *intra*-northern differences. Resort to the historian's favourite mantra, 'more research is needed', seems appropriate here.

Finally, it is worth speculating about the relationship between regionalism and the search for status and mobility within the class hierarchy. The prominent role of the lower-middle class in western nationalist movements has been widely acknowledged and it has been argued that a powerful strain of popular imperialism typified that class in late Victorian and Edwardian Britain.[39] In the later context, the suggestion is that national and imperial sentiments and the sense they bring of belonging to a widespread and powerful community are especially attractive to a group notably prone to social insecurities and status anxieties. In the light of this, it would be interesting to examine the social background of those 'regional activists' – the leading figures in county-based dialect societies, supporters of regional devolution and so forth – in order to ascertain whether the region offers a particularly suitable site for status enhancement amongst a grouping stretching from the upper-working to the middle-middle class. 'Regionalism', if the word can be thus used to define a loose body of related activities and aspirations, certainly provided rich opportunities for the garnering and exhibition of skills that could be obtained without recourse to expensive training or elite social networks. It is possible to imagine how this might allow either aspiring social groups or socially aspiring individuals much valuable cultural and social capital and capital that could be accrued in an arena that felt comfortable and manageable. Just as it has been suggested that some areas of regional literature provided a convenient avenue for women authors denied access to the national sphere, so it might be that the 'middle' geographical domain between the local and the national offered those in its social equivalent a potentially empowering space.

This study has paid only slight attention to the place and role of racial and ethnic groupings within the North. The largest single groupings have comprised the Irish who came in particularly significant numbers in the 1840s and 1850s (especially to Lancashire), but who have continued to migrate to the region at certain times since then; the eastern European Jews who arrived from the late nineteenth century and established communities of about 30,000 in Manchester and 20,000 in Leeds by 1914, and the Afro-Caribbean and South Asian communities established mainly from the 1950s.[40] Individual towns and cities have also seen the establishment of distinctive populations such as Liverpool's West African community, which dates back to the early eighteenth century, and the Yemenis of Sheffield and South Shields. The largest northern concentrations of immigrants and their British-born descendants have always been found in the larger towns and cities and within the industrial areas of west Yorkshire and east and central Lancashire in particular. Many smaller country towns and almost all rural areas have experienced very little immigration and, since 1945, virtually none at all.

All groups contributed to the texture of the North even if many of their organisations and institutions have for obvious reasons largely served their own specific communities. The great exception here is provided by Liverpool, whose distinctive accent owes much to the influence of Irish migrants in the nineteenth century and where, as already noted, Irish influences have been crucial to both the realities and the myths that make up the city's history.[41] Especially since the 1960s and 1970s, at least a surface degree of multi-culturalism has become a hallmark of the modern northern townscape as religious buildings, restaurants and shops testify to changing demographic and cultural patterns. It would be difficult, however, to argue that the various black and Asian communities have ever been, or felt, fully part of northern culture in the sense of shaping it or connecting with its major institutions and forms of expression. Although individuals may speak with powerful local accents and have integrated at various levels, the strength of pre-existing personal and group loyalties combined with the experience of some hostility from sections of the indigenous population will have often rendered the search for a 'northern' identity largely irrelevant.

Diane Frost's rich study of Liverpool has shown how 'Scouseness' has often been an exclusionary device of white working-class Liverpudlians, forcing the complex matrix of black communities to forge their own identities in response. The 1980s and 1990s, for example, saw much comment on the marginalisation and/or exclusion of black spectators (and, indeed, players) from one of the city's greatest cultural practices, professional football.[42] Cricket, another key part of northern culture, has also provided much evidence of racial exclusion in the late twentieth century at both recreational level and within the first-class game. These issues have had especial resonance in Yorkshire where the game has always provided such a strong focus for county identity. Although the County Club has made strenuous and genuine efforts to improve its links, particularly with Yorkshire-Asian cricketers, the continued failure of a local Asian player to break into the first team and the ill-advised remarks of some senior ex-players and officials have combined with wider racist currents to persuade many that Yorkshire cricket wants to remain exclusively white. One Bradford Asian claimed that 'if oil was found under Bradford companies like BP and Shell would be straight here to use that resource, but there are thousands of kids who are passionate about cricket and no-one is trying to tap into that'.[43] Cricket, then, remains a feature that happens to be shared across largely separate black, white and Asian communities, rather than a unifying strand within a wider northern sporting culture.

In recent years sections of the Asian community, particularly young Muslim males, have been deemed as a problem within and for the North in ways that add a distinctively racial twist to traditional images of the region's failure and decay. Indeed, press coverage of disturbances involving minority ethnic groups in 2001 to some degree defined racial tension as a northern problem. Although only five northern communities experienced actual violence headlines such as 'A long hot summer: how violence has swept the North' and references to the 'northern riots' stigmatised the region as whole and defined it as the key site for the nation's contemporary social ills.[44]

It would be foolish to argue that northern identities are always necessarily devices of racial exclusion; staying just within the sporting context, many clubs and their white fans have put enormous efforts into fighting racism and trying to build multi-racial communities of support.[45] It should be acknowledged, however, that regional loyalties – and not just northern ones – have the capacity to add a potent ingredient to banal racism. Evidence to support this is not easy to assemble, as it is a sensibility more likely to be hinted at in casual conversation than in written form. This author first became aware of it in the 1970s when hearing the organiser of a Yorkshire folk dance group defend his decision – later rescinded – to exclude a young Pakistani applicant on the grounds that 'it wasn't traditional'. Similar comments have been made in the context of cricket. The retreat to an idealised version of a regional culture allows individuals to deny any racist intent by taking emphasis away from race and nation. Similarly, while it would be ridiculous to accuse all modern readers of dialect literature of a tendency to racism, there is no doubt that such literature can have an appeal for those seeking a nostalgic retreat to an 'ethnically purer' past.[46]

Attempts to theorise the relationship between regionalism and race have been almost non-existent but one interesting example occurred in the initially unlikely source of the *Yorkshire Dalesman* magazine in August 1939. In a piece entitled 'In praise of Yorkshire', William Harbutt Dawson – significantly, perhaps, holder of a Konigsberg doctorate who described his life's work as 'interpreting Germany to English people' – expounded upon the relatively common notion of 'County and even parochial patriotism' serving as a building block for a wider national identity. Dawson goes beyond the normal discourses here, however, in his consideration of how allegiances might serve 'the larger patriotism which we owe to the common fatherland'. The role of such patriotism is to

> prove an effective antidote to the sentimental and irrational cosmopolitanism which is so much in vogue in these days, and which finds dangerous expression in the endeavours of certain elements in our population – in part impelled by interested motives – to open our borders, and even our highly-prized citizenship, indiscriminately to the riff-raff of Continental humanity. If we do not wish to see England lose her individuality in a hotchpotch of dissimilar ethnical groups, we should regard it as no less a misfortune that our beloved Yorkshire should cease to hold its distinctive place in national thought and life, civilisation and culture.[47]

His own rather inchoate solution was to encourage the Yorkshire universities and colleges to create 'their own traditions' in order to sustain the county's individuality. In Dawson's worldview 'Yorkshireness' becomes a first line of defence against racial degeneration, its distinctiveness a guarantee of national unity and purity. It is an extreme and idiosyncratic view and very much of its period, but is worthy of attention if only because it demonstrate that regionalism does have the potential to take on some of the more problematic elements of nationalism as well as the more rational, inclusive and progressive formulations that supporters of regional self-government tend to stress.

The future of the North

The North of England entered the twenty-first century in a far more positive and creative mood than was conceivable just ten or fifteen years earlier. The cultural and, to varying degrees, economic renaissance of major cities such as Leeds, Liverpool, Manchester and Newcastle has earned much media attention, stimulated tourism and genuinely improved the quality of life for their more affluent citizens. There has been, too, a more general 'greening' of the north as de-industrialisation and the imaginative uses of subsequently redundant buildings have combined to produce a radically different physical environment. Ex-pit villages and small textile towns have thus become desirable dormitories, allowing many more families to enjoy the peculiar blend of rural/semi-rural setting within easy distance of urban resources long acknowledged within the North as one of its greatest strengths.

There have also been early signs of new thinking about relationships within the region. In a shrewd assessment, Caunce has argued that rivalry 'has served the North well in the past, and it can continue to do so, but it is essential to acknowledge that the rivals need each other and continue to learn from each other'.[48] A number of initiatives suggest that this crucial lesson is being learnt. 1998, for example, saw a major exhibition entitled Art Transpennine 98 that placed works of art in a variety of venues in an area bounded by Lancaster and Sheffield in the north and south and Hull and Liverpool in the east and west. Although intended as a freestanding event, it was also designed to draw attention to the common interests of this 'Transpennine' region and its wider connections to Northern Europe. The broad agreement of co-operation in the wider interests of the north-west signed by civic leaders of Manchester and Liverpool in September 2001, represents another potentially significant moment.[49]

For some, a further and crucial source of optimism has been provided by the increased possibility of regional self-government. Although devolution for the English regions was briefly fashionable in some circles in the aftermath of the First World War, with C. B. Fawcett's still fertile *Provinces of England* (1919) both symptom of and inspiration for such tendencies, it was effectively a dead issue until the last quarter of the century. The Campaign for the North in the 1970s partially revived it but it was the political and economic changes of the 1980s that proved crucial. The intellectual space opened up by the post-imperial mindset; the so-called 'democratic deficit' caused by the loss of local government powers and 'quangoisation' from the 1980s; the stimulus to local initiative caused by the sheer scale of the economic problems faced and the realisation that central government would do little about them; the inspiration of the newly created Scottish and Welsh parliaments and the clear lead given by the European Union, all played a role in pushing regional government further up the political agenda.[50] Although the Conservative Party remained largely resistant to the 'Balkanisation' of England, the Liberals have always been enthusiasts and the Labour Party slowly and sometimes uncertainly moved towards an acceptance of a greater autonomy for the regions during the 1990s. That process culminated in the long-awaited White Paper, 'Your Region, Your Choice', in May 2002. Using the eight regions created for the Government Offices for the Regions in 1994, this proposed assemblies of some 25 to 35 members elected by proportional representation with executive responsibility for their respective Regional Development Agency (established in 1999) and some financial responsibility in such areas as housing, tourism, sport and culture. The north-east, the region furthest from London, the most socially deprived and the most frequent to claim colonised status, has the largest body of advocates for self-government in the seven-county North. The aspiration of some there for a bigger world than 'the south-bound trip to London to beg for jobs and out-relief', and one embracing Scandinavian-type social democracy and reinvigorated historic trade and cultural links with Ireland, Scotland, Scandinavia and the Baltic, certainly generates a sense of freshness and excitement.[51] 'Europe of the Regions' is a slogan that has liberated many thoughtful minds.

Whether optimism on all these fronts prefigures a genuine shift in the fortunes and status of the North or merely another of the false dawns that have punctuated its recent history is unclear. The factors to be overcome are considerable. The issue of regional self-government, for example, is fraught with difficulties. There are innumerable technical issues to be resolved and not least the likely need to abolish existing County Councils, in some cases sources of pre-existing loyalty and affiliation, and the question of relationships with central government. A number of critics have warned that devolution could result in a decline in the share of national resources for some regions with no guarantee of the assumed 'economic dividend'.[52] Yet again, although the three northern regions have some coherence, boundary disputes will be inevitable and there are still those who would prefer a system based on a far larger number of smaller units built around specific cities and towns. More importantly, there has been little obvious grass roots enthusiasm for the devolutionary project at any stage. While the *Daily Telegraph* was not entirely accurate in depicting Labour's 2002 plans as attractive only to 'a small army of "constitutional experts", academic zealots and Labour politicians who see the opportunity for further self-aggrandisement', it does to an extent capture the weakness of English regional and sub-regional political consciousness.[53]

Many, of course, favour regional devolution as the best method of combating the excessive power of London but even a well funded and strategically astute network of provincial governments might have trouble restricting or even beginning to balance the capital's power. There is little evidence of a halt to the flow of provincial talent to London and no sense that many southern residents are willing to take advantage of the north's cheaper prices and environmental benefits noted above. This is not simply a matter of staying on to enjoy better economic or cultural opportunities. The psychological capital of being at the centre, even if its resources are little used, is immensely important. As the journalist Hywel Williams put it, 'Go beyond this domain and you're out of it. What you may gain in manners you will lose in edge and pace.' Defining London as stretching from Chelmsford to Reading and from St Albans to Crawley, with Oxford, Brighton, Colchester and Milton Keynes as its suburbs, he argued that 'The difference between Londoners and the English are now as great as between the British and the Italians. This is not a city. It is a nation.'[54] While this might be an exaggeration it is a helpful one and is indeed accurate in specific contexts. With an economy larger than that of Denmark, Finland, Sweden, Poland, Portugal and Greece, by the late 1990s London had 'reached a level of importance where it should be considered as an economy in its own right'.[55] At the same time, there has been no diminution in central government's wish to see London as the centre of the nation's key symbolic sites. While it was the apparently limitless expenditure on the Millenium Dome rather than its location at Greenwich that most angered critics in provincial England, the decision taken in 1995 to site sport's National Stadium at Wembley met with more general concerns about metropolitan bias.[56] To a large extent, decisions of this type are driven by external concerns. Even the *Guardian*, still a powerful voice for the regions, argued in 1995 that 'for foreigners [London] is the only place in England they want to visit or bring international sports events to', a sentiment it repeated seven years later when arguing that 'London remains the only place for a National Stadium'.[57]

It is, then, not surprising that throwaway comments have once again been made about moving the capital from London, with one commentator suggesting Newcastle as an alternative.[58] Such suggestions are attempts to provoke debate as much as serious blueprints and the most likely outcome for the North in the foreseeable future is largely a series of variations on the story as before. The economic situation will be mixed and patchy with those cities and sub-regions that show the most willingness to moderate old hostilities and forge new alliances emerging as the strongest; whether any future system of regional government facilitates or inhibits this will be the touchstone of its effectiveness. It will certainly need to be accompanied at least initially by some central direction of higher-value industries into northern conurbations if the issues of regional imbalance and the outward migration of talent are to be even partially addressed and redressed.

Cultural battles between North and South (and within the region) will inevitably continue in some form, too ingrained and too essential to a whole family of myths ever to disappear. For northerners, the emotional capital engendered by a sense of exclusion is often too potent to be easily relinquished while, for outsiders, the North has been 'other' in too many ways and for too long to allow for rapid changes in attitude. The real skill will be in learning to look beneath the clichés and habits of imagination that lie at the heart of these myths, to see the real problems that arise when one part of the country is associated with success and another, no matter how affectionately and even enthusiastically it might sometimes be viewed, with backwardness and low status. It is essential that the theatre of North–South rivalry becomes a necessary source of creative tension and not, on the former side, a device for sometimes facile explanation of difficulties, and, on the latter, an excuse for failing to see genuine needs and problems. Only then will the North fulfil its potential either within the confines of the nation-state or within a future 'Europe of the Regions'.

Notes

1   *The Times*, 18 June 1912.
2   *British Bandsman*, 18 October 1930. Important here are C. Waters, 'The Americanisation of the masses', *Social History Curators Journal*, 17, 1989–90, pp. 22–6 and 'J. B. Priestley, 1894–1984: Englishness and the politics of nostalgia', in S. Pedersen and P. Mandler (eds), *After the Victorians* (London: Routledge, 1994), pp. 209–26.
3   G. Stedman Jones, 'The "Cockney" and the nation, 1780–1880', in D. Feldman and G. Stedman Jones (eds), *Metropolis London. Histories and Representations Since 1800* (London: Routledge, 1989), pp. 272–324.
4   P. Dodd, 'Lowryscapes: recent writings about "the North"', *Critical Quarterly*, 32, 2, 1990, pp. 17–28.
5   A musical appeared in 1982, written by Alan Price, and in 1988 Keith Waterhouse scripted a TV series starring James Bolam.
6   His weight drifted up to 25 stone in some stories. This description is from *Way of the World. The Best of Peter Simple* (London: Johnson Publications, 1963), p. 52. I am grateful to John Walton for loan of material. Wharton worked on the column from 1957. See his autobiographies, *The Missing Will* (1984) and *A Dubious Codicil* (1991), published in a double edition (London: Hogarth, 1992).
7   Wharton, *Way of the World*, pp. 66, 246–7.
8   *Sunday Times*, 5 January 1975.

9 *Bill Tidy. Drawings, 1957–1986* (Liverpool: Walker Art Gallery, 1986). I am grateful to Andrew Hobbs for this reference.

10 Quoted in *Yorkshire Post*, 14 April 1970.

11 J. Belchem '"An accent exceedingly rare: Scouse and the inflexion of class', in his *Merseypride. Essays in Liverpool Exceptionalism* (Liverpool: Liverpool University Press, 2000), p. 56.

12 'The perils of Armpit United, a strange and terrible place', *Evening Standard*, 8 January 1998.

13 T. Mason, 'Football, sport of the north?', in J. Hill and J. Williams (eds), *Sport And Identity in the North of England* (Keele: Keele University Press, 1996), p. 50. The essays in N. Kirk (ed.), *Northern Identities* (Aldershot: Ashgate, 2000), certainly suggest that a sense of being northern was inferior to other forms of identity.

14 Melvyn Bragg, *Speak for England. An Essay on England, 1900-1975* (London: Martin Secker and Warburg, 1976).

15 C. Harvie, 'English regionalism: the dog that never barked', in B. Crick, *National Identities. The Construction of the United Kingdom* (Oxford: Blackwell, 1991), pp. 105–19; L. Castells and J. K. Walton, 'Contrasting identities: north-west England and the Basque Country', in E. Royle (ed.), *Issues of Regional Identity* (Manchester: Manchester University Press, 1998), pp. 44–81; P. J. Taylor, 'Which Britain? Which England? Which North?', in D. Morley and K. Robbins (eds), *British Cultural Studies* (Oxford: Oxford University Press, 2001), pp. 127–44; R. Weight, *Patriots. National Identity* (London: Macmillan, 2002), pp. 591–8.

16 M. Bradford, *The Fight for Yorkshire* (Beverley: Hutton Press, 1988).

17 N. Mansfield, *English Farmworkers and Local Patriotism, 1900–1930* (Aldershot: Ashgate, 2001).

18 A. D. Smith, *Nationalism and Modernism* (London: Routledge, 1998), p. 62.

19 C. Harvie, *The Rise of Regional Europe* (London: Routledge, 1994), p. 14; Taylor, 'Which Britain?', p. 145.

20 Weight, *Patriots*, pp. 595–6.

21 'United we stand?', *Northern Review*, 9 & 10, 2001, p. 13.

22 See *County Monthly* editorial, October 1902, for a statement of aims.

23 J. Osmond, *The Divided Kingdom* (London: Constable, 1988), p. 68.

24 D. E. Allen, *British Tastes. An Enquiry into the Likes and Dislikes of the Regional Consumer* (London: Hutchison, 1968), p. 39.

25 *Liverpool Echo*, 20 April 1964; G. Turner, *The North Country* (London: Eyre and Spottiswoode, 1967), p. 299. The speaker was a Stockton-on-Tees alderman. One Hull trawlerman interviewed by Turner, p. 193, claimed that he 'set' Londoners 'with the niggers'.

26 M. Saler, 'Making it new: visual modernism and the "Myth of the North" in Interwar England', *Journal of British Studies*, 37, 4, 1998, pp. 437–9.

27 *Northern Review*, 3, Summer 1996, pp. 79–80, 82.

28 K. Wrightson, 'Northern identities: the long duree', *Northern Review*, 2, Winter 1995, p. 25.

29 J. Paxman, *The English. A Portrait of a People* (London: Penguin edn, 1999), p. 157; Taylor, 'Which Britain?', p. 136.
30 Quoted in A. Briggs, 'Local and regional: the story of broadcasting in the north of England', in his *The Collected Essays of Asa Briggs, Vol. 3* (London: Harvester Wheatsheaf, 1991), pp. 169–70.
31 A. Mitchell, 'Manifesto of the North', in S. Chan and T. Wright (eds), *The English Question* (London: Fabian Society, 2000), p. 46.
32 J. Hill, 'Rite of spring: cup finals and community in the North of England', in Hill and Williams (eds), *Sport and Identity*, p. 108.
33 J. Black, 'Northern identity and post modernity', *Northern Review*, 2, 1995, p. 23.
34 On populism in general, see P. Joyce, *Visions of the People. Industrial England and the Question of Class, 1840–1914* (Cambridge: Cambridge University Press, 1991).
35 Quoted in his autobiography, *Recollections and Reminiscences* (London: Williams and Norgate, 1924), pp. 249–50; *Bradford Telegraph and Argus*, 10 October 1938.
36 *Bradford Telegraph and Argus*, 15 January 1997; *The Times*, obituary, 19 March 2002.
37 *The Times*, 19 March 2002.
38 Turner, *North Country*, pp. 83–4.
39 P. J. Taylor, *Political Geography. World-Economy, Nation-State and Locality* (London: Longman, 1989 edn), p. 185; R. Price, 'Society, status and jingoism: the social roots of lower middle class patriotism, 1870–1900', in G. Crossick (ed.), *The Lower Middle Class in Britain* (London: Croom Helm, 1977), pp. 89–112.
40 P. Panayi, *Immigration, Ethnicity and Racism in Britain, 1815–1945* (Manchester: Manchester University Press, 1994).
41 Belchem '"An accent"', pp. 40–6.
42 D. Frost, 'Ambiguous identities: constructing and de-constructing black and white "Scouse" identities in twentieth century Liverpool', in N. Kirk (ed.), *Northern Identities*, pp. 195–217; D. Hill, *'Out of his Skin'. The John Barnes Phenomenon* (London: Faber and Faber, 1989).
43 Quoted in J. Williams, *Cricket and Race* (London: Berg, 2001), p. 192.
44 *Observer*, 8 July 2001.
45 B. Holland, L. Jackson, G. Jarvie and M. Smith, 'Sport and racism in Yorkshire: a case study', in Hill and Williams (eds), *Sport And Identity*, pp. 165–86.
46 P. Salveson, 'Region, Class, Culture: Lancashire Dialect Literature, 1746–1935', Unpublished PhD thesis, University of Salford, 1993, pp. 512–13.
47 *Yorkshire Dalesman*, 1, 5, August 1939, p. 11.
48 S. Caunce, 'Urban systems, identity and development in Lancashire and Yorkshire: a complex question', in Kirk (ed.), *Northern Identities*, p. 65.
49 *New Statesman*, 9 January 1998, p. 54; *Guardian*, 27 September 2001.
50 J. Osmond, *The Divided Kingdom* (London: Constable, 1988), pp. 44–7; J. Mather, 'Labour and the English regions: centralised devolution?', *Contemporary British History*, 14, 3, 2000, pp. 10–38.
51 Preface to B. Lancaster and R. Colls, *Geordies* (Edinburgh: Edinburgh University Press, 1992), p. xiv. For more mixed views, 'A Geordie nation?', *Economist*, 27 March 1999, pp. 26–8.

52 K. Morgan, 'The English question: regional perspectives on a fractured nation', *Regional Studies*, 36, 7, 2002, pp. 797–810.

53 *New Statesman*, supplement 'Sowing the Seeds of English Devolution', 26 June 1998. *Daily Telegraph*, 10 May 2002.

54 'Capital Offence', *Guardian*, 27 December 2000.

55 Douglas McWilliams, Chief Executive of the Centre for Economics and Business Research, quoted in the *Sunday Telegraph*, 12 October 1997, B5.

56 In this case it is main rival-bidder Birmingham, rather than the North, that has the greatest complaint.

57 *Guardian*, 31 October 1995; 24 May 2002.

58 George Monbiot, 'Move the capital', *Guardian*, 2 September 1999.

Index